The Good Enough Life

The Good Enough Life

Daniel Miller

polity

Copyright © Daniel Miller 2024

The right of Daniel Miller to be identified as Author of this Work has been asserted in accordance with the UK Copyright, Designs and Patents Act 1988.

First published in 2024 by Polity Press

Polity Press
65 Bridge Street
Cambridge CB2 1UR, UK

Polity Press
111 River Street
Hoboken, NJ 07030, USA

All rights reserved. Except for the quotation of short passages for the purpose of criticism and review, no part of this publication may be reproduced, stored in a retrieval system or transmitted, in any form or by any means, electronic, mechanical, photocopying, recording or otherwise, without the prior permission of the publisher.

ISBN-13: 978-1-5095-5964-0
ISBN-13: 978-1-5095-5965-7 (pb)

A catalogue record for this book is available from the British Library.

Library of Congress Control Number: 2023934604

Typeset in 10.5 on 12.5 pt Sabon
by Fakenham Prepress Solutions, Fakenham, Norfolk NR21 8NL
Printed and bound by CPI Group (UK) Ltd, Croydon, CR0 4YY

The publisher has used its best endeavours to ensure that the URLs for external websites referred to in this book are correct and active at the time of going to press. However, the publisher has no responsibility for the websites and can make no guarantee that a site will remain live or that the content is or will remain appropriate.

Every effort has been made to trace all copyright holders, but if any have been overlooked the publisher will be pleased to include any necessary credits in any subsequent reprint or edition.

For further information on Polity, visit our website:
politybooks.com

CONTENTS

Acknowledgements	vi
Introduction: Cuan and Kant	1
1 An Exceptionally Free Society?	34
2 Philosophers of Freedom	64
3 The First Satiable Society	78
4 Philosophers and Consumerism	105
5 Inequality, Drugs, and Depression	120
6 Justice as Fairness	153
7 The Body and Sports	177
8 The Origins of Philosophy in Sport	199
9 Creating Community	211
10 Placing Heidegger	231
11 Engaging with the World	243
12 The Stoics and Epicurus	261
Conclusion: Hegel, Anthropology, and Philosophy	282
Notes	301
References	326
Index	344

ACKNOWLEDGEMENTS

I am especially grateful to Pauline Garvey, who carried out a parallel ethnography in Dublin and jointly wrote our project book, from which many ideas and passages have been used in this volume. Also to David Prendergast and Adam Drazin. Special thanks to my wife Rickie Burman, who participated in the fieldwork and helped to edit this book.

I would like to express my gratitude to countless people in Cuan. I cannot list you all, but in particular Maria A., Monica A., Edel B., Eric B., Lawrence B., Peter B., Rachel B., Hilda C., Helen D., Mary G., Pat G., Peig, Aiden H., Suzanne H., Dierdre J., Carol K., Eleanor K., Marie K., Sian K., Bob L., Deidre L., Catriona M., Dominique M., Geraldine M., Eamon M., Eugene M., John M., Katherine M., Michael M., Norma M., Oliver M., Raymond M., Vincent M., Catherine N., Kevin O., Michael O., Martin R., Bob S., Henry S., Noel S., Liam S., Maria S., Paul S., Janet W., and Serena W. Maria A. and Henry S. also helped me find additional research participants amongst migrants and in the new estates respectively.

Thanks for comments on the manuscript by Maria A., Rachel Miller, Mathew Doyle, Haidy Geismar, Pauline Garvey, Richard Miller, Sheba Mohammid, Felix Ó Murchadha, Maria Nolan, and especially Martin Holbraad, Bob L., and the readers from Polity Press. I am also extremely grateful to Justin Dyer for his impressively conscientious and detailed copy-editing.

Special thanks to Laura Haapio-Kirk, who painted the front cover for me as a birthday present.

While writing this book, I was very concerned that I would be publishing detailed discussions of philosophers without any personal background or training in academic philosophy, which was likely to lead to misrepresentations and distortions. It seemed essential therefore to have the manuscript also read by someone trained in disciplinary philosophy. I am very grateful to the philosopher Jeremy David Bendik-Keymer for helping to eliminate some of those misunderstandings and misrepresentations from the chapters concerned with philosophy. Any remaining misrepresentations and failures are mine alone – a classic caveat that remains particularly true and pertinent in this case.

Funding for the ethnography came from the European Research Council (ERC) under the European Union's Horizon 2020 research and innovation programme (grant agreement No. 740472).

INTRODUCTION
Cuan and Kant

This book sets out to compare two potential sources for understanding how life could and should be lived: the writings of certain philosophers about the good life; and an ethnography based in a small Irish town of people living what will be described as the good enough life. The discipline of Western philosophy is generally considered to have developed from the sixth century BCE in classical Greece and its colonies with a focus on the question of how to live well, exemplified by Aristotle's discussion of the term *eudaimonia*, generally translated as living well or a good life. Fortunately, *eudaimonia* resonates with an ambiguity in the English word 'good'. When we say, I am living the good life, we mainly refer to happiness. But when we say, I aim to live a good life, we mainly refer to virtue and ethics. Early philosophers were concerned with the relationship between these two. Socrates stated that,

> Seeing that all men[1] desire happiness, and happiness, as has been shown, is gained by a use, and a right one, of the things of life, and that the right use of them, and good-fortune in the use of them, is given by knowledge – the inference is surely that everybody ought by all means to try to make himself as wise as he can?[2]

Aristotle, in the *Nicomachean Ethics*, confirms both that *eudaimonia* is the ultimate aim of life (1097 15–21),[3] and that the sound use of reason will allow us to flourish through *aretē* (excellence/virtue), demonstrated above all through thoughtful action by a harmonious, well-habituated soul.

INTRODUCTION

These are philosophical ideals, but what of life as lived? Today, we might feel less confident about the relationship between virtue and happiness. Could a selfish and greedy person still be happy and is a virtuous person necessarily happy? As it happens, most of the people who contributed to this ethnography seemed to share the ideal of *eudaimonia* that a virtuous life was also the most effective route to personal happiness, though the examples of virtue discussed in this book come from activities such as grandparenting and environmentalism rather than through an abstract philosophical concept of 'reason'. The people in my fieldsite do, however, make considerable use of the principle of 'being reasonable' as a foundation for being judged as wise. But it was a different observation that was the starting point for this comparison between philosophy and ethnography. From the very beginning of fieldwork, I was struck by the sheer love of this community for the town in which they lived and their identification with it – a sentiment reminiscent of the foundation of so much Greek philosophy, which took for granted that the good life was based on citizenship associated with a particular city-state, known as a *polis*.

This volume is therefore constructed through juxtaposing chapters about well-known philosophers or schools of philosophy with other chapters drawn from an ethnography of the retired population of this small town in Ireland, people who would never consider themselves to be either philosophers or exemplars of the good life. Anthropological ethnography differs from most social research because the emphasis is on observations of what people do, rather than what they say. The portrait of these people's good enough lives has been extrapolated mostly from their everyday actions, rather than interviews. It is the life they lead that provides our evidence. The premise for this book is that there may be advantages to considering a population that actually exists as against ideal models of what society might or should be. This gives ethnography a potentially important complementary role to certain philosophical questions. Within the discipline of philosophy, a consideration of the good life subsequently took its place alongside logic, epistemology, politics, and a multitude of other considerations as philosophy grew in breadth and depth. The concern of this volume is, therefore, with only a small element of contemporary and historical philosophy. A final unusual quality of this book follows from the use of ethnography to exemplify the good enough life; increasingly, social science seems to be dominated by critique, while this will be largely a book of praise.

INTRODUCTION

The people presented in this ethnography are all Irish. This does not mean that they are necessarily representative of the population of Ireland. I spent sixteen months living amongst these retired people in a small town on the east coast of Ireland, which has been given the pseudonym of Cuan. I didn't have a car and hardly ever left the town. I therefore cannot say how typical they would be of Irish people more generally, although my findings were generally consistent with a parallel and simultaneous ethnography by Pauline Garvey in an area of Dublin with a similar demographic.[4] Furthermore, most of my informants were not born in Cuan but migrated from other parts of Ireland or in some cases from abroad. I will sometimes use the term Cuan as a convenience to describe the people I worked with, but the arguments apply only to my research participants, who were mainly retired, and not necessarily to the rest of Cuan.

The ethnography characterizes this population as an example of the 'good enough' life. The semantics are not ideal. The phrase 'good enough' might be seen to imply sufficiently good, which would make this a rather complacent exercise, as though we could not aspire to do a good deal better in achieving virtue. This is not the meaning of 'good enough' intended here. The phrase is mainly known in academia through the work of the psychologist Donald Winnicott in reference to good enough mothering.[5] His point was that we could praise rather than condemn a mother who, under often difficult circumstances and faced by all the contradictions of parenting, manages to develop a reasonably sensitive response to her infant, creating a secure and nurturing environment. The phrase 'good enough' is also important as a means of differentiation from the way philosophers consider the good life in reference to how a society should ideally be. By contrast, anthropologists tend to comparison with other existing societies, rather than against some ideal. This book is therefore not trying to suggest that Cuan is ideal; rather that, for all the faults that will be described, it is hard to find another currently existing society that is demonstrably better.

Individual chapters of this book will focus on particular components of the good enough life. John Rawls (chapter 6) helps us to consider justice and fairness, when set against the inequalities and other problems found in Cuan (chapter 5). Socrates helps to explain the centrality of sports to the people of Cuan (chapter 8). Heidegger is contrasted with the way Cuan has been constructed as a place (chapter 10). The Stoics and Epicurus discuss what we should do

INTRODUCTION

with our lives as we age, in comparison to these retirees (chapter 12). Other philosophers have been selected because of their commentaries on the nature of freedom (chapter 1) or affluence (chapter 3), both qualities of this population to which chapters have been devoted. The capabilities approach associated with both Martha Nussbaum and Amartya Sen is found to have some aspirations in common with this ethnography, as does the book *After Virtue* by Alasdair MacIntyre. In the conclusion, Hegel is deployed to try to resolve some of the key differences between these philosophical approaches and what has been learnt from the ethnography. In every instance, it is only my attempted interpretations of these philosophers that can be offered in the course of these comparisons. I have no training in academic philosophy.

Why write a book on the good enough life right now? We live in a restless world. Over the centuries, hundreds of millions of people have migrated in search of a better life. Consider those who have over time colonized the lands of North America, reducing the indigenous people to a small remnant. Or consider the 250 million people who more recently have migrated to industrial regions of China and were the subject of a wonderful study by Xinyuan Wang comparing their migration from rural areas to work in factories with their simultaneous migration from offline to online.[6] Many contemporary migrants are refugees from war and oppression. The most impoverished rarely have the resources to undertake such migrations. The majority, such as in the case of the vast Chinese migration, move in search of 'a better life'. What this term 'a better life' implies is that they seek the security of a higher income or a better health service or the opportunities of education for their children, as well as escape from struggle and coercion. For many such migrants, the aspiration is to seek a largely middle-class and suburban lifestyle,[7] which they hope to achieve over one or more generations.

This then raises some rather important questions. How should we regard this middle-class, suburban, settled life that most of the world now aspires to? Is this a perfectly reasonable ideal, the sort of life that pretty much everyone could and should emulate? Is there some plausible concept of the good enough life, or of life purpose, that this lifestyle corresponds to? Or is it an illusion or a trap, an image created by the wider political economy, these days often glibly termed 'neo-liberal capitalism', in order to sell us a lifestyle to which we sheepishly conform? Rather than reaching some ideal, have we

4

fallen into a muddy rut along the way? In the past, the only way of conceiving of an ideal life would have been through sketching out some version of a speculative utopia. But in the twenty-first century, quite a few migrants have largely achieved the life they sought, in countries where that is how much of the population now live. Instead of speculative utopias, we are in a position to appraise the very ordinary lives of millions of people, living in versions of a middle-class, suburban lifestyle within a welfare state. If this lifestyle already exists and can be observed, then we have reached the point where we can consider the value of such lives.

Ireland is a largely middle-class country with a centrist government and a welfare state. Cuan could be considered suburban in that it is within commuter distance from Dublin. The population who form the backbone of this book seem to correspond, then, to these migrant aspirations. One of the groups deliberately included within the ethnography were migrants from outside of Ireland who have settled in Cuan. There were not many such migrants because Cuan is a relatively expensive place to live, but those who became research participants regarded the town as a clear fulfilment of their ideals as migrants.

On occasion when discussing this book with other social scientists, the result has been a horrified expression. Why am I not studying people in poverty or the highly oppressed? Don't I know how much people around the world are suffering? As it happens, most of my previous work has been with such populations. I have lived for considerable periods with people who had no toilet of any kind other than the fields, only intermittent electricity, and could afford just two meals a day rather than three. I have published a book about a hospice whose patients had received a terminal diagnosis and were dying.[8] It is important to observe and report on deprivation, struggle, and suffering. But it is also important to write about lives outside of these conditions. One of the limitations of disciplines such as psychology and much social science is that, if we are mainly engaged with the problems and pathologies of modern life, in order perhaps to assist in such situations, the result is a strange perspective that sees so much in the world from the viewpoint of pathology. By contrast, the remit of anthropology is first and foremost to explore the cultural diversity of humanity and help all of us to understand empathetically what it means to be other than who we are. Anthropology is currently trying to make this a more egalitarian pursuit in repudiation of its colonial and privileged origins. All populations should be equal in the possibility of becoming the subject of some inquisitive anthropologist and also in the possibility of becoming an anthropologist. This was another reason for embarking on a study of a population that is slightly more affluent than the UK, where I live.

Whenever I hear people tell me (as they often do) that, 'Oh, they would be of interest to an anthropologist, you should study them,' I sigh, because anthropology should regard no population as more authentic or interesting than any other. It is essential to anthropology that we, too, should be examined for our weird cultural beliefs and assumptions that other people find astonishing and in need of explanation. Otherwise, we will assume that somehow our beliefs are more natural and obvious, and it is only others who require such investigations. Like most of my research participants, I am middle class and suburban and I found many things that we held in common. But I also found people in Cuan to be remarkably different in their approach to life than those I had written about in a previous ethnography of a similar-sized population in a fieldsite just outside London.[9] (I am myself a Londoner.) It is reasonable to see Cuan as the kind of society many people aspire to, but beyond that it is hard to regard it as typical. Often in contemporary social science, the context of neo-liberal capitalism is appealed to as the cause of some observation. But the populations who live within neo-liberal capitalism seem just as heterogeneous as those who don't. If Cuan is remarkably different from the English settlement that I had recently written about,[10] it could hardly be because of some fundamental difference between British and Irish capitalism.

One of the reasons for alternating the ethnography with discussions of sometimes analogous and sometimes contrasting philosophy is that the aim of this book is not just observation but also appraisal. Appraisal required some kind of yardstick against which Cuan could be measured, and this is provided by philosophy.[11] There have been many previous attempts to juxtapose philosophical questions with anthropological approaches, and there has also been a recent growth of interest within anthropology in topics such as virtue, happiness, and ethics. The closest parallel is probably a recent edited collection by Harry Walker and Iza Kavedžija which explicitly addresses similar questions regarding the relationship between happiness and *eudaimonia*.[12] As might be expected from an anthropological collection, there is no attempt to measure the good

INTRODUCTION

or happy life. Rather, ethnographies demonstrate a plurality of values and priorities. Older Japanese people may be more concerned with tranquillity, seeking a balance between autonomy and dependence, and focus on modest aesthetic aims within everyday practices. That makes them very different from the association between happiness and excitement of young people in the US. Humanists link happiness more closely to virtue, while Chinese parents try to decide whether to focus on their happiness or that of their children. Most people see happiness as the by-product of other aims and not necessarily enhanced through explicit discussion, a conclusion that will be reinforced by the evidence presented in this volume. There are many other anthropologists concerned with various aspects of the good life,[13] as well as works that examine different dimensions within the relationship between anthropology and philosophy.[14] I am not aware, however of any that adopt the precise structure of alternate juxtaposition that is employed here. I apologize that this book only examines Western (itself a highly problematic term) philosophy and that I possess none of the knowledge that could permit venturing beyond this. Given that I have no formal background in academic philosophy, it already felt like an act of considerable hubris to try to engage with the range of philosophers who will be discussed, but at least these were mainly figures I had encountered during decades working in social science.

If anthropology has a record of engagement with philosophy, there are also movements in the other direction. A notable influence has been the philosopher Alasdair MacIntyre's critique of previous attempts by philosophers to create a more general or universal approach to virtue.[15] MacIntyre argues that our ideas of virtue are inculcated by our socialization into particular traditions and cultural values. This would give licence to anthropological approaches that extrapolate *eudaimonia* from studies of culture,[16] and that analyse virtue through observing practices such as sharing.[17] Similar arguments about the necessity of culture and comparison may be found in the writings of Martha Nussbaum and Amartya Sen, notwithstanding their own philosophical differences.[18] By the end of this book, it will be apparent that the example of Cuan differs from some of the expectations that have emerged from this literature. Virtue for this population will turn out to have much less to do with tradition than might have been anticipated. The arguments of the conclusion lie closer to what will be suggested were Hegel's arguments for virtue and freedom as derived from the way society collectively creates culture and thereby creates itself.

In using the term 'yardstick', a curious other possibility arises. If a range of philosophical discussions are set against the ethnography, then it could equally imply an appraisal of these philosophers through examining how their ideas measure up against an actual population. This volume will pay equal regard to both possibilities. The ethnography will be employed to reconsider the contributions of some philosophers, while philosophers such as Rawls will be deployed to make judgements about Cuan. This is, then, two books in one. If you find yourself falling asleep when reading the sections on philosophy, you have the option of just reading the alternating chapters devoted to the ethnography, and vice versa.

It is possible that my research participants are going to be a little horrified at being employed in such a manner. Generally speaking, they are quite a modest lot. I can't think of a single one of them who would see themselves as representing any kind of ideal life, let alone having the hubris to compare themselves to the great philosophers. As far as I could tell, they do not regard themselves as special in any way. But, of course, that is precisely why they serve this purpose so well. There was no search for an ideal society. The value of the ethnography lies in understanding a 'good enough' society that people might feasibly aspire to. I must apologize to my friends and research participants whom I am setting up here as Irish 'Davids' against the 'Goliath' of Philosophy. It should be crystal clear that this is entirely an author's conceit exploiting their very modesty by making that virtue part of their qualification for being utilized in this fashion.

As already noted, it was an early but then sustained observation about Cuan that became the catalyst around which the ambitions of this book crystallized. This was the degree to which the people of Cuan seemed besotted by Cuan itself. There was not even the germ of a plan to write a book on the topic of the good enough life at the start of a very different research project. This book arose mainly from the evidence that while people in Cuan did not describe their individual lives in glowing terms, they constantly went on and on about how Cuan itself was the ideal place within which to live a good life. This seemed to correspond to the relationship between the good life and the *polis* in the Greek city state. This book is not a detective story; it can start with its conclusion: that to the degree to which these

INTRODUCTION

research participants live the good enough life, the principal cause turns out to be the manner by which they have created the town of Cuan.

The Love of Cuan

I settled in Cuan for an entirely different purpose. I was running an international project, funded by the European Research Council, called ASSA: The Anthropology of Smartphones and Smart Ageing. As part of this comparative project, I would study this topic in Cuan, while my Irish colleague, Pauline Garvey, who teaches Anthropology at Maynooth University in Ireland, would carry out a parallel project in a Dublin suburb. Subsequently, we wrote up our findings, which turned out to be largely identical, in a book called *Ageing with Smartphones in Ireland*[19] as one of a series of monographs that derived from the ASSA project. I apologize for the fact that in writing this volume it has been essential to reprise some of the themes already discussed in that earlier volume, but it is likely that book will mainly be read by those interested in either smartphones or ageing, while this volume is frying up some bigger fish.

One of the joys of traditional anthropology was its aspiration to a holistic methodology. The method known as ethnography or participant observation consists of living with a population, in this case, as mentioned, for sixteen months, during which most days are spent in their company, engaging in activities alongside them, but also sometimes interviewing them directly. The anthropologist arrives with a topic that requires studying, in this instance ageing and smartphones. But an ethnography implies examining those topics as part of everyday life. In order to understand the consequences of smartphones, the vast majority of research has to be about people's offline lives, since we cannot know in advance whether it may be family life, religion, education, gender, or something else entirely that will help us interpret what people are observed to do with these devices. We therefore need to investigate everything else that goes on in their lives in order to be confident about our explanations for smartphone usage and consequences. After all, no one lives inside an academic topic; they live all these things at once. I call our method holistic contextualization. Ethnography is unusual as perhaps the only academic research method that seeks to correspond to life as it

INTRODUCTION

is actually lived. It is almost the exact opposite of hypothesis testing, which would reduce research only to variables already known about. Ethnography is also a qualitative method that refuses to reduce observations to data, or things which can be counted. As a result, it can have no pretensions to be akin to natural science, and indeed ethnography is often looked down upon by other disciplines because it has little that they would consider as hard data. What it contains instead is a grasp on life that is not a result of any kind of artificial parameter or encounter. We simply spend around sixteen months swimming in their sea. (As it happens, most people in Cuan do swim in the actual sea and considered me completely wimpish because I found it too cold.) For many anthropologists, even interviews are suspect as artificial research contrivances. Instead, we mostly trust observations based on life as it unfolds around us and overhearing conversations that are naturally taking place between others.

It follows that often the most rewarding part of an ethnography is the encounter with topics that could not even be envisaged. Ethnography then becomes a voyage of discovery. This book is full of topics that were never intended to be studied, not just the good enough life, but pet dogs, bingo, cocaine, sports, or where people choose to go on holiday, all of which came into the frame as general background. But none of these made quite as strong an impression as the observation that slapped me straight in the face within days of arrival: the love of Cuan felt by the people of Cuan. They were also pretty keen on the fact of being Irish. Most of the current inhabitants of Cuan are themselves migrants from other parts of Ireland. They are referred to as 'blow-ins'. Soon after arrival, I heard many versions of 'I didn't know anything about Cuan when I moved here, but it turned out to be a magical decision.' For the entirety of my stay, this sentiment dominated all others. Almost everyone wanted to make sure that I was aware of just how much they loved Cuan. Cuan has turned out to be such a perfect place to live that they could not now imagine living anywhere else. None of this was a response to any research question. It just seemed important to so many people to drop this sentiment somewhere into the conversation. Over time, it also became clear that this is something they frequently did amongst themselves and was not just mentioned for my benefit. The people of Cuan are simply besotted by Cuan; the term 'heaven' is not infrequently used. As in the initial quotation, a common refrain was that this was an example of simple good fortune, because they had

INTRODUCTION

not known any of this in advance of moving there. They had just lucked out.

The praise took many forms. One of the most popular statements concerned the range of activities. The claim that Cuan has everything except a swimming pool, a hotel, and a cinema was heard at least a hundred times, always with those same three caveats. The iconic Cuan walk is along the seafront. This was felt to be an infinite pleasure as the sea presents a different aspect however many times one stares out at it from one's walk. This particular walk would also inevitably lead to social encounters such that a ten-minute walk could take hours as people stop to chat. Other commonly cited virtues included the lack of crime, the suitability of Cuan as a place of retirement, and the weather relative to other parts of Ireland. Another popular refrain was that, if any individual wanted to develop some new craft or activity, there would always be others who would come together to help make this happen. The claim, however, that dominated to a degree that it ends up as the bulk of chapter 7 in this book was that Cuan is heaven because of the range of sports available.

The emphasis on sports was closely related to another heartfelt form of praise for Cuan. This was the hope amongst older people that their children would return. People living in small towns in every region face the fear that their children will one day leave in search of something bigger and better. The children of Cuan mainly do leave when they go to college or first obtain jobs. By the end of their teen years, they are bored to tears by the town and claim there is nothing to do there. But, in many cases, it seemed that once they contemplate having children of their own, then they wish to return to the town so that their own children might replicate their positive experience. Much of this rests on the success of sports as providing enjoyment and purpose for younger children. A silver lining of the economic crash in Ireland was said to be that children of Cuan were then able to purchase properties in the town that otherwise had become unaffordable for first-time buyers. My study of the newest housing estate suggested that, despite the expense, around a third of purchases were from people originally brought up in Cuan. This will not be the only example of the town's virtuous circles. In chapter 9, we will see that this sense of positive community led to it being differentially favoured by government grants, which meant it was becoming a still better place to live.

INTRODUCTION

The sheer level of praise for the place might have seemed extreme. But another piece of evidence made this still more strange. If Cuan as a very heaven was an almost universal view of those who had lived for some years in the town, it was not a view shared by anyone outside. Even today, Cuan is a largely disregarded place. On my rare forays to Dublin, people always expressed surprise that I should have chosen this out-of-the-way fieldsite for my research. It is not a place I have found referenced in tourist guides to Ireland. People are aware that it was a seaside destination in their parents' day but can't really see much reason to go there now, given the weather is so much better in Spain. There are plenty of good beaches and more swish-looking towns much closer to Dublin than Cuan. It is as though Cuan is surrounded by the river Lethe, so that only those within it are aware of its glories. No one ever suggested Cuan as the kind of place that would be 'of interest' to an anthropologist – which seemed as good as any reason for settling there.

How could a place be so well regarded internally and so disregarded externally? I confess that I, too, could have voiced these sentiments. My choice of Cuan as a fieldsite related to logistical convenience and the reputation of its age-friendly group, since I planned to be working mainly with older people. Yet I ended up liking the place just as much as everyone else and wondering which star to thank for my fate. At first, all I felt was some bemusement in the face of this enthusiastic self-love of Cuan. But as an academic it clearly required explanation. Not just why are people in Cuan besotted by where they live, but also, if this is clearly experienced as the good enough life, what does this tell us about the way people consider the meaning and purpose of life more generally? It helped that one of topics within our project on ageing and smartphones was also about life purpose – a topic that arose naturally from a project devoted to retirement, when people are more likely to be confronted by questions of what more they want out of life.

As fieldwork progressed, I realized that not only was I coming to share something of this fondness for Cuan, but I also shared many of the values and interests of my interlocutors. I am not Irish and have no Irish ancestry, though, being Jewish, I don't identify with being English to the same extent as people in Cuan identified me as being English. I do have Irish grandchildren, which was one of the reasons I wanted to live there, to explore another part of my family identity. More generally, though, I am of a similar age to these

INTRODUCTION

research participants. Perhaps bizarrely, I write books about being retired instead of retiring myself, but that seems to make me just as happy as retirement makes them. I come from a similar liberal left-leaning orientation, and most of my informants seemed sympathetic to the woes of the British Labour Party, of which I am a member. I am at a similar level of comfort and income, with common interests in taking holidays and the wider world. We watched the same TV series and the same Premier League football matches, and often read the same newspaper (*The Guardian*). I support my wife in her work with a project to help asylum seekers, which parallels the kind of philanthropic work common in Cuan. More than any other ethnography I have carried out, I could see myself mirrored by my research participants and increasingly could see myself living happily in Cuan. This obviously raises the question of whether I will be expressing the values and opinions of the people in Cuan or my own. My advice to the reader is that when the values and practices you encounter in this book are those you approve of, you should see them as emanating from Cuan, but when you cringe at what you regard as complacent naïvety, assume that is me.

Introduction to Ireland[20]

This book is certainly not intended only for people interested in or knowledgeable about Ireland. This presents a problem since it would be hard to fully appreciate the ethnographic chapters without some knowledge of Irish history. Fortunately, a truly excellent account of that history was published while I was writing this volume. Fintan O'Toole's *We Don't Know Ourselves* is enormously helpful equally for the degree to which it is the background to this ethnography and the degree to which the ethnography turns out to be so different from what this history might have presaged.[21] It is a wonderful read because of the author's facility in interweaving his personal history, the political and economic history of Ireland, and the more general shifts in the lives of the Irish. It is particularly important that this is quite a personal history, because the Irish who appear in my book are of a similar age to O'Toole. The life that is recounted in his book is in large measure the life that my research participants have lived through, with some of them born in a similar part of Dublin to O'Toole. You will therefore certainly have a better appreciation of what follows in this book if you have previously read his book.

The Republic of Ireland, with a population of almost 5 million, shares the island with Northern Ireland, a part of the UK with a population of around 1.8 million. Ireland declared independence from the UK in 1919, and this was acknowledged in 1921. The capital city of Dublin has a population of around 600,000, while that of Dublin county is around 1,300,000. Cuan is within one hour's travel from Dublin. Ireland became a member of the European Union (EU; back then the European Economic Community or EEC) in 1973. The lifetime of most of the research participants has been an economic rollercoaster. Younger people find it hard to comprehend the social and economic transformation that Ireland has undergone within living memory. At the time of independence, 58 per cent of employed men worked in agriculture.[22] O'Toole points out that no one really expected this to change. Ireland was destined to remain a low-income agricultural backwater to Europe. Many of my research participants were born in rural locations and tell vivid tales of poverty both on farms but also in Dublin during that period. They couldn't possibly have imagined becoming the people we encounter today. O'Toole also stresses the ubiquity of emigration as a hallmark of twentieth-century Ireland, creating a diaspora that is widely dispersed around the world,[23] to the extent that there was serious discussion about the possibility that the Irish of Ireland might more or less disappear. A striking feature of the time in which these people were born was that since 1922, the newly independent Ireland under the tutelage of Éamon de Valera systematically replaced the colonial authority with the authority of the Catholic Church. The Church ran almost the entire education system and had such a strong grip over government and the everyday life of the people that the country could be considered an effective theocracy. For example, a marriage bar introduced in the 1930s meant that until 1971 women in the civil service were legally obliged to give up work on getting married, in order to encourage them to concentrate on rearing children and caring for families.[24]

Many respondents commented on the deeply conservative beliefs held by their parents, and often initially by themselves. Not infrequently, differences of opinion about religion led to rifts within families that spanned decades and left lasting scars. Catholic bodies such as the Christian Brothers oversaw their education and their

INTRODUCTION

general behaviour. The Pope's visit of 1979 seemed to reflect this degree of devotion. The explanation for this theocracy lay in the primary aim of the Independence movement to assert a complete break from British colonial domination. The Catholic Church was being granted power that it seemed to have earned from its relative suppression over the previous centuries of colonial rule by the Protestant English. Similarly, a huge effort was made, and continues to be made, to spread usage of the Irish language, though in this area to little effect. I never heard a single sentence uttered in the Irish language as part of casual conversation in Cuan, though I would have done had I been on the west coast rather than the east. My impression was rather that in Cuan the Irish language has become a kind of performative sacred language that is the effective replacement for Latin within modern secular Ireland.

What is astonishing is how quickly a rural theocracy, without even the expectation of change, has become something else entirely. The sociologist Tom Inglis argues that, in one generation, Ireland has transformed from being an isolated Catholic agrarian society to being a liberal-individualist, secular, urban society revolving around business, commerce, and high-tech transnational corporations.[25] By the early 2000s, Ireland was identified as having an open global economy. The Church didn't so much decline as abruptly collapse in its claims to authority subsequent to a series of scandals from the 1980s onwards.[26] This perhaps reached its apogee during my fieldwork in 2018, with the convincing vote to repeal the constitutional ban on abortion.[27] The scale of such change is evident in that as late as 1993, homosexuality was illegal in Ireland, but just twenty-two years later, in 2015, it represented the first country to legalize same-sex marriage by popular vote and was hailed as being in the 'vanguard' of social progression by the *New York Times*.[28]

The term 'rollercoaster' is appropriate since the experience of Ireland was not simply one of consistent economic uplift. It included the boom years of the 'Celtic Tiger' but also the mauling of that tiger by the severe economic crisis after 2008. This recession, sparked by the economic freefall of the banking system, led to a bailout by the International Monetary Fund and EU.[29] The period was characterized by high levels of unemployment, mass emigration, a collapse in domestic construction, and austerity measures imposed by the European Central Bank.[30] By 2017, when the fieldwork began, the recession had largely passed but had left many scars. Austerity had led to increasing levels of inequality and the proportion of the Irish population at risk of relative (if not absolute) poverty had risen to 21 per cent. Yet property prices in 2016 soared to rates of increase that mirrored the earlier 'Celtic Tiger' period. Economic growth for 2017 was among the highest in the EU (at 7.3 per cent). Economic figures for Ireland can be misleading, however, due chiefly to the distortions represented by the activities of the IT sector, which was flourishing thanks to the country's low taxation rate for such companies. Domestic activity was also up 4.9 per cent and there was strong employment growth. A long history of emigration had been halted by the attractions of Ireland as a site of immigration during the 'Celtic Tiger' period. With recession, this was again reversed, only for the tide to turn once more as Ireland recovered its economic prosperity, such that by 2013 there were renewed invitations for emigrants to return.[31] My fieldwork coincided with a new confidence, although the shadow of the recession was still present in many people's lives.[32] I heard about people who had committed suicide during the recession out of despair regarding their future prospects. Yet in the post-recession era, Ireland became the fastest-growing economy in Europe, while still dealing with the legacy of recession. This was their rollercoaster. Another important factor was that I was conducting fieldwork in a place where people received a higher pension than the English with whom I had previously worked. Whatever the past, today they were reasonably comfortable.

The shift from theocracy to modern, largely secular Ireland was equally dramatic. The clerical scandals in the 1990s and 2000s, including the sexual abuse of children, the treatment of 'fallen' women in the Magdalene laundries, and the deaths amongst children left in care, have all undermined the credibility of the Church. A reversal of past attitudes to same-sex marriage, divorce, and cohabitation have led to newly established norms.[33] What is distinctive about Ireland is not these liberal values, but the fact that they developed later and faster than in most other regions.[34] Yet here change should not be exaggerated. While there has been a growth in secular values and some forms of liberal individualism,[35] the two-parent nuclear family is still the most typical environment in which children grow up in Ireland.[36] Divorce rates remain low (6 per cent) when compared to trends in other European countries. While most countries in Europe are concerned with a growing aged population and low birth rates, Ireland's population is relatively young and fertility rates are

INTRODUCTION

among the highest in Europe[37] at around 1.9 children per woman.[38] Intergenerational ties remain strong.[39]

The period of fieldwork was one that reinforced a positive sense of European identity set against a dramatic decline in the international reputation of the former colonial power of Britain. The decline in any respect for the British that resulted from the Brexit débâcle is discussed in chapter 1.[40] But this also meant renewed anxiety about the future of the Northern Irish border, and the potential economic slump of a no-deal Brexit. Additionally, fundamental state services such as housing had been cut during austerity, while health and welfare provision are still quite fragile. The word 'crisis' was a common adjective to describe both health and housing. Housing represents a particularly potent cypher for the state–citizen contract in Ireland[41] and economic boom and bust seems to be measured in the popular imagination in bricks and mortar. The fact that Ireland saw the highest percentage increase in property prices during 2017 of any developed country, at 12.3 per cent, seemed reminiscent of the pre-recession unsustainable property boom. Accounts vary in discussions of income inequality in contemporary Ireland and I am not expert enough to judge between them. Chapter 5 in this volume will, however, describe in detail how such inequalities present themselves within Cuan itself.

By contrast, Irish politics had become relatively stable, with nearly a century of fairly predictable alternations between two parties that had origins in the bitter civil war that followed independence: Fianna Fáil and Fine Gael. Despite these roots in savage conflict, they are today generally regarded as two sides of a centrist coin. Cuan, being mainly middle class, would be strongly reflective of this largely liberal consensus. The main political shifts concerned an oscillation between Labour, the Green Party, or Sinn Féin as people searched for a credible opposition; the specific ideology of these three parties may have been less important than their potential for this role.

A further conspicuous factor is the sheer size of the Irish diaspora, which dwarfs the local population as a result of the more recent emigration to the UK in the 1950s and again in the 1980s, along with the better-known and earlier migration to the US.[42] By contrast, migrants from outside Ireland were rare in Cuan owing to high property prices, though women from Eastern Europe were increasingly evident within the local labour force, particularly in catering and childcare. A nearby town to Cuan reveals a sharp contrast. Its older

17

INTRODUCTION

proletarian history is now overshadowed by extensive immigration, with migrants from Africa and Asia representing around 15 per cent of the population.

Today, there is a generally positive sense of Irish identity at home and abroad. An increasingly strong European identity was boosted not just by the decline in respect for the English but also by the sense of European support of the Irish position during the Brexit negotiations. There is a keen interest in travel abroad, where the Irish generally find they are regarded as genial and egalitarian. At the same time, many people either retained or were developing interests in icons of specifically Irish culture. These included Gaelic sports, such as hurling, alongside a substantial revival of traditional music. People in Cuan took pride in the fact that Irish music and literature punch well above their weight, with figures ranging from the novelists Sebastian Barry and Sally Rooney to post-punk musicians Fontaines D.C., alongside a generally positive, albeit romantic and often crudely stereotypical, American-Irish identity that has been disseminated through film and television and is much discussed by Fintan O'Toole.

The importance of O'Toole's book lies just as much in what it does not presage. My research participants are of a similar age and lived through everything he recounts. Both tell a story of how conservative, theocratic rural Ireland could finally become my ethnography of secular, urban, and urbane liberal cosmopolitans. On the other hand, O'Toole pays a good deal of attention to the rise of mass consumption and the interest in wealth, status, and materialism that grew alongside this history. It is not a book that would predict chapter 3 in this volume, which claims that by far the most important measure of status in contemporary Cuan is environmentalism and anti-consumption. O'Toole's book has extraordinary stories of veniality, corruption, and scandal, yet this ethnography is of a population of such probity and citizenship that Cuan would have garnered the approval of Weber.

More complex is the relation between the ethnography and the fundamental theme of *We Don't Know Ourselves*. O'Toole's book tells of a people who above all kept things swept under the carpet; a refusal to acknowledge what was nevertheless at some level well known. He argues this through case after case from the heights of politics to what people didn't acknowledge in the streets around them. On reading chapter 5 of this volume, which examines deep

INTRODUCTION

inequalities within Cuan and the incidence of cocaine usage and other problems, there is some continuity with O'Toole's thesis. But I have never been to a place that didn't turn something of a blind eye, for example, to lower-income housing within its midst. Instead, I would argue that, taking a more general overview, the people of Cuan have shown, if anything, an admirable self-perspicacity and an openness about (most of) their vices and virtues. In conclusion, there will be shown to be some remarkable contrasts between the portrait painted in this volume of Cuan and that of O'Toole's entirely excellent and plausible rendition of the recent Irish history which my research participants lived through.

There is, also, an important point where our accounts converge, appropriately since O'Toole's final chapter is dated 2018, the same year that I spent in Cuan. At this point, O'Toole is remarking on how Ireland both repealed the ban on abortion and granted same-sex marriage.[43] He draws attention to the number of over-sixty-fives who voted for the repeal. This tallies with a wider claim that the contemporary Irish possess a legacy based more on embracing constant change, rather than just referencing back to any fixed indigeneity or their own historical narrative. This in turn explains why our accounts are ultimately quite compatible. Because while the focus of O'Toole's book is on the refusal to acknowledge what was happening, this took place within a narrative of quite remarkable change over his lifetime. If much of the ethnography that follows in this volume contrasts with the Ireland that he has portrayed, it merely confirms that there has been no let-up in the pace of change. It follows that this book's claim to be contemporary will also soon be out of date.

Cuan

Cuan was, for some periods of its history, an important fishing port, but this peaked in the eighteenth century. Towards the late nineteenth century, the boats were used to trade cargo such as coal. The surrounding area is fertile, but was dominated by English landowners under a tenants-at-will ruling that meant that they could be evicted without notice, making life more precarious. Generally, the area was poor, as was most of Ireland, but perhaps a bit less food-poor and so less impacted by the Famine in comparison to the west of the country. The historical record emphasizes the heroism of those who supported Republican calls, for example, in the 1916 uprising, with streets named after associated martyrs. Less discussed were the splits, even within families, represented by that period and the subsequent civil war, which may well have led to the emigration of those who ultimately supported the losing side. This was combined with the destructive impact of the First World War.

The population before the modern expansion was around 2,300. When most of the research participants were born, Cuan had become mainly familiar as a holiday destination, where local people often rented out their homes for the summer and lived in a smaller dwelling built within their own garden. During that period, Cuan was known for its holiday camps, and the associated ballrooms and music scene. This proved highly significant when the first private estates were built, since many of the people who chose to purchase these houses knew of Cuan because either they or their parents had taken holidays there. The holiday industry was well developed by the 1890s but collapsed quite quickly when people in Ireland started taking cheap vacations abroad in the 1970s, resulting in this current situation of Cuan being largely disregarded and having practically nowhere where people can stay.

There was never much by way of manufacturing industry in Cuan. Its class identity was mainly a result of geography. People saw themselves as higher class than the more proletarian town on one side and lower class than the more upmarket towns on the other side, which continue to draw holiday makers from Dublin. This geography has a considerable impact on how the people of Cuan understand themselves. The feeling that they are middle class is partly derived from being literally in the middle between the posh and the proletarian. With respect to internal class divisions within Cuan, there have been two major state housing projects, the first built conspicuously outside what would have been the town boundaries at that time. Private housing really took off in the 1970s, and during this period the population doubled. From that time on, there has been almost continuous building of new estates, as remains the case today. The result is a major expansion of the population, which currently numbers around 11,000. Much of the state housing has been sold off, with fewer than 200 such homes remaining. It is common for adult children in Cuan to leave in their twenties but return when they want to have families in their thirties. Many people from the new estates commute to Dublin to work or study. Around 700 individuals

INTRODUCTION

in Cuan stay at home to mind their family. A feature of note is the degree to which community activities tend to be dominated by the 'blow-ins' attracted by the housing estates and commute to Dublin, who are now the majority population. People remain very conscious of whether someone is Cuan-born or a blow-in. Again, this will be the subject of chapter 9.

The town is well served with restaurants and pubs, which are generally more upmarket than those in the surrounding villages and towns, unless one goes closer towards Dublin. Otherwise, the high street is fairly typical of Ireland, with one large and one more local supermarket, one garage, two banks, and a good number of hairdressers and pharmacies. The most official expression of the love for Cuan comes from the huge interest in the nation-wide Irish Tidy Towns competition. Politically, this is a fairly liberal area, whose votes reflect much of Ireland, fluctuating between Fine Gael, Fianna Fáil, and Labour, though with a marked increase in the Green vote in recent years and some support for Sinn Féin.

Today, there are four main types of housing in Cuan. The first is the old town, representing around a third of the whole. This is extremely mixed, including some very large fine period housing and equally large new housing built by wealthier people to exploit the views over the sea. It also includes much smaller houses and is the district with the most bungalows, often the original cottages, some of which still have thatched roofs. Second come the big estates built from the 1970s to 1990s, mainly reasonably sized three- and four-bedroom houses, with little variation. The third is the aforementioned state housing, mainly the Vartry Estate, with smaller, mainly three-bedroom houses. Finally, there are the big new Brittas estates, on the edge of Cuan, again mainly three- or four-bedroom properties, but on a much larger scale, approximately a third of which have been purchased by Cuan residents or their children.

Cuan's housing is more expensive than most of the towns and villages nearby but less expensive than middle-class Dublin and some of the towns between Cuan and the capital. A three-bedroom property sells for around €350k, a four-bedroom for €450k, a house with a sea view for €550k. Over 90 per cent are houses, rather than apartments. The population is fairly homogeneous as only around 8 per cent are foreign-born, the largest group of these being British (often of Irish descent), followed by people from Eastern European countries often working in the town. Analysis of the census shows overall income levels slightly above the national average. The result is a largely middle-class town with a central pocket of state housing that as a whole can be regarded as reasonably representative of contemporary Ireland. Although not strictly a suburb, if we think of suburbia as a compromise between urban and rural life, including commuting to a city but with easy access to the countryside, then the term is appropriate.[44]

Field Methods

Ethnography consists primarily of participant observation, in this instance simply living in Cuan for sixteen months. I started by volunteering for the local theatre to make tea, hanging around the two local cafés where groups tended to meet up, and then joining more and more activities. The ones I most frequently attended included: the active retirement group for playing bingo; the Men's Shed; the ukulele group; various trad music sessions, including one in which I participated through reading song lyrics and poetry; local walks; a set dancing class; a book reading club; a film club; the local historical society; attending mass at the Catholic church; the sailing club talks; and litter picking for Tidy Towns. After a while, I started to receive more invitations to people's homes, at which point I followed Pauline Garvey's advice to always bring a *brack* when visiting someone at home. *Brack*, a kind of sweet fruit bread, was particularly appreciated by my older participants, and for some it carried memories of childhood treats and rural living.

Secondary to participant observation, I recorded one or more interviews with around 170 individuals. With a smaller group, I tried to include three interviews on the topics of smartphones, ageing, and health respectively. In addition, it was helpful to interview people with specialist knowledge. These ranged from pharmacists, hairdressers, vets, the Garda (police), physiotherapists, volunteers, nuns, and alternative health practitioners. Each provided perspectives that might not be available in day-to-day fieldwork. For example, some men who were struggling with issues around retirement would only open up to psychotherapists, so it was only through interviewing the latter that it was possible to learn about the depth of these problems.

Participant observation is primary, since what people say is better regarded as more of a legitimation than a description of what they

INTRODUCTION

actually do. As previously noted, the people in Cuan in turn observed me, and initially this was mainly to brand me as English, to a degree I had never previously experienced. As people came to know me better, I became a more singular individual in their eyes. Did my English background matter? In one way, this fieldwork was an experiment. I am an older English male, while Pauline Garvey is younger, female, and entirely Irish. She carried out her fieldwork with a very similar population, but within Dublin city itself. We met occasionally, but the fieldwork was largely independent. Yet when we came to write our joint book, there was a remarkable degree of cohesion. We essentially agreed about both what we had seen and our interpretation of what was going on. Around the only differences we encountered related to the slightly younger profile of her research participants. As a result, writing a joint book was remarkably easy. This suggests that what is termed the 'positionality' of the ethnographer was not an important factor in this case. What mattered far more was our shared training as professional anthropologists.[45]

While most of my fieldwork was situated in the core area of old Cuan, I made a concerted effort to include those living on the newest estates at the far end of the town as well as low-income households living in social housing, and recent migrants mainly from Eastern Europe. These three additions were intended to ensure the breadth of the ethnography. There are lonely people in Cuan, or people who have lost the art of sociality. It was important to find and include such individuals, because of a potential methodological bias in ethnography that might focus on the more socially active people encountered in the types of public activities in which an ethnographer can most easily participate. Given that one of the arguments in this volume concerns the degree of social involvement, it was important to ensure that this was not an artefact of the methods employed.

My emphasis was on older people from their fifties to their nineties as long as they were not 'vulnerable'. As an estimate, I probably spoke at some time or other to at least a quarter of those aged over sixty-five in Cuan. I followed the protocols of my university and funding ethics committees with regard to obtaining consent. My main ethical concern, however, is not with compliance with the requirements of committees but the injunction not to cause harm. In general, the degree to which an account has been anonymized in this volume is relative to the degree to which a person's identification might cause harm. Anonymization is secured through changing details about people that are not relevant to the point that is being made through their inclusion in the text. In these days of search engines and online maps, it would not be hard to work out where Cuan is, but I would ask readers to respect the pseudonym as assisting in this ethical aim of protecting the anonymity of individuals.

A Joke on Kant

This book consists largely of an ethnography. Apart from the previously mentioned yardstick that would allow us to judge philosophy against ethnography and vice versa, there were two other reasons for developing this juxtaposition with my readings of certain philosophers. The first was a by-product of my approach to ethnography. Influenced by anthropologists such as Pierre Bourdieu and sociologists such as Erving Goffman, I am drawn to activities regarded as relatively unimportant or background. I believe that often people's values are manifested by those mundane parts of life they just take for granted and are therefore unchallenged, rather than issues they might explicitly debate such as politics. You will read here descriptions of playing bingo, walking dogs, choosing holidays, and grandparenting. One purpose of considering these in relation to philosophy is to make the case that these pursuits, which would otherwise be dismissed as mundane, are precisely where people engage with many profound issues explicitly discussed in philosophy.

The second aim was to promote a re-set in the relationship between anthropology and philosophy more generally. I read philosophy often in awe, as do many others. This results in a tendency to look up to it and its more general and abstract discussions. This book is intended to proselytize for a more equal and sideways relationship between anthropology and philosophy, by focusing upon the insights gained when philosophical questions are reconsidered within the messy context of everyday lives. What will be presented here are merely my own readings, mostly of the original texts (well, the English translations). These should certainly not be taken as any kind of authority on those philosophers. But I hope that what amounts in some cases to the 'gist' of the philosophical arguments is sufficient to help view the ethnographic material in a very different light, and that justifies their inclusion. As I am an amateur, there are undoubtedly misrepresentations and areas of ignorance within these sketchy accounts of

INTRODUCTION

philosophical texts and I both take full responsibility and apologize for these.

If the people of Cuan were in thrall to Cuan, I was in my earlier days in thrall to philosophy. A childhood love of Greek and Roman myths and legends led me to an early interest in Socrates, then the Sophists and other classical writings. When I was a teenager in the 1970s, Sartre and existentialism were clearly *à la mode*. Later, as an undergraduate student in archaeology, I took part in endless debates about positivism and epistemology. Teaching anthropology had always involved trying to keep abreast of philosophical movements that were influencing the discipline, such as post-modernism and post-structuralism. My most concerted effort to embrace philosophy was an involvement with the debates within Western Marxism that were dominant when I started work as a lecturer in material culture studies at University College London, transitioning from archaeology to anthropology. This shifted into an abiding fascination with Hegel, who was the core influence upon my first more theoretical book *Material Culture and Mass Consumption*[46] and who has continued as a source of inspiration ever since.

Why, then, are the philosophical sections of this volume introduced with a discussion of the German philosopher Immanuel Kant (1724–1804)? One influence was that Kant has become an icon of philosophy, the figure who stands for my imagination of philosophy itself. The main reason, however, was that rereading Kant inspired a rather lame joke about what is *a priori* to Kant, given his obsession with the *a priori*. This 'joke' will be played on Kant later in the following section because it encapsulates perhaps the single most important feature of anthropology itself, which will be juxtaposed with the discussions of philosophers throughout this book: the study of sociality and social relations.

It is likely that most people who have engaged with Kant's writing, even at my superficial level, have started with his best-known work, the *Critique of Pure Reason*.[47] The *Critique of Pure Reason* considers the problem that we cannot know about things in themselves. What we know is first mediated by our faculties, which determine the impression they make upon us. If an object existed in another dimension, we simply would not know of it, since we possess no faculty to perceive that dimension. We therefore cannot claim to begin from the principles of pure reason, since reason itself relies on a series of *a priori* conditions or fundamental categories through which we obtain perception. Our minds precondition us to take in things as they appear to us. The types of categories analysed by Kant included our sense of time and our orientation in space. Kant argued that the objective world must in some manner conform to the conditions of these same *a priori* categories that we bring to the perception of the world. We see things in space and time and therefore at least imagine that space and time are a quality of those things.

So far, so what? There is no particular link between these arguments and the ethnography. But they are important because when it comes to reading Kant's moral philosophy, it seems that this was largely modelled upon similar principles. Kant's discussion of the fundamental categories that lie prior to reason is called theoretical philosophy. The field of morality is known as practical philosophy. The *Critique of Practical Reason*[48] follows a parallel logic to the *Critique of Pure Reason*. Once more, Kant asserts that we cannot directly observe the fundamentals behind morality, including the God we may believe in. These are again *a priori* categories. In the *Critique of Practical Reason* and allied writings, Kant looks at the conditions of rational action based on *a priori* assumptions. He proposed what he called a 'categorical imperative', which structures practical reason and equates to the simultaneous demands of both duty and rationality. Only morally dutiful action is truly rational. For the purposes of this juxtaposition with ethnography, what seems surprising about Kant's approach to the fundamentals of morality is that 'all moral philosophy rests wholly on its pure part. When applied to man, it does not borrow the least thing from the knowledge of man himself.'[49] This implies that in the search for moral fundamentals, Kant is seeking principles that transcend both context and history.

This suggests that the starting point for an apprehension of morality is to insist on the autonomy of persons. They are even held to be autonomous from any specific desire. This autonomous freedom is taken to be an *a priori* property of us being rational beings, something that is not granted to us, but inherent.[50] To understand the fundamental moral law, we have to pare back to universal principles that give us morality and not be deflected by the consideration of any specific context. The same applies to Kant's insistence upon freedom as a primary condition. Freedom is not just the conscious sense that we could have acted differently from the way that we did, implicating a judgement as to how to act. To be properly equated with freedom, it supposes that moral judgements are universal principles, irrespective of cultural conditions.

Kant thinks that moral people should rise above their specific circumstances and make a judgement based on some maxim or underlying principle that applies to all people. There are some basic principles that should become evident to us all as rational human beings. For example, it is appropriate to link the maxim that 'I will not lie' to an ideal that everyone should avoid lies.[51] It is less appropriate to suggest that I should borrow money to cover a debt, because we would ask ourselves what would happen if everyone took this action. Morality is, then, a categorical imperative, which we come to understand if we test it by the criterion of how it would work as a universal law and the likely consequences of its universal application. In practice, of course, we may act on specific desires rather than as we categorically should.[52]

The core to Kant's *a priori*, whether in relation to reason or to morality, is the presumption of a mind capable of making judgements; a mind that is situated within an individual, whose relationship to the world as a universal is Kant's concern. The fundamentals that lie *a priori*, with respect both to the cognitive categories and to the moral law, are identical for all beings. Given this emphasis upon a purely free individual, it is not surprising that Kant is often regarded as a core figure in the formation of philosophy as an essentially liberal discipline. The insistence on the autonomy of each individual to make moral choices outside of external influences is quite similar to the conventional model of the individual making consumption choices without reference to other conditions within the discipline of economics.[53] Chapter 6 will give more direct consideration to this link to liberalism and morality through a discussion of the work of Rawls and the principles of a liberal state that claims to respect the freedom of the individual will.[54] A counter-argument might be made that this style of discussing individuals in relation to universals goes back to Aristotle and is a genre of philosophy rather than a reflection of any historical period.

What Lies *a Priori* to Kant?

On reading Kant, an idea struck me first jokingly and then more seriously. In view of the continuous appeal to the *a priori* throughout his writing, it might be intriguing to look and see if there is anything that could be considered *a priori* to him. Is there something analogous within anthropology that corresponds to an *a priori*? I believe there is such a candidate for this *a priori* without which one cannot account either for this ethnography or for anthropology as a discipline. Conspicuously to the fore amongst my research participants is the constant presumption of sociality. Everything starts from social relations. Sociality is *a priori*. No one comes into the world alone; they wouldn't survive. Some societies do then allow more of a drift towards individualism. Less so people in Cuan.

The ethnography of Cuan only really began to make progress when I acknowledged the specific way sociality was understood as *a priori* for this population: when I came to appreciate that the key to understanding Cuan society is what happens when two strangers meet. At first, they are generally quite wary and the greeting may be relatively superficial. What really matters is establishing that they know specific people in common. Once that overlap of social networks is established, everything relaxes and people's engagement becomes more friendly. At first, people viewed me with considerable suspicion. Often they would start by saying things like, 'Oh, you are the Englishman people are talking about,' not an especially positive categorization in an Irish town with its colonial past. What helped wasn't just that I came to know more people, it was the way I learnt to deploy this knowledge. Very quickly in any conversation with a person I had just met, I would say something like, 'Oh you live on so and so street, so I guess you know ...,' or, 'You play that sport, do you, well I understand from so and so ... .' Once I could establish that I knew individuals in common with this new person, then I was no longer 'The Englishman', I was someone they could potentially relax with and chat to. This was the main reason why the first six months of fieldwork were quite frustrating and not so rewarding, but by the time it came to the final three months, things were 'grand'.

I have worked as an ethnographer in many other countries and noted similar practices. But none quite the same as the way this operated within Cuan. For example, in Trinidad, there might be a latent instrumentalism concerning why it could be useful for both parties to know of another individual.[55] This is very different from the way social networking operates in Cuan, where there is no such instrumental component. Making a comparison between Ireland and Trinidad provides an equally important contrast to Kant. Having asserted the priority of the social over the individual, the anthropologist will also avoid the implications of universality, because what we mean by sociality will be with reference to some regional context. Social etiquette operates as an expression of specific cultural and normative values. For anthropology, even the concept of individualism has its own *a priori*, because anthropologists will first examine specific cultural ideas about individualism. An example is the book *After Nature* by Marilyn Strathern.[56] Strathern's discussion was influenced by the research of her colleague Alan Macfarlane into the origins of a specific English individualism that stretches back to medieval times and was in stark contrast to the European conceptual and institutional comprehension of the individual.[57]

This approach is not intended to detract from an appreciation of individuals. Characterization of people through reference to a group or to 'an ethnography' will clearly over-generalize and could diminish our respect for the particularity of each individual. This is why ethnographies usually include stories based on specific and always unique individuals. Furthermore, as already noted, there are lonely people in Cuan and there was a commitment to find them. But doing so required considerable effort. This study was conducted as part of my second large-scale exercise in comparative ethnography. Five years previously, I also led a project of a similar scale designed to study the nature and consequence of social media, a project called 'Why We Post'.[58] For that project, I spent sixteen months carrying out an ethnography of an English fieldsite of comparable size (though the English would call a settlement of 11,000 a village and the Irish a town). Most of my writing about that English fieldsite consists of an examination of the increasing isolation and loneliness that became apparent,[59] especially in the study of hospice patients that formed part of the larger research.[60] My argument was that there are particular qualities in Englishness itself – for example, the respect for each individual's privacy within their own home – that had led to this problematic condition. In the English study, it had required no effort at all to find lonely or isolated people.

Both the people in the English and those in this Irish fieldsite expect in retirement to take up additional hobbies, interests, and activities. At a celebration of International Women's Day in Cuan, as well as many similar occasions, the speaker exhorted women to develop new interests primarily for this purpose of extending their social networks. They really didn't need any encouragement. One of the key differences was that in the English village certain new hobbies, such as painting and writing, tended to be viewed as essentially individual pursuits whose primary purpose was individual self-expression. In Cuan, however, these same hobbies of writing and painting were generally undertaken as social activities. In the cafés, it was common to see a group of painters on a break from their classes. In a creative writing group, people exchanged their drafts and discussed them. The emphasis in Cuan is on the collective nature of these retirement pursuits, which flourish alongside the sheer scale of public involvement in bridge, bingo, Tidy Towns, and countryside walking. Then there is all the sociality that needs no excuse or associated activity but develops around the weekly or sometimes daily meetings in cafés with friends and family around the town. When I returned to Cuan after the pandemic, one of the most common responses to a question about the main impact of Covid was that they had met new friends while taking their frequent walks around the beach as daily constitutionals.

There was a clear contrast between Cuan and the equivalent fieldsite in England. People in Cuan could imagine the kinds of problem of isolation and loneliness that had been shockingly common within the English study, but they always referred this to the condition of older unmarried male farmers somewhere deep in the countryside, the one Irish group notoriously prone to loneliness and isolation.[61] This was not envisaged as a possibility within a place such as Cuan where someone would always be keeping an eye on any given property and its residents. The hospice where I carried out research in England had to deal with funerals that no one came to, not even close family, though these were an extreme. In Cuan, by contrast, a funeral was an event that commonly packed the substantial church to its rafters.

These examples are characteristic of the way anthropology would approach the *a priori* of sociality in practice. It is possible to make the general assertion that sociality is always *a priori* and oppose this to Kant's autonomous individual. But then the apparent universalism of this claim is instantly negated because the anthropologist immediately asks about the different forms of sociality or individualism that pertain to each population where they work. The English may have cultural values that tend to foster individualism, but that does not contradict the more fundamental principle of sociality as an *a priori*. In England, too, loneliness and isolation were considered as failures and problems rather than the proper nature of society.

INTRODUCTION

Posing sociality as an *a priori* is, then, equally fundamental to the perspective of anthropology as a discipline as it is to the characterization of Cuan.[62] A perfectly reasonable definition of anthropology is to describe it as the study of social relations. If anything, the problem in social anthropology has been our tendency to reduce everything to social relations. Often theorists such as Émile Durkheim or Mary Douglas are critiqued for being just a bit too assiduous in their desire to bring whatever they are studying back to some kind of reflection of more fundamental social relations.[63] The origins of anthropology lie in the study of small-scale societies that almost inevitably used kinship itself as their fundamental organizational principle. In conclusion, both the societies that anthropologists study and also the discipline of anthropology itself take social relations and sociality as an *a priori*. Persons are understood as relational before they are understood as individuals. This includes cognition and reason, the other concerns of Kant. The relationship to the world starts, at least according to Melanie Klein, from a baby's initial consciousness of either the presence or the absence of its mother's breast.[64] Only later do we come to see ourselves as individuals.

These points, then, situate an ethnography in a middle field somewhere between the two main units employed by Kant: his imagination of the pure autonomous person and also his universalism. There are good reasons why philosophers may want to imagine conditions abstracted from the context of sociality in order to logically construct universal arguments. Kant is thereby able to achieve many things that anthropologists would not attempt. He was not trying to distance us from life, but to provide a mechanism for going more deeply into the conditions that allow us to create our sense of common decency that everyone should agree to. But it is important to simultaneously remind ourselves that such conditions are speculative, as none of us live outside of our messy contexts. This opens the door to the complementary role of anthropology based on the ethnography of extant populations.[65] In an ethnography, an examination of how people make rational and moral judgements becomes mainly a question of the *a posteriori* rather than the *a priori*, because judgements are always founded within the constraints and the possibilities given by established convention and their consequences for subsequent decisions.[66]

As just noted, Kant's reliance upon the de-contextualized individual making moral decisions feeds into what becomes the premise behind most discussion within modern academic economics, which also tends to theorize and create models based on the premise of free choices made by autonomous individuals. Today, however, there would be very few defenders of such assumptions within contemporary social science – it is after all called *social* science. By this point, it might also be expected that there would therefore have arisen some similarly aligned critical discussions of Kant coming from within the discipline of philosophy itself. An example can be found in the writings of Catriona Mackenzie and her colleagues, who propose to replace Kant's notion of individual autonomy with that of relational autonomy.[67] Their critique has focused primarily on the emergence of a feminist reading of Kant which lies closer to an anthropological sensibility.

To conclude, the immediate inspiration for arguing that sociality must be seen as *a priori* came not from reading earlier versions of the same argument that has been common at least since Durkheim, but from observations made during the ethnography of Cuan. These arguments do not detract from Kant's crucial contribution to our understanding of what an individual 'should do' in the face of moral dilemmas. Kant was not trying to limit ideals to present reality, but trying to provide ideals by which to judge reality.[68] But for the very same reason, it seems important to complement his discussions with others that begin from a rather different *a priori*. There are two primary qualities of the anthropological *a priori* that will be found throughout this ethnography. The first is the presumption of sociality and social relations. But as a study of a single town in Ireland, this is joined to the presumption of culture in opposition to any universalism, evident in anthropology's general tendency towards comparison, as in the above contrast between Cuan and a similarly sized fieldsite in England, but also cultural relativism, even when we are aware of the problems posed by pure relativism.[69]

A reminder of certain caveats. First, I have no evidence that the people of Cuan with whom I worked are representative of Ireland or even of Cuan. Second, a discussion of Kant and of a style of writing based on the relationships between the individual and the universal may apply to certain philosophers, but certainly not to the entirety of 'Western' philosophy. Each individual within the ethnography and each philosopher within the canon of philosophy is unique. But it is still possible to analyse at the level of typicality and that which is characteristic. In the conclusion, it will be suggested that there are common traits to philosophy that differ from typical anthropological discussions and the presumption of many people in Cuan: for example, that many philosophers, not surprisingly, tend to favour individual contemplation and philosophizing itself as a goal in life. This has very little in common with the Irish ideal of good *craic*: having an enjoyable time in the company of others.

A final question might be posed as to the selection of philosophers who appear in this book. Why those and not others? I have deliberately tried to include a range of philosophers from classical philosophy, including Socrates and the Stoics, through to post-Enlightenment philosophers such as Hegel, but also founding figures of modern philosophy such as Heidegger, Adorno, and Sartre, as well as more contemporary philosophers such as Alasdair MacIntyre and Martha Nussbaum. The second criterion was to locate a body of philosophy that seemed to be a plausible match for the ethnographic material presented in the preceding chapter to which they are being compared. This is why Socrates is considered in relation to sport, Sartre in relation to freedom, and Rawls in relation to inequality. Readers may well consider alternative philosophical contributions that could also have served. But I wanted to write a book that was reasonably clear, focusing in each case on a particular philosopher or philosophical movement rather than attempting a more comprehensive survey. The overarching aim remained a comparison between philosophical approaches to the good life and an ethnographic approach to the good enough life.

Chapter 1

AN EXCEPTIONALLY FREE SOCIETY?

The argument of this chapter is that a group of retired people from one small Irish town represent an exceptionally free people – in some ways freer than any previous historical population. These statements are not quite as extreme as they sound. The word 'represent' acts as a caveat here. These people are not unique. They are an example of populations found not just in Ireland, but increasingly around the world, who in various ways have gained this unprecedented degree of freedom, each with respect to distinctive histories and through overcoming specific constraints. Taken collectively, these populations represent a small minority of the world's population. It is to be hoped, but it is by no means assured, that they represent a trajectory that will continue to grow. In the meantime, this chapter is dedicated to asking what we can learn from such populations as already exist and are open to research.

What does it mean to claim that a population represents an exceptional or an unprecedented state of freedom? The term 'freedom' refers not to the release from any one particular burden or constraint. Rather, it is the sheer range of simultaneous disengagements from a very wide range of prior constraints and obligations, coupled with an increasing capacity to fulfil their desires, that justifies these claims. As will be true of several of the chapters of this book, some of the examples that follow were previously discussed in my book with Pauline Garvey.[1] Also, one of the significant elements that contribute to freedom of this community – their relative affluence – will be discussed in more detail in chapter 3. There have been wealthy populations throughout history: the elites of the Roman Empire or the Chinese mandarins under imperial rule, for example, both of whom may have had more money than they knew what to do with. But contemporary affluence is not just a matter of finance. Today, we live with health services, transport systems, digital communications, and a host of other facilities that historically money could not buy. Living with access to painkillers, cars, planes, and the internet represents a colossal break with the past. These, too, are important components that warrant this claim of unprecedented freedom.

The aspects of freedom that were most fully discussed in my book with Pauline Garvey included freedom from work, freedom from family, freedom from religion, and freedom from age. These will therefore be only briefly reprised in this chapter. Instead, there will be a focus on an area not discussed in the earlier book: freedom from politics, including identity politics. While this may be the only example to be considered in depth, the overall aim of the chapter is to convey the entire constellation of freedoms that in combination makes this claim to unprecedented freedom plausible.

Freedom from Religion

For this Irish population, perhaps the foremost and most conscious element of freedom, since it corresponds to our common colloquial use of that term, would be the freedom they feel they have gained through their own historical trajectory. They frequently compare their present circumstance with memories of when they were young and the degree of theocratic control over so many aspects of their lives that they had experienced at that time. As described in the introduction to this book, the context was partly a legacy of the Independence movement and the bloody civil war that followed. When Éamon de Valera became the key figure in the formation of independent Ireland, he pursued a single-minded quest to create an authentic Irish identity, free of British colonialism, and central to this was the reinvigoration of Irish Catholicism, a vision supported by all sides in the Independence movement. This resulted in a period of theocracy in which government decisions on almost all matters were strongly influenced by the Church, which directly ran elements of the state at the local level such as education. The Catholic Church (and the Jesuits in particular) clearly influenced the drafting of the 1937 constitution, which recognized its 'special position' until this was removed by the Fifth Amendment in 1973. Listening to informants, not only did they recall their experience of a Church-dominated education, but it seemed as though almost everything that had occurred during their youth, ranging from which public buildings were approved to what theatrical performances were staged, implicated a Church figure in the background. A much more detailed account that effectively conveys the implications of this theocracy for ordinary people is found in O'Toole's *We Don't Know Ourselves*.

One of the retirees of Cuan wrote a book about the years he spent in the Christian Brothers, who were a major force in the Church's control over education. Although he decided to leave this organization, his book is at pains to show that during those years he saw nothing that suggested the kinds of sexual and other abuse that have subsequently come to light. It does show, however, how for his generation it was quite natural to join such an order at a very young age, with many also becoming monks or nuns. In many large families, the expectation was that at least one sibling would join the Church, making religion an even more integral and intimate part of their lives. This situation was not uniform. Most of these retirees attended mass in their youth as something basic and compulsory. Yet one individual, born in Cuan, told how he and his mates managed to get away with rarely going to mass, and a few were secular from the time of their parents' generation. The overwhelming sense, however, was of intense religious observance, a political theocracy, and a time when most forms of authority were ceded to the Church.

Having said that, Cuan was one of the earliest towns to take a liberal turn away from the Church, probably influenced by the tourism that only ended once people from Ireland could afford to take summer holidays in Spain in the 1970s. Prior to that, the town had been seen as a hub of popular entertainment, the regional site people flocked to when they wanted to go out dancing and enjoy themselves, often in defiance of the Church. The shift to liberalism may, then, have been both earlier and more gradual within Cuan compared to much of Ireland, where it was experienced as a more precipitous collapse in Church authority associated with a series of massive scandals. In Cuan, too, everyone has had to deal with their personal shock and re-assessment as scandal after scandal came into the public eye. O'Toole suggests that the impact of these scandals was yet more powerful in that they required an acknowledgement of things that in some degree may have been known but were repressed.[2] The scandal over sexual abuse by the Christian Brothers was critical because of their control over education. One of my research participants had spent her life working with the now elderly victims of another scandal: the neglect of illegitimate children given over to the Church. Today, even those with faith observe the subsequent lack of religiosity amongst the young and see themselves as perhaps the last observant generation. The Cuan region voted by a solid 72 per cent for the repeal of the Eighth Amendment: that is, the legalization of abortion.

This figure leaves 28 per cent who didn't vote for abortion rights, and it is likely that these would lie mainly within the demographic that dominated the ethnography. Based on my attendance at church services, I estimate that between 600 and 800 people go to one of various masses in most weeks, almost entirely older people, out of a population of around 11,000. Many of those attending, however, go for social reasons and meet others for tea afterwards in one of three or four regular sites, including tea provided within the church after the service. For them, the church plays a role as the centre of community life – a role that is celebrated in popular culture such as the TV series *Father Ted*, a comedy where the Church is portrayed as far from its own ideal, but perhaps the more benign as a result. For many older people, religion means the comfort of familiar custom, which continues even when the underlying faith is less relevant. The current priest in Cuan is fully aware of the necessity for transformation within the Church itself. His work is now mainly devoted to developing social support and conveying a more general and often quite ecumenical sense of moral responsibility and ethical awareness. The Church seemed to serve these purposes effectively.

As noted in my book with Pauline Garvey, one of the most common refrains heard in Cuan was a variation on the expression, 'I was born Catholic, but as a result of the Church's self-destruction through scandal and abuse I am now free to be a Christian.'[3] This seems intended to convey that they had been brought up within an extremely disciplined and authoritarian Catholic Church, with its traditional emphasis upon sin and damnation. Today, by contrast, they would prefer to see Catholicism as a more general ethical aspiration to be a good person, concerned with others through actions that arise from their own volition. Even those who are entirely secular in belief might espouse this general sentiment of trying to be a good Christian. The result is a very different and generally more acceptable contemporary alignment with the Catholic Church.

AN EXCEPTIONALLY FREE SOCIETY?

What matters most for the purpose of this chapter, however, is the sheer scale of this transformation. Both at a national and a local level, Ireland had shifted from being one of the most deeply religious countries in Europe, when these people were young, to becoming a nation in the vanguard of liberal values today.[4] For the people of Cuan, those born there, but perhaps even more so for the many who had migrated from rural backgrounds, this was the most important example of a palpable sense of freedom, because it was the underlying context to so much else in their lives. Becoming liberal and secular meant freedom of thought, and felt like an almost visceral enlightenment, to the degree that they had personally once experienced the precise opposite.

Freedom from Work

Two other key components of unprecedented freedom relate to work and to the family, these two activities which dominate much of an adult's life. Freedom of thought is fine, but one also needs time to think. Once individuals were old enough to enter the workforce, then employment had taken up much of their day and often became central to their identity. They had become shopkeepers, sports physiotherapists, or school caretakers. This was less true for women, at least earlier on, but the next section on the family demonstrates a commensurate freedom.

One of the primary aims of the ASSA project was to acknowledge the consequences of increased life expectancy. In most regions, retirement is viewed as a sort of add-on to life, while real life is identified with the earlier periods of work and parenting. Our project benefited from being able to view retirement from a comparative perspective. This revealed a stark contrast between the findings of the study based in São Paulo as compared to Cuan. Marília Duque found that in São Paulo, when people retired, their first concern was to retain the status and identity built up through decades of employment.[5] They often sought new kinds of work, or new ways of ensuring that others did not cease to see them first and foremost through this identification with their previous employment. Your work was who you were. The setting is crucial here, since of all the cities of Brazil, São Paulo is the one most generally identified with the success and prosperity derived from hard work. It has a very different vibe from, say, Rio de Janeiro.

By contrast, I spent around a year going weekly to the meetings of the Cuan Men's Shed, an organization specifically intended for retired men. One of the most striking observations was that I simply would not have known, without directly asking, what the prior occupations of these men had been. Importantly, there was no attempt to assert the status of some of these men, who had held very senior positions, as against those who had relatively low-paid or manual occupations. The only time that the contrast became apparent was when the group was faced with tiresome bureaucratic procedures which stipulated that, to conduct voluntary work, the Men's Shed had to abide by all sorts of data protection rules, insurance policies, police clearance procedures, and similar requirements. It then became apparent that some of its members had extensive managerial experience, and, as they were very familiar with such requirements, they volunteered to deal with them.

It was not that people hid their past employment. Some of the groups of men who met in the town cafés on a weekly basis had bonded around their common legacy. For example, one such group had been working in education and another in the civil service. Quite commonly, people took on some relevant role for a few years after retirement, such as helping audit new teachers or acting as a consultant for the government ministry where they had previously worked. But within a relatively short time this ceased and for all intents and purposes life began again, devoted entirely to developing the novel activities permitted by retirement.[6]

These activities, which ranged from learning a musical instrument to taking up more serious photography, joining a walking group, or researching a talk for the historical society, generally had no relationship to any past employment. If anything, the attraction of new retirement activities was that they enabled people to engage with a range of experiences that felt like an expansion of life. The core argument of my book with Pauline Garvey is summarized in its subtitle: *When Life Becomes Craft*. This was not a reference to the number of craft activities retired people engaged with, but rather an argument that the core craft that dominates all others is the capacity to now craft one's own life. The skill these retirees were developing was that of organizing their social lives, activities, holidays, and free time, adding and subtracting interests that in effect sculpted them anew. Our point of reference was the role of the smartphone: WhatsApp and Calendars and all the other apps turned out to be crucial to this ability to keep order within what were often remarkably busy retired lives. All such activities were freely chosen, in marked contrast to the experience of salaried employment, which had dictated much life on a daily basis. Already with this example, we can see how much the experience of freedom is about freedom *to* and not just freedom *from*.

Because extended retirement is of relatively recent appearance, we have rarely come to terms with its consequences. Given the extensive years of education required for many more professional occupations, increasingly people may be well into their twenties before they commence salaried employment, while many of those who participated in this ethnography had retired in their late fifties. As a result, a good number of these retirees could expect around thirty years of retired life, having perhaps spent no more than thirty years in salaried employment. If the life of retirement is of equal length to the life of labour, it should be considered of equal importance. Yet this is clearly anything but the case in academia, in the media, or even in the general population. There are probably a thousand books about work for every one about retirement. The sheer longevity of retirement also impacts on the proposal to view it as life craft. This is a craft that can now be refined over decades. It is not simply what someone chooses to do when they first retire. It equally may include an interest they decide to develop after twenty years of retirement.

Freedom from Family

If there was a previous constraint on free time that sometimes surpassed even the requirement of employment, at least for women, then it would surely be the obligations of kinship. Most women could recall periods of life that had been exceptionally demanding when they had been mothers, often of three or four children in turn. Anthropological studies of kinship have tended to focus on issues of classification and the social obligations that follow from one's position within kinship. As a result, we may have neglected the way kinship itself has developed in recent years, changes which require us to pay more attention to kinship as experience.

In the lives of people in Cuan, kinship is now a somewhat intermittent experience. In between the intensity of being a child or a parent comes the period of late teenage years or early twenties, where it is quite common for an individual to have very limited contact with family. In Cuan, people at this age are likely to be spending time abroad or at least at some distance from their home town. Many then return to Cuan to have their own families because, as already noted, they see the town as ideal for parenting in view of their own experience as children. In addition, in Cuan they will have the practical support of their own families. When the children grow up and leave home, kinship may once again diminish, returning to a variable extent with active grandparenting. A final period of intense kinship may follow as one cares for elderly or dying parents and then in turn is cared for in one's own last years. In short, kinship is far more than a classification. There are periods of life dominated by kinship and others where it barely registers.

A common observation amongst these retirees was that they had been looking forward to the freedoms associated with retirement. But the time of retirement then coincided with the frailty of their parents, sometimes involving dementia, whose incidence has markedly increased with growing life expectancy. Dementia and other frailties may place exceptionally heavy pressures upon children that mostly they were simply not prepared for, with often accompanying tensions between the siblings because of their differential ability or willingness to take on the burden of caring for their parents. Following the death of their parents, however, they can then take up the freedom that had beckoned with the prospect of retirement.

In a separate paper,[7] Pauline Garvey and I have argued that perhaps the key kinship category associated with retirement, grandparenting,[8] has become a rather more profound element of kinship than had previously been acknowledged, especially in relation to this experience of freedom. This is not because of the relationship to the grandchildren themselves, but because of the way grandparenting plays a role in resolving a person's prior experience of kinship. In that paper, we document how grandparenting resolves the previously sometimes problematic relationship to one's own children, not only because children are now pleased to acknowledge the help and support of their parents in grandparenting, but also they may become more appreciative of what was involved when they were parented as children, thereby creating a more empathetic relationship with their own parents. Further, we found that this led to a reassessment of the way the grandparents had themselves experienced being children, parented in often low-income, large families with varying degrees of alcoholism and subjected to sometimes quite traumatic experiences.

What was equally striking was the effort that grandparents made to ensure that grandparenting could become an expression of, rather than the suppression of, their personal freedom. This was achieved by ensuring that active grandparenting came to be viewed as their willing contribution, not merely an obligation of kinship. Amanda affirmed her sense of agency by noting that her grandparenting was neither too demanding nor too light. She or her husband would drop off or collect their granddaughter from nursery. On some days, she looked after her between nursery ending at noon and her niece taking over childcare around 3.00 p.m. She was more than happy to be involved, but grateful that this didn't impinge too much upon her wider freedoms. This ability to create balance and choice reflected the relative affluence of both the grandparents and the parents. It would not be the case in some other parts of Ireland.

This concern with freedom may be a reflection of the grandparents' prior experience of parenting. Olive, a sixty-four-year-old living on the relatively low-income Vartry Estate, felt she had been a good parent to her three children. But having successfully discharged her responsibilities as a parent, she did not feel obliged to undertake extensive grandparenting. Her daughter was desperate to go back to work and could only afford to do so if her mother took over the care for her own child full-time, but Olive had steadfastly refused:

> I have never minded my grandchildren, well I did mind one for a year but then the mother became pregnant and was looking to me to take over and I said no, no it's not going to happen. I would rather do my own job [cleaning in a shop]. She wanted to go back to work but you would be getting the two children at 7 in the morning and you would have them to 7 in the evening. Instead of being their granny I would be their mammy. I was sixty at that stage and I am not going to become a mother at sixty, simple as that. She is still not back to work. She will have to do what I did, which is wait till they go to school.

Turning grandparenting into an expression of freedom brings two major benefits. The first is that those involved can then perceive their grandparenting as an expression of love, both for the grandchildren and for their own children. If their labour is taken for granted as obligation, it is less explicitly about love. Curbing routine commitments also allows them to make exceptional efforts if the need arises. Grandparents often talk about how they will drop everything when someone is ill or there is some crisis. They are well aware that interventions at critical times tend to be more appreciated, while routine care can soon be taken for granted. This is why Olive refused to do 'formal babysitting', but always made an effort to help out when she was needed, typically, when a child was sick and couldn't go to school. She described this as 'just filling the gaps as they arise'.

The wider context to these observations is the way friendship is supplanting kinship as the dominant idiom for social relations.[9] Similar to these retirees, when I was a child, I would be introduced to 'Auntie' this and 'Uncle' that, individuals who were actually friends of my parents, not relatives. Today, however, someone might introduce 'my sister or mother, but also my close friend'. This replacement of kinship by friendship as the dominant idiom has arisen precisely because we can choose our friends but not our relatives. It represents an underlying shift from obligation to voluntarism as the foundation for the authenticity of a relationship. In the past, being a grandparent was defined by its classificatory obligations, the way anthropologists would have represented and understood it. Today, it is preferably expressed as love, found in grandparents' individual desire or willingness to help under a condition of relative freedom. In all of these ways, grandparenting is turned into an idiom of freedom, when it might well have been largely a constraint.

As retired people age, it becomes more likely that their own parents are now deceased. Their grandchildren will in turn have reached an age where kinship is relatively attenuated and even resisted as they go out into the world. This does not mean that there are no affective involvements with family. Almost invariably, these retirees told me that relationships with their family remain their strongest bonds of love and affection unto death. But kinship may diminish as an active component of everyday life and there may be older people who feel they don't receive as much family attention as they would like. This may be in part a negative consequence of that shift from obligation to freedom. Even if they are engaged with family on a daily basis, this may be mainly through WhatsApp or shorter visits that occupy a small proportion of the day. Overall, women continue to spend far more time cultivating routine family relations than their husbands. But they are also most likely to appreciate the freedoms they now enjoy, compared to the unremitting labour of being a full-time mother, and will talk enthusiastically of all the new activities through which they are now crafting their lives.

Freedom from Age

The topics of freedom from religion, work, and family are discussed within my work with Pauline Garvey, but the dominant theme of that book was freedom from age itself. In summary, the argument was that, historically, ageing was experienced through the medium of traditional categories of identity, because most societies, including the parents of these retirees, had clearly designated roles and expectations that pertained to the old. They had become the elderly or the senior citizen. These categories had some positive connotations of maturity or even wisdom, as well as negative associations such as suggestions of senility. A sepia photograph of a grandmother in a rocking chair, with her family around her, may have shown someone still in her fifties, but the photograph situates her in an established role and position that both defined and constrained her.

In recent decades, these cultural constructions of ageing are much diminished. Informants told how they expected to feel old when they reached sixty, seventy, eighty, or ninety, but these decennial birthdays came and went. Instead of entering a new dimension of age, there remained a feeling of continuity from youth. Thanks to digital technologies, they could re-engage with experiences associated with their actual youth, listening on Spotify to the music of the seventies in their seventies. I knew several retired people who made good use of a dating app called Plenty of Fish. At the same time, they had lost the attribution of cumulative wisdom which came with the respect for seniority and experience. The skills revered today are likely to concern new technologies rather than farming. Yet this loss of wisdom might have a positive consequence in creating a more equal relationship that takes little note of age. If an older person contributes to a discussion in a committee that runs a voluntary association, their opinions are valued only to the degree they seem worthwhile, irrespective of age. They have become valued for what they can contribute rather than for who they are.

Given the gradual elimination of identities based on traditional categories of ageing, the core parameter of difference among my informants became frailty. People maintained a continuity with youth until some reduction in health meant that things they used to do or be were no longer possible. A time might come when they could no longer drive, or walk, or remember, any of which would be a significant break with the person they had been up until then and would eventually be a harbinger of the decline that would lead to their death. But, prior to such deeper frailties, there were increasing numbers who even in their early nineties felt that the continuities with youth far outweighed the impairments that had been experienced up to that time. They remained an aggregate of that which they had developed over their life course, be it a reputation for bad jokes, or a respect for their knowledge of astronomy, traits which might have developed in their thirties or in their sixties. In the language of gerontological studies, they were in their third age rather than their fourth age.[10] This freedom from age is one more example of a freedom that is unprecedented.

More subtle is the question of whether at a certain age there comes an existential dividend to ageing. There are limits to what can be said with any confidence, even after sixteen months of ethnography. Do people worry less about their future when there is less future to worry about? Have they become more accepting or more terrified by the prospect of mortality? Is what they commonly say true about being far more afraid of dementia than death? One reason it is so hard to determine what people actually think about such matters is that they probably don't know themselves. I, too, couldn't say whether the things I tell myself about these issues are what I actually believe. So how can I expect that of others?

Freedom from Politics

The Civilized Irish: Politics with a Capital P
At this point the discussion will move from topics discussed in some depth in my book with Pauline Garvey to other fields which also express the form and nature of contemporary freedom. An additional benefit of now giving consideration to freedom from politics is that as part of the general trajectory of this volume, it leads us towards a freedom *to*, rather than just a freedom *from*. As mentioned in the introduction to this book, the period of fieldwork included what should have been one of the more contentious political discussions of modern Ireland, known as the Repeal of the Eighth. The Eighth

Amendment of the Constitution Act 1983 was an amendment which in effect enshrined in law the political opposition to abortion, making this virtually illegal. It was passed in 1983 after a bitter referendum campaign that ended up with 67 per cent voting in favour to 33 per cent voting against. The campaign to reverse this amendment took place during fieldwork in 2018 and resulted in almost the exact opposite figures.[11] As noted above, Cuan was particularly liberal, achieving a 72 per cent vote in favour of the repeal.

Although there were many posters on the streets put up by the respective campaigns, there was surprisingly little active discussion, even amongst the older people, who might have voted against. Just once, I recall a visiting folk singer being chided for her explicit pro-abortion song, but even that was more out of concern that someone else might have been offended. People recalled how the debate had been livelier the first time around, but by now they mostly knew each other's opinions. There was never much doubt about how the vote would go, so there simply wasn't a good enough reason to prompt divisive discussion.

It was not that people failed more generally to discuss issues that could be considered political. The retired people who met in the cafés had endless discussions on topics such as the housing problem or the health service, what had gone wrong, and what should be done. They all knew the longer historical background to such problems. While such discussion usually included criticism of whoever was in power at the time, they were not politicized debates intended to foster support for one political party over another. This was the period of Trump in the US and the Brexit débâcle in the UK. Everyone was aware that outside of Ireland, in the two countries whose news they most carefully followed, things were increasingly not just politicized but polarized. Politics had never been so foregrounded and divisive. There was a horrified fascination with both Trump and Brexit; people were often glued to the news about both. These examples served to remind everyone of what were regarded as the unremittingly negative consequences of such divisions.

There were also older and deeper reasons for avoiding divisive politics. It was unclear how many refugees had settled in Cuan because of the 'troubles' in Northern Ireland, but there were certainly some, and probably far more in the wider region. There was one particularly striking phrase that one could often hear in people's discussions of Northern Ireland. At some point, a person might make the claim that 'the Catholics are just as bad'. It seemed it was important to people in Cuan to distinguish themselves from the behaviour associated with populations of Northern Ireland of all stripes. Even if they support Sinn Féin – and some of the people I came to know well did – this was to do with its success as a credible alternative to the current dominant political parties, rather than any espousal of its historical commitments. It was entirely compatible with the belief that Northern Ireland remained troubled because of its adherence to division itself. If people in Northern Ireland were regarded as over-politicized, this fostered a self-image of the people of Cuan as comparatively apolitical.

In such discussions, the point of reference seemed to be the ideal of being 'civilized'. Northern Ireland was being exploited to confirm that Cuan people were above all civil, in showing a fundamental respect and concern for each other that transcended any political adherence. These ideas around the civilized and civil society were not passive. They incorporated an ideal of active concern and responsibility for others. It was the same sentiment that arose during the Covid-19 pandemic when people would closely observe everyone else's degree of compliance with government restrictions, sometimes exceeding the Garda in this. Ensuring everyone else was compliant affirmed their role as good and dutiful citizens, adding to the way they affirmed their status as conspicuously civilized through drawing a contrast with Brexit, Trump, and Northern Ireland.

As I was not present then, it is difficult to make claims about the past, but there were hints of a prior time when political discussion had also been muted, but for completely the opposite reason. When people referred to politics historically, it was overwhelmingly dominated by portraits of a heroic struggle for independence from the British. Almost everyone seemed knowledgeable about and could recite in very considerable detail the events that culminated in freedom for Ireland. There are streets in Cuan named after the martyrs murdered by the particularly thuggish Black and Tans. It was rare to have a music session in one of the pubs without the rendition of songs of praise to the heroes and heroines of that struggle. I was quite surprised that no one had actually demolished a monument in the town set up by an especially rapacious colonial landlord and also to learn that some properties still paid lease rents to English landlords. There was every reason why an Englishman such as myself should have been treated with suspicion and bitter resentment. I could be seen as the scion of an erstwhile colonial power. Behind these events lay centuries of oppression, the Famine, and, prior to that, the destruction wrought by Oliver Cromwell in the seventeenth century.

But these uses of history become far more difficult when reference is made to the period after independence, which was followed by a particularly brutal civil war during 1922–3, with many atrocities and reprisals in which more people lost their lives than in the independence movement. Cuan is situated in a region likely to have included many people on both sides. This probably meant that by the end of this war it would have been very difficult to engage in political discussion as many families would have had members fighting for the losing side. One heard occasionally of those who then left Cuan only to return many years later, if at all. This implied a legacy of avoidance of political discussion at a time when it was simply too divisive.

The situation today could hardly be more different, notwithstanding that the two dominant political parties, Fianna Fáil and Fine Gael, are actually the descendants of the opposing forces that fought that civil war. They later became the natural parties of government. Since the 1920s, there has been no other majority government in Ireland. Over time, both parties relinquished any radicalism that stemmed from their origins to become equally mainstream and very similar to each other. For several decades, the Irish population has mainly voted for two alternative versions of centrist politics. As one became contaminated by its mistakes or failures in government, the other would be voted into government. Even traumatic events such as the depression of the 1980s did not result in any real distinction between these parties. Votes would be given to alternative parties such as Labour or Green, but once they agreed to become coalition partners, the inevitable result was disillusion, as they in turn took some responsibility for the problems and compromises of participation in actual government. Cuan had become a place where people could discuss politics and vote, but could equally pride themselves on a kind of civilized and largely apolitical life.

The International Context

A further contribution to this freedom from politics was the repositioning of Ireland within the international arena, as it shifted from a negative orientation to the UK to a positive orientation towards Europe. In England, I was born at a time when the Irish were often perceived as construction workers or skivvies, and jokes and insults at their expense were commonplace. When I first arrived for my project, I had intended to drop into my conversations, as early on as possible, that, while I have no Irish ancestry, at least my descendants were Irish: my daughter is married to an Irish man. In my head, this was going to be my identity security blanket.

I expected hostility and suspicion based on history. But gradually I came to realize that in many ways the attitude was quite the opposite. There is a short-term history as well as the long-term one. Most people, when they consider the Irish diaspora, focus on the US. But the main waves of emigration from Ireland in the 1950s and 1980s were to the UK. The US 2016 census found 125,840 Irish-born citizens, but in the UK 2001 census the number was 869,093. Today, around 10 per cent of the UK population believe they have Irish ancestry.[12] Many people in Cuan have family in the UK, often married there. Many of the newspapers available in Cuan are local versions of UK papers. One lecturer admitted it was difficult to teach a class unless he could claim allegiance to one of the English Premier League football teams. People watched the same TV serials, such as *Line of Duty* or the latest Netflix drama, and they mostly bought the same brands as I did in London alongside Irish products.

Ambivalence about the English often arose through humour. At the end of my fieldwork, I held a farewell gathering in a pub for around forty of my research participants. During the party, one of them came up and said to me, 'Of course we came to celebrate. We are getting rid of a Brit without wasting a bullet.' As an Englishman, I was the butt of various jokes, but my sense was that these jokes expressed affection, a willingness to include me, rather than take aim behind my back. The most consistent negative attribute that people sometimes shared with me was that the English could not and should not be trusted. There remained, however, a general respect for the English as people who managed to get things done quite effectively. The period of the ethnography witnessed a remarkable shift in that perception, mainly due to the débâcle over Brexit.[13]

Almost everyone in Cuan saw themselves as having done pretty well out of being within the EU. It was viewed as contributing considerably to their economic success. Today, people in the town mostly enjoy higher incomes and better welfare, including higher pensions, than their equivalents in the UK. In contrast to the difficult relationship with the UK, people could now have a positive sense of themselves as European, without this detracting from their identity as Irish. A strong European identity also contributes to this release from the prior colonial identification. Being European had become taken for granted as an integral aspect of being Irish. The political posters attached to lamp-posts at election time vie in their promise to work for Ireland in Europe.

For all these reasons, the Brexit vote seemed incomprehensible. How was it that the English didn't 'get it' with regard to the benefits of European membership? Why would a country simply shoot itself in the foot? These questions arose immediately after the UK referendum. But that was just the start of the débâcle. Over the sixteen months of ethnography, daily news broadcasts reinforced the feeling that the British government was spectacularly inept, as was the failure of the UK Parliament to unite in opposition to a hard Brexit. The then leader of the opposition was viewed as equally ineffectual. Month after month, the newspapers reported how, having got themselves into this hole, the British reaction was always to dig deeper. People in Cuan watched these farcical political shenanigans with jaws wide open. Bit by bit, this evolved into a general realization that the English were in fact more inept than anything or anyone had previously given them discredit for. The subsequent denigration was given 'more in sorrow than in anger'. I turned from being the object of suspicion to the recipient of sympathy. Again and again, I tried to reassure people that there was no way a hard Brexit would actually happen; it would surely be just tokenistic. This was my own entirely mistaken belief at the time, and I, too, proved to be just one more stupid Englishman.

Of course, opinions varied. There was the rare exception who congratulated the English on their perspicacity in this positive rejection of Europe. More common was the way Brexit reinforced views about not trusting the English, who once again were treating the Irish with a mixture of ignorance and contempt. There seemed no understanding at all in the UK of the genuine fear of violence and recession that was felt in Cuan as a consequence of Brexit. But as the prior view of the English as effective and able to get things done crumbled away under the Brexit tide, it perhaps had a silver lining. It had become a catalyst in changing how the once colonized understood their erstwhile colonizer. Brexit may prove to have been an important contribution to the long-term decolonization of Ireland. Perhaps, after all, colonialism had nothing to do with any particular qualities of the English, but actually had been no more than an exercise of brute force. To a degree, then, this was yet one more contribution to freedom, a more genuine freedom from the English.

Good Enough Government
Often in those café discussions, individuals might express horror at mistakes made recently in Ireland around medical testing or the events leading up to the depression that followed the fall of the 'Celtic Tiger'. But given the two centrist parties, these were viewed as evidence of incompetence rather than arguments for any alternative political ideology. The unspoken implication was that such centrist politics had delivered good enough government. These governments could make horrible mistakes but were more to be trusted than governments driven by ideology. The best role for more idealistic parties such as the Greens, Labour, and Sinn Féin was their constant snapping at the heels of government to prevent complacency.

It may be that, having been born in one of the poorer European countries, people in Ireland were particularly appreciative of their current condition. They were aware that, apart from the lack of a national health service, in most respects they were better off than the English. Rightly or wrongly, people believed that the Irish state had one of the most progressive taxation regimes that fostered relative equality, making them a much more equal society than, for example, the US. As admirably demonstrated in the book *The Spirit Level*, affluence brings a sense of more general wellbeing only where it is combined with relative equality.[14] With the rise of social media and higher education, people are more likely to be held to account by those whom they know within this relatively small country. To this extent, government feels more human and approachable; it is harder to simply project onto it as an entirely alien and oppressive force.

The government at the time of the ethnography reflected the general liberal ethos of the Irish. The Taoiseach (prime minister), Leo Varadkar, as a gay man of Indian origin, seemed the proper embodiment of these ideals. I never once heard a negative comment about who he was (though plenty about his actions as Taoiseach). As a medical doctor, he seemed to accord with the general desire for competence directed to welfare as the essence of what people expected of government. While not the case for Cuan, in some rural regions there was a very different experience of what could be termed bad enough government, with evidence that 'in some areas the Irish state has been so weak in terms of service provision that communities have always had to go out and create the services and facilities that they want for themselves'.[15]

All of this provides further evidence for a relative freedom from politics. Under conditions of good enough government, the activities of governing tend to fade into the background. Someone would sooner or later sort out the road systems, the provision of services such as water and electricity, the Garda or fire officers. The hospitals and the care homes were there, even if intolerable waiting lists were too. The state was expected to take responsibility at the national level and just get on with the job, not brilliantly perhaps but in its good enough manner. This was seen as especially good enough when compared to Johnson, Trump, and Stormont, but also in comparison to the recent severe economic depression, which had been profoundly shocking. The fear was more that property prices would over-heat again – which rather sounds like a problem of being too successful. Brexit's silver lining was that Dublin could now proclaim itself as the largest English-speaking city in the EU. It is perhaps easier to live good enough lives alongside good enough governments.

Politics with a Small p
Everything that has been written so far might appear to be leading to a conclusion that the concept of freedom from politics equates to a population becoming politically inactive, perhaps even complacent. A result of all that could be called 'freedom *from*'. It is therefore of considerable significance that this ethnography confirms the very opposite. Cuan may have become unusually depoliticized in relation to national politics, party politics, Politics with a big P. But this had mainly resulted in the rise of a 'freedom *to*', such as a freedom to voluntarily engage in politics with a small p. This was an astonishingly active community in terms of political involvement. The single most common commitment was to Tidy Towns, a national competition traditionally concerned with keeping litter off the streets and the overall appearance of Cuan, but that was shifting towards the incorporation of various environmentalist criteria. More important was the sheer range of volunteering: an individual might be helping the lifeboats; assisting with autistic children; organizing a sports committee; helping with the school; launching environmental projects; delivering meals on wheels; or organizing a poetry festival or the bridge club. It seemed that people were more comfortable

being active in citizenship precisely because being a citizen was relatively free from politics.

The single clearest evidence for this distinction was the working of the Cuan Community Association (CCA), which was by far the most important 'political' organization in representing and helping organize the town. I was only able to attend the annual general meetings of the CCA rather than its more regular committee meetings, but I came to know several of the past chairs of the association well, seeing and interviewing them many times. In addition, there were many other research participants who had served at some time on various CCA committees. Without exception, everyone spoken to made the identical claim about the working of the association. They asserted that the CCA was resolutely apolitical. It took strong measures to be as autonomous as possible from association with any political party. The phrasing used several times was that those kinds of political affiliations were left at the door when people entered the room.

Yet the CCA was remarkably successful as a political institution that was constantly involved through lobbying and interaction with wider political bodies. This could be the local regional council but also sometimes central government. As a result, politicians were often present in its discussions, but the CCA simply refused to be used as a platform where established politicians could make their pitch. At the annual general meetings, it couldn't stop local councillors doing their level best to ignore such constraints, but mostly politicians were reduced to echoing their fulsome support for the various initiatives that the CCA had itself been involved with during the past year, or aimed to take up in the following year. They competed mainly over who could show most support for the association.

In the week-to-week workings of the CCA – for example, developing a new school, improving access for the disabled, making provision for bicycles, finding a new way to disseminate information to the population, and countless other activities – there was not a hint of political adherence. There was only concern with doing whatever was required in order to forward the agreed policies and aims. As in almost every other organization that could be observed in Cuan, taking on leadership roles was regarded mainly as a chore that people would temporarily agree to because it was their turn. This applied to the role of chair, secretary, treasurer, or as the lead for some particular task such as providing information for developing a policy on local transport. There was absolutely no attempt to gain status through leadership.

This also meant that the association was free of anything other than token elections, which were reduced to affirming usually unanimous agreements as to who should do what. This is not always a welcome mode of action. It could have raised complaints around the lack of representation, or undemocratic traits in self-perpetuating and self-reproducing governance. But mostly people in the town recognized that committee members and leaders were engaged in quite tedious matters that heavily encroached upon their free time and were grateful that anyone was prepared to volunteer to undertake such tasks. The same applied to smaller-scale projects. The chair of the Men's Shed had made abundantly and frequently clear that he felt he had done his share and that someone else should take over the role. But having failed to persuade anyone to actually take this on, he had become resigned to not yet resigning. He finally found his replacement after the end of the ethnography.

I recall a conversation with one ex-chair who was brought up in another part of Europe and had found this equally astonishing. After talking about the raucous politics of her homeland, she noted that, 'by contrast, the CCA is completely non-political. Everybody knows the people around the table have political affiliations. Everybody voted hopefully. But we never actually talk about that. It's always the "what's for the good for the community".' With respect to actual politicians, she noted they 'come and make their pitch, which they [the committee] see as a bit of joke, but indulge it since they need to have them on their side'. The constitution of the CCA has clear formal regulations against any form of party-political involvement and takes regular steps to ensure this: for example, at one point constraining the posting of political posters on a particular street.

One of the reasons I found this so striking is that I have carried out ethnographic work in many other regions of the world that included observation of equivalent local associations. Although these varied, they would mostly present the exact opposite characterization. Local politics was mainly exploited for developing individual reputation and power and was constantly subject to factionalism, public and private antagonism, and rivalry. It was often seen as providing a springboard for party-political advancement. Based on these prior ethnographic experiences, if anyone had told me that the state of affairs I have just described in Cuan was even possible, I would have dismissed them as naïve and assumed they had simply failed to excavate down to the hidden recesses where such politicized and competitive status-based activities were really taking place. I would have regarded this description as evidence for poor-quality fieldwork. But after sixteen months living in Cuan, and knowing many of these individuals reasonably well, I am confident that what I have described is the dominant ethos and practice of the CCA.

This lack of division was reflective of the wider community. I spent a good deal of time constructing an oral history of Cuan. The recollections of genuine disputes were so few and far between that only two stood out. One concerned the kind of activities that should be put on by the local theatre group. The second was a dispute over a possible one-way system for the traffic. The latter was one of the very few occasions which had resulted in some public protest. But this soon calmed down in the face of detailed policy discussion that forced people to consider the complex and often contradictory arguments involved in trying to come to a decision. Again it was really hard to believe that the only historical disputes were one argument over traffic and another over theatrical musicals.

As it happens, one further dispute did arise during the course of the ethnography itself. This concerned the issue of trees on the pavements. On one side were those who wanted to cut down trees whose roots created uneven pavements and thereby an impediment to mobility vehicles for the disabled. On the other side was the much more vociferous support for the protection of the trees as an essential part of Cuan's landscape. The initial dispute was impressively engaged, with people chaining themselves to railings and painting protests on the trees. Walking down the street meant being accosted by the writing on several of these trees purporting to be the trees' own protests and laments regarding their anticipated fate. The target was not the CCA but the regional council. The tension was soon diffused by the actions of the CCA, amongst others, which ensured that there would be a series of genuine consultations and compromises. Soon discussion was more focused on which particular species of tree might work best, where replacements were required, and what sizes of saplings were needed. The dispute was never politicized and was dealt with in an exemplary fashion based around the ideal of consensus.

A similar conclusion came from ethnographic interviews with two aspirant Cuan politicians, both of whom have since come to prominence within Irish politics, one at a national and the other at a regional level. At the time of fieldwork, I had no idea that this was likely, and I am pretty sure neither did they. What was abundantly clear was their sincerity and indeed integrity. Neither seemed driven by personal aggrandisement or ambition. For both, it was simply a continuity in a trajectory of civic duty. Standing for local election was an outcome of activities they had been engaged with for many years. One of them had worked previously for an NGO supporting immigration rights, the other had worked to support people with mental health problems within educational services. They had gradually developed a deep concern with current political issues, in one case especially around environmentalism and in the other around gender equality. Becoming a politician came from a sense of frustration that no one was really taking the kind of pro-active leadership necessary in issues such as combating climate change or helping neglected populations. Maybe it was only by becoming a politician oneself that an individual could try to ensure that such actions might be realized in the future. Though these two individuals were forged from this Weberian crucible, I found on a recent visit that since they have become successful they have been subject to a mainly cynical population, who refuse to believe that any politician could be sincere.

There were also already established politicians who were somewhat less pure. The most successful was a figure who made great efforts to gain credit for whatever good deeds had occurred. When performed at the annual meeting of the CCA, this caused considerable cynicism. I was quite shocked at his rather brazen claim to have been heavily involved in a venture that I had myself been involved in for over a year. He had been consulted and perhaps even done a little bit of lobbying for the cause, but he was essentially peripheral to the success of this venture. But should I have been shocked? It is easy to be hypocritical about politicians. They are hardly alone in trying to claim credit for actions they consider benign. The nature of democracy is such that a failure to gain credit could mean being voted out of office in the next election. As someone who has attended countless tedious Labour Party meetings in London as a party member, it is hard not to feel aggrieved by those who constantly critique but would never bother undertaking such responsibilities themselves. Then again, I was living in the England of Boris Johnson, where politicians are often even more craven and deceitful than others claim them to be.

AN EXCEPTIONALLY FREE SOCIETY?

An important factor in explaining this degree of positive involvement in both informal and formal political activity lies in the background of this population. A high proportion have previously worked in public sector areas such as education, health, and the civil service – all major employers within Ireland, much of whose economic development was state-led.[16] Others had worked in managerial positions within fields such as banking and commerce. The consequences were evident at a meeting held to develop a project concerned with housing for older people. The committee behind this initiative had been active for a while but felt they had so far lacked success partly because they still didn't have the requisite experience and networks. They therefore held a public meeting with the express purpose of recruiting two new individuals with experience in the financial and organization functions that would be required. Astonishingly, the meeting was an instant success in recruiting those with the requisite skills, one of whom had previously been the chief financial officer for a decent-sized company. It seems to be yet another silver lining from more extended retirement that many voluntary organizations now benefit from the accumulated experience and continued sense of responsibility of such professional retirees.

In conclusion, freedom from politics turns out to be very different from what might have been envisaged. There is that initial freedom both from the oppressive constraints imposed by less liberal governments and from the possibility of freedom from party politics when government consisted of the alternating of two centrist parties. Political complaint is mainly about incompetence, sometimes with tragic consequences, but not political ideology. As the people of Cuan become free of Politics, they use that freedom to engage in *p*olitics. As found in the previous chapter, there is simply no connection between freedom and individualism. At a local level, the retirees of Cuan had developed an exemplary commitment to active citizenship and collective community responsibility, based on a remarkable level of consensus derived from the foregrounding of the pragmatic at the expense of the ideological. Caveats will be found in chapter 5, which delves into evidence for inequality. But these will not lead to a rejection of this largely positive portrayal of Cuan politics. As will be argued in the conclusion to this book, freedom from politics was a condition which enabled my research participants to build Cuan as their '*polis*'.

Freedom from Identity

Gender

From the previous discussion, it seems as though Cuan was becoming less polarized politically at the very time when much of the world was moving in the opposite direction. A similar argument can be made with regard to trends within identity politics, though in this case the contrast is with generations rather than with regions. Older people of Cuan have experienced significant changes in regard to identity over the last two or three decades. This chapter will examine gender and Irish identity. Class will be discussed in chapter 3.

On my first arrival, it seemed that, if anything, gender differences were more marked in Cuan than I had anticipated. Public sociality was often gender-segregated. Many women would meet up for coffee and a chat with other women during the week, not just in twos but often through established groups, such as women who had just come from celebrating mass. Until recently, the male equivalent was mainly socializing together in pubs, but this was no longer the case. The cafés were now also places where groups of retired men met regularly, for example those who had worked in the same profession, or who lived in the same street. When one walked into a café, many of the non-family groups would be single-sex, although by no means all. Those taking a break from an art class or bridge class would be mixed. But even in my weekly ukulele session, almost inevitably, men gravitated to one side of the room and women to the other.

Over time, however, this observation came to feel misleading. In most societies, after a while, it is possible to pick up on the ways in which men and women send signals to each other: signals of appraisal and awareness of possibilities. Even while appearing apparently oblivious to these signals, one can discern a constant hyper-awareness of the implications of the slightest gaze or orientation of the body. Sexual possibilities are fundamental relations, and while not always at the forefront of thought, they are hard to dislodge as a constant latent aspect of consciousness. Yet it became evident that the older people in Cuan were simply far more relaxed when it came to gender encounters (or perhaps just even more subtle). They appeared to have been able to slough off that meta-level of sexual frisson and increasingly enjoy each other's company in a manner that transcended gender identity to a degree that is probably impossible for younger people, who may never be free of the consciousness of the possibilities of sex. It is very hard to know whether sexual activity actually decreases with age,[17] but given the relentlessness of sexual desire evident in various public scandals and the sheer number of cases in which people have engaged in activity they subsequently regret (balanced, of course, by those they may not regret), it seems reasonable to see any such decline as a kind of additional freedom – at least to the degree that sexual desire is experienced as something that controls people, rather than is under their control. But this is all highly speculative.

More amenable to ethnographic enquiry was evidence for increasing gender equality. Partly this reflected decades of feminism as it was absorbed into the more general self-consciously liberal ethos of this community, where equality was in and of itself a commitment. An example already considered was grandparenting. One of the many impacts of second-wave feminism, as it had become normalized since its emergence in the 1960s and 1970s, was the retrospective acknowledgement of the asymmetry of parenting. Men were as likely to reflect wistfully upon this past as women. While women might have felt that they were more exploited, men talked of having missed out on a potential highlight of their lives. The evidence that this was more than an affectation was to be seen in how grandparenting emerged as largely gender-equal, with men sometimes more keen on being involved than women. For example, Gráinne recognized how her husband, who constantly worked late as a father, subsequently felt guilty for neglecting his children, and was expiating this through his devotion to his grandchildren. By contrast, she felt that it would be only too easy for grandmothering to become the same kind of routine obligation that would reprise the resentment she experienced as a mother in the form of endless self-sacrifice to her children. She saw how this could intrude on her positive relationship to being a grandmother.

There were many such examples of how prior gender differences had declined, further evidence for which will be discussed in chapter 12. For instance, while a group called the Men's Shed might have exacerbated gender differences, in practice the men were keen to go to cookery classes and visit flower shows, in part because on retirement both genders appreciated that they had only one life and that the existence of gender as a cultural distinction had deprived them of certain experiences that they could perhaps now attend to. The same sentiment was bringing more women into the pubs and both sexes might now equally participate in activities such as walking, yoga, or cycling. While men had been favoured financially when younger, at this stage in life sociality mattered more than income and it was women who had traditionally dominated active sociality which now protected men also from loneliness or isolation.

The overall result can be described as freedom from gender itself. At this stage of life, it simply seemed to matter less whether one was a woman or a man. This was not entirely the case: some inequalities persisted. The clearest example of these were retained differences in expectations around who would do most of the practical care when it came to looking after frail parents. Generally, though, gender had shifted from being a category of identity imposed by others to become an attribute that an individual could highlight or ignore as they preferred: A woman might wear unisex blue jeans one day but an attractive dress the next. If anything, it is now the change in male behaviour and attitudes that represents the culmination of such second-wave feminist ideals. The striking contrast is with young people, where, at least in the student world, there has been a considerable rise in the politics, self-consciousness and projection of identity categories, seen, for example, in the rise of self-selected pronouns. It is possible that this has become a means by which young people attempt to gain independence and separation from what they may regard as the more complacent forms of feminism associated with their parents.

Choosing to be Irish
An equally complex story emerged around another other obvious point of identity: being Irish. It may be strange to imply that there is a new freedom from being Irish as an identity at a time when perhaps people in Ireland have never been as proud to be Irish as they are today. Many people in Cuan were learning the Irish language (though it is never used in casual conversation). The primary sports in terms of rates of participation were Gaelic football and hurling. I often went with friends to listen to Irish traditional music at several of the Cuan pubs, which hosted trad music sessions. The point, though, is that, as in the case of gender, there was a shift from identity as obligatory, imposed upon a person by others, to identity as something people have the freedom to align with only to the degree they choose. Two contributory factors have previously been discussed. The first

is that it was easier to be relaxed about being Irish within a larger, encompassing, but entirely positive sense of also being European than being Irish based partly on an ambivalent historical, post-colonial relationship to the English.[18] The second is that there has been a shift in international views around the connotations of being Irish so that it has become one of the most positive of all national stereotypes, both at the personal level of being taken as warm, funny, and genuine, but also at the cultural level, ranging from the exceptional presence of accomplished Irish novelists to the popular culture of Irish pubs.

The primary reason this is experienced as freedom came from the evidence that this population had previously experienced being Irish as a relentless political education campaign. On one occasion, a group of older people on a collective allotment started to compare their experience of Gaeltacht. This was a compulsory period spent by young people in an Irish-language school, often during the school holidays and often in the west of Ireland, where Irish language retains its place in everyday life. The dominant recollection was of violence. It was a conversation about beatings – whether personally experienced or observed – including which kind of wood or other instrument had been used, mainly by the nuns. They also recalled the insistence that only the Irish language was supposed to be spoken and the ways they had managed to get around that constraint. This may explain why, despite decades of government attempts to inculcate the Irish language, it had never become accepted as part of ordinary conversation. Things have changed and young people today have a very different experience of Gaeltacht. But these conversations recall the absolute authority of the Catholic Church in education as part of de Valera's deliberate and systematic attempt to construct Irish nationalism across all domains.

If, then, today Irish identity is flourishing, this may be precisely because, with the decline of both Church and state authority, it has become more elective. Today, people feel free to choose, and generally do choose to devote themselves to any number of activities that have strong national connotations. They might spend ages on ancestry.com establishing their links with the Irish diaspora. They might seek out places of Irish heritage and learn songs from the nationalist struggle and the traditional instruments that accompanied these, or seek to improve their Irish language skills; but equally they might not.

Conclusion

It was suggested at the start of this chapter that the strength of the argument for describing this population as exceptionally or unprecedentedly free was to be made through the simultaneity of all these different examples of freedom. In aggregate, they amount to more than the sum of their parts. To summarize: retirement life is becoming as extensive as working life. We may have decades when we do not need to work or bring up families. The sense of freedom was palpable because the Irish had themselves lived through a time when poverty, large families, and often rampant alcoholism were enormously constraining, as was the control by an effective theocracy. This meant that, so far from feeling entitled, retirees in Cuan could really appreciate the rise of secularism and affluence as freedom. They also now enjoyed the advantages of a relatively de-politicized modern welfare state. Finally, they had the freedom of extraordinary capacities given by science and technology, as became clear from our study of the smartphone and the ease with which things could now be accomplished using a device they carried in their pockets and handbags. Equally, there are the extraordinary advances in health care and relative freedom from pain and debilitating illness. There has never been a historical elite with the range of advantages found in this ethnography and in other analogous contemporary populations.

The discussion of politics in this chapter made clear that freedom is characterized as much around freedom *to* as freedom *from*. This point is strongly connected to the emphasis on freedom as a collective endeavour, rather than being presumed to be a movement towards individualism. As has been hinted at but will be more fully discussed in the conclusion to this book, freedom as an integral part of the good life is understood as something that is fostered by the way people in Cuan have collectively constructed their own conditions of freedom, which have become the foundation for Cuan as the site of the good enough life.

No research participant ever made the claims to freedom found in this chapter's title. It is entirely this author's contention and extrapolation from the ethnography. But these arguments sometimes found resonance in their discussions. For example, Justin, retired from a successful commercial career, was now much devoted to philanthropic activities in the developing world. He often described himself as a member of 'the Golden Generation', which certainly implies relative freedom. Others often made jokes about the advantages that had accrued with age: 'If I had known life would be so good in my seventies, I would have hurried to get here,' or 'I have reached a point where the government gives me money just for still being alive.' Older people wondered whether young people, who hadn't the same experiences of poverty and theocracy, could feel appreciation of these freedoms to the same degree. The young, by contrast, would probably hear this phrase 'the Golden Generation' and note how much more difficult it had become to afford their own property, worrying that 'the Golden Generation' might be the last and not just the first of its kind. At the same time here, as in wider Irish studies, intergenerational relations were found to remain mostly supportive.[19]

Some predicted that the next generation would enjoy freedoms that they couldn't even imagine. Others had a more nostalgic view, emphasizing an entirely different trajectory that started from their imagination of true community and happiness that had been the condition of the past, compared to a selfish, narcissistic, and unhappy present. In public discourse, the smartphone was almost always presented as a loss of humanity, even though the actual use of smartphones implied something quite different. Not surprisingly, most people had several such contradictory narratives that they brought out according to the context of the discussion.

Cuan is merely one example of many populations around the world that might also be considered to have achieved exceptional freedom but are very much a minority with regard to the world at large. Each of these populations is obviously unique with its own historical trajectory. Others will not have experienced the same kind of theocratic state or come from an agrarian background. Each may have had their own long treks to freedom that followed quite different paths. Hopefully, more populations will be enabled to become more like Cuan in the future, but in their own way. Finally, freedom may be foundational to the good enough life, but all of this raises the question of what we might mean by freedom. To answer that question, the next chapter complements the ethnography by considering the way that freedom has been imagined in philosophy, as opposed to how it is experienced and practised by this population.

Chapter 2

PHILOSOPHERS OF FREEDOM

The nature of freedom is a perennial concern of philosophy, and this chapter will briefly reprise (my limited interpretation of) a few of philosophy's many profound contributions to the subject. I had hoped that the ethnographic material presented in the previous chapter might then provide some additional perspectives to these considerations of freedom. This proved a difficult alignment whose possibilities may not fully emerge until towards the end of this chapter. The chapter begins with two philosophers closely associated with the questions raised by the ideals of freedom: Jean-Paul Sartre and Isaiah Berlin. After showing why it was difficult to associate their contributions with the discussions of freedom found in the previous chapter, a more congenial linkage is found with the capabilities approach of Martha Nussbaum and Amartya Sen. In turn, this provides a possible route to exploring what the ethnography of Cuan might add to such philosophical debates.

Sartre

One of the television programmes I most enjoyed in my youth was called *The Roads to Freedom*, an adaption of three novels by Jean-Paul Sartre (1905–80), a philosopher strongly associated with the place of freedom in understanding humanity. The obvious point of departure for engaging with Sartre seemed to be the 800-page opus that made his reputation as a philosopher: *Being and Nothingness*.[1] Sartre is the only philosopher associated with the movements of phenomenology and existentialism who will be considered here. An enjoyable introduction to these philosophical movements, which helpfully situates the contribution of Sartre with those of many relevant contemporaries, can be found in Sarah Bakewell's book *At the Existentialist Café: Freedom, Being and Apricot Cocktails*.[2]

It doesn't take anything like 800 pages to realize that while *Being and Nothingness* is an extraordinarily impressive work, unfortunately it may not serve the purpose of this particular investigation. The problem is that the retirees of Cuan present a particular state of freedom that is of interest because of its contrast with historical conditions: freedom relative to conditions that were less free. By contrast, Sartre is primarily concerned with an ontological argument: the place of freedom irrespective of circumstance as an aspect of the very definition of being human. Much of *Being and Nothingness* is concerned with concepts developed for the purposes of his argument, such as contrasting 'being-for-itself' with 'being-in-itself', though there are also wonderful sections that don't require deep immersion in his terminology, such as the discussion of our desire to be loved.[3]

One of the reasons Sartre is so difficult to apply to this ethnography follows from the previous discussion of Kant as a typical philosopher in the introduction. The majority of Sartre's discussions concern universal claims made on the basis of the being of the individual. While Sartre is perhaps unusual in the degree to which he is also concerned with the individual's relationship to others, in being-for-the-other, his main orientation is rather to burrow deep within the individual, to the extent that this work could be regarded as a contribution to psychology as much as to philosophy. Above all, freedom is a responsibility to choose one's attitude to one's circumstance: the 'existence' which existential philosophy understood people as having been thrown into. This might have corresponded to a judgement on how people in Cuan have responded to their specific condition, but the principle is far more important to Sartre as a universal. He is arguing that the necessity of responsibility lies irrespective of one's condition. Even when faced with being executed, the individual is responsible for using their freedom to determine their attitude to their fate: a theme taken up in the novels that were serialized as the *The Roads to Freedom*. The primary role of freedom for Sartre is as a source and foundation for an individual's authenticity. The key consequence of freedom is understood to be responsibility, which in turn is the foundation for his contribution to moral philosophy.

A good deal of Sartre's work concerns the way people can be authentic to themselves as opposed to the condition of bad faith, a theme explored further in his later work *Anti-Semite and Jew*.[4] Over the course of his oeuvre, Sartre shifts from the universalism of *Being and Nothingness* as he becomes more politically involved under the influence of Western Marxism. He subsequently grew more interested in concrete instances of sociality, as found in his later philosophical opus *Critique of Dialectical Reason*.[5] But it is the day-to-day furtherance of freedom and sociality that dominates the evidence presented in the previous chapter, and these concern rather more mundane events than the revolutionary praxis that became the focus of Sartre's later work.

This makes it hard to claim that the ethnography and Sartre's philosophical work shed much light upon each other. A different approach might have been through Sartre's fictional writings, which also contain considerable philosophical insights. The novel that stands out as a contribution to his thinking about the nature of freedom is *Nausea*.[6] In this novel, it is the burden of radical freedom that gives rise to that experience of nausea for the book's protagonist, Antoine Roquentin. Through this portrait, Sartre presents the problems of freedom that emerge when contemporary urban life gives rise to the possibility of a largely purposeless and de-socialized wandering individual, burdened and literally sickened by this experience. At the end of this chapter, it will be suggested that this represents a more profitable and significant place for comparison with the lessons about freedom learnt from Cuan, but mainly by way of stark contrast.

Berlin

Following this initial failure, a second attempt to find a productive alignment was made through reading another writer generally associated with understanding the nature and consequences of freedom: the Russian-British philosopher Isaiah Berlin (1909–97). In particular, I focused upon an essay called 'Two Concepts of Liberty',[7] originally delivered as a lecture in 1958, but best read alongside the caveats added in a later volume titled *Liberty*.[8] Berlin's best-known contribution comes through his analysis of what he calls negative and positive freedom. Negative freedom is found in the striving to remove all obstacles to the ability of a person to act as they would wish. This would seem to reflect the degree to which people in Cuan achieve a condition of 'freedom *from*' relative to their past. Berlin's discussion of negative liberty leads to a wide series of debates as to whether we should be aiming for a minimum space of inviolate freedoms, such as freedom of religion and the protection of basic rights as a citizen, or whether we should be striving for a much larger ambition that expands these freedoms to encompass as much of life as possible, through a liberal politics that constantly forces an authority such as the state to defend any policy that might curtail the freedom of an individual. Another key concern for Berlin is the determination of how far we should limit one person's freedom in order to protect the freedom of those this person might oppress. Berlin recognizes that people with limited money or resources may have little that they can do with freedom, which may therefore not be their first priority. At the same time, he wants to retain the distinction between equality and freedom, arguing that while equality is desirable, it should not be conflated with freedom.

The most original of Berlin's contributions is perhaps his idea of positive freedom or positive liberty. If we take freedom as the ability to fulfil desires, we face the problem that perhaps some people need further education or some wider institutional support before they could even know what their desires are or should be. Perhaps they need help in finding their 'proper' desires. For example, if Kant assumes that people in a state of complete autonomy will understand the precise moral path that accords with reason itself, who has authority to decide whether they have in fact chosen the right path that properly derives from reason? Would it ever be justified to coerce a person into making the choices that are dictated by reason in order to make that person free? For example, is it is justified to force a person to be vaccinated against Covid because that is the choice that would be made by an abstraction we call 'reason', or because of a concept of the collective freedom (in this case freedom from Covid) as opposed to the individual good?

Berlin sees such problems arising from Rousseau's assertion that we are born free, and yet everywhere we are in chains.[9] How should we regain our birthright of freedom? For Rousseau, as for Kant, an individual can become free by forming desires that follow from reason itself, which will become evident because they have become the general will. This can easily segue into the idea that the general will has authority to dictate freedom to each individual. In short, it allows a higher authority to decide where freedom lies and coerce an individual back onto that path. As realized historically, this became the tyranny that followed after the French Revolution. The leaders of the revolution were convinced that they were the embodiment of the trajectory of freedom implied by reason itself and were thereby authorized to coerce the French into manifesting this ideal. Left to themselves, people could not be free since they had not been given sufficient capacity of reason to appreciate where real freedom lay.

Similarly, Berlin credits Hegel with responsibility for what becomes manifested through Marx as the claim to know the true path of history and in particular the historical purpose of the proletariat.[10] Others argued that because of their oppressive condition, the proletariat, or in China the peasantry, couldn't know their own true desires and would have to be coerced into both the awareness and the consequences of that knowledge.[11] These two cases demonstrate the problem of positive freedom. Once we reach the point of arguing that an individual who does not desire what reason dictates they should desire can be said to not know themselves as they truly are, then we open the gates to a totalitarian order that claims to be the true path to reason.

Berlin therefore proposed a more modest, but to his way of thinking safer, conception of freedom that recognized a more plural outcome whereby people might end up with all sorts of beliefs and values that others might not wish for, but what mattered was that they were free to do so. Negative freedom needed constant protection from positive freedom. This is his justification for keeping the ideal of freedom separate from other laudable values such as equality. Berlin may have underplayed the degree to which pluralist versions of positive freedom are still subject to distortion and abuse,[12] but the more immediate problem is that, however worthwhile these ideas are as philosophy, it once again seems hard to equate them with the active agency of my research participants and what they were found to do with their condition of freedom. The previous chapter documented such a depth and breadth in the forms and experiences of freedom cultivated in Cuan. They are far closer to the types of situations most people find themselves in with regard to issues of freedom. Rather than trying to equate them to some abstract concept of reason, it would seem more valuable to try to understand what they have contributed to the experience of freedom and how they might then add to such philosophical discussions. Fortunately, a third approach does seem to be more focused upon that active agency vouchsafed by freedom.

Nussbaum and Sen

This third approach is derived from the works of Martha Nussbaum and Amartya Sen, while acknowledging the many differences between them. The previous chapter suggested an analogy between Cuan itself and the centrality of the *polis* to the development of philosophy in classical Greece. To return to this starting point, there is another possible point of departure in a 1987 essay by Nussbaum[13] based on her interpretation of book seven of Aristotle's *Politics*.[14] Here, Aristotle tries to link his general discussion of what constitutes the good life as developed in his *Nicomachean Ethics* with his arguments about the ideal *polis*. Nussbaum focuses on the idea of the *polis* as a distributive institution. Seen in this light, it can be viewed as an early contribution to what becomes known as the 'capability approach' to human welfare, developed by Nussbaum herself and Amartya Sen. Aristotle recognized that it was the responsibility of politics to ensure the conditions for citizens to live well – a practical consideration not, as with Plato, a utopian one.[15] Politics should also encompass a more holistic conception of the good life.[16] Merely giving people wealth and office is insufficient. What matters is what people do with such advantages. Nussbaum suggests Aristotle thereby helps us to consider two different kinds of capability. The first is internal to the person, their intellect, character, and sense of virtue, which will enable them to choose well how to use their capabilities. These are developed through education. But there are also the external conditions that give them the means for having capabilities that they can then employ. This is where the distributive responsibilities of the *polis* come to the fore.

Sen's approach was certainly sympathetic to Nussbaum's general orientation, though Nussbaum has also noted important differences.[17] In his book *Development as Freedom*, Sen argues for a robust form of freedom as agency.[18] One of his most significant contributions to the welfare of our world is that in his work as an economist he has been instrumental in changing the way economists think about what it is they are trying to achieve. More specifically, bodies such as the United Nations had tried to improve welfare through criteria such as increasing the gross national product. Sen showed why they required a much broader conception of what people needed and wanted from life. As suggested by the book's title, he proposes freedom as the ultimate aim of development, which should commit to removing barriers to its realization. These barriers might include poor economic prospects, the state's neglect of public facilities, and the political conditions that prevent people from determining their own welfare goals, from being or doing what they would wish. Freedom is 'both the processes that allow freedom of actions and decisions, and the actual opportunities that people have, given their personal and social circumstances'.[19] Sen sees an intrinsic value to human freedom, not just its instrumental effectiveness. The manner by which he links freedom also to justice will be discussed in chapter 6 as part of a discussion of John Rawls, who is an important influence upon his thinking.

These approaches seem insistent upon making those linkages between freedom and equality that were resisted by Berlin. They also take further Berlin's response to the problems of positive freedom in that both Nussbaum and Sen have an even more avowedly pluralistic conception of freedom, with a stress on ensuring that people are able to determine for themselves the goals that they wish to be free to accomplish. Nussbaum is a little more structured than Sen in her response to the question of what constitutes capabilities, perhaps because she regards it as the philosopher's responsibility to delineate the central human capabilities.[20] She is also more explicitly concerned to retain certain universalistic principles as against mere cultural relativism,[21] while arguing that this is compatible with their commitment to pluralism. As well as preventing an authoritarian claim to positive freedom, pluralism is the key quality within the capabilities approach that makes this more appealing to anthropologists than those approaches previously discussed. Pluralism respects cultural diversity as the source of values that drive the capabilities desired by any particular population or indeed individual. These are often exactly what the anthropologist hopes to uncover through ethnography. Every example of freedom discussed in the previous chapter was contingent upon the particular histories and trajectories of this population and their subsequent cultural values.

Sen outlines some of the key tasks required to achieve freedom. An obvious example is the need to reverse the current neglect of women's agency, which had included depriving women of the opportunity to work, a topic also central to the wider writings of Nussbaum.[22] Both authors recognize that if freedom is associated with human rights, then we must acknowledge that human rights impose reciprocal responsibilities on the individual, including a commitment to society. In contrast to Sartre, Nussbaum and Sen are concerned with practical substantial freedom rather than abstract or ontological freedom.

All of this feels like a more appealing point of departure for thinking about how to see this ethnography as a contribution to philosophy. If pluralism is central to the capabilities approach, then it has to remain open-ended, without over-specifying the substantive nature of capabilities. Otherwise, we cannot respect people's freedom to determine these for themselves. What follows from this requirement is that an evaluation of these ideas about freedom requires more than just the ideas themselves. We would need to examine an actual instance of a real population that can be used to exemplify what people then do with substantive capabilities. An individual may use their retirement by working for the benefit of Cuan, as described in the previous chapter, but equally they may be going on holiday or spending time with grandchildren. What matters here is that the logic of this philosophical approach effectively cedes authority to actual populations to whom we must turn. There is, then, a case to be made that Nussbaum and Sen's approach requires books such as this one that seek to extrapolate values and goals from the practices of an observable population.

For a population to exemplify the capabilities approach, they must first live under those condition of freedom vouchsafed by external conditions. An important consideration then will be that presented in chapter 5, which confronts the evidence for problems such as inequality and depression as part of the context for thinking about freedom. Only then would that population be able to demonstrate their character (i.e. Aristotle's inner capabilities) as manifested through their actions. One important caveat, which Nussbaum and Sen also acknowledge, is that any judgements about this population should include normative moral conditions. We would need evidence that freedom is being used for good rather than evil, incorporating that population's own moral cosmology. So later chapters will also investigate the nature of cosmology and desire found in the ethnography. Finally, we would need to see how far we can retain the relative contributions of virtue and happiness that dominate the classical consideration of the good life, as, for example, in Aristotle, with these or their equivalents as extrapolated from this ethnography of the good enough life.

Cuan, the Philosophers, and Freedom

Already the previous chapter has set out to consider Cuan as the fulfilment of those conditions of freedom implied by the capabilities approach. Evidence was provided that not only have these retirees sloughed off the constraints associated with daily employment, family obligations, and financial constraint, they have also made full use of the resultant freedoms to actively develop their capabilities, most noticeably through their actions in developing Cuan itself through their active volunteering and taking civic responsibility through their involvement in local political and community activities.

To fully appreciate the achievements of these retirees, it may be helpful to return to the initial discussion of Sartre. Above all, the freedom that was vouchsafed to my informants emerged from the rapidity with which the Catholic Church largely collapsed as the normative and moral framework for life, and with it the loss of religious authority. This collapse of religious authority could have become an example of the condition of unmoored freedom that concerned not only Sartre but also sociologists such as Durkheim and many post-Enlightenment thinkers, intellectuals who worried that radical freedom based on the collapse of traditional moral authority would inevitably lead to an egoistic individualism without wider life purpose. Durkheim and other social scientists who were developing a theory of society around functionalism argued that religion had had an important role in maintaining social cohesion, which implied that its loss would have repercussions. In his study of suicide,[23] Durkheim problematized the condition of unmoored anomie.[24] Where Durkheim saw anomie, Sartre imagined nausea, especially within an urban setting which permits extreme individualism and detachment. Antoine Roquentin stood for a condition that included a pointlessness and absurdity to life that haunted French 'Left Bank' authors such as Albert Camus and Jean Genet and the Irish playwright Samuel Beckett, alongside the philosophers. There is a legacy of this in the contemporary use of the now colloquial term 'existential crisis', implying the loss of any purpose to life. Kant's moral philosophy serves as a precedent to these concerns in so far as it was forged in part to prevent the collapse of moral authority that the rise of science seemed to presage. To conclude, the decline of religion seems to have been accompanied by an equal lack of conviction in our ability to sustain society without the support of some structure that could substitute for faith. The overall consensus seemed to be that in a sea of radical freedom and rampant individualism, people were much more likely to sink than to swim.

Thank heavens, then, for the retirees of Cuan. It is hard to imagine any other group that experienced a more radical or rapid collapse from a highly theocratic government that controlled every aspect of everyday life. Yet it is equally hard to imagine a society that seems less troubled by problems of anomie or nausea. The decline of religion has turned out to be profoundly inconsequential, demonstrating that religion had by no means acted as some kind of functional glue for society that required a replacement for society to cohere. It is not just that radical freedom looks nothing like the figure of Sartre's Antoine Roquentin. Cuan represents a still more profound intervention as a repudiation of the tendency within philosophy and much of social science to associate freedom with individualism. So far from freedom leading to a retreat from sociality, these retirees took their condition of freedom as the possibility to more fully embrace and cultivate sociality. They sloughed off the forced sociality of the workplace to replace this with the freedom to construct their own community, making community itself an idiom for the expression of freedom. They were not trying to be free from the normative and the collective. They employed freedom to facilitate both, in something more akin to the ideals of social democratic Scandinavia and certain versions of socialism. Cuan makes it possible to see how sociality itself can be as much a manifestation of freedom as can individualism. This is what makes it such an important complement to at least some philosophy of freedom.

How can sociality manifest freedom? An example I have discussed elsewhere that is not specific to Cuan concerns the shifting ways in which we conceptualize and prioritize our primary social relationships.[25] The dominant idiom for social relations in the past, for most societies, derived from kinship. As noted in the previous chapter, many societies had the practice of fictive kinship[26] that I experienced when I was young. Over the last few decades, however, friendship is generally replacing kinship as the dominant idiom for sociality. The reason for this shift is precisely because freedom itself has become a more significant factor in adjudicating the authenticity of a social relationship. It was suggested that friendship now dominates over kinship because, as people will frequently say, they can choose their friends, but they can't choose their relatives. Once again, we see how social relations can become an idiom for expressing freedom rather than obligation.

A further example also detailed in the previous chapter was found in the manner by which retired people understand the obligations of grandparenting. In the past, this was a relationship that mainly expressed kinship as obligation. But in contemporary Cuan, grandparents are clear that they don't want their care for their grandchildren to be merely taken for granted. They want to have it seen as expressive of their love and care for both their children and their grandchildren. For this to be the case, grandparenting had to shift to something that is freely given and thereby emblematic of freedom as a condition of sociality. But voluntarism is not individualism; it is in this case a shift in the medium by which we practise relationships. These grandparents are just as committed to their children and grandchildren; they just want this to be an expression of love rather than obligation. There is, then, no intrinsic link between freedom and individualism. There are many different ways of engaging in social relations such that they become an idiom for freedom instead of constraint. More broadly, if we understand the way the people of Cuan have created Cuan itself through the work of bodies such as the CCA and how this has consequently provided the conditions for their good enough lives, we have not strayed that far from the way Aristotle understood the role of the *polis* and in turn its contribution to capabilities.

Most of my research participants would also agree with Nussbaum and Sen that the inverse of the coin of freedom is responsibility. They have created a society in which the behaviour of an individual remains tightly regulated by their peers. Within this intense sociality, it was very clear who was doing what. It would be noted who had not volunteered for Tidy Towns, who was not helping to look after the elderly, who had refused the request to help start up a new photography group. Cuan is a highly normative society. As noted above, during Covid lockdowns, people excelled in taking on the mantle of the Garda in watching to see which of their neighbours had failed to isolate in the manner prescribed. They had replaced imposed external and structural constraint with an ideal of communally held consensual constraint. This brings us back to a different dimension of the capabilities approach that examines freedom through a discussion of cultural values, implying this more social and normative basis for the experience of freedom and of wellbeing. Overall, then, there is very little in common between freedom as extrapolated from this ethnography and most colloquial definitions of freedom as equated with individual choice.

The contribution of the ethnography to philosophy is further enhanced if consideration is now extended from Sartre to Berlin. Berlin's primary interest was in political freedom. Negative freedom is largely imagined as the ability of an individual to be free from politics in order to engage in their own individual desires and aspirations. Positive freedom would have prevented this if it gave licence to some larger authority's claim to be the sole mantle of reason. Yet just as people in Cuan employ their freedom to cultivate sociality rather than individualism, they also use their political freedom not to disengage from politics, but to create their own politics of engagement. Mostly, they do feel an unusual freedom from Politics with a capital P: that of newspaper headline party politics and the state government As we saw in the previous chapter, in stark contrast to the heated polarization that has engulfed others, Ireland had seen decades of relatively centrist politics based on a comparatively generous welfare state. This means that generally government is left to get on with governance.

Yet so far from this freedom from 'big P' Politics leading to an absence of politics, people in Cuan cultivate an impressive sense of civic responsibility. If politics includes reference to an individual's personal involvement, then they have become more political as a result of their freedom, not less. The amount of time they give to community associations, activities such as Tidy Towns, helping a youth sports team, or meals on wheels is prodigious. The CCA has become a pragmatic and collective concern to get on with the job of improving schools and pavements, but with the clear instruction never to discuss party politics. I gave two examples of individuals who subsequent to the ethnography became significant conviction politicians concerned with environmentalism and poverty. In conclusion, if Berlin does an excellent job of showing us what positive liberty *should not mean*, Cuan does a pretty good job of showing us what positive liberty *should mean*.

Cultural pluralism is an important component of the philosophy of Berlin, Nussbaum, and Sen. There has been no suggestion in the book so far that other populations would necessarily follow a similar trajectory to Cuan. Freedom in itself enhances the possibilities of cultural heterogeneity. Unfortunately, rather more populations have voted for conservative and nationalist governments that promise to return them to a nostalgic condition, often based on repudiating the cosmopolitanism that comes with the liberal freedoms espoused by Cuan. There are many other populations that appear in their turn to be textbook cases of ever-increasing individualism and perhaps anomie. This ethnography as an exercise in anthropology accords with Nussbaum and Sen's own emphasis upon the comparative as opposed to a single normative ideal, or what Sen calls the transcendental approach to justice.[27] The complementarity between philosophy and anthropology is also apparent in that this ethnography will never achieve what has been accomplished by some of these philosophers. Nussbaum and Sen have had a significant impact upon bodies such as the United Nations. They have changed the world for the better to a degree that no anthropologist could expect to achieve, and they should be admired for that. Arguing for a complementary relationship between anthropology and philosophy is about acknowledging all that each discipline can more easily achieve than the other.

What is implied by using the term *polis* in relation to Cuan? Suggesting an analogy between the two is clearly problematic. The ancient *polis* was a city state and in political terms would be more equivalent to the Republic of Ireland than to Cuan – with the stark difference that only a minority of the population of the classic *polis* were citizens. The analogy remains useful, however, to the degree that it allows for certain comparisons to be made with classical philosophers such as Aristotle, based, for example, on the evidence of the previous chapter that many people in Cuan are involved in civic activities that relate to the town rather than just their obligations as citizens of the Irish state. The analogy also seems warranted because this book is premised on the evidence for the way people identify with Cuan and see it as the source of both their happiness and virtue, the constituents of *eudaimonia*. More surprisingly, as this book unfolds, what will come to matter is not that Cuan seems to be less than the classical *polis*, but that in some respects the relationship to its population is even more profound. Chapter 8 will demonstrate how, unlike the classical polis, where people were citizens by dint of birth, Cuan in its modern form was largely created by its blow-ins: that is, migrants to the town. This sets up the arguments found in the concluding chapter of this volume. There it will be shown how in the course of their commitment to Cuan what was actually created were the people I had come to study. We will need to understand not just what the people of Cuan do, but what makes them those people. This is why the discussion of freedom within this chapter remains incomplete. The conclusion to this book will therefore add one more philosopher to this mix. Hegel provides the missing jigsaw piece that can complete the picture of how this population was created. Hegel draws out the dialectical process by which a people are made free through the way they create the world around them. In the meantime, the conclusion of this chapter is that if we want to learn about freedom not just abstractly and conceptually, but in terms of its implications for how we might live our lives in the contemporary world, then there is much to be learnt from philosophy. But there is also a great deal to be learnt from ethnography.

Chapter 3

THE FIRST SATIABLE SOCIETY

Satiable Consumption

In several respects, this chapter is a continuation of the arguments of chapter 1. It concerns another domain within which humanity has conventionally been regarded as driven by various external and oppressive forces. It will again provide evidence that we have failed to acknowledge the degree to which this situation has radically changed. Freedom will be shown to come not just from becoming an affluent society, but primarily through becoming the first satiated society. Not freedom to consume but freedom from consumption and the burdens of consumer choices. Evidence will be presented that to the degree to which people in Cuan compete for status and reputation through emulation, this process has shifted from competition over conspicuous consumption to competition over conspicuous *anti*-consumption used to demonstrate a person's environmentalist credentials. A final section will explore the way consumption has shifted from an expression of breadth to one of depth as a characterization of our relationships with the non-human world.

By far the most long-lasting and influential approach to the study of modern consumption was *A Theory of the Leisure Class* written by Thorstein Veblen in 1899.[1] This is the book from which terms such as 'conspicuous consumption' arose. Veblen directed attention to the nouveau riche, who, unlike the older aristocracy, had worked for their wealth. He sensed that these nouveau riche, under the influence of aristocratic status, now wanted to display their distance from that same world of work which had enabled them to become rich. This would be achieved through an emphasis on leisure activities and vicarious consumption, all of which was much to the consternation of Veblen, who inherited the Puritans' positive valuation of work itself, which the leisure class sought to repudiate.

As Veblen demonstrated, in any society where status is important, the key mechanism for linking status to consumption is emulation. People lower down the social order copy the consumption of people higher up in order to appear more like them. This is one of the forces that makes consumption insatiable. Take the example of bread. For centuries, wealthy people ate refined white bread because the lower classes could not afford to. When, however, everyone could afford white bread, the higher classes developed new consumption preferences such as more expensive wholemeal or organic bread partly to retain their distance from the lower classes. Emulation remains a primary mechanism in explaining the findings presented in this chapter.

Veblen was by no means the only social scientist to offer theories that linked status to consumption or to explain the insatiable nature of consumption. Under the influence of both Marxist philosophers (who are the subject of the next chapter) and more general critical studies, the focus switched from mechanisms within populations such as emulation, to an exposé of the vast forces within contemporary capitalism, such as advertising, which were principally intended to ensure that consumption demand remained insatiable. Economists such as J.K. Galbraith[2] argued that capitalists had realized that if they were going to invest a good deal in a new commodity, they first had to ensure the creation of a population that would desire that commodity. Only by creating demand could they protect their investments. Most of the academic emphasis today remains on how corporations persuade us to buy their goods and services. These processes of production and consumption could work in tandem. Colin Campbell wrote an influential book arguing that surprisingly what might have seemed like the counterculture ethos of the 1960s actually turned into a desire for novel experience such that whatever we purchased never quite lived up to our expectations.[3] This would again drive us into always wanting something more. A third significant academic contribution arose from social scientists and especially anthropologists such as Pierre Bourdieu,[4] Mary Douglas,[5] and Marshall Sahlins,[6] who argued that we create a plethora of different goods in order to exploit them for expressing social distinctions such as gender or levels of education. There are, then, several plausible theoretical explanations for what is regarded as the intrinsically insatiable nature of modern consumption and its subsequent role in social relations.

When it comes to the retired and relatively affluent population of Cuan, however, what is their relationship with consumption? As soon as we engage with people in Cuan, perhaps joining them in their daily walks along the streets or beaches, we encounter a problem with these academic characterizations of consumption. The vast majority of clothing that the people we meet are wearing is not particularly differentiated. We would have difficulty estimating their cost or knowing their brand. I have written about this more extensively elsewhere,[7] but if there is one garment above all that characterizes the modern world it is surely blue jeans. There exist expensive versions of blue jeans, but it is highly unlikely that one would encounter these amongst the older population of Cuan. The attraction of blue jeans is simply that they are regarded as nondescript. Unlike any other garment, all clothes can 'go' with blue jeans. Blue jeans reverse all three of the most common approaches to consumption. They wear well and do not go out of fashion, reducing the need for clothes shopping. They are relatively cheap and resist the blandishments of the vast fashion industry, refuting the idea that we merely follow capitalist injunctions to consume. They also fail to accord with anthropological discussions of semiotic differences, since the whole point of wearing blue jeans is that they are effectively undistinguished and say nothing at all about us. Blue jeans are reasonably common amongst Cuan retirees, but the clothes they mostly wear, styles which began as sports clothing but have descended into generic everyday wear, have these same three characteristics. They are generally undistinguished, reasonably hard wearing, and have little connection with current fashion.

When retired people talked about where they purchased their clothing, three shops stood out as by far the most common preferred sources, such that hardly any other locations gained much of a mention. These were Penneys, Marks and Spencer, and Dunnes Stores. If other shops were mentioned, then they were likely one of the few clothing shops that are to be found within Cuan itself. But Cuan is not blessed with many clothing shops. As I discovered on one weekend, there is a not a single place in Cuan where it is possible to buy men's underwear. Few people outside of Ireland are aware that Primark originated in Ireland, where it retains its original name of Penneys. But pretty much everyone would know of Primark as about the cheapest place around to buy clothes. This was in and of itself viewed as a positive. A young woman was happy to announce, 'Penneys is my favourite place in the world.' Dunnes Stores would be more expensive but is probably the best-established general department store in Ireland, rather than a brand that people would use to display their wealth. Marks and Spencer is also most easily related to the ordinary and the everyday. A common expression for personal taste was 'middle-of-the-road'. Young people would now supplement these stores with online clothing sites such as BooHoo and Pretty Little Things. The four clothing stores within Cuan are more expensive, as small independent shops tend to be, and are used more for special occasions. As a middle-aged woman of middle income put it, 'Perhaps it's good to have an option outside of the big names, you know it's all the same in the shopping centres, for like a special location or something.' Several other people suggested that, yes, they might go to the Cuan clothing shops, but only ever during sales.

At the book reading group I attended, alongside only one other man, there was a woman who stood out in terms of her stylish wardrobe. It is likely that some of her clothing was quite expensive, but it was also clear that this was not the feature to which the other women paid any particular regard. What was admired was simply that for this particular woman getting dressed was her craft, just as others might take up photography or gardening. She was able to put together an assemblage that we all agreed worked well and suited her, and that everyone enjoyed seeing. Another example, not from this group, was a woman who was now quite frail in her late seventies, but was still known for the elegance of her clothing, and especially her shoes. People recognized the importance of this continuity of self-respect in the face of ageing and the deterioration in her looks and health. She had recently suffered quite severe health problems that had often left her in bitter tears of frustration at the subsequent incapacities. But if anything, she had become still more adept at choosing clothes, putting them together in assemblages, understanding the role of shoes as the point that at least other women (almost never men) appreciated where this sartorial aesthetic came together. Her mannerisms and behaviour had an elegance that matched her couture. Her generation would refer to her as 'refined'. Similarly, there were some men who tended to wear more conservative apparel which went with other traits and behaviours that led people to regard them as 'gentlemen'.

It was likely that most of the other members of this book reading group could have afforded similar clothing if they had so chosen. But generally, women's clothing in Cuan was similar to men's clothing in being largely generic and unpretentious; decent but not really special. Not so much blue jeans, but simple slacks and blouses, while men favoured t-shirts. If one saw a group of people in standout finery, the single most likely cause was that the Cuan church was hosting a First Communion service, and the smartest of all would be the seven- or eight-year-olds taking part.

Men in Cuan, as in so many places today, appeared mostly in clothing best described as unpretentious to the point of being drab. There were exceptions. If there was one genre of clothing that probably was still used for display, it would be the elaborations on this otherwise generic sportswear. As will be argued in chapter 6, sports had such a central role in Cuan that it was not surprising that much of people's everyday attire was influenced by sports-styled clothing. On one occasion, a man noted that a friend was wearing a jacket from The North Face, a relatively expensive brand within that genre. This was viewed as an example of conspicuous consumption and the remark was critical. It was also unusual because mostly people would not be able to recognize the brand of someone else's clothing. It was much of a muchness.

Clothing, then, stands for what is meant by satiable consumption. To develop a sufficient wardrobe of such ordinary clothing from the most common retail sources such as Penneys was not particularly expensive. This older population had already accumulated garments over decades. They therefore had little reason to go shopping for any more clothes, other than for very special occasions, if then. They would buy replacement clothing and occasionally buy an item if they happened to see something they especially liked. Clothing might continue to come as gifts or as a kind of souvenir from a trip abroad to warmer climes, but, overall, the demand for clothing was essentially satiated and certainly satiable. Clothes shopping was largely finished.

These same observations apply to many other genres of consumption. By the age of retirement, most people had also accumulated pretty much whatever they needed by way of home furnishing and goods required for whatever tasks they were engaged in. A new activity might require some additional goods such as starting an allotment or taking up painting, but these were quickly acquired. People remained susceptible to chance purchases, however. There was a very funny song circulating at the time of my fieldwork with regard to shopping at Lidl supermarket. Shopping at Lidl is a curious experience since it often seems like a random juxtaposition of mundane and specialist goods. The song suggested you could end up with 'a pack of streaky bacon and a crate of Russian stout. And a portable generator just in case the lights go out.'[8] People did certainly end up with goods they couldn't quite remember even intending to buy, but again this was exceptional. Today, conspicuous consumption is increasingly associated with vulgarity and a failure to uphold the more important claims to equality, as when a middle-aged woman from one of the older Cuan families remarked,

> So the attitude is that being materialistic is vulgar and retrograde, but as long as they don't show off and there is good *craic* when they are together it is forgivable. When we are all sitting together it doesn't matter if you are wearing a Gucci handbag or whatever. So, consumption is like a burden rather than an asset.

We have reached a point where a person is far more likely to be looked down upon than looked up to because they have flaunted an expensive item.

All of this was just as well for those research participants whose only income was their government pension. It was important that they had sufficient for their needs. The fact that they mostly claimed this was the case was clearly enabled by the observation that there was no more pressure to consume driven by status emulation. It also helped a great deal that Ireland has a relatively well-functioning welfare state. The main failure in this respect was the lack of a national health service, such that for older people the costs of medical services could be a significant drain, especially as most felt they needed medical insurance. For those with clearly limited income, however, there would be a medical card which partially covered medical expenses. Reliance on state medical services meant that these were free, but the waiting lists could be horrendous. Outside of the health service, the welfare state had helped the cause of satiable consumption. Older people had a free TV licence, and they were generally appreciative that at a certain age they could travel for free on public transport anywhere in Ireland. They could also get a free passport and assistance towards their energy costs. In summary, most retired people saw a good enough life as entirely achievable based on the state pension and services and whatever else they had by way of savings.

There were consumption differences. A survey I carried out of cars in the highest- and lowest-income areas of Cuan showed that cars in the wealthier areas were of more recent purchase and there were a few expensive models. The survey also showed that the differences were not ones that seemed of any great practical importance. The lower-end models were generally just as effective for driving as the higher-end models. The whole issue of inequality will be discussed in chapter 5, but a critical point is that even lower-income households living in state housing would not have been short of items that people regard as essential or necessities. The ethnography included a focus upon those living within state housing, so I was quite often sitting inside the homes of the less well-off residents of Cuan. Their kitchens and bathrooms were a bit smaller than in private housing, as were the windows, but not significantly different, and not without the appurtenances that could be seen in the kitchens and bathrooms of wealthy residents.

Lower-income households could still usually afford at least one main and some smaller holidays. For example, a taxi driver living in the area of state housing whom I knew well still expected, on an annual basis, to take his family to Las Vegas and himself to the horse racing at Aintree near Liverpool. Unlike wealthier households, this family would not have expected to go to Machu Picchu in Peru or to have a second home in Spain. But there was no suggestion that such things mattered that much, or that life was deficient without such luxurious forms of consumption. They would not be used to indicate status. During the ethnography, questions of unaffordability came up mainly in respect to health, as noted above, or otherwise because of expenditure on children. Children in Cuan had the choice of countless sporting activities, but these often incurred costs. A parent noted that 'This child is in the Sea Scouts and that's €170 a year and they just assume you can come up with €170 as though it's nothing.' For some, this was a significant burden, but not for most.

The same arguments would apply to electronic goods. People would recall how important it had been once to keep upgrading their computer until computers more or less equated with all that we expected of them. A few years later, the same happened with smartphones, but now the annual improvements in smartphones were of only specialist interest. Most people in Cuan had either an iPhone or a Samsung Galaxy. Once one had paid for the device and a plan, usage was not related to cost, and could not thereby be used to express conspicuous or differential consumption. What was striking in our smartphone research was that incremental improvement did continue, but entirely through the development of apps that made a host of things easier, such as driving, shopping, photography, and knowing when a bus was coming. All of these apps were free. Similarly, smart TVs were now large enough and there were no major new technologies that were deemed essential. In short, there was simply nothing going on in the world of production that disrupted the overall sense of a satiable condition. There was nothing people really wanted that they could not afford. Retired people are in any case generally quite conservative when it comes to consumption and would be unlikely to be tempted by anything that wasn't a marked improvement upon their capacity to achieve a goal.

As always, caveats are required. Status marking based on conspicuous consumption had not completely disappeared. It could be represented in wine connoisseurship or foods purchased at a delicatessen rather than a supermarket. Of the various activities people were involved in, golf certainly used to have a strong connotation of status and the annual membership fees would have been well beyond most people. Today, fees are far lower than in the past, but there is certainly still some status involved. For some people, having a presence on the golf course was still probably experienced as having a 'place' in the world. Sailing could obviously involve considerable expenditure, but it was something of a passion amongst a large group of people within Cuan and it was the skill and knowledge that commanded deep respect, not the expenditure. Owning a large boat without the requisite skills would be more derided than admired. The people of Cuan made a point of the fact that they had a sailing club, not a yacht club. Most of the popular activities, however, such as joining a ukulele group, involved hardly any outlay. Becoming a serious photographer might involve more expense, but there was little sense that expense would be a significant factor in deciding which activity to favour. All of this meant that most retired people were under no pressure to continue to engage in work in order to finance themselves, just as there was no real social pressure to have additional goods.

To conclude, in respect to both goods in general and their day-to-day activities, the older people of Cuan had become a blue jeans population. The term 'blue jeans' also implies relative freedom from choice itself as choice can be oppressive. One of the ways people in Cuan explicitly differentiated themselves from what in conversation they generalized as the culture of the United States was that the US was assumed to be a place where choice was valued in and of itself. Going into a restaurant in the US often meant being confronted with a litany of choices. Diners delighted in finding versions of what was on the menu specific to their preferences. By contrast, in Cuan, people were likely to regard excessive consumer choice as a chore of no special importance. They mainly wanted a clear menu without further elaboration and to just order from that, unless there were specific dietary reasons for making special requests.

For many older people, it was not just that conspicuous consumption had become vulgar. In as much as they were involved in status competition, it was more likely to be over their skills in the cultivation of thrift. Most retired people could tell stories of where they bought something cheaper than someone else or how they crossed the border to Northern Ireland in order to save on the cost of medicines. One of the most common words that people used to describe their situation was 'comfortable'. Comfortable is a word often denigrated in more academic circles as associated with complacency. Consider the phrase 'the comfortable middle class'. Yet this was a population that was probably far more involved in community activities and generous acts of assistance to others than would be the case in most places where people do not regard themselves as comfortable. They worked extremely hard to make elderly parents, visitors, and friends comfortable. Where comfortable implies satiable, then there is no reason to regard this as other than a virtue.

Age is an important component in these arguments regarding the satiable society. In every study I have conducted on consumption, children were found to be highly susceptible to advertising, and there is no reason to think this would be different in Cuan. There are certainly young people in Cuan who are involved in conspicuous consumption, and in chapter 5 this will be discussed in reference to cocaine use. Two of the most successful Instagram 'influencers' in Ireland are from Cuan and I see them almost every day appearing on my Instagram in different outfits. There was one quite flashy bar in Cuan with an eye to its visiting celebrities, and restaurant food in general is expensive. As a migrant from Europe noted, 'It's the older people who are more casual and it's the younger ones who are that way with material things, but I think that's everywhere.'

This corresponds also to the way older people like to claim that the young have become addicted to the latest gadget or fashion and are seen as thereby more superficial, trivial, and individualist, if not narcissistic. But the effect of all this moral condemnation only serves to make older people even more committed to maintaining this differentiation so as not to be tarred by their own brush. It was noticeable that people in Cuan tended to direct these barbs mainly at a kind of generic 'young people'. The actual young people of Cuan were more often admired for their sporting and educational prowess, and one's own children were not usually seen as either extravagant or superficial.

A chapter in my book with Pauline Garvey is dedicated to the topic of downsizing.[9] It presents evidence that older people are actually keen to maintain quite a high level of property possession and are not in fact given to downsizing. If they move house, it tends to be to secure more modern homes that are easier and cheaper to maintain. They feel that the achievement of this level of lifestyle and comfortable property has been hard won and they want to remain at a certain level with respect to their basic living conditions. Satiable often means reaching a certain plateau which is then maintained thereafter. Houses are akin to computers and smartphones in this respect.

Two further factors may contribute to these findings. The aforementioned emphasis upon sport often involves espousing a lifestyle which is more inclined to austerity, to challenging the body in difficult exercise that confounds expectations of the constraints of age. The very idea of luxury may connote something insipid and flabby, while people in Cuan were almost invariably trim. Another factor noted in the introduction to this book is Cuan's geographical position between a more proletarian town on the one side and somewhat upmarket towns on the other. For anyone who was drawn to conspicuous consumption, there would be simply no point to remaining in Cuan, a place where their efforts were more likely to be derided than admired. They would almost certainly have migrated to a town closer to Dublin or more likely to South Dublin, which would be the appropriate sites for displaying luxury. People had a variety of stereotypes through which they described both Cuan and its neighbours. For example, it was commonly suggested that the wealthy farmers of a nearby town would be rather more materialistic than would be the case in Cuan. Cuan in the past was not at all wealthy and the majority of blow-ins came to the town precisely because housing tended to be cheaper with increasing distance from Dublin.

In Cuan, retirement was dominated by people who had worked in the public service or management within the commercial sector. But there were certainly some who made a living through entrepreneurial activities. There is an obvious reason why business entrepreneurs tend to conspicuous consumption. A major factor in business success comes from the display of pecuniary confidence. The perception of strength and likely future growth is what drives stock markets often more than actual assets and performance. But even at very low levels in economic activity, people have to decide whether a person or a firm is a safe investment or a risk. The appearance of doing well is therefore more important in attracting further investment than actually doing well.

Mostly, however, business in Cuan was relatively small-scale, such as the ownership of a local retail outlet. There were one or two families who owned several restaurants or other businesses and had very impressive and extensive properties in and near to Cuan. These families, however, were highly integrated into the general life of the town. Some members of the very same families were not nearly as well-off and, apart from the size of their homes, were not otherwise given to conspicuous consumption. Good evidence for the lack of any significant local circuit of status was the absence of organizations such as Rotary or the Freemasons that elsewhere are usually the preserve of successful business people or the higher levels of certain professions. The issue will be returned to in a more general discussion of the place of egalitarianism in chapter 5.

The argument for the retired people of Cuan as representative of a satiable society may now seem complete. In fact, we are only halfway there. This is because an equally strong body of evidence may be derived from a field of behaviour that is only starting to emerge as an arena of status competition: the supersession of conspicuous consumption by conspicuous *anti*-consumption. Recall the example at the start of this chapter that when everyone can afford white bread, the highest class will turn to wholemeal and organic loaves. Today, the primary exemplar of emulation is undoubtedly in the field of environmental activism with its clear message of anti-consumerism.

Environmental Emulation

Cuan is an energetic town, as later chapters on sports (chapter 7) and other activities (chapter 9) will make clear. But on settling there, it did not take long to be struck by another source of abundant activity that galvanized people into new commitments and collective action. It seemed as though every couple of weeks one heard about some fresh environmentalist venture.[10] At the Men's Shed, an enthusiast came to speak to us about the prospect of setting up a repair initiative to help people restore objects they might otherwise have just thrown away. The next week one would hear about a subsidy for local bee-keeping or monitoring energy use.

This rapid expansion of interest in green issues was helped by being a matter of both popular sentiment and encouragement from the state. The evidence for the latter was especially clear from discussion with the stalwarts of what was undoubtedly the most important of all Cuan's public commitments: the Tidy Towns competition.[11] A sizeable proportion of the retired population that formed the research participants of this study were also volunteers for Tidy Towns. As a volunteer myself, on the day when I was returning my borrowed litter-picking equipment I found that I knew a good number of the other volunteers who were hovering at the meeting. This was a prime activity for retirees in Cuan. Most of us were allocated a patch of a few streets for weekly inspection and cleaning. Tidy Towns is taken deeply seriously across Ireland. Started in 1958, it was originally an annual competition concerned mainly with the public appearance of Irish settlements. More than 900 communities compete in Ireland for the award and Cuan expects to do well. Nothing else has quite the same traction. The Tidy Towns Facebook site is one of the most active for Cuan with over 800 followers.

In discussing this with the Tidy Towns committee, it became clear that they had seen the priorities shift in recent years. They explained this as a reflection of the shunting of Tidy Towns from one government department to another. The current Department of Environment, Climate, and Communication needs to demonstrate to the European Commission how Ireland is fulfilling its obligations to the environment. The committee suspected that this had led the department to put pressure on Tidy Towns to demonstrate the government's positive commitment to these European demands. Today, for the judges of Tidy Towns, 'sustainable waste and resource management' or 'wildlife, habitats, and natural amenities' count for as much as 'residential streets and housing areas' (all fifty marks each).

Some members of the committee were ambivalent about this shift. The ideal of retaining a wild area on environmental grounds doesn't necessarily equate with the ideal of a pretty area as a Tidy Towns priority. Furthermore, such was the prominence of Tidy Towns that committee members tended to be landed with the organization of whatever initiatives were relevant. For example, they found themselves liaising with the school on an initiative concerned with micro-plastics in the ocean. One committee member opined, 'To my mind it's just ridiculous. Tidy Towns is somebody tidying up the place. It's nothing to do with the bees and the butterflies and the sustainability and the whole thing. It needs a new title, but they say you can't change it.'

This view was unusual. Mostly, this top-down pressure was pushing at an open door, since it was largely these same people who were constantly developing their own initiatives around environmental causes. Others in Tidy Towns recognized that it was precisely because it was now more aligned with sustainability issues that it retained its vanguard presence as the premier national initiative and thence the natural base for such wider commitments. A meeting held by Tidy Towns specifically directed at sustainability attracted 800 people. It is now green issues that are bringing people on board to Tidy Towns.

Another burgeoning initiative was Sustainable Cuan. The group emerged from the influential 'Transition Towns' movement that started in the UK around 2006 and is aimed at developing greater self-sufficiency in response to problems of climate change. Typical activities would be trying to work with local supermarkets to reduce plastic; developing a vegetable box scheme based on local growers; encouraging people to harvest rainwater; developing initiatives concerning food waste; or encouraging the organic side of the allotments. There were also initiatives to encourage bee-keeping to support pollination. The appeal to the Men's Shed concerning the repair of goods was linked to a consideration of upcycling and related initiatives which simultaneously re-fashion traditional ideals of thrift – something that would reconnect older people with virtues garnered from their initial upbringing in poverty. Enthusiasm for environmental causes had its limits, however, when a clash arose with private interests. For example, parking charges aimed at reducing the use of private cars were resisted.

The rise of environmentalism was a major point of discussion in my book with Pauline Garvey, for two main reasons. First, the very idea of 'sustainability' proved perfect as an appeal to retired people who were increasingly concerned with personal sustainability as their health deteriorated. Consequently, eating healthy foods or taking up cycling could comfortably bring personal sustainability and planetary sustainability within the same orbit. Second, the shift to environmentalism played a major part in the ability of these retirees to in some sense get younger. Initially, climate change was viewed as something especially associated with young people galvanized by the very young Greta Thunberg. The logic was that young people would have a more natural concern with the long-term viability of the planet. But in practice retired people had more time to become actual environmental activists and could in effect outdo the young in their displayed commitment. Similarly, younger people were accumulating possessions, especially when they had children. It was retired people who could conspicuously divest themselves of possessions and embrace anti-materialism through various strategies of decluttering and dispossession such as taking things to the charity shop.

The ethnography made apparent that older people to some degree resented the way that traditional respect for seniority had been traduced by the new digital skills which were deemed as natural attributes of the young, sometimes making them feel stupid by comparison. It felt to me as though the degree to which older people could constantly outdo the young with respect to a conspicuous environmentalism had helped to restore some balance. This perhaps partly explains the zeal with which the retirees were taking up every kind of environmentalist challenge. This is, however, clearly supposition and not something anyone expressed openly.

All of this also became a public demonstration of older people's repudiation of the values associated with consumerism or the blandishments of capitalism. But this wasn't merely anti-consumption; it was often conspicuous anti-consumption – an activity which returns us to the initial arguments of Veblen about emulation. When it comes to status display and status competition, there is simply no reason why conspicuous anti-consumption cannot serve just as well as conspicuous consumption. Whether intended or not, active environmentalism had become by far the most important dimension of status differentiation in Cuan. It tended to be those who were most educated and most in touch with contemporary trends who were at the vanguard of these initiatives, sometimes because of the influence of their university-educated children. By contrast, several overheard remarks revealed how people living in the Vartry Estate were branded by the middle class as caring little about rubbish in the streets or the problems of climate change. This was not necessarily true: I came across passionate advocates of environmental causes, such as using seaweed for fertilizer, on the Vartry Estate. But this did not prevent the rise of a general prejudice among the middle class that assumed lower-income or less educated people would not care as much for the environment as they did. This allowed environmentalism to emerge as an effective proxy for class differentiation.[12]

Sometimes consumption and anti-consumption were not opposites but reinforced each other in relation to status display. An example was organic food, which was generally more expensive than non-organic food. Investments in alternative energy and other green initiatives could also come at a price. In such instances, greater wealth could be deployed to demonstrate one's superiority in the field of anti-consumerism. Alternatively, thrift and other forms of anti-consumerism could be regarded as skills in their own right. Knowing how to get bargains from charity shops or cooking from basic healthy ingredients rather than shop-prepared meals was often used as a claim for respect. There have by now been a fair number of studies of the relationship between environmental activism, status, and class. Several of these are set in countries such as Norway and Sweden, which are probably comparable to Cuan in favouring collective as against individualist values. They replicate this evidence for status competition through environmentalism. It will be interesting to see what happens when anti-consumption becomes the primary drive towards status in a rather less egalitarian context.

Ultimately, there is one huge advantage that anti-consumerism has over consumerism within a process of status accumulation through emulation: anti-consumerism comes with powerful ethical associations that make absolutely clear the moral superiority of its advocates. As noted above, consumption emulation in the sense of keeping up with the neighbours is now more likely to be associated with vulgarity. With anti-consumerism, people set themselves up to be a 'good example' to others in order to encourage emulation of their actions. Environmentalism is driven by a sense of belief, on occasion purloining moral ideals from religion, in that the very idea of being a good, decent, moral person is now measured by degrees of environmental commitment. All of this clearly contributes to a sense of life purpose for people who, as they age, are growing increasingly conscious that life is finite. A goal of sustainability is a gift to those concerned with what they should be doing for their rest of their time on earth. This is in stark contrast to the historical situation, where it has always been difficult for wealthy people to assert superior morality on the basis of their greater consumption or higher status.

To be clear, nothing snide or denigratory is intended in this characterization of status competition over environmentalism. There is no suggestion that the commitments to environmental goals are insincere or reducible to virtue signalling. Environmentalism is a positive and indeed essential thing to be competitive about. It was yet another reason to be constantly in awe of the good citizens of Cuan and make them subject to a book of praise. There is no contradiction in observing the degree to which environmentalism now dominates social status and its genuine moral necessity at a time when climate change is the single most urgent problem for contemporary humanity. Indeed, this alignment may be no bad thing. I am happy to cede status to those who work harder to secure the future of the planet than I do, acknowledging their moral superiority, if that makes me want to emulate them.

As with several previous examples, Cuan seems important in showing how processes assumed to assert individualism may not do so. One of the effects of all these movements and initiatives, whether Tidy Towns or Sustainable Cuan, is that they bring people together around a common cause whose very ethos is opposed to what has become seen as an over-individualized society, which is in turn seen as symptomatic of the influence of that rather glib category 'neo-liberal capitalism'. This is a story about the creation of new cultural normativity and the moral pressures on individuals to conform to these ideals. It is compatible with the previous chapter on freedom since involvement is largely based on volunteering, but mostly volunteering for what are community projects and under strong normative pressure. The good enough life is the good society/ *polis*, not just the good individual. Cuan is a Tidy Town.

Why Calling Ourselves Superficial Is Superficial

So far, this chapter has developed two main arguments: that consumption in Cuan is largely satiable; and that anti-consumption has replaced consumption as a primary goal in life. But there is a third argument, which is central to any wider understanding of people's relationship to objects. A major part of the critique of consumption has been that it makes people more superficial; that in the presence of this massive array of goods we replace depth with breadth. This has been a common assertion at least since the time of the German sociologist Georg Simmel.[13] The latest iteration of this argument has come with the rise of digital technologies. The same set of arguments about increasing superficiality seems to have become even more prevalent and forceful for the critique of digital society as for that of consumer society.

Both the previous discussions pertain to the quantity of possessions. The word 'satiable' suggests the capacity to limit the number of new commodities, while the environmentalist concerns go beyond that, towards an attitude of positive divestment of possessions. Older men could become quite boring in their constant assertion that, for example, these days they only needed two good pairs of walking shoes and the rest had gone to charity shops. But equally important is our qualitative as opposed to our quantitative relationship to things: that our relationships in some supposed historical time were deep and authentic and now they have become shallow and inauthentic because we live in a consumer or digital society.

To consider these questions, additional evidence will come from two rather different sources that help break down the simple dualism that focuses upon the relationship between people and things. We might gain a better understanding of these relationships if we consider some cases that don't fit easily into either category but are a kind of in between. The first of the two fields that serves this purpose is something that is not human but is very much alive: our pet dogs. Then we turn to something that is certainly not alive but has developed a quite unprecedently intimate relation with the human beings who use them: the smartphone. A link between the two will be the argument that our relationship to pets is all about anthropomorphism, while our relationship to smartphones can be understood as something that takes us beyond anthropomorphism. In both cases, however, the primary point being made is in repudiation of assumptions that the depth of our relationships has suffered as a result of the increase in breadth.

Pet Dogs
Dogs were by no means the only pets that people kept in Cuan, but they clearly dominated. The evidence around having dogs as pets comes both from observations of people with dogs and discussions with dog owners and from interviews with the two veterinary practices that had a base in Cuan. The number of pets registered with these vets would suggest that the majority of households in the town had a pet. The importance of pet dogs was also evident from the fortnightly magazine *Cuan News*, which had a 'Dog of the Week' item with a photograph of the hound in question and then various factoids, such as the following (a composite of two cases):

Name: Milo
Breed: Cavalier King Charles
Age: Four months
Favourite toy: His ball and his little red dinosaur, but really he is a typical pup and loves eating and playing with all the adult items that he shouldn't be near!!
Favourite treat: Cheese, carrots and crisps
Loves: Giving kisses, running around the garden and finding new places to leave little unwanted surprises for his mam and dad.
Hates: He has a genuine fear of other dogs (unless of course they are significantly smaller than him, i.e. maybe a timid Chihuahua or a rare 'shy' Yorkie).
Special Because: He arrived at his new home just before the recent Covid distancing and lockdown measures and is giving his new family so much joy during a challenging time. They would be lost without him.

Dogs featured a fair bit on community Facebook accounts, both because people asked questions, such as recommendations for a dog groomer or suggestions for dog grooming clippers, but also in the form of complaints about insistent barking. According to the vets, around 70 per cent of their time was taken up with dogs, 20 per cent with cats, and 10 per cent with rabbits, ferrets, and a range of exotic pets. Most dogs for older people were common breeds such as spaniels, Jack Russells, terrier crosses, or Labradors while those buying dogs because they had children were more likely to take one of the cross-breeds such as labradoodles or cockapoos. Typically, these were bought for children between two and four years old who had often become jealous of their friends who had dogs. There were also quite a few dogs that impressed others, such as huskies and miniature schnauzers, which were paraded and much appreciated.

Dogs might cost anything from €300 to well over €1,000. The vets were well aware when people bought cut-price puppies from illegal puppy farms, since these often quickly fell sick and required treatment. Further costs included around €40 a month in food, or €70 to feed a large dog. Even with basic worming and vaccines, dogs could cost around €150 a year to keep healthy. Less than 20 per cent seemed to have health insurance and health bills could become exorbitant. Aileen in her eighties lived on the Vartry Estate on her pension. She had to look after her son, who had quite severe mental health problems, but he in turn was besotted by a fourteen-year-old dog that had severe health problems of its own. Between the arthritis and heart tablets, the dog set them back around €100 a month, which was pretty much all that her son contributed to the household as he had difficulties working. Most people could not afford the expenditure that came when, for example, their dog had cancer and so they decided to have it put down. But some would decide on treatment and this could be between €4,000 and €5,000 a month for several months. One of the vets during my fieldwork was dealing with a dog from a family with three children. There was an orthopaedic surgeon for dogs who could have operated, but the family simply couldn't afford the €2,500 that would have been required.

The fact that these sums may be spent on dogs might seem to contradict earlier sections of this chapter and equate with what Veblen called vicarious consumption, demonstrating the affluence of their owners. The purchase of very fancy breeds might equate with conspicuous consumption, but this was rare. Mostly, large expenditures required by dogs was not an issue of status rivalry, because this was a private concern that others would have known little about. Instead, it seemed to be evidence for the way people expected to treat their dogs as more analogous to their treatment of people. It formed part of an increasingly anthropomorphic sensibility extended to dogs.

There were four main examples of this trend. The first was the way dog sitting had become more like babysitting. It used to be that families went on holidays and took their dogs to kennels. But the dog had become so fully integrated into family life that the absence of the family was now much more traumatic. People in Cuan preferred to leave the dog either with a regular friend or relative, or with a dog sitter, who was again regularly used, so that the dog had an independent relationship with the person they were staying with and the experience was much less traumatic. Some might even accompany the dog for the first time and watch how the interaction appeared to be progressing to ensure that the dog seemed comfortable, just as they might watch their infant when employing a babysitter for the first time.

A second example links dogs back to the discussion of environmentalism. This has several parallels with the treatment of dogs. For many people, the high-status dog was no longer a pure breed or expensive dog, but rather a 'rescue dog', perhaps one that had been left because the previous owner had died, or the children had rejected their Christmas present. Many people in Cuan now actively sought out such 'recycled' dogs in preference. They were keen to let others know that these were rescue dogs, which seems to confirm the arguments presented earlier regarding status and environmentalism. The vets would no longer agree to euthanize healthy dogs and said they managed to place 99 per cent of such dogs with new owners. A further development was that those who opposed bio-medical health interventions had similar views when it came to their dogs. One of the vets in Cuan employed an acupuncturist and there were other complementary therapies in relation to dogs' physical but also mental health. One Irish website lists ten vets who deal with complementary therapies for dogs, including homeopathy.[14]

A third example is best understood in relation to a wider cultural trait of Ireland, where funerals play a very significant role in communities. It seems that even people who have great difficulty affording veterinary bills will pay the extra €200 to have their dogs cremated and to retain the ashes. Mostly, these are kept on mantelpieces, but ashes are also scattered over favourite spots, as is increasingly the case with human ashes. Finally, there is the rise of concern for mental wellbeing and recognizing conditions such as depression in dogs, evidence of which might be constant staring at a wall or even dogs banging their heads against a wall. Occasionally, treatment may extend to prescribing anti-depressants, but mostly it is about developing mental stimulation for the dog through giving it tasks. For what it's worth, my impression was that dogs barked less in Cuan than any place I had previously lived, which the vet would interpret as showing that dogs are happier and have more attention than in most regions.

For at least one of the vets, this anthropomorphic sensibility seemed very natural. She had herself been brought up in a family where there were never fewer than half a dozen dogs, and, as with many residents of Cuan, she regarded a real or natural family as one with dogs. When she talked about problems such as depression and head-banging, there was no doubting her compassion and empathy. This was also evident in her language. For example, when explaining why most people don't train their dogs (something she regarded as necessary for highly intelligent breeds such as Labradors and collies), she stated, 'They can easily become extremely bold, because they know how to work you and to work the system.' Similarly, when she explained the new hydrotherapy pool that helps dogs' rehabilitation after orthopaedic surgery or the employment of their dog acupuncturist, it was evident that these stemmed from the same basic empathetic engagement with her animals. There might be vets elsewhere who were more concerned to make profits from gullible and anxious pet owners, but in Cuan it felt like these veterinary concerns were, rather, an extension of love and compassion.

Mostly, older people acknowledged that pets stood both as companions and as an important reason for daily exercise. A vet told a story of an older person who simply stopped walking once their pet had died, which led to their own decline. Also important was the way dogs provided people with a sense of responsibility, some mental stimulation, and a kind of social interaction. People also talked of buying a dog for their children in the hope that this would help to develop their facility at relationships and some understanding of responsibility.

What can be contested are suppositions, frequently heard, regarding the consequences of dogs for the development of social relations. A research participant, Patricia, who became a good friend, was a sixty-year-old woman living on her own, whose primary relationship was undoubtedly with her dog. She had arrived in Cuan six years previously and was quite clear that she hoped that having the dog would be a catalyst in developing her social relations with people in the town. Certainly, she seemed to have hugely benefited from the direct relationship with her dog, irrespective of any such additional social consequences. On occasion, I would accompany both her and her dog on their walks. As we walked along the beach, around 15 per cent of the other walkers had dogs with them, around the same proportion who had accompanying children. We also passed a large number of single people using this stretch for exercise. Many of the people we passed called out Patricia's dog by name as readily as calling out her own name. It was unimaginable that a walk would not include some social encounters, and these frequently included chatting about the dog. A younger woman, Valeria, joked that 'the important thing is not you but the dog', since much of the conversation was almost inevitably about the latter.

However, in all those six years, nobody Patricia had encountered through dog walking had ever migrated from that relationship to become a friend who would be seen in other contexts. Other attempts by Patricia to develop friendship though volunteering had been highly successful, as Cuan is a very friendly community, but encounters based on dog greeting remained just that. This is not to suggest that such encounters are without significance. The degree to which people greet each other and stop for a chat while walking is seen by pretty much everyone in Cuan as important in establishing the character of the town, as it does provide daily social encounters. It was one of the most common pieces of evidence that people used to justify their extravagant praise for Cuan itself. Many people tried to walk at the same time daily in order to meet with other regulars, and this might be a highlight of that day's sociality. However, the assumption made by most people regarding its effect as a catalyst for deeper friendship proved not to be the case either for Patricia or for several others to whom I put this question directly.

There are many histories of our relationship to pets and dogs. One of the most influential is by Keith Thomas, who documents the rise of pet dogs as substitute children in England.[15] There are also histories of farming or hunting that document how dogs have enhanced the capacity of humans as kind of technology. From the Cuan perspective, the utilitarian aspect of dogs had diminished, though they still encouraged older people to take walks and could be a major asset in helping them remain fit and healthy. More recent factors that encouraged dog ownership included dogs purchased as gifts for young children. Later on, couples were also said to have dogs as 'practice babies', implying that from the besotted way they acted in relation to their pet, the observer could easily surmise that within a year or two the couple would have an actual baby. For older people, however, they were primarily companions.

Smartphones
The core to digital technologies is that they make many things far easier to replicate and to share. As a result, we now have an ever more diverse array of cultural forms in the world. Instead of a hobby around gardening or painting, a person can be absorbed by a specialist social media platform such as Twitch or a sub-Reddit group that most people have never heard of but which takes up much of their lives. Although the digital is now a foundational part of our infrastructure that we just take for granted, most of the discussion about its impact on our lives has consisted of an exploitation of the digital in order to engage in various forms of moral condemnation. An ever more insistent critique, especially of young people, who are particularly associated with the digital, is that they are losing their humanity as they replace people with screens. Young people are castigated as the superficial generation with nothing more than a TikTok[16] attention span. If the first half of my career was taken up in opposition to such comments with regard to consumption, for the last two decades I have been fighting a rear-guard action in particular on behalf of young people through the use of ethnography to study how they engage with digital devices, once again with the aim of repudiating these assumptions, to show how it is the accusations that have become more superficial, not the people. For example, there was a period that seemed obsessed with the critique of the selfie, a word which conveniently sounded like 'selfish'. This seemed proof positive that young people were becoming narcissistic. In my work in secondary schools, however, I found that five times as many posted selfies were actually of groups rather than individuals and that the 'ugly' selfie on snapchat was being used to create strong bonds within the group.

I have no desire to offend dog owners. Smartphones may not be alive, but there are grounds for juxtaposing them to dogs as a means for examining the extension of an anthropomorphic sensibility. The way people in Cuan related to their smartphones will help us appreciate an analogous humanizing of our relationship to objects. Relatively little is included in this volume about smartphones, given that this was the primary topic of research in my book with Pauline Garvey, where more extensive discussion can be found.

A useful bridge between these topics of smartphones and dogs was a digital pet called the Tamagotchi. This was a fashion that lasted a few years around the turn of the millennium. The idea of the Tamagotchi was that it required constant care from its owner, under which it would thrive and without which it was doomed. If you stopped 'feeding it', after a while it 'died'. The Tamagotchi was thereby explicitly intended to be analogous to a pet. Gardening acts as another bridge in that plants are living but can't really be described as pets.

Few people care about nurturing their smartphone as though it was an external creature such as a dog or even a Tamagotchi. Yet the smartphone has inveigled its way into becoming if anything still more intimate. First, it has become an important instrument in the way we care for others, especially those who do not live close by. The use of WhatsApp by people in Cuan to organize care for elderly parents quickly became seen as essential. But the true intimacy of the smartphones lies rather in the degree to which they become integrated into the person or relationship. The concept of 'beyond anthropomorphism' was employed in our volume *The Global Smartphone* to show how smartphones can become an extension of the self, something closer to the idea of an avatar.[17]

Perhaps the ideal analogy that links the dog and the smartphone comes through the fiction of Philip Pullman. His best-known book series *His Dark Materials* is set in a world where humans have animal 'daemons': avatars that both reflect their personality and give them capacities they would not otherwise possess, such as an owl that can see better than its human in the dark. We might have expected such intimate and affective relationships with robots that are anthropomorphic in the sense of looking to some degree like people. But appearances are by definition superficial, and the point of the phrase 'beyond anthropomorphism' is that the intimacy with the smartphone is not dependent in any way on appearance. A smartphone looks nothing like a person, while a dog certainly can.

A chapter in our collective volume *The Global Smartphone* provides several examples of how the smartphone acts as an avatar.[18] There is the way an individual's personality or interests become expressed through the phone. A highly professional woman in Cuan turned her iPhone into a marvel, a tightly organized encyclopaedic prosthetic to her life, so that anything she might want to attempt could now be done more seamlessly and with better information. She had set up her smartphone so that when it was time for her to pay a bill, a whole series of apps and information sources connected up to make this a smooth operation. She had organized her smartphone to become a life manual that linked websites, calendars, and notes to express her sense of herself as a consummate professional. She had never secured the employment that would have recognized her abilities as she saw them. It was only through the smartphone that she had created the representation of herself as she believed herself to be.

By comparison, there was the gruff hyper-masculine descendant of Cuan fishermen whose refusal to use any other than the most essential smartphone apps became an expression of his masculine minimalism and antipathy to such fripperies. The research explored the way a smartphone could capture what had become special about a Cuan man whose life was devoted to engineering, or the way an eighty-year-old woman now used Instagram to facilitate her relationship to art, both her own and others. In a remarkably short period, it became possible to investigate the degree to which an analysis of their smartphone felt like knowing the individual behind the smartphone – a question that is also commonly asked when we see a person next to their choice of pet dog.

Behind this comes an appreciation that the smartphone is also a work of craft, not by its designer so much as by its consumer. The smartphone is unprecedented in the degree to which it can be changed post-purchase through adding or subtracting apps, changing settings, and creating content. This is what allows for such an intense personalization within a very short time. Starting from this highly individual relationship, the evidence is then presented to show how equally adept the smartphone has become as the avatar of relationships, such as couples or intergenerational relations. The intimacy between a couple who have been together fifty years is evident when it no longer matters whose smartphone has any particular app. The inconsiderate grandchild is revealed by the unsuitable games that now populate the grandparent's smartphone. Finally, *The Global Smartphone* considers how smartphones also embed cultural values. Generalizations around gender implied when one talks of masculine smartphones are in fact Irish gender stereotypes that might be different elsewhere. To the degree that a person embodies the normative values of their society, so in turn does their smartphone.

Just as once we respected the book collection or record collection as an external expression of the individual, their values and interests, so a young person might judge their friend through appreciating the nuances of their particular smartphone. We also increasingly cede cognitive functions such as memory to smartphones. Knowing how to find facts becomes more helpful than memorizing the facts themselves. A capacity that developed first through the invention of writing and then through the invention of printing and the creation of libraries is now hugely extended by the smartphone and associated search engines. The smartphone thereby develops as an extension of cognition. All of this suggests that the smartphone has become a powerful prosthetic element for both bodies and minds, justifying this label of 'beyond anthropomorphism'.

The following chapter will return to these discussions of the pet dog and smartphones to consider the implications for philosophy and the depth of our relationships more generally. But already it should be clear why it is the critique of the smartphone rather than the smartphone itself that is superficial.

Conclusion

This chapter has presented three primary arguments. The first is that it is possible to have a satiable society with respect to our demand for goods. The second is that the primary source of emulation today is not consumption but anti-consumption. The third is that our relationships, whether with each other or with the world around us, may not have become more superficial. The evidence presented came from Cuan, but in considering whether these three arguments are plausible, a reader can certainly reflect upon their own experiences and changes observable in the world around them. The problem is that even people who use smartphones all day long for helpful and what are increasingly seen as essential purposes, such as driving, looking up information, and keeping in contact with others, may still adhere to a public discourse that presents these devices as making us more shallow, trivial, and anti-social. Similarly, it is possible that readers of this volume live in a society where environmentalism has become critical to status claims in ways at least analogous to those that have been presented here, but may not wish to acknowledge the relationship between environmentalism and status if they feel that reduces the integrity of their genuine moral commitment.

It will also be rather obvious that the content of this chapter fails to accord with common presumptions about the consequences of living in a capitalist society. Most of the examples, such as wearing blue jeans, becoming satiable, or even transforming smartphones into what we want them to be, rather than what companies intend them to be, seem to portray capitalism as rather ineffective. In fact, there is nothing in this chapter that detracts from the critique of capitalism *per se*. The newspaper I read daily (*The Guardian*) provides constant evidence for just how rapacious and cruel business interests and the search for profitability remain in countless areas. I believe we are partly responsible for this. As long as we continue to buy the cheapest example of a product, we are complicit in the capitalist logic of businesses paying the least for raw materials and for labour that they can. I wish there was as much concern for fair trade as for environmentally friendly goods. The evidence presented in this chapter is not in any way an argument that capitalism is benign, but it does show that we cannot simply write off every society glibly as neo-liberal because the underlying political economy is neo-liberal.

This is not, however, a book about how businesses operate. As already noted in the introduction, the striking contrast between the individualism of the English and the sociality of the Irish would be hard to link to any difference in the nature of the neo-liberal capitalism found in these neighbouring regions. What has been consistent throughout this chapter is a concern with the way critics of capitalism and of digital technologies have often quite unnecessarily shown no respect at all for the abilities of ordinary people who live in this consumer and digital world. The primary contention of the following chapter's discussion of Western Marxism is that the critique of capitalism should not require a condescending set of assumptions about populations. There should be some space where we can accord respect for the people of Cuan, their strident environmentalism, and their satiable consumption.

Chapter 4

PHILOSOPHERS AND CONSUMERISM

Dialectic of Enlightenment

The critique of the consumer society has been a major component of twentieth-century writing in both philosophy and social science. Over three excellent volumes, Daniel Horowitz traced the rise of a critique of American consumer culture over a still longer period.[1] It is not surprising that there are roots beneath this critique that stem from within philosophy itself, as will be suggested in chapter 12 on the Stoics and Epicurus. Many philosophers have maintained a fairly consistent leaning towards asceticism. This may have had limited relevance for much of history since most people lived in conditions we would now consider as poverty. Even the comparatively wealthy of the past would have had no access to the vast array of consumer goods, science, and modern technologies that we now take for granted. Over the last century, however, consumer culture has taken central stage in our moral debates about the direction of humanity. There are many candidates for exploring this tendency through philosophy. In this chapter, the focus will be on some of the most influential voices found within the Marxist tradition. These were selected partly because this was the genre of philosophy that I was personally attached to when I was a student, and partly because it is the branch of philosophy most clearly directed against the rise of what was seen as insatiable consumerism.

These philosophers are often described under the category of Western Marxism in order to differentiate them from Marxist ideology within the Soviet Union, which was more concerned to overtake the West in the development of mass consumption.[2]

Furthermore, this anti-consumerism is not directly derived from the writings of Marx himself. If anything, he celebrated the capacity of industrial production to expand the possibilities of humanity. The issue for Marx was not the quantitative growth of cultural forms represented by such goods. It was that the proletariat could not enjoy the fruits of their labour since capitalism had sundered what should have been the intrinsic link between such products and those who had created them as value. It was Western Marxism that subsequently turned this critique of capitalism into a more general critique of capitalist consumer society. While there were many impressive political philosophers within Western Marxism, such as György Lukács and Antonio Gramsci, the movement that focused most fully on the critique of mass consumer culture was known as the Frankfurt School,[3] within which a key philosophical text was *Dialectic of Enlightenment* by the German philosophers and social theorists Theodor Adorno (1903–69) and Max Horkheimer (1895–1973).[4]

This chapter will therefore start with *Dialectic of Enlightenment* and then add discussions of two influential figures in the further development of these critical perspectives: Jean Baudrillard and Walter Benjamin. As a student, I was greatly influenced by these figures. But when I recently re-read *Dialectic of Enlightenment*, I found it to be one of the strangest of well-regarded philosophical works. By far the most consequential section of this book concerned the culture industry, but prior to that essay there are 120 pages that are really quite peculiar. Although Adorno and Horkheimer on several occasions rail against Kant, they share a similar concern with what they regard as certain negative possibilities emergent from the Enlightenment. Kant wanted to retain a place for religion and morality. These authors are concerned to protect art and wider human values from this same reduction to the relentless progress of science. They portray the world around them as submerged within a totalitarian construction based on domination, within which thought itself has become a mere commodity. As the book title suggests, Adorno and Horkheimer see much of what they detest about modern life as a legacy of the Enlightenment. But what feels strange about their argument is that their discussion of the Enlightenment seems to include so much that most people would assume the Enlightenment opposed, such as myth.[5]

The starting point of their exposition is that human endeavour, of necessity, requires domination over nature, which simultaneously becomes the instrument for securing the domination of people by people. From the time of the Enlightenment, science becomes the primary instrument of that domination and of a relentless disenchantment of the world, 'For the Enlightenment,' Adorno and Horkheimer claim, 'whatever does not submit to the rule of computation and utility is suspect',[6] until meaning itself is renounced. Culture itself has become merely a manifestation of business rationality, whose results are superficial to the point of meaninglessness.

Adorno and Horkheimer begin with a dialectical analysis that stretches far back in time to try to find the origins of the dilemmas that face the contemporary world. They argue that these lie in the ultimate unity between the Enlightenment and its foe, myth, as the original form of human conceptualization. Myth and early religion were attempts to bring order to the world and thereby assert the sovereignty of humanity over nature, often vicariously through imputing powers to spirits and deities that then represent the authority of humanity. Adorno and Horkheimer suggest that early magic can be viewed as attempting to achieve similar aims to science, though mimesis. This argument is then used to suggest that the Enlightenment is the heinous source not only of developments in science but also the very things that most enlightenment philosophers would have seen as abhorrent.[7] The earlier section also includes a lengthy discussion of Odysseus, who comes to hear the Sirens, while the rowers, as labourers, do not. This is followed by a bizarre attempt to argue that Juliette, an anti-heroine created by the Marquis de Sade, in her engagement with various appalling sexual practices that neglected no orifice, is actually bringing a kind of enlightenment ethics and order to the construction of orgiastic practices. In modern parlance, this is a seriously weird book with some very strange engagements with the topic of temptation.

These sections lead up to the best-known essay within their book: a discussion of the culture industry. Under the guise of a critique of domination and inequality, the authors take up a highly elitist position that condemns as worthless the mass culture of ordinary workers, the very people who according to Marxism were supposed to be re-credited with value. The term 'culture industry' asserts that cultural forms are principally created through capitalist business, whose sole motivation is profit. As noted in the previous chapter, the argument was clarified subsequently by the economist J.K. Galbraith.[8] Any industry will secure its profitability by first ensuring that its audience, primarily workers, are receptive to its products. They don't want to risk investing large sums of money in a product without being sure it will be consumed. The original critique of Marx concerning the potential reduction of our humanity to exchange value in industrial production here becomes a more totalizing critique of all culture as the vehicle for exchange value. The culture industry constructs a humanity engineered to passively receive its creations. As the authors put it, 'Culture now impresses the same stamp on everything. Films, radio and magazines make up a system which is uniform as a whole and in every part.'[9] They argue that radio allowed the charismatic character of Hitler's speeches to create a homogenized mass and appreciative response in the same way that the printing press allowed for the spread of the Reformation.[10] It is a strange analogy. Books may well have helped spread totalitarian versions of the Reformation. That is hardly a reason, however, for rejecting books *per se*. Under the culture industry, there are no individuals and there is no spontaneity, and, importantly, there is no critique (other than the authors' own) that cannot be incorporated by the culture industry.

There is another unwarranted assumption within *Dialectic of Enlightenment*. There is no logical reason why the culture industry might not have succeeded in its task by producing culture of such high quality that everyone would indeed be united in their desire for and appreciation of cultural products. If anything, that would have enhanced the profits of the culture industry even further. After all, no one has suggested that the science produced by the Enlightenment cannot be really good-quality science. But Adorno and Horkheimer sneak in their own severe cultural prejudices by always assuming that the result must be of the lowest possible worth. They continually return to the defence of high art, both classical music such as Beethoven and avant-garde music such as Schoenberg. The implication is that the contemporary mass working class now represents the lowest possible taste. Thanks to the culture industry, 'the misplaced love of the common people for the wrong which is done to them is a greater force than the cunning of the authorities. … By craftily sanctioning the demand for rubbish it inaugurates total harmony.'[11]

Adorno and Horkheimer are appalled that a jazz musician such as Benny Goodman could appear with the Budapest string quartet.[12] They even manage to include some avant-garde art in their critique[13] and refuse to accept that film innovators such as Orson Welles were genuinely experimenting in any challenging way. They would probably see our contemporary 'sampling' culture, represented by platforms such as TikTok, as the final descent into the hell of debased superficiality. In short, these authors are amongst the purist embodiment of what Bourdieu called the 'aristocracies of culture',[14] sitting around contrasting their avant-garde and difficult modern art with worthless pop culture or football. They are surely the most egregious example of a denigrating dismissal of the very working class they claimed to support.

This is even more astonishing in the light of their own historical circumstance, the Weimar Republic, which prefigured the complex mix of critical and capitalist production that we see today. Already Fritz Lang could be popular but certainly not predictable, whilst avant-garde painters could appear in mainstream galleries. This was the period that saw the work of Thomas Mann and Herman Hesse, not to mention Bertolt Brecht and the astonishing Bruno Schultz. This dismal disparagement of ordinary people as cultural consumers was never really a requisite part of their cultural critique. The importance of Adorno and Horkheimer's work, especially at the time, was that the culture industry had such a glamorous and beguiling façade: those gorgeous black-and-white posters of Hollywood's leading stars. It was very hard to see that behind these lay a ruthless capitalist business that was driven by competitive studios whose true focus was the bottom line of profitability. People needed a book such as *Dialectic of Enlightenment* to pinch themselves awake from such dreamworlds; to acknowledge the realities of what lay behind these cultural façades. But this does not excuse such appalling and unnecessary elitism and denigration of those who viewed these films.

Baudrillard and Benjamin

Over the next several decades, other figures within Western Marxism extended these arguments to a more general critique of consumer society. Some, such as Wolfgang Fritz Haug, provided detailed analyses of commodity aesthetics in order to show how these goals of debasement were achieved.[15] But perhaps the most influential figure in the critique of the commodity was the French sociologist and philosopher Jean Baudrillard (1929–2007). In books such as *A Critique of the Political Economy of the Sign*, Baudrillard argues that even Marx failed to appreciate how his analysis of use and exchange value, developed to characterize the exploitation of workers, could also apply to their life as consumers.[16] Consumption had been quite neglected in Marx's own writings. Baudrillard, if anything, goes still further than *Dialectic of Enlightenment*. Commodity culture has become merely the mass production of signs. Advertising ensures that some trivial difference between two versions of a commodity has become the apparent experience of choice. We have become merely the requisite vehicles which allow these signs to colonize the world. The clothes we wear and the objects within the homes we invite people into have become the most effective branch of the advertisement industry that saturates the world with the sign system of capitalism: once we have purchased them, we become the walking, talking adverts for them. Capitalism has created insatiable consumers who become as fully superficial as the commodities through which they live, and whose propagation has become their purpose in life.

The very titles of some of the most influential works in this tradition, such as *One-Dimensional Man*[17] or *The Culture of Narcissism*,[18] make clear how relentless and sustained this criticism of most people's tastes had become. In 1987, I suggested that these writers had simply failed to observe consumption itself.[19] Consumption is a process. We don't just buy clothes; we then wear them. We don't just buy houses; we decorate them and turn them into homes. Consumption may start with the purchase of entirely alienated objects from shops. But after purchase we use these goods to create families, living rooms, and cultural interests, and through these processes we negate this initial state of alienation. The shirt that we have worn when out on a date is a very different shirt from the one we purchased. It is now 'my shirt', suffused with the experiences of wearing it. You can't have it, or even borrow it, for love or money. Consumption is often a long-term process which turns commodities back into the means by which we develop our humanity through our creation of the external world – that is material culture. I made this argument analogous to a return to the Hegelian arguments that preceded Marx and which will be discussed in the conclusion of this book.

In short, consumption is not, as these theorists argued, a continuation of the alienation found in production, its superstructure. Consumption can be its negation by turning an alienated commodity into an inalienable possession. Later, I argued that the most typical day-to-day shopping, which had traditionally comprised a housewife buying what would be turned into a family meal, should mostly be regarded as a technology for the enactment of love.[20] English families traditionally did not like to discuss their love for each other abstractly. It was sometimes through the care and attention given to buying the precise goods that matched the preferences of each family member that love was manifested. Supermarket shopping should thereby be regarded as a technology for shaping love.

To return to the original figures associated with the Frankfurt School,[21] the other highly influential intellectual was the German cultural theorist and philosopher Walter Benjamin (1892–1940).[22] Benjamin's most influential essay, *The Work of Art in the Age of Mechanical Reproduction*,[23] alongside his most sustained study, *The Arcades Project*,[24] taken as a kind of precursor to the shopping mall, both lead us in very different directions to *Dialectic of Enlightenment*. Adorno, who often assisted Benjamin financially, on several occasions tried to draw the latter back into his more conservative version of the Marxist critique. But while Benjamin would acquiesce in the idea that under capitalism the potential for consumer culture remains in a kind of frozen, unrealized state, he nevertheless insisted upon turning our attention towards its positive potentials. It was the magical array of shop windows along the arcades that fostered the rise of the wandering *flâneur*. If mass production threatened the original aura surrounding the work of art, it also laid the foundations for a potential democratization of art, making it accessible for mass populations.

A typical lyrical and attractive essay by Benjamin is called 'Unpacking my Library'.[25] Examined closely, however, it still retains problematic elements, at least when it comes to juxtaposing this tradition with what can be gleaned from the ethnography of Cuan. For most people, books are commodities only in as much as they initially pay for them. Once purchased, they are usually treated as inalienable personal possessions. We are often reluctant to part with them, and if we finally do so, it may be to charity shops, since we wish neither to sell them nor to throw them away. This is precisely the argument I had put forward regarding the process of consumption as the negation of alienation. My well-thumbed copy of *Jane Eyre* is now more than its text.

In 'Unpacking My Library', Benjamin celebrates being reunited with his library after his books had been packed away for two years. Benjamin not only read books, he was also a collector. He bought and sold volumes, implicating values such as investment possibilities that don't impinge upon mere readers. There are many kinds of collector, and Benjamin downplays the ideals of order and competition that drives other collectors. For him, the appeal lies more in the disorder and sense of serendipity that come from chance encounters.[26] He discusses values for the collector connected to memory and imagination, rather than mere utility. But when Benjamin exemplifies this relationship through the argument that the character of the true collector is seen in the possessions of many volumes that he never actually reads,[27] then it is hard not to conclude that those books are also being regarded as a commodity. Benjamin in his constant browsing of catalogues is imagining the possibilities of possession. What this requires includes money, expert knowledge, but also flair, knowing what is just the right book for him in particular to buy.[28] Money certainly comes to the fore in his description of the auction and his awareness of the competitors or his excitement in the process of bidding for books.[29] The sense of insatiable consumption is also present in his fascination with unpacking more and more books and the difficulty of stopping this activity. Benjamin even argues at one point that the best relationship is one of inheritance, since that gave a sense of responsibility for these collections. After reading this essay, one might even start to have some sympathy with Adorno's anxiety about where exactly Benjamin was going with all this.

I would not want to begrudge Benjamin his pleasure in collecting. The problem was that, despite writing sophisticated theoretical papers about the potential democratization of art, there is little in his writing that suggests that he, any more than these other elite thinkers, could imagine that his experience as a collector might be replicated by similarly sophisticated forms of consumption amongst the less privileged: that a lab technician could be a connoisseur of Chinese ceramics; or that the office discussion of yesterday's Premier League football match covers an extraordinary depth and appreciation of 'the beautiful game'. Starting with *Dialectic of Enlightenment* and ending with 'Unpacking My Library' is a way of acknowledging a breadth to the Frankfurt School, but it is hard to see where within that breadth we can locate most people who live in this world.

The Value of Mass Culture

How do these views stand in relation to an assessment of contemporary culture? Even before turning back to the ethnography, I should confess to my own values. Mostly, after a day writing this book, I, like so many others, will spend at least some of the evening watching television. According to the authors of *Dialectic of Enlightenment*, the main contribution of television is that it will 'intensify the impoverishment of aesthetic matter'.[30] I admit that I often relax watching Korean drama, of which I am inordinately fond, or Arsenal playing football. I also prefer to listen to the latest pop music[31] rather than to classical music. But I refuse to see contemporary television as merely debased. A recent competition for the best television series in the UK was between Michaela Coel's *I May Destroy You* and Steve McQueen's *Small Axe* – both masterpieces of critical drama and both of them mainstream television series.

Most of my research participants also watched a good deal of television, some with important consequences. Fintan O'Toole tells how a talk show called *The Late Late Show* influenced the shift away from theocratic control in Ireland.[32] A quality entirely missed by books such as *Dialectic of Enlightenment* is that precisely because people in Cuan can now assume that most of their friends and neighbours are watching the same mass-produced television, these programmes contribute to the maintenance of sociality. If we have run out of things to say about the weather, politics, or sports, then there is that new BBC detective series, or an Irish comedy such as *Father Ted* or *Mrs Brown's Boys*, that can extend their tea or Guinness while they enjoy the conversation of their peers.

Mostly, these retirees were children of blue-collar workers, and in some cases farmers, generally not industrial proletarians. They had almost always started as relatively low-level salaried employees such as clerks, accountants, ancillary nurses, or primary school teachers – people whose work was traditionally devalued and whom the Frankfurt School and other Marxist scholars claimed they would liberate. But even at that period of their life, they had more in common with the Frankfurt School writers than the latter would ever have credited. They often reflected on their early exposure to literature, even within families oppressed by poverty and alcoholism. They came from the Dublin of Joyce or the countryside of Yeats and felt close to such Irish literary traditions. They often worked into their conversations their pride in the books that they had read when young.

There were several book discussion groups in Cuan, one of which will be described in chapter 11. More surprising are the sheer number of Cuan authors with an international reputation, alongside many other authors whose books may not extend beyond a local readership. I encountered over twenty people in Cuan who had published books. Those were just the ones I knew of. There is a flourishing annual poetry festival, and two creative writing groups, where people would read out their latest compositions for comment and support. Cuan doesn't have many shops, but one of these is an independent bookshop. Walter Benjamin imagined this distributed creativity in the mass population as something for the future, presently a frozen capacity within the disenchanted realm of purely capitalist production. That was certainly not the case for Cuan.

The gulf between Cuan and Western Marxist philosophers seems even greater when we turn from culture to the wider world of commodities. For writers such as Baudrillard, people are mere mannequins wearing and thereby advertising capitalist products and ensuring an insatiable demand for new goods.[33] There is no imagination or comprehension of a possible satiable society concurrent with capitalism, a society where most people feel they now have the things they need or want and shop mainly for replenishment, plus a smattering of gifts or souvenirs. Chapter 11 will explore unfulfilled desires among the retirees of Cuan when it came to holiday destinations, but they expressed no great concern were these to remain unvisited.

With the rise of digital technologies, there are trends towards de-commodification as well as commodification. Whether entertainment through YouTube, education online, or access to news and information, once the background payments are made for the internet and smartphone, most of what follows as content is experienced as free.[34] Yet users have developed their own complex responses to these trends. For example, with few exceptions, research participants responded to my direct question that they would never pay for a smartphone app. It is a rather astonishing finding. Many very useful apps that would certainly have made their lives easier cost no more than a cup of coffee. Why, then, would they refuse to pay anything at all for an app? This can only be because these retirees are active in their sensibility towards issues of commodification. This is not necessarily positive. In our unwillingness now to pay much for music we listen to, we bear some responsibility for the mere pittance music creators gain from music streaming. This is not to detract from the primary role of neo-liberal capitalism in currently extending global inequalities,[35] but we also need to acknowledge the degree to which we collude in the reproduction of inequality.

There is also some potential for a rapprochement between ethnographic observations and this philosophical tradition. The passion for environmentalism and the current emphasis upon divestment from goods is fostered by a similar critique around the superficiality and insatiability held to be intrinsic to consumer culture. It was striking just how many of the retirees mentioned a kind of hippie phase in their youth.[36] The problem of climate change has clearly validated this critique, if on very different grounds. To some degree, then, these philosophical traditions may take some credit for their subsequent influence upon this population. Within contemporary philosophy, there are voices such as Kate Soper who argue for a new version of the good life based on an alternative, environmentally conscious form of consumption, while incorporating much of the Marxist critique.[37] None of this, however, detracts from the inexcusable and condescending elitism of the Frankfurt School and its lineage.

Are We Post-Human?

Walter Benjamin learnt a great deal from his books, but that is not what 'Unpacking My Library' is about. It concerns the way his relationship to books transcends the utilitarian to become a component element in his self-creation. Similarly, our book *The Global Smartphone* is not just about what people do with smartphones. It concerns the way smartphones facilitate who we can become.[38] The final section of the previous chapter provided the evidence that, so far from assuming that there is an increasing superficiality, we can see an extraordinary depth to the relationship between people in Cuan and some objects. If Benjamin found that books could become a profound component of his humanity, notwithstanding their status as commodities, so can other sources of knowledge such as the smartphone. The smartphone, too, is a step change in our ability to know more about the world, with search engines akin to a mobile library, just far more useful.

The term we created in order to express this depth of relationship was 'beyond anthropomorphism', since smartphones look nothing like people.[39] In philosophical discussions of post-humanism,[40] the primary concern is rather different. This is a project that desires humanity to reach beyond the anthropocentrism of seeing only humans as the measure of all things, arguing that we also need to the consider the perspectives and welfare of the non-human. Post-humanism is popular today well beyond philosophy because it would seem to favour environmentalist concerns and also expose historical and contemporary cruelty to the animal world.[41] Post-humanism seems to mean various different things depending upon the author and the academic discipline within which it is being employed,[42] though most of these share this idea that we need to see the world from a less anthropocentric viewpoint, which usually also implies a more empathetic relationship to nature. An influential example of these views as they pertain to our pet dogs has been the recent discussions by Donna Haraway of dogs as companion species.[43] Haraway shows the consequences of thinking about dogs as more than just pets and seeing them as other beings we live amongst with their own viewpoints and experiences.

Does the ethnographic evidence around the deepening of the relationship between people in Cuan and their pet dogs, as described in the previous chapter, support this argument? Not really. It suggests that while arguments around post-humanism remain significant aspirations, they are not yet descriptions of these relationships. The ethnographic evidence accords better with an extension of anthropomorphism rather than a repudiation of anthropocentrism. It shows how we now treat dogs in a similar fashion to the way we already cared for children, and how we impute similar psychological conditions to dogs as to persons. Certainly, this results in better treatment of dogs, because we extend empathy by thinking of them as more like ourselves. But this is not at all the same as considering what a dog perspective on the world might be. My ethnographic evidence for being cautious about the use of post-humanism in relation to pet dogs is supported by other studies more grounded in the close observation of the everyday treatment and consideration of these companion animals. They show the problem in, for example, extending our concepts of kinship into a kind of petship.[44]

A similar conclusion would arise from the ethnographic evidence for our relationship to smartphones. This is one of mutual change. Smartphones take on our character and personality: for instance, the minimalist smartphone of the gruff male that thereby expresses his sense of his own masculinity by making sure he uses no more apps than he absolutely has to. At the same moment, we are changed as human beings by virtue of the way smartphones enhance our capacities: for example, the ability to remain in constant contact with non-proximate others. As a result, we now include within the term 'human being' the capabilities that have been enhanced by possession of the smartphone.

There is a lesson here. One problem is that every time we encounter the latest iteration of these media technologies, we hear two contradictory claims: either that we have now become some kind of cyborg that is beyond human, or – the opposite and more common argument – that digital devices represent a loss of our true humanity, that face-to-face encounters are more natural or authentic. We claim smartphones are anti-social even if we use them to actually extend our social engagements through their screens. Perhaps the problem is that our conception of what it is to be human is essentially conservative, as though human beings are merely that which we have been in the past. Yet a definition of humans as unable to fly was refuted by the invention of aeroplanes. A better definition of being human might be one that encompasses all the capacities that we will one day attain as each new technological advance makes them possible.[45] We have neither become more than human, nor lost our humanity. We have simply had our capacities enhanced by our continual development of technology – something that has been true since the Stone Age – and every new technology will bring simultaneous positive and negative consequences.

Conclusion

This chapter represents the second pairing between a particular philosophical approach and the ethnography. As in all these pairings, the discussion concerns only a few philosophers and cannot stand for philosophy more generally. This was a particularly critical chapter because it felt important to contest attitudes that are inimical to anthropological sensibilities. Adorno and Horkheimer could hardly be more removed from the anthropological furtherance of human empathy, respectfully trying to appreciate the way others see and experience the world. *Dialectic of Enlightenment* claims to be in support of the liberation of ordinary workers but turns out to be a highly elitist and condescending characterization of people as mass culture. A far better point of departure should surely be respect for the way people in Cuan have developed a positive environmentalism as an issue that can galvanize popular concerns and also actions, and have found a plateau for their consumption despite the blandishments of capitalism.

The final part of both this and the previous chapter comes to a rather unfashionable conclusion, but on empirical rather than philosophical grounds. There is a groundswell of support for a concept of post-humanism that implies a kind of dualism. It suggests that we have previously been thoroughly anthropocentric and that has been the cause of our failure to respect the planet and the non-human. The initial discussion of pet dogs and smartphones was intended to show that we retain a depth of relationships and are not becoming more superficial. But the analysis then suggests something beyond this. The extraordinary compassion and concern that people show for their pet dogs was found to have developed from an anthropomorphic sensibility. The retirees of Cuan are classically humanist in the colloquial meaning of that term which implies empathy and care for other humans. But so far from blinding them to that which lies beyond the human, this seems to be the resource that proved amenable to extension. Humanist empathy seems to be the foundation for this depth of consideration now applied to animals. When smartphones first arose, it was easy for older people to claim the young with their selfies were becoming selfish or narcissistic. Now these phones are also the technology of older people, we can see that accusations that we were replacing people with screens are themselves superficial. We use those screens to be more in touch with and express our care for others.[46] Smartphones also show that the boundaries between humans and objects are fluid and complex as technologies become prosthetic and extend what it is to be human.

The same observation could be applied to anthropology itself, if one believes the premise of anthropology should be empathy, the desire to understand the experience and values of other peoples. Anthropologists have provided many ethnographic portrayals of societies living in less dualist or Cartesian relationship to their worlds, and there is an abiding interest in their relationship between society and nature.[47] The empirical evidence of this chapter suggests that perhaps it is the same extension of humanist concern that also helped the population of Cuan develop its environmental passion over recent years. Keen gardeners do not just exploit plants for anthropocentric purposes. If they fail to try to understand how plants behave, they will be poor gardeners. Just as anthropologists try to see the world from the perspective of other people, but also include the agency of spirits and environments, so, too, the people of Cuan have used their humanistic sensitivities to become remarkably single-minded in their dedication to saving their planet. Though one branch of philosophy seems to believe that concern for the rights of non-human species and the planet should arise from the repudiation of humanism, the trajectories of Cuan suggest that in popular sentiment these rights are more likely to emerge through an extension of humanism.

The extraordinary dominance of environmentalism in contemporary Cuan is not just a shift in values, it is a volte-face. It was really not very long ago that most people were striving to increase conspicuous consumption rather than conspicuous *anti*-consumption. Fortunately, this discussion of philosophy can end on the rather upbeat note of the previous chapter, where it was argued that environmentalism will always have a distinct advantage over conspicuous consumption as a means of allocating status. At last, we have a criterion that can comfortably align with claims to moral superiority, something that the wealthy have struggled with throughout the previous history of humanity. For which reason, even without the imperatives of climate change, environmentalism is unlikely to be merely a passing phase. It represents a significant and welcome change in the future of status and reputation which will hopefully ensure the sustainability of our planet. Once more, while we can learn from philosophers such as Soper, suggesting how our future ought to be, it really helps to have Cuan show us just how profound a change has already occurred in the everyday lives of an actually existing population.

Chapter 5

INEQUALITY, DRUGS, AND DEPRESSION

Inequality and the Vartry Estate

The ethnographic evidence presented in previous chapters has suggested an overwhelmingly positive appraisal of the retirees of Cuan which accords with the title of this book as an investigation of the good enough life. That same title was, however, intended to differentiate this study from any investigation of the good life, acknowledging that there were bound to be faults in any actual population that would need to be equally considered. The purpose of this chapter is to ensure that any overall assessment of Cuan shouldn't neglect any and every aspect of Cuan society that might contradict this positive appraisal. Is there evidence from the underbelly of Cuan society – its fundamental inequalities or social problems such as drug addiction and depression – that challenges the way these retired people are being presented and the conclusions that are being drawn?[1]

Two approaches were used when attempting to ensure coverage of these negative aspects. The first was to structure the ethnography such as to include the full diversity of the town. It would have been only too easy to limit coverage to these older, more affluent retirees since they are the most conspicuously present group. They are the people you tend to see during participant observation in community, voluntary, and even leisure activities. To prevent any such blinkered vision, three groups were designated as additional components to be included in the ethnography, with a minimum of ten research participants in each case. The first consisted of the newest estates on the fringes of the town. The second were migrants born outside of Ireland.

INEQUALITY, DRUGS, AND DEPRESSION

The third was an area of state housing given here the pseudonym of the Vartry Estate. Of these three, it was probably the Vartry Estate I came to know best as several of my closest friends happened to live there. The other methodological strategy to ensure wider coverage was to seek out professionals who might have knowledge of difficult issues not otherwise evident in the public domain, such as depression and drug addiction. This meant interviewing as many as possible of the relevant professionals working in Cuan, including social workers, psychotherapists, lawyers, Garda officers, and pharmacists.

The Vartry Estate was the key to understanding the foundational inequalities of contemporary Cuan.[2] This was not the first state housing built in Cuan. Postcards and maps from earlier periods reveal how the first government housing estate was built in a position noticeably apart from the rest of the town at that time. But almost all those houses are today privately owned and Cuan has grown to encompass this area. The later and larger Vartry Estate consists of around 330 houses, of which around half are now privately owned, many purchased on favourable terms by their original tenants, but others sold on through the open market, many to blow-ins. As a result of such policies, there is a general shortage of state housing in the overall district within which Cuan is found, with around 10,000 on the district waiting list.

State housing such as the Vartry Estate was originally assigned to less well-off local people. One of the first individuals to be moved into the estate recalled the harshness of those days. She had worked at times as a carer in a nursing home but struggled to bring up her three children. Her brother died of a drugs overdose, and when she didn't have work she was given vouchers that could be exchanged for corned beef. For her and other families, an important resource was a potato field in an area now covered by one of the newest estates. The farmer there allowed them to glean potatoes for free. She also had a strong memory of 'those fecking hairy blankets' they would get issued from social welfare. The estate's houses consist mainly of three-bedroom houses, smaller than those of the new private estates but generally viewed as quite reasonable accommodation. In some respects, the estate residents have been less subject to the extreme changes in the Irish economy. They didn't rise so far during the Celtic Tiger boom since they had no assets, but nor did they fall so far during the subsequent recession because they have been more reliant on state welfare. Yet, as will be seen below, the area was certainly impacted by that depression and also by the more recent rise in incomes, as can be documented through the changing pattern in the consumption of illegal drugs.

The estate retains a legacy of when it was regarded by many others in Cuan as an area of largely dysfunctional families. When a crime is committed in Cuan, the first place people will point a finger at is the Vartry Estate. Families who are involved in crime are indeed to be found on the estate, which also includes households of single mothers who have struggled to bring up difficult teenagers who then get into trouble. The important point today, however, is that it is doubtful that one could find more than twenty out of these 330 households that fit such stereotypes of what is generally termed by my informants 'dysfunctional households'. But the fact that any exist at all has consequences for the reputation of the area. Cuan also includes some older men who might once have been fishermen and labourers, but who now spend much of the day sitting at one end of a particular pub watching the fate of their betting slips. This leads to some ambivalence, since many people in Cuan simultaneously hold quite a positive – even romantic – sense of what they characterize as the rough-and-ready ways of the estate, including tales of past brouhahas. They have become an icon of one version of Irish authenticity.

It was evident throughout the ethnography that although the Vartry Estate lies pretty much in the middle of Cuan, it represented a quite separate world. A striking example came from a conversation with a person who otherwise exemplified the philanthropic liberal ethos of the dominant Cuan community. This was a man who, while still fully employed, had done an enormous amount of voluntary work to help improve the community facilities in Cuan, driving it in the direction of greater accessibility and equality as well as being a prominent member of the CCA and the various good works accomplished by the association. The story he told was of walking past the main Cuan church and observing a well-attended funeral. What astonished him was that he simply didn't recognize most of these mourners. By this stage, given how involved he had been within community activities, he would have thought that this was just not possible. He had simply assumed that by then he knew most people in the town at least by sight. After a while, based on those he did recognize, he realized that this was a funeral of a Vartry Estate resident, which was where almost all the mourners had come from. The experience came as a personal shock and a revelation of how it was still possible to have missed coming to know this particular segment of the Cuan population.

A similar story was told by a woman also known for her philanthropic activities, though in this case through involvement with development projects in Africa, rather than anything local. She recalled how the school she had attended as a child in Cuan had been reasonably broad-based and that several of her school friends had been children from the Vartry Estate. Yet in the course of our conversation, she came to appreciate through my probing the extent to which she had subsequently lost touch with all of those friends, while remaining in contact with most of those who lived in other parts of Cuan. On reflection, she said, 'My first friends just happened to be from the Vartry Estate, but you just drift apart.' These stories were by no means universal, as several of the people I came to know best and who were part of the same circles and networks as these two individuals themselves lived on the Vartry Estate as private homeowners. They had reasonable connections equally with people living in state housing or in private housing.

According to a community welfare officer who had been responsible for this area some decades previously, around the 1970s, the estate was then characterized by deserted wives and single mothers who struggled to get men to pay their child maintenance. They were mainly from this region as, unlike some other state housing, the estate was not being used to 'dump' problem families from difficult areas of Dublin. The estate would subsequently be the target of various government initiatives as well as help from charities such as St Vincent de Paul, the largest charitable organization in Ireland.

Crime itself is generally very low in Cuan and most lawyers are much busier with issues of property litigation and divorce. There had been one murder on the Vartry Estate, but everyone knew that this involved someone with specific mental issues, and people living on the estate were resentful that it was nevertheless used to blacken their reputation. Still today there are people in Cuan who talk of walking the long way around in order not to walk through the estate itself, especially at night, some even saying that they have never once walked through it. There was a time when one's child would have been strongly discouraged from an unsuitable liaison with a possible partner from the estate. People relate stories such as when the teams in a local rugby match on the estate had left their belongings in a pile while they played, only to find afterwards that these had all been stolen. The environmentally conscious middle class talked of how people on the estate threw rubbish out and failed to support Tidy Towns (a major crime in the context of Cuan). Mostly, though, the speaker in question would then add something like: 'Ninety per cent of it is grand, but there's just a small element that give it a bad name, it is a small element.' Some felt that if they themselves were associated with golf or sailing, they would be automatically subject to being slagged off by people on the estate for being 'too posh', which was sometimes the case. Surprisingly, given its reputation for egalitarian inclusivity in sports, there were people on the estate who had not even used the Gaelic Athletics Association, seeing it as not for people like them.

Many of those who had been brought up on the estate were scornful of the way it was discussed elsewhere in Cuan. OK, so a few lads on the estate had once tried to emulate a kind of 'wild child' look and language. But that hardly justified the way others in Cuan circulated rumours about the 'freedom fighter' gang and their exploits. Within the estate, opinions varied regarding the few households who clearly still enjoyed fostering an anti-establishment ethos. Some saw them as victims who were never listened to or given the support they needed. Others saw them as having a chip on their shoulder that harked back to a time when they lacked community or state support, and had failed to acknowledge the degree to which this was still no longer the case. Yet there are various ways in which support is clearly lacking and there are new forms of bureaucratic discrimination. For example, obtaining a credit card or bank account can be hard if at some point you have fallen foul of the criminal justice system, or you don't have necessary evidence relating to certain kinds of expenditure. One underlying issue was that as Cuan has shifted to a generally high level of affluence and property prices, this may have exacerbated the feelings of inequality felt by those on the estate, as might the number of estate homes being occupied by private purchase and then gentrified. As already noted, however, the national census shows Cuan as only slightly better off than average, taking Ireland as a whole.

At one stage, in an attempt to get to know people on the Vartry Estate better, Pauline Garvey and I tried to initiate classes on smartphone use for older people there and received every support for doing so from the estate's community centre. But despite leafleting and other attempts to interest people, almost everyone who actually came was someone I already knew personally and their friends. This was possibly no bad thing, since I (unlike Pauline) proved pretty inept at trying to help people improve their smartphone skills. But the initiative was prompted by our project's evidence for a growing digital divide. As government, commercial, and other services are increasingly placed online, people without access to, or confidence in using, the internet are simply unable to access state services. This is exacerbated if, as in some cases, they have never learnt to type.

Whatever the opinions about the Vartry Estate itself, the more left-leaning group amongst the research participants were constantly complaining that there was a lack of state housing for those who needed it. This was quite clearly the case. In particular, they often discussed the various ways private developers had managed to evade regulations regarding the proportion of state housing they were supposed to include in their plans. This was seen as an ongoing problem of Irish governance more generally. The question of just how common deprivation remains on the estate will be discussed further below, since exploring a specific issue such as drug addiction probably helps provide a more accurate picture. Overall, attitudes had mainly settled into a somewhat embarrassed acknowledgement of separation described in vaguely euphemistic terms such as when one person opined, 'You have a lot of people with very different interests and lifestyles. Maybe they're not the kind of people who like to spend their afternoons sitting in a coffee shop in ... street, while a lot of people in Cuan do.' Given such condescension, it is important to meet the actual people of the estate.

Five from the Vartry Estate

Bob is the first example of someone living on the Vartry Estate, but since he was the subject of a film included in my book with Pauline Garvey,[3] the details of his story are only summarized here. Briefly, Bob worked mainly as a butcher and then finally as a school caretaker. But the major transformation in his life came during his retirement when he became a successful poet, an activity to which he was entirely devoted. He was now as comfortable in going to an opera in Dublin as in taking me to the Cuan betting shop. He hadn't really changed his class identity through becoming a poet (which hadn't brought in any kind of income). Rather, he showed the way it was possible for someone on the estate to simply live within two class cultural milieux simultaneously and, as far as he was concerned, unproblematically. This is something that is perhaps more possible in Ireland than in countries with a stronger history of class divisions.

Aileen, who was introduced in chapter 3, was in her eighties and had been a waitress for her entire working life. With five grandchildren and a couple of well-employed children, she might have hoped to settle into quiet retirement, but, as described above, she lived with a son who suffered from depression and was much attached to a dog that was now itself quite elderly with expensive medical costs. As it happened, however, the dog had proved its worth the evening before I had first come to visit her in her house. There had been an attempted break-in through the back door which was abandoned when the dog had gone over to investigate the noise and barked enough to scare off the intruders. Aileen knew of another household not far away that had been less lucky and the intruders had 'smashed everything'. She was clearly still shaken and glad of my company. At least, however, the house was her own, as she paid off the mortgage not long after the death of her husband. Her son did manage some kind of work, which helped a little towards the bills for the dog, but her main worry was that, given her own prospects of mortality, how would her son survive without her and also without the dog?

Martin and his family moved to the Vartry Estate in 1992. As a fisherman, he would have preferred to be in a nearby town which is where he actually fished from, rather than Cuan, whose people tended to look down upon anyone from that town. As with many others, his feelings about the Vartry Estate were ambivalent. He knew there remained some stigma and that there could still be trouble from a few heavy-drinking households. But when he compared things to twenty years previously, he regarded them as much improved. The principal reason, as he saw it, was not so much the more liberal and accepting perspective of the wider Cuan society as the way in which an estate had its own internal trajectory. At one time when there were a lot of young teenagers in the same cohort, they made 'a fucking[4] nuisance of themselves'. But they had grown up now, and the older problem individuals with their drinking were nothing like as much an issue. Anyway, as he noted, he could tell quite a few horror stories about what had happened behind closed doors in other Cuan families that saw themselves as a step above the estate.

INEQUALITY, DRUGS, AND DEPRESSION

Sinéad was very wary about her neighbours ever since one of her daughters had had to hastily retreat home from a 'sleep-over' when the man of that house had returned drunk with a friend who immediately tried to be 'friendly'. She also despised what she called the 'carry on' represented by certain single mothers in the area and their out-of-control children, though this may well have again referred to things as they had been decades before, rather than any contemporary events. On the other hand, recently a near neighbour had insisted on Sinéad taking her telephone number so that she could ring for assistance if there was any trouble, though of course she never would.

Alice had lived in the original state housing estate before the Vartry was built, a time when there was not even lighting between there and the then village of Cuan. She had worked in factories and more recently house cleaning, which she still did now in her sixties. (A neighbour was still cleaning offices in her eighties.) She remembered when popping into neighbours for 'a bit o' sugar or teabags or coal'. She felt that the estate's problem had always been alcohol rather than drugs. In those days, many people were fishermen or worked on the land. Contrary to generalizations found in this and other chapters, she never liked bingo and she was a Tidy Towns volunteer. She had been on the committee of various charitable institutions and much involved in helping children with special needs take holidays. One of Alice's main roles was as the organizer of a Christmas savings club. Traditionally, such rotating credit schemes were developed to help people pay for the extra costs of presents and food at Christmas. Currently this involved 120 people, most of them from the Vartry Estate. Alice collected variable sums of money from each, on a weekly basis, and gave the proceeds back to them on the first week of December. In return, she kept the interest from the savings account. This required a certain amount of flexibility and forbearance as not everyone felt able to pay up every week, though only five or six failed to see the whole year through. As a result, she certainly knew a good many people on the estate. She knew who was actually struggling and who wasn't, how responsive the council was to residents and how this had changed. No one had ever tried to 'take advantage'.

The case of Alice is especially important when considered against the initial comments by the Cuan stalwart who failed to recognize people from the estate at a funeral. While the Vartry Estate may be shunned by many others, it certainly has its own internal networks of friendship, neighbourliness, and support. One of the people I worked with on the estate had suffered from depression for some years because of family issues. She noted how people would often come around to check on her. She would always say, 'I'm fine' or 'I'm grand.' But the more perceptive would look beyond that and insist they had a cup of tea together. There were other women who had taken to drinking at home regularly who were more recalcitrant and difficult to connect with, though I equally encountered them in other parts of Cuan.

To conclude, the Vartry Estate is less homogeneous now that half the houses are in the private sector. While people were less involved in the Celtic Tiger and recession, they have seen gradual but incremental improvements in their living standards and prospects, with many of their children benefiting from the high level of local education, since there is only one secondary school in Cuan which they equally attend.[5] Outside of this are perhaps twenty households that remain bereft of any such uplift and highly suspicious of any kind of establishment, while regarded by everyone else as dysfunctional. Increasingly, then, in terms of the key divisions, people undertaking government work in the area no longer see things as a contrast between the Vartry Estate and the rest of Cuan. This has become replaced by a distinct group of households often referred to as 'pockets' of poverty and problems that remain, notwithstanding the overall improvement in living standards and life chances for most others on the estate. What also remains, however, is a stigma, as perceptions take much longer to change. This stigma impacts on how people on the estate more generally are perceived and treated. Some time after fieldwork, one of my closest friends on the estate came close to a heart attack when the Garda suddenly broke down his front door and burst in. We subsequently learnt that this had happened because another estate resident had deliberately given the Garda the address of one of the least likely residents as a 'helpful tip-off' in revenge for something the Garda had done to them. But what my friend and I knew was that if he had been living anywhere else in Cuan, the Garda would certainly have made more checks before taking such violent action.

Class in Cuan: Bingo and Bridge

To expand beyond the single case of the Varty Estate and consider the issue of class relations in Cuan more generally, it is hard to reconstruct these from the history of the town, because this is not really what groups such as the historical society tend to focus on. Overall, my conclusions from an attempt at some oral history is that inequalities in Cuan developed not just because some people were fisherman and farm labourers, while others were lawyers or had a better education. What seems to have mattered most was whether one had some basic asset whose value could rise. If you actually owned a fishing boat or owned some land or a house, then it was very likely that your fortunes would have steadily advanced with the growing fortunes of Ireland as a whole with the huge rise in asset values. But if you only worked on that fishing boat or on that land or were an assistant in that shop, then you were never the beneficiary of this uplift to anything like the same extent. You simply never had the initial resources that enabled you to purchase a property. As such, you were more likely to have ended up being allocated state housing. Over decades, then, people who might once have been relatively close to each other, in terms of their financial situation, gradually grew further and further apart.

A generation or two previously, many families in Cuan had had the experience of trying to rent out their homes to incoming summer tourists, mainly from Dublin, building small accommodations in their own garden plots for themselves to live in over the summer months. At the time, this would have made householders feel members of a lower rather than a higher class. But given the value of properties in Cuan today, those same houses have cemented their owners' position within a comfortable middle class, as long as they own them. Originally, there may also have been an element of 'upstairs-downstairs' in that two of the people I knew on the Vartry Estate had worked as cleaners for other households within Cuan.

To this growing internal differentiation within the original Cuan population would be added the blow-ins from the 1970s, most of whom had a good salary and later on a decent pension which would have placed them in the main middle class. They tended to be at the lower end of the emergent middle class, since otherwise they would have moved to a higher-status location closer to Dublin. Some blow-ins had bought properties within the Vartry Estate because they were easily the most affordable properties in Cuan. Class is, however, far more than simply differences in income and relationship to the state. It is both more nuanced and more cultural, related to other kinds of differences such as accent, attitudes, and the places you frequent. For this reason, having started with this obvious and overt distinction of income levels, the example of a distinction that will serve for class more generally is deliberately taken from activities that no one in Cuan ever explicitly linked to class. That is the point. Class is important partly because it is in the unspoken and unthought differences that people just pick up on from day-to-day life and that lead them to frame other people in categories with differential expectations. As an example, contrast bingo and bridge.

Early on in this ethnography when I asked for suggestions of activities I could engage with that were particularly important to older people, I was recommended to attend the weekly Active Ageing Group, and that title sounded promising. I duly started to participate in their regular weekly meetings. These comprised up to seventy people, but often I was either the only male or there were just one or two others. Their meetings were dominated by playing bingo. There were occasional other activities: for example, a four-night trip to the west of Ireland (including a tea dance), a visit by an actress who entertained them with a monologue, and a competition to mark St Patrick's Day. Some also went to a weekly session of indoor bowls. Nevertheless, bingo was so dominant that everything else felt like an appendage.

Furthermore, the group were fiercely protective of bingo. A suggestion to develop some computer classes at the expense of bingo was immediately rejected by popular acclamation as even a possibility. There was an undercurrent in the response that the group might have wanted a bit more of an active role in their own organization, rather than being told by the organizing committee what they 'ought' to be doing. Such groups often create solidarity through grumbling about committees. But more important seemed to be the continued enthusiasm for bingo itself. The weekly session included a token contribution to the attendees' more general health and welfare, as it always started with some very gentle exercises, carried out while seated, such as could be accomplished by the very oldest members attending the group. A casual survey suggested there were roughly equal numbers of people in their seventies and eighties with fewer in their sixties.

Usually, the organizers of the bingo would be the ones doing the calling, while the rest of us were the punters, sitting on tables of six. After the bingo came tea and biscuits. When not playing, there was plenty of banter, which, as was often the case in Cuan, could include humorous put-downs about an individual's appearance or reputation. But the game itself was played in silence. The bingo comprised a whole slew of familiar calls, such as 'two little ducks – 22', 'legs 11', and 'sweet 16'. The use of 59 – the Brighton Line (referring to a city in England) – suggests their antiquity. False claims to have won were not uncommon but treated with understanding. People tended to take their tea back at their tables and then leave rather than engaging in any wider socializing at the end. There was a small fee to join and the prizes were also small, often groceries, though I once won an Easter egg.

To understand this emphasis upon bingo requires some historical context. People sometimes reminisced about what had been a far more extensive presence of bingo in the region; a time when the church used to hire a nightly bus to take people to bingo in the surrounding areas so there was practically never an evening without the possibility of playing. The impression gained was that they mostly represented the original inhabitants of Cuan rather than the blow-ins, and from relatively low-income households where a prize of groceries would be worth something. The key to understanding bingo is that it is purely a game of chance. People might make mistakes in thinking they have won, but there are no skills or strategies that can increase an individual's chance of winning. As a result, the game is fully egalitarian. It thereby gives value to the idea of fate or luck as an appropriate arbitrator for determining results. The popular writer Marian Keyes had a hilarious radio monologue about playing bingo. Her key observation was that winning was OK, but winning too often led to murderous glances from other players as this was considered completely inappropriate and somehow the fault of the individual, who was thereby making themselves appear superior to the rest. As Carrie Ryan has noted recently,[6] the upsurge of bingo during Covid was a sign of its virtues in helping build community and bonding precisely because it is seen as an enjoyable game without dividing people into winners and losers, skilled or unskilled.[7]

I did not attend bridge regularly as I don't know how to play (even I can manage bingo), but on one occasion I was given special dispensation to watch others play. I also observed some bridge lessons. This was an important moment for bridge in Cuan. There were three separate venues but now they were bringing them together within a single site. The current organizer started playing with his wife in their forties. Now they were in their seventies and had seen the initial club run out of space. The general age profile would be a little broader than bingo. There were a smattering of people in their forties or younger, but mainly the players were in their sixties, seventies, and eighties. They took pride in the fact there were also accomplished players in their nineties who attended regularly, saying things about them like, 'Yes, he's ninety, and bloody sharp as a razor!'

Bridge is around 70 per cent female compared to the nearly 100 per cent of bingo. There are around 150 to 200 stalwarts playing at least once a week. Between these three clubs, there is bridge on almost every night, usually starting at 7.30 and ending at 11.00, with an individual playing around eighteen to twenty-one games per session. There had been plans for bridge to be included in an expansion of the community centre, but these never came to anything. The clubs' members therefore decided to raise the requisite funds. A combination of raffles and reduced prize money for their regular bridge raised €100,000 and then there were donations and interest-free loans from members. Eventually, they were able to buy a dedicated property that would allow them to unite the three bridge venues into one.

To the outsider (well, me), bridge is an extremely repetitive game consisting essentially of winning tricks by having a card with a higher value than one's opponent. But for its cognoscenti it is considered more like chess in the degree of strategic evaluation of the longer-term game plan that leads to victory. Still, it did feel ironic that people who regularly condemned the young for the sheer amount of time 'gaming' on smartphones actually managed a prodigious amount of cumulative game playing of their own. The main emphasis was local, but Cuan included players who would go to competitions both elsewhere in Ireland and internationally. Clearly there were some for whom bridge had become the dominant activity of their lives and an object of both great dedication and veneration.

Bridge can also influence and reflect relationships. Since pairs move tables after each game, they end up playing with a range of abilities. The choice of partner is key and there can certainly be blame apportioned for the failure to win. There are jokes about the kind of marriage one needs to have where it is even imaginable that one's partner in life can also be one's partner in bridge. There is, however, also a higher etiquette that sees anyone losing their cool as that very Irish version of the idiot, an 'eejit'. As David Scott and Geoffrey Godbey note elsewhere, there is a mix of those who see the game as primarily social and those who focus on what they see as serious bridge.[8]

It is simply unimaginable that the bingo players would be backed by the kind of resources that would have allowed them to pay for a centre of their own. It is equally hard to imagine groceries being seen as a suitable prize for bridge. One of the organizers for the bridge was entirely unaware that bingo even existed within Cuan. The difference in class ethos is equally evident in what each game represents. As just noted, bingo players resisted anything that suggested they subjugate their game of luck to a higher instrumental purpose, such as learning to use computers. By contrast, one of the most common discussion points around bridge would be the various ways in which the game was 'good' for a person. Increasingly, this is dominated by the idea of bridge as brain training. As people age, they increasingly fear the onset of dementia. They believe regularly exercising their brains can diminish this possibility. As a kind of mental keep-fit, bridge fits the way an ageing and strongly environmentally conscious middle class commit to sustainability, starting with self-sustainability.

Bridge is fiercely competitive because ultimately it is seen as testament to skill and ability. It reflects a principle of meritocracy: that people gain a position in life commensurate with their abilities. This is an entirely different ethos from resolutely egalitarian bingo, which exports the adjudication of outcome to fate or luck: the universe is responsible for what happens, irrespective of ability. This game of skill may be related to claims for the emancipation of humanity by a meritocratic middle class over an aristocratic *ancien regime* based on birthright, on having parents with position, power, and property. These remain contemporary issues. Inheritance is still often the force that determines power, now more commonly reproduced indirectly through having the money or influence for one's children to go to a good college, where education gives at least the appearance that subsequent success depends upon merit.

Even if and when, however, merit finally triumphs over breeding, this can merely represent the replacement of one unfair system by another, since ability and skill are often themselves a birthright. Some people are simply born cleverer than others or with skills that others do not possess. People are fully entitled to believe that there is no fairness in a system where people who happen to be born with fewer skills should thereby be condemned to less in their life.[9] A fair society would imply that, if anything, benefits should go differentially to those without such abilities as a compensation for the bad luck of birth. In that sense, bingo, while coming from a very traditional and in some ways stultifying past, might represent a form of liberatory future that has rarely been even enunciated, let alone realized. The principles discussed in these two paragraphs will be considered again in the next chapter, because they are central to the arguments of the philosopher John Rawls.

Using the contrast between bridge and bingo to stand for class relations in Cuan confirms how class is not merely a quantified scale based on differential income or education. Class is a cultural phenomenon, important precisely because it contributes imperceptibly to a constellation of values and experiences. The premise of meritocracy as the foundation for a good society is fundamental to the values of the middle class and their denigration of mere luck and fate as exemplified by bingo. The moralities of class distinction were equally evident in chapter 3, where it was shown how claims to environmentalist virtues as anti-consumption have displaced consumption as the basis of claims to higher class status. Consumption had allowed people to transfer economic capital into cultural capital as a conspicuous claim to status, while environmentalism shifts class to a closer alignment with moral virtues. All of this is of a piece with common opinions overheard in Cuan that the Vartry Estate remains the site of older vices such as not caring about rubbish and recycling more than of contemporary virtues, thereby ignoring the people on the estate who share deep concerns over the environment. But such is class in Cuan.

Migrants

If the intention had been to use this ethnography to investigate the plight or struggles of migrants in contemporary Ireland, then Cuan was not the appropriate fieldsite.[10] The price of property was too high and the state housing too full. As a result, there was little chance of a low-income migrant family settling in Cuan. Migrants were present, however, and around 10 per cent of my interviews were with migrants from abroad. The census shows that the two most common sources of immigration were people from the UK, often with Irish ancestry, whom I did not count as migrants, and people from Eastern Europe of Catholic faith, who were included. Ireland is unusual in that the majority of migrants are from within the European Union.[11] But the migrants I came to know best were families from Mauritius, of South Asian and African origin, since, by sheer coincidence, both of my immediate neighbours happened to be from that island nation.[12]

A typical Cuan initiative was the provision by volunteers of English-language classes to migrants. This was situated in the Vartry Estate community centre. The result may not have been quite as anticipated in that almost all the students were actually au pairs doing child-minding for affluent households in Cuan and the immediate surrounds rather than the struggling migrants this initiative was intended to support. The location was significant. As one volunteer put it, 'I felt slightly threatened by the Vartry community centre. There were always youths hanging outside where I would park the car and it was a kind of side of Cuan I don't usually dip into. And anyways I was horrible at trying to teach them, the foreigners, to improve their English. It was not for me.' Yet back in the day she had been one of those who had gleaned free potatoes from the field on the outskirts of Cuan because they had struggled for food, as well as scouring the town dump for spare nappies.

Most migrants who had ended up in Cuan had come through fairly arbitrary routes, such as knowing someone who worked in a bar there. But soon they mostly became part of the mainstream chorus talking at length about how lucky they were and what a brilliant place Cuan was to live in. The largest group, from Eastern Europe, generally retained many links to their homeland, quite apart from family and friends. The one fly in the balm of the Irish ointment was the cost of medical care. Several migrants mentioned that they therefore retained their dentist, optician, or doctor from their country of origin. For any kind of expensive medical investigation, they would consider returning to the much cheaper health service of their natal home. Some also worried that their imperfect English might result in misunderstanding health advice or their GP visits. This was less the case if they had more fluent children. These days more continuous contact was usually maintained with family and friends in their natal home through social media such as Facebook. As in most migration studies, the main point of integration came with their children, who generally saw themselves as essentially Irish, which could entail a certain distancing from their parents.

The degree to which migrants wanted to keep in contact with other migrants from their own country would vary. One Hungarian in Cuan was aware of around twelve other Hungarian families in the general region as well as a Hungarian school in Dublin. He met other families occasionally and expressed a concern common amongst migrants about whether his children would retain language fluency in their mother tongue. Migrants usually had at least three or four apps on their smartphones that related to their country of origin, which might concern health, shopping, entertainment, or social communication. They made little mention of racism, and white Catholic Eastern European migrants might well have had little experience of it. Often a migrant would come from a family that now included other diasporic migrants. Social media became even more important when contact was not just with natal countries, but also with siblings or cousins in Australia or Spain. A very different set of migrants came from relatively wealthy professional families. If someone from Cuan had been posted by their company for a while to Spain or Poland, they might have married there, usually to someone with a university education. It seemed much more common for Irish men to bring wives from abroad, while Irish women were more likely to stay in their husband's country.

My two Mauritian neighbours had some additional concerns. Being religious, it was very important for them to have good access to a mosque, in one case, and a church, in the other. They also had relevant religious apps on their smartphones. They appreciated the local health services, and it would not have been possible to return to Mauritius just to deal with a health issue. An older man who had several health problems was heavily involved with the Irish health system, and this had become a major financial burden for his family. In one case, the children went to school and college in Dublin, and although they lived in Cuan, they may have felt that it was important to keep metropolitan and not just provincial networks. Many Mauritians came up to help them celebrate important family events in Cuan, which is where the wife in one family worked. They also had family in England and France, so the initial choice of Ireland came more from the happenstance of where they could find a place that would accept them. One of them had simply come on holiday, paid for by her brother, and then decided to stay. Ending up in Cuan had to do with rental costs and job availability.

The presence of migrants didn't particularly impinge upon the lives of most of the research participants now they were retired. But as many of them previously worked in the public sector, they often had considerable experience of migrants in their past. Compared to most populations, they evinced neither a negative nor – as one finds in some liberal populations – a kind of affected positive discourse about migrants, though critiquing racism was generally a badge of honour. Mostly, though, immigration was the kind of topic that they knew came up frequently in less liberal and what they saw as less middle-class contexts, and perhaps that was the reason they chose not to focus upon an issue which was not particularly germane to Cuan.

Alcohol and Drugs

The topics discussed in this section were difficult to research simply because they are either illicit or hidden. For that reason, a considerable effort was made to go beyond what people would say in an interview situation and find other kinds of evidence. One of the most important sources were a number of psychotherapists who see patients in Cuan. The problem was that psychotherapists are equally a distortion since they only see people who feel they are developing a pathology. A similar issue arose around interviews concerned with suicide or drug abuse. The situation was very different regarding depression, since people today take pains to show just how open Cuan has become in engaging with this problem. Overall, then, the evidence discussed in the following sections was conscientiously researched, but that doesn't mean that I am confident in the accuracy of what is portrayed.

Alcoholism

Any discussion of alcoholism in the context of Ireland is fraught, because alcoholism is central to historical derogatory stereotypes about the Irish, which people now obviously resent.[13] Yet at the same time it was a leitmotif in the way this generation discussed their own parents, suggesting that the historical prevalence of alcoholism is also a truth that has to be acknowledged. Not surprisingly, this led to considerable ambivalence in the way people talked about pubs and alcohol. On the one hand, there was almost a pride when describing the number of drunk people circulating the streets after St Patrick's Day or the capacity of a particular individual to drink excessive numbers of pints. It was easy to find stories about the fishermen of yore who were paid on a Friday and didn't go out to sea again until the entirety of their wages had been drunk. This may be why the ethnographic evidence suggested a good deal less alcoholism in Cuan than most people claimed. Today, there are six pubs alongside quite a number of bars found in sports clubs and restaurants. But just recently two pubs had closed and the shift from pubs to coffee shops as key sites of sociality was palpable. There was a clear pattern amongst older men whom I met for sessions in a pub that we would almost all drink two pints of Guinness over the course of the evening, rarely more or less. Even when we met in a pub, the women from my book group drank so little that the pub might have been somewhat affronted at being exploited as the location for these meetings.

One contested question which was impossible to resolve was the incidence of alcoholism amongst women drinking wine at home purchased from supermarkets, where it is a good deal cheaper than in pubs. Many women confirmed that they drank at least a glass of wine regularly, which mostly meant daily, at home. Some certainly observed how many bottles of wine other women had in their baskets at the supermarket check-out. I met at least one woman who seemed relatively isolated and whose best friend could be said to be a Chilean called Merlot. This is radically different from the past, when alcohol was almost entirely associated with men in pubs and there were no off-licences – a time when drinking was essentially a public rather than private experience.

There was certainly some under-age drinking, but as with youth crime it was almost always something done in another town, where the youth in question were less likely to be recognized. This was an observation confirmed by the Garda. What was shocking was the sheer numbers of people who described their parents as alcoholics and talked with great sadness about the consequences for their families as they were growing up. So, if the evidence suggests that there is some exaggeration of the levels of drunkenness today, it appears that in the past Ireland was just as mired in alcoholism as both Irish and non-Irish people have claimed. As was often pointed out, historically there was just very little else to do in Cuan. Alcohol consumption remains a major part of everyday life in Cuan, and the pubs are a key site for social activities, as are the sporting clubs. But the impression of a steep decline in alcoholism is reflected in the number of pub closures and the number of drinkers in each pub.

INEQUALITY, DRUGS, AND DEPRESSION

Cocaine and Other Drugs
This section of the book has no basis in direct observation. The evidence is entirely from interviews and conversations. No topic garnered a greater diversity of responses than that of the incidence of cocaine in Cuan, from those who suggested it was barely present at all, to those who suggested it was so ubiquitous as to be unavoidable. Both were equally adamant. When I mentioned that a young person had claimed that they simply never came across cocaine, others said that they must be lying. One older male claimed that 'Cuan is one of the places in Ireland where it is most available' and that:

> I know of friends who have had to re-mortgage their houses. I can tell you there's quite a lot of families in Cuan who have had drug dealers standing at their front doors threatening to kill them and the children have to be sent to Australia or New Zealand and go on these grand tours off travelling because of drug use and having to get them out of the town before they bring serious violence on the family.

Yet the very same individual's son claimed to have barely ever come across the drug. Cuan is a place where people can hang out mainly with the like-minded. It is perhaps possible that an individual could thereby be quite oblivious to what was going on elsewhere. I concluded that both scenarios could co-exist. Cocaine has been around at least since the 1970s and today the habit of snorting lines before going out on the weekend is something one could associate with many thirty- or even forty-year-olds as well as twenty-year-olds.[14]

A common observation was that Cuan was a fantastic place for children to grown up in, for reasons that will be described in chapter 7 about sports. But at around sixteen years of age, there typically emerged an almost inevitable sense of boredom; the feeling that Cuan was a place where there was simply nothing at all to do. This was when the teenagers started with their vodka shots. Since Cuan is a relatively affluent town, some drug or other at €15 a pop was generally affordable. By contrast, young people often felt that drinking in pubs was far too expensive for them and was something that only really came into life once one was earning a salary. If people regarded Cuan as a more affluent middle-class town where drugs were affordable, they also saw these as factors that meant most people would be more likely to be able to cope with the consequences.

The protagonist of Marian Keyes' popular novel *Rachel's Holiday*,[15] who simply can't see why anyone would see her cocaine usage as any kind of problem, would have been quite at home in Cuan. This observation was reinforced by the psychotherapists and counsellors, who felt that a major issue was the degree to which drugs were not seen as a problem. The way cocaine has become simply a part of going out partying or clubbing today seems to be reasonably similar to the common use of marijuana in the 1960s or 1970s, which was also regarded by users as relatively unproblematic. Yet, as in that earlier period, there were clearly individuals whose relationship to marijuana then or to cocaine now had developed a far more problematic side.

Ultimately, the psychotherapists were far more concerned that there was another group of users who had taken up with the drug while still young teenagers and had come from difficult backgrounds, which generally meant they were living on the Vartry Estate. For these reasons, the psychotherapists and other professionals tended to be involved mainly with people from what were described above as these 'pockets' of deprivation: specific households or clusters. These were seen as critical, since the pattern of drug use was so different. In mainstream Cuan, cocaine represents a drug of relative affluence, increasingly associated with the lifestyle of thirty-something-year-olds. But in the 'pockets', cocaine and other drugs are the addiction issues of teenagers. The starting point might be twelve- or even eleven-year-olds smoking weed and taking ecstasy, quite possibly before they are drinking alcohol, and then getting into cocaine at around thirteen or fourteen – an age at which it tends to be devastating. Cocaine use had been severely reduced in the Vartry Estate until around the time of fieldwork because of the long legacy of the recession, leaving marijuana as the most common drug. But marijuana itself has become stronger over the years and there are those who are smoking more or less all day long, a practice strongly associated with depression (whether as cause or effect).

As the recession has faded and money is more available, cocaine is coming to replace a strongly entrenched and highly problematic distribution of MDMA and ketamine. Alongside are various 'tablets': the 'uppers' and 'downers' and prescription drugs. There was no ethnographic evidence that the opioids that have devastated the US had become common in Cuan, nor for much heroin use, but these might have been missed. It seemed that in some cases the parents of these younger problem drug users had themselves been heroin addicts in the past. These were families that might have had children in and out of care for generations and rarely had two parents present. These children had also mainly dropped out of school. But to reiterate, this was not characteristic of the Vartry Estate, the vast majority of whose residents led very different lives. These were the 'pockets', who represent very few people today.

For those outside of these 'pockets', young people are mostly finding cocaine circulating around the colleges at more like eighteen years old, well after they have started drinking. The problem at this stage is that someone who wants to avoid contact with drugs may find it quite hard to find friends. Older people were not immune to addiction. A psychotherapist noted someone of almost forty who really couldn't go out because of the degree of cocaine addiction. At whatever age, the general assumption was that, apart from getting professional help, these people needed social support and ideally some kind of sport or activity that might provide an alternative, more virtuous focus.

Overall, then, the evidence suggested that cocaine usage was probably substantial and widespread.[16] The problem remains assessing its impact. On face value, it seemed as though it was commonly devastating for those with few resources in life, while most of the older middle-class users had become more like Keyes' figure Rachel. They viewed it as a recreational drug that was similar to the marijuana their parents had used but with a slightly higher status. It seemed to be something that they could 'handle' and would almost certainly have far less devastating impacts than the alcoholism of their grandparent's generation. It wasn't possible to be clear as to how many 'Rachels' there were and how far this should be termed addiction. In any case, the externalities of cocaine are clear enough, not just in violence and crime in Ireland, but in the place where I have carried out most of my past ethnographies, Trinidad. This was an island that was relatively law-abiding when I first worked there in the 1980s, but has since been devastated by the constant fear caused by very high levels of murder, kidnapping, and other crimes. All of this arose as a result of Trinidad becoming a conduit site for cocaine, some of which might well be destined for places such as Cuan. As this crime wave has touched the lives of many of my friends in Trinidad, I am constantly aware of the tragic consequences of cocaine.

Depression

In his classic work *The History of Sexuality*, the philosopher Michel Foucault argued that at a time when we had assumed that the topic of sex was severely repressed, actually people couldn't stop talking about it and investigating it.[17] This would not hold for Cuan, where the topic of sex remains quite repressed, at least compared to some other regions of the world. But when it comes to the issue of depression, there is a close parallel. People often said that there was a kind of conspiracy of silence in failing to discuss and confront depression. Yet throughout the ethnography, depression arose as a remarkably common subject of conversation and analysis. Curiously, while people seem to regard a key aim in life as happiness, the achievement of which is a measure of their lives, there is very little discussion of happiness as an overt quality. To discuss happiness *per se* seems rather crass and perhaps complacent. By contrast, almost everyone seemed driven to talking about depression with some frequency. Often in Ireland when people are discussing depression, they still focus upon the kind of rural depression in Western Ireland that was subject to an important and highly controversial work by the anthropologist Nancy Scheper-Hughes.[18] Cuan may be within the same country, but to all intents and purposes it seemed more like another planet in terms of its distance from that kind of context when it came to its own discussions of depression. Equally, Cuan is also quite different from some other contemporary middle-class societies, where going to see a psychoanalyst or having depression seems to increase an individual's status amongst their peers. There are, however, clear modish elements to depression, evident in the ubiquitous presence of mindfulness at this period.

There are at least three different ways of discussing depression, each of which implies a specific theory of causation. The first is to regard depression as an essentially medical problem: for example, a genetic disposition or an association with an imbalance in hormones. The second is to consider it as a social scientist might, as something that arises because of the wider context, such as poverty or oppression. The third would be to understand it in terms of personal circumstance, such as mourning a lost relative or failing to attract the person one is in love with. All three are common in everyday conversation in Cuan, though people would mainly focus on the third element because that involved detailed discussion of some individual. After saying a person was suffering from depression, they would narrate something that had happened to them that explained this: for example, the son who never recovered after the death of his sister in a car accident, partly because the last time he saw her they had had a quarrel and he said some horrible things to her; or a woman living on the Vartry Estate whose son was in constant trouble with the Garda and this had led to her own depression.

In other discussions, people often opined that depression was essentially genetic, suggesting that people in Ireland were generally more prone to depression, with the corollary that this was linked with the weather. It is hard not to agree that getting through the winter in Cuan can be depressing. Importantly, it seemed that people didn't generally support the social science approach: that someone living in difficult conditions was more likely to be depressed than someone with wealth. It was mostly the professional experts who were likely to assert these correlations with poverty or struggle. There is evidence for high rates of depression in Ireland, though not especially in the area of Cuan.[19] The ethnography suggested that depression is particularly prevalent amongst young people. The retired community I was working with included many who talked about depression as something they suffered from at an earlier age. Several had severe problems because of children or in some cases grandchildren with depression. But in accordance with national statistics, the retired demographic generally seemed much happier and less prone to depression – a situation that statistics suggest mainly changes only when people become frail and face difficult health challenges, mostly in their late eighties or nineties.

As the *Cuan News* demonstrates every fortnight, this is an amazingly high-achieving town on almost all measures. There are the levels of success in national school exams, or Cuan as the place that has spawned significant figures in activities ranging from Instagram influencers to internationally regarded music bands and authors. People assume that this rebounds as considerable competitive pressure on young people. Young people are also said to be presenting with problems because they are involved in too many activities with too high expectations. There is considerable concern with the pressure to excel at school since, with homework, that could mean studying from 8.00 in the morning through to 7.00 or even 9.00 at night. Because this pertains to a much larger population, it is probably a significantly greater cause of depression than drugs. The results of the national school exam at age eighteen are made public. In addition, Cuan, like so many places in Ireland, has had some shocking incidences of sexual abuse related to people in authority over the young.

Just as impressive as the sheer frequency of discussion of depression is the level of community response. There are several dedicated organizations focusing on problems of youth depression. Cuan sees a considerable turn-out for an annual walk that takes place around dawn called 'Darkness Into Light' based on a national organization that deals with youth depression.[20] One of the most experienced psychotherapists, who worked within a doctor's surgery, noted the high incidence that followed the Irish recession and that still hadn't really tailed off, but also the annual cycle that reflected the weather. Friends I made in Cuan also told how much more difficult things were during the damp and dank winter months, when there were days of such strong winds that it could be dangerous to step outside for anyone with a frail constitution.

The position of psychotherapy is a complex one. Being called a psychotherapist does not necessarily mean that one has undergone the kind of training that could eventually lead to full qualification as a psychiatrist or psychoanalyst. There is no clear governing board assessing certification. As a result, it includes a range of practitioners (around nine within Cuan), some of whom would be closer to complementary medicine in beliefs and style and some closer to bio-medical training or formal psychology, including the aforementioned individual who practises from within a GP's surgery. Common words used by the others in describing their approach are 'eclectic', 'systemic', and 'compassionate'. Their presence is generally quite discreet and the building where several of them operate from has no external signage. It is a mainly, but not exclusively, female profession. In Cuan, they tend to the 'softer' end of the profession with concerns such as drama therapy, art therapy, or play therapy partly reflecting that the main demand is for children's services.

Mostly, therapy is private, but there are some schemes where people with medical cards (based on means testing) can qualify for up to a dozen sessions. But clearly services are highly restricted for those unable to pay, who certainly would not receive the kind of three-year weekly sessions that a psychotherapist might recommend. It's a field where increasingly people have looked things up on Google and come to professionals thinking that they have 'got' some condition. But more than that, they are simply often frightened or panicked by how they find themselves to be. They present different forms of anxiety, often including relationship issues and stress related to high expectations, as well as the problems of a small town where people know each other. The professionals recognize that the more middle class are likely to come with their own views and expectations these days, often associated with approaches such as mindfulness and cognitive behavioural therapy (CBT). I was struck by how often my research participants explained themselves to me through directly quoting either Bowlby[21] and Winnicott[22] and discussing the quality of their 'attachments'. Clearly, personal experience has in part been moulded by the popularity of such once mainly academic discussions.

Incidents of suicide were also commonly referred to during the ethnography, especially those of young adults. As one person noted, it 'put the terror into the hearts of every parent in the town because everybody had somebody who was a bit, you know, a bit vulnerable and not feeling great about themselves, and it just, it just scared the living daylights out of everybody'. In every case, there would be considerable discussion trying to piece together the personal circumstances. One discussion was about whether the problem was the rivalry between two brothers where one never seemed to achieve what the other seemed to effortlessly accomplish, whether in sports or in education. Another concerned someone who simply never could clamber out from the pit of grief that followed when their partner was killed by a car.

Again, what was impressive was the level of response within Cuan to these traumas. It led to the foundation of a town group solely dedicated to recognizing and addressing the problem of suicide, especially amongst young people. A parent who had experienced this loss was one of the major figures in furthering the response. At the time of fieldwork, the group had been so successful in raising funds that it was able to hire a specialist psychotherapist and counsellor to work in this region. She was one of several whom I interviewed and already had an impressive understanding of the local situation. I felt she was making a significant difference amongst some of the most troubled teenagers on the Vartry Estate. This is especially helpful since counselling sessions are otherwise quite expensive and it is generally felt that many such sessions are required in turning around the life-course of an individual. I was not the only person impressed by this. The response that the town had made to youth suicide was one of the examples that was frequently cited as evidence for the strength of Cuan as a community.

Loneliness

By far the most common response to discussions about loneliness was that, while this was a well-known condition for single males in rural areas, Cuan was a town where everyone kept at least an eye on everyone else. When one case was found of a male whose death went unnoticed for a while, it was followed by the explanation that the individual concerned was notoriously anti-social and had made considerable efforts to secure this level of isolation. Many of the retired community, including some who looked frail enough to be recipients, were actually involved in delivering meals on wheels, and they reported back on any individuals whom they had reason to be concerned about. There are plenty of Cuan residents whose family now live in other parts of Ireland, the UK, or further afield, but they will likely know enough people in Cuan through other channels. The church would also be an important element in keeping watch over its flock. Community initiatives such as the Men's Shed were formed because of the feeling that it is men in particular who are prone to isolation when they are older, if, for example, they have been widowed, and that bonding over shared labour was effective.

Loneliness as a topic raises questions about the more ambivalent attitude around neighbours. I have written elsewhere about both the historical and contemporary relationship between neighbours in the UK.[23] People in England commonly make claims about the superior quality of neighbourly relations in the past. But mostly this reflected economic need. Once people became more self-sufficient, they would express this partly through shunning the neighbours they had once depended upon and celebrating the degree to which they could now select their friends by choice rather than by juxtaposition. This sentiment was also apparent in Cuan, though less pronounced. Generally, friendship was based on other forms of association, which were not hard to achieve given the sheer level of community activity. But people still kept an eye on neighbours. This was not perhaps as benign as the way relations between neighbours in villages had often been nostalgically portrayed in literature and oral history. Nor was it as malign as implied by a notorious novel which gave a very different image of life in such villages, called *The Valley of the Squinting Windows*, which scandalized Ireland when it was published in 1918.[24] The impression gained was that if someone was not on holiday and yet had not been seen for a while, someone else would likely have taken note and made sure they were OK. Overall, loneliness was probably not a common experience within Cuan.

Egalitarian Ireland

This chapter has documented the degree of inequality that exists within Cuan. Yet when seen from a comparative perspective, Irish society, and Cuan society especially, may be unusually egalitarian. As already noted, most Cuan residents would have been born in poverty themselves and there was therefore none of the sense of entitlement found in inherited privilege. Even if they retired from senior positions, they mainly started at the bottom of occupational hierarchies, as clerks or nursing assistants. A man who now lives in an enviable house, with a wonderful sea view, recounted how, not far from that house, he used to help with gutting fish to earn pin money for his mother as his father drank all the household wages. He had shifted throughout his career between social and community work and what proved quite profitable entrepreneurial ventures. Today, he is involved in several Cuan community activities.

Perhaps the strongest evidence for the changing relationship to class and the Vartry Estate was the case of Fintan. Fintan was a stalwart of the estate and one of the leading figures in helping develop the football club, a sport he was passionate about. He had had his own struggles and fully acknowledged some of the more problematic social elements in the estate. But as a generous and caring individual, he also understood the structural inequalities that they represented and the need to help people out of those conditions. In the 1970s, he had started a local residents association for the estate and promoted attempts to provide the children living there with some sort of holiday in the summer. For many years, he had felt that the estate was comparatively neglected and he had seen the CCA as a bastion of that other segment of Cuan that tended to prefer not to really acknowledge that the estate existed, while no doubt doing plenty of good work elsewhere. He told a story about when he tried to book a sporting event at the CCA on behalf of people from the estate and was told it was full for the whole season. When he then tried the same thing while pretending to represent the football club, suddenly they had room for his booking.

But, over time, Fintan was gradually co-opted as someone who did valuable community work and eventually himself became the Chair of the CCA. At that point, he was able to see the records of their previous work and fully acknowledged that he had been wrong about them. He could see that the association had been well aware of the Vartry Estate and had worked hard to support the area, though clearly that attitude may not have included all their employees, as the story of the sports booking indicates. Fintan, together with the CCA, was then able to raise funds for the building and staffing of the Vartry Estate's own community centre, which was where the English classes were held and where Pauline Garvey and I tried to initiate smartphone classes. Although they came from what is often called 'different sides of the railway track', Fintan and the rest of the CCA were actually very similar examples of the wider community-minded retired group of citizens who gave exorbitant amounts of time voluntarily helping to develop the Cuan community.

Several other egalitarian practices, for example regarding autism, will be described in the next chapter. My reason for going to Cuan in the first place was the exemplary work of the local age-friendly chapter.[25] But you could see this egalitarian ethos in almost any community event. At a poetry slam, the selection of the winners seemed based entirely upon merit, but it was clear as the event proceeded that much effort had been put into including some younger or newbie poets. Even their parents might have admitted the poetry wasn't great, but would have been pleased in the way this recognized that everyone needs a chance to begin somewhere. It was clear that if somebody was evidently a migrant or in some way disabled or disadvantaged, they would be given encouragement to take part in such events and that attitude would be expected of the organizers by the community at large. Just as in the examination of class, however, it is useful to have some cultural or vicarious indication of whether and how egalitarianism operates in Cuan, which accounts for the following discussion.

The Importance of Insult

One of the most powerful mechanisms for ensuring social equality seemed to lie in a well-developed proclivity for personal insult. This was not the first time I had encountered such a relationship. Trinidad, where I have been working for over thirty years, is in this respect quite similar to Cuan. People constantly pulled down the pretentiousness and status claims of others through barbed remarks. I had found this a challenge. Insulting people doesn't seem like the best way of ingratiating yourself as an anthropologist into a community. Yet the best sign that as an anthropologist I had reached the desired level of integration was probably when I felt comfortable in insulting Trinidadians and they felt equally comfortable in insulting me.

Similarly in Cuan at first, I found the level of insult shocking. One figure in particular stood out. He was a regular at the 'session' that I attended fortnightly at a pub where everyone took turns at singing.[26] The insults that he threw out at everyone except myself (indicating my failure to be fully integrated) were astonishingly direct and sometimes quite painful to hear. Typical would be his comment when addressing one of the older singers: 'When you were still alive, could you actually get the notes right?' or 'You make music like Elvis; it's just a pity you have the body of Lazarus.' The aim is for a quick and equally cutting retort. Failing that, the protagonist may themselves feel they have been too cutting and then employ self-deprecation to fill in for the lack of response. In this instance, after waiting a few minutes, the speaker recounted how he had auditioned for a part in a Passion play and was offered the role of the cross, since his acting was so wooden. There again, if a person exaggerates their self-effacement by claiming, for example, that they really can't sing very well, another will note, 'Well, that never stopped you singing in the past.' Such behaviour is more characteristic of men, but I have certainly observed women throw their barbs with gusto.

Banter seems particularly important when someone is appointed to a position of authority. Then they will almost always try to undermine themselves by jokingly exaggerating their sense of power. For example, on one occasion, people in the Men's Shed were occupied in painting something for display and were being rude about each other's efforts:

Kieran: It's your turn to be inspector.
Finian: Right then, I am claiming inspectors' wages. Oh, look at that rust you have left there. I think you need to start the whole thing again.
Kieran: What, are you impugning my painting?
Finian: Clearly, the way you lot work I should spend my entire time standing around inspecting.

In another setting, a teacher of adults exaggerated how affronted she was by an interruption, shouting out, 'Are you giving me lip again?' The best way to dispel any apparent claim to authority was to exaggerate it to the point of absurdity.

Why does this matter, and why is it characteristic of societies such as Cuan or Trinidad? Harsh insult seems to be associated with such egalitarian societies, suspicious of authority. In Cuan, people accept that someone needs to be the chairperson or the teacher, but only as the occupant of that role. What they resist is the sense of entitlement. In the UK, for example, with its aristocratic lineages and class traditions, individuals are more likely to assume that authority is natural to them and a quality of their person. It emanates from the depth of who they are. In Cuan or Trinidad, by contrast, it is important that authority is understood as a transient possession, to be kept on the surface. It belongs to the role and not to the person. In Cuan, people do not deserve to be the chairperson; they are simply taking their turn in the chore of chairing. What they deserve is to be finally relieved of this task.

How do you keep such things on the surface? The insults above could have been deeply wounding, but the recipients were expected to respond with humour and to hope to take their turn in this tournament. By taking people down the moment they show pretension, or take their authority too seriously, equality is preserved as the principle of social encounter. A parallel process is involved in, on the one hand, keeping the insult on the surface, not letting it get deep inside you, and, on the other hand, keeping the role one has been assigned to on the surface, not letting it fool you into thinking this is who you really are. At the same time, to the degree that men feel more comfortable and accomplished at this performative insulting than women, it becomes evident that what can be egalitarian at one level can be divisively unequal at another. In observing people in Cuan, one might be tempted to see banter and insult as superficial, but the consequences of keeping things on the surface are deep.

Conclusion

Most of social science is quite properly directed to problematic topics such as poverty and depression both in order to draw attention to these issues and in the hope of contributing to their resolution. As previously noted, however, this creates a clear distortion in how the world is represented. To write a book about people who generally describe themselves as happy is partly a conscious intention to redress something of that bias. In that context, this chapter has a special significance, because without it there would have been a danger of a bias from the opposite direction: towards complacency or a whitewashing over the problematic conditions of Cuan. The people of Cuan live directly alongside the inequalities, drugs, and depression that have been discussed in this chapter and that therefore must be addressed. The evidence suggests that they should be characterized neither only as saints nor only as sinners. A high incidence of depression is not necessarily incompatible with the presentation of Cuan as comparatively ideal. To the degree to which depression, for example, may be caused by quite specific experiences such as unrequited love, a model society may still have a high incidence of depression because there never will be a society that can guarantee the absence of unrequited love.

These issues, then, have to be separated from the evidence for conditions which are by no means inevitable and mostly reflect continuing inequalities in Cuan society. How do relatively affluent retired people see themselves when sitting alongside very different conditions of life? The evidence suggests that one response is to turn a blind eye. Even though the Vartry Estate is slap bang in the middle of Cuan, there are people who skirt it both physically and mentally: the individual who in an interview recalled the people he was once at school with and suddenly realized that it was those from the estate who had somehow subsequently fallen out of view; the key individual in developing the Cuan community who was astonished by seeing a funeral in the town where he recognized almost no one at a time when he would have assumed that was just not possible. Whether we blame local people, the local council, or perhaps most of all the structures of political economy that foster inequalities of this kind, there is a problem if the people who most need support are not in view.

Yet the very same two individuals mentioned above were extraordinary people in the degree to which they sincerely dedicated themselves to public service, whether it was spending long periods working in Africa to help alleviate difficult conditions, or doing sustained difficult bureaucratic work to help ensure funding for better and more egalitarian services within Cuan. Fintan had both the best evidence for the neglect of the estate and yet when he took over the role of Chair of the CCA, which he held for six years, equally the best evidence that the CCA had been paying much more heed to the estate than he had previously realized. The most impressive help I witnessed, the support that is going directly to the most vulnerable and depressed young people on the Vartry Estate, is being paid for not by the government, but by voluntary donations from within Cuan. If judged against an ideal, this chapter has revealed much in Cuan that falls short and could be condemned. Yet if judged comparatively against most places in the world, then those same institutions and practices might be lauded as amongst the most impressive of any region and to be admired and emulated. At this point, it seems reasonable to turn to philosophy to see if there is some yardstick against which any further adjudication of Cuan might be attempted.

Chapter 6

JUSTICE AS FAIRNESS

Is it possible to attempt some kind of adjudication both of Cuan and simultaneously some strands of Western philosophy based in this instance upon evidence for the relative treatment of the various constituent populations of Cuan? For this purpose, the concept of 'justice as fairness' would seem an especially apposite juxtaposition with this ethnography. It stands as the summation of the contribution of the American philosopher John Rawls (1921–2002). The book which is the key to Rawls' reputation was *A Theory of Justice*, published in 1971.[1] In this work, Rawls develops an approach which he claims to have derived in large measure from Kant. Several of the other philosophers discussed in this book, including Amartya Sen, have in turn written detailed critiques of Rawls. The task, then, for this chapter is to determine how far Rawls helps us to judge Cuan, and to what extent this attempt to directly apply his book to an extant population in turn helps us evaluate the worth of *A Theory of Justice*.

Rawls' contribution is not confined to a single book, and his later work included important points of clarification and implementation. But the 500-plus pages of *A Theory of Justice* were his primary contribution. It is a consummately philosophical work, and a reading soon makes clear that, while the intention here is to deploy the book as an assessment of a contemporary population, its foremost concern was an internal dialogue within the history of political philosophy. Rawls seems to have intended his book to be a major response to the centuries-long dispute between two philosophical traditions. One was represented by Locke, Rousseau, and Kant and is termed 'contractual'. This is the tradition to which Rawls regards himself as an heir.

JUSTICE AS FAIRNESS

As to the opposing tradition, this is personally very familiar since I have spent my entire working life at University College London (UCL). One of the best-known features of my university is a cabinet found in one of its corridors containing the stuffed skeleton and wax head of Jeremy Bentham.[2] Bentham was one of the founders, alongside his esteemed follower John Stuart Mill, of the approach known as utilitarianism, which has also had a considerable influence on the discipline of economics. Though Bentham is perhaps best known to many contemporary students through Foucault's description of his infamous panopticon model, the more benign side of this philosophy is echoed through Bentham's presence here at UCL. He stands for the values which led it to become the first English university to welcome women, Catholics, Jews and non-conformists into university education. Rawls considered that the culmination of the utilitarian approach lay in a late nineteenth-century book, *The Methods of Ethics*, by Henry Sidgwick,[3] and that is the work against which he is mainly writing. The critique of the utilitarians is a constant motif within Rawls' *A Theory of Justice*.

As I understand it, the utilitarians argued that political morality should be based on trying to ensure the maximum happiness for the greatest number of people, where utility describes the desirable end of any action. Against this idea, Rawls pitches a rather older tradition perhaps best known from the title of Rousseau's book *The Social Contract*, though the version that is most prominent in *A Theory of Justice* lies in the premises of Kant's various works on morality. While, then, there are deep historical roots to Rawls, his book is equally immersed in the values and institutions of the America in which he lived, and much of it seems to assume that there is now an established historical condition for the realization of contractual morality which lies in the kind of property-owning democracy represented by the US.

The fundamental argument behind Rawls' work has an elegant simplicity. It starts from the premise of justice itself and the insistent opposition to everything that is unjust. Rawls regarded utilitarianism as unfair to the degree to which some smaller fraction of society might become oppressed as part of the same process which led the larger fraction of that society to achieve greater happiness. Happiness for the greater number as espoused by the utilitarian approach is therefore neither just nor fair. At the same time, fairness for Rawls is not the same as absolute equality. He argued that it is perfectly fair for some to be wealthier or more fortunate than others, but only when their rise in fortune is also of benefit, or at least not detrimental, to the least fortunate member of that society. For example, a capitalist could justify a system which differentially rewarded successful entrepreneurs, whose efforts have also thereby improved the lot of their workers. But Rawls would condemn a system where an entrepreneur succeeds through exploiting those workers to their detriment. The starting point which allowed some to be successful entrepreneurs and others to become their workers should also be egalitarian, otherwise this would not be fair. People should not be favoured merely because they happen to start with the initial benefits of their birth, either historically through inherited wealth or through higher natural intelligence. As he put it, 'Those who have been favoured by nature, whoever they are, may gain from their good fortune only on terms that improve the situation of those who have lost out.'[4]

A contractual society is one based on mutual advantage, which would then mitigate the condition of natural ability.[5] This is a caveat which surely sets Rawls apart from the modern 'liberal' positions often favoured in the US, which tend to advance a position of meritocracy. Rawls does remain liberal, however, in the sense that his idea of a social contract is one entered into by individuals shorn of any concept of a transcendent object called society that has interests distinct from or superior to its members.[6] He thereby espouses the theoretical individualism of classic liberalism and of Kant. Rawls also refutes the idea that these conditions can be left to a pure market system, recognizing that such a system will result in externalities, such as a deleterious impact upon the natural environment.[7] He does, however, seem to regard the market system as an effective way of connecting supply and demand, but argues that it should also have limits. This suggests that he would not preclude the possibilities of, for example, a feasible market socialism as advocated by Alec Nove.[8] These approaches favour increasing prosperity, provided that no one is harmed in order to obtain it. We would certainly now include potential harm to the planet in that deliberation.

Once justice is secured, Rawls leaves open the principles by which a society will determine the proper distribution of advantage, including thorny issues such as how to allocate the inevitable burdens between the different generations – a topic that has come to the foreground since his time as a result of our response to climate change. Rawls' own fundamental concern is that whatever these secondary principles turn out to be, they should accord with the underlying principles of what he calls 'the original position', which is his rendition of a hypothetical initial social contract. 'The original position' is based on trying to imagine a situation in which everyone is allowed to choose freely the principles which should govern their society while aiming for a political order based upon fairness. The fundamental unit here is mostly the same liberal individual who was the foundation of Kant's writings on morality. There is, then, a secondary level of discussion in Rawls which applies to the consideration of many other issues, such as the duties and obligations that subsequently apply to each citizen: for example, whether civil disobedience is ever justified. This is the topic of chapter 6 of his book.

According to Rawls, justice comprises all that which has to be mutually agreed upon in order to fulfil 'the original position', creating the basic structure for any society that claims to be just. In turn, this implies a free, reasonable, and rational population who could have determined these conditions of justice.[9] These conjectures require a population that contains none of the differences between people which might have led them to have differences of interest in formulating this contract. If, for example, men had a different interest from women, or older from younger people, they might not settle on the same preconditions for justice. Against this, Rawls ask us to imagine a 'veil of ignorance' with regard to who we might actually be. At this point, we have returned to a position that feels very close to the way Kant argued for the creation of a universal morality by speculatively imagining an ideal condition where every individual is also a philosopher, embodying pure rationality de-contextualized from culture as the condition from which they make moral choices.

When it comes to specifics, the circumstances under which Rawls lived are clearly germane. He tends to specify conditions such as the right to vote, the right to hold property, freedom of speech, and freedom from assault,[10] which he presumably felt were enshrined in the US as a country that did in fact have a founding set of principles. But he also insists on the right to a strictly egalitarian educational system in order that class does not constrain access to knowledge[11] – a condition that would not be at all true of either the historical or contemporary US. Much of his discussion applies to institutions rather than to individuals: for instance, ensuring that there are no conditions which make access to any office less available to some than others. It seems important to Rawls in ensuring this 'difference principle' that we constantly bear in mind what he calls the 'least advantaged representative man'[12] and consider the impact of any discussion of justice or fairness upon that individual.

When Rawls focuses on the position of the least advantaged member of society, his philosophy would seem left-wing to the point of utopianism – a reasonable term given that 'the original position' is quite explicitly utopian. But there is still a problem, in that even if the position of the least advantaged is raised by the actions of the more advantaged, the effect remains one of potentially increased inequality – a situation that the economist Thomas Piketty argues corresponds to the contemporary world.[13] If people are increasingly unequal, then we also have to address the evidence of books such as Richard Wilkinson and Kate Pickett's *The Spirit Level* which clearly demonstrate that there is a debilitating impact of inequality itself on, for example, people's health, even when the lower fraction are also experiencing improvements in their welfare. The lowest fraction may be doing better, but when they see others doing far better, they may not regard their situation as either fair or just. This might seem to directly contradict Rawls. Theoretically, Rawls could simply come to accept the evidence of *The Spirit Level* and add the consequential argument that inequality itself has to be curbed to the degree that it creates disadvantageous consequences that outweigh any material benefits that have accrued to society's least advantaged person. This would then come back into alignment with the overall proposition of justice as fairness.

Yet there is a reason for thinking Rawls would not have responded in this way. At several points in *A Theory of Justice*, he argues in principle against the position of envy, since he suggests it could be corrosive to an acceptance of the legitimacy of any political order.[14] Indeed, he seems to suggest that if a society fulfils all his conditions, then it is almost 'unfair' to his theory that anyone should nevertheless feel envy at someone else's advantages. So, while Rawls is careful to protect the fundamental property of equality as good, it may be that he was influenced by right-wing critiques of socialist ideals at that time. Right-wing ideologues have always tried to disregard socialist critiques of inequality as mere envy. Rawls' discussion of envy is followed by his laying out the grounds for prioritizing liberty,[15] which again perhaps reflects his prioritization of certain liberal values in the US. There are many other assumptions derived from situating examples in the kind of society he lived in which render him easily subject to critique from left-wing arguments: for example, around the basic inequalities of the prevalent economic system such as position in the workforce.[16] Nevertheless, as a theoretical philosophical discussion, the slant remains consistently utopian beyond even the dreams of socialism, a method Rawls considered as 'ideal theory'.

Before juxtaposing Rawls with Cuan, it is important to acknowledge that there have been trenchant subsequent critiques of Rawls, including Michael Sandel's *Liberalism and the Limits of Justice*.[17] In her book *Frontiers of Justice*, Martha Nussbaum argues that even such necessarily abstract theories of justice must also be responsive to the urgent problems of our contemporary world.[18] She therefore examines three distinct areas which she argues have been insufficiently considered by Rawls: the disabled, the non-human, and people who live beyond the boundary of any given state. Nussbaum argues that her 'capabilities approach' properly demands a more active application of moral sentiments such as benevolence and compassion.[19]

In his volume *The Idea of Justice*, Sen argues that if our primary concern is with reducing injustice, then it is better to consider this comparatively and contextually rather than against some measure of perfect justice, which in Rawls (and Kant) amounts to a transcendental institutional investigation.[20] A comparative approach would also permit a plurality of views,[21] which accords with the discussion in chapter 2 of Sen's insistence on giving people a voice in what should be their values and aims in life. We should include their concept of freedom, not just the means to achieve freedom. There are a host of other concerns that Sen brings to bear on Rawls, including the overemphasis on institutions and the lack of consideration for those who live beyond the boundaries of a particular state, as well as issues around the imagined 'original position' that echo points made above. As noted in chapter 2, Sen's focus on the comparative and contextual is also an argument for a more anthropological approach.[22] Yet for all his trenchant critique, Sen still feels that Rawls remains the best foundation for such as discussion. Sandel brings out similar points and, along with other communitarian philosophers, is concerned to counter the claims to universal principles with a recognition of pluralism. This is a point that Rawls conceded in his later writings,[23] while hoping to retain a common ideal of decency. Given that so much of this critique implies the need to consider Rawls in relation to the plural values that exist around us, this seems to be the right moment to consider him against a particular example of the good enough society. What follows here is thereby hopefully at least indirectly supporting some of the arguments of Nussbaum, Sen, and Sandel.

Rawls and the Family

How, then, are we to apply Rawls to the good enough life? This will be attempted in stages, moving from smaller to larger social units, considering first the implications for the family and ending with the relationship between Cuan and the world. In the introduction to this book, it was noted that, while for philosophers such as Kant and Rawls it is axiomatic that all humans come to the philosophical table as equal individuals, for both the people of Cuan and the anthropologist it is equally important to assert that there are no individuals outside of social and other relations. We are born as children and citizens. So even to theoretically consider a contractual morality poses the initial problem of whom we imagine this contract is with. An individual will not consider those people they love or who are their kin as identical to people they will never meet in a distant country. They will not regard even the citizens of their own country in the same way as those who live in their town, even if they may never actually meet these more proximate others. We primarily care about people to the degree to which we identify with them as my family, my town, my nation, my gender, and so forth.

The existence of the family therefore poses an insuperable problem to any abstract argument between contractualism and utilitarianism. Both of these camps stem from a political morality in which the aim is to maximize happiness. Rawls' definition of happiness is summarized as 'a person is happy when he is in the way of a successful execution (more or less) of a rational plan of life drawn up under (more or less) favourable conditions, and he is reasonably confident that his intentions can be carried through'.[24] Yet at least with respect to my own messy life, I recall the main occasions when I have found myself unexpectedly happy are those when my rational plans for myself have had to be thrown into the dustbin by what seemed the entirely irrational desires of my children. On their behalf, I have had to care more about winning battles against imaginary dinosaurs than writing the next academic paper. In my previous study of shopping as what I called a technology of love,[25] I tried to show how the very nature of love is its capacity to find greater happiness through subsuming the self in a relationship than in trying to cultivate the self as an individual. As noted in chapter 4, the person buying the weekly shopping in a supermarket is translating their care and affection for the people in their family into efforts to find that which will most please them, even at the sacrifice of their own desires and their own time. What they thereby gain is only understandable in the context of love. But there are good reasons for thinking that love, as in love for one's children, can be the consummate source of happiness in life. I believe I have ultimately gained more happiness from being a parent (and now grandparent) than from being an author.

Is it theoretically possible to incorporate these caveats within Rawls' approach? If it is my primary source of happiness, then my love for others is certainly rational. But sourcing happiness in self-sacrifice does feel like a twist and there is not a whole lot about love in Rawls. These problems are evident when he makes statements such as 'Happiness is also self-sufficient'[26] or considers how we choose holidays, as though this is based on the merits of a place in relation to our personal desire, rather than a long negotiation between all the members of the family involved in that holiday.[27] This is often a process of such fraught complexity and contradiction as to defy much philosophy or indeed rationality.

If the primary concern was to remain congruent with Rawls' arguments, then this would likely lead to Véronique Munoz-Dardé's suggestion that we should consider abolishing much of what corresponds to the contemporary family.[28] The family is, after all, riddled with inequalities of gender and generation. It is not remotely close to any 'original position' and it is hard to imagine how it ever could be. The traditional Irish family, known as the stem family, as portrayed by early anthropologists such as Conrad Arensberg and Solon Kimball,[29] was a bastion of inequality favouring the interests of a single son who inherited all the land, as against his siblings, who inherited nothing.[30] Many of my research participants recalled with unhappiness their upbringing in very large families – which were the result more of a lack of contraception than any desire of their parents to have many children. We cannot assume that people wanted large families in the past if large families were in fact no more than the inevitable outcome of the desire to have sex.

The historical family in Ireland makes a mockery of any 'original position', but it is also nothing at all like the experience of the family that was encountered in this contemporary ethnography. We may learn a good deal, however, from the subsequent trajectory of the Irish family that started from the condition the Irish were born into and ends with the family as it presents itself today. There is a case to be made that this history consists in large part of an attempt to come closer to the conditions espoused by Rawls. Over time, thanks to contraception, the size of the family came to better reflect the intentions and desires of parents. As people become more affluent, they were able to also develop family relations according to an ideal rather than the struggles of necessity. The original stem family had much to do with the small size of peasant landholdings, which is not of particular concern to contemporary Cuan. Discussions with lawyers in Cuan around practices of inheritance suggested a clear shift towards egalitarianism. For example, a more relevant disparity in recent times concerned the fate of the youngest daughter. There had sometimes been a generally unspoken idea that the youngest female might stay unmarried and instead look after her elderly parents. In return, this daughter would theoretically receive a favourable inheritance, for example the house, although, according to the testimony of the lawyers, often no such expected reward was actually included when it came to reading the will.

By the time of this ethnography, however, all these inequalities had pretty much disappeared in favour of a family based on a more absolute equality. The modern principle is that all siblings should be treated the same. In the spirit of Rawls, they should not be differentiated, whether on the grounds of natural ability or subsequent fortune. One should simply divide the inheritance equally regardless. This goes still further. The working morality of the family in Cuan now seems to be that every member is free to follow their desires and interests as long as they do not lead to deleterious consequences for another family member. For example, it is at least hoped that if one of them gains a university degree, then that will have benefits for the rest: for instance, the more educated might be expected to help the parents when it comes to filling out some complex government form. A notable finding of the ethnography was that in almost any issue regarding health, people would try to identify a family member who had an education or a job that might have led to some superior medical knowledge, such that they could be contacted to help interpret some health advice that a family member had read on the internet or been given by their doctor. Just as argued by Rawls, a differential trajectory in the fortunes of family members is understood as acceptable as long as the least favoured also benefits from the better fortune of the most favoured. This is pretty much the opposite ethos to that described by Scheper-Hughes and still earlier anthropologists for the traditional rural Irish family.[31]

The contemporary family in Cuan is also founded upon assumptions about love similar to my own expectations and experiences. The family is the project which ideally teaches an individual that happiness is better realized through an orientation to others than to the self. Of course, the ideal may not correspond to the actuality. In practice, these families may be riven by strife and competition, including sibling rivalry, where each is convinced that the other has benefited at the expense of themselves. This is something perhaps common to families everywhere. There were many conversations during the ethnography that were bitter and resentful in relation to descriptions of what was happening in that family. Because of the age group that this research focused on, these were typically disputes about who was having to spend the most time caring for elderly or dying parents. But it is still possible to assert that such inequalities are far less common than was the case in the past and that there has been quite a remarkable change in the ideals and models of family life.

The conclusion of this discussion of the family is that historically almost all the changes that have occurred can now be recast as movements towards the ideals laid out in *A Theory of Justice*. This is not to claim that the contemporary family is consistent with those generally rather utopian ideals, but rather that Rawls has helped us discern a clear trajectory in family history that can be better understood when we view this in relation to those abstract ideals. To that extent, the philosophy has certainly been helpful in understanding the lives of people in Cuan. Does this also apply to other levels of identity amongst this community?

Fairness in Rawls and in Cuan

Attempting to apply Rawls as a theoretical philosopher to an appreciation of Cuan itself is difficult, since just as was the case for the family, there is no sense in which Cuan ever complied with his 'original position'. There was no contract made by the townspeople shorn of all interests and relationships to come together in a spirit of pure equality and reason. Nevertheless, there are perhaps unspoken contractual elements that have become implicit for contemporary residents of Cuan. One way of discerning these comes through the degree to which residents of Cuan comparatively disregard those who are not from Cuan or not Irish and presume that they have commitments within Cuan and to other Irish citizens that they do not have to the citizens of Japan or Argentina. There are currently quite a few people active in hosting families and individuals who have fled from Ukraine. But only two people were found to be sufficiently concerned with issues of poverty in Africa or South Asia to have gone and provided personal support. It follows that any more general discussion must include a caveat: that justice and fairness are applied as criteria only to the degree to which people identify with others. This is institutionalized in the way being an Irish citizen binds those who thereby share the associated laws, rights, and obligations. Any application of Rawls is therefore segmentary. People feel the strongest contractual relationship with their family and friends, then with Cuan, then with being Irish, and finally as potential citizens of the world. Of all these levels of identification, the one that is most important to the discussions of this volume would be the identification with Cuan itself. Two questions follow. To what extent can we consider this as an imagined contractual relationship? And if it is contractual, then does it apply equally to all those living within Cuan including groups analogous to his concept of the least advantaged persons? For this purpose, I will consider two examples: the first considers people with autism and the second considers the evidence presented in the previous chapter with regard to the Vartry Estate.

The first example that might fit this designation of the 'least advantaged representative man' can be considered through the treatment within Cuan of people on the autistic spectrum. As in almost every example discussed within this chapter, the most extraordinary finding is how far the present seems to be anything but a continuation of the past. Modern Ireland is far better explained through an emphasis upon repudiation.With respect to attitudes towards mental health, a novel such as Sebastian Barry's *The Secret Scripture* reveals the appalling conditions for people with mental health issues or whose social behaviour had led them to be categorized alongside those with mental health issues.[32] Historically, treatment involved taking those with such issues as far from the community as possible, placing them in institutions where they were never seen. In starkest contrast, perhaps the single most positive expression of concerned citizenship in contemporary Cuan is the attitude to people with autism. The contemporary ideal is that those designated as on this spectrum should be at the heart of the public community and just as visible as any other citizen. Quite early during fieldwork, I was struck by their very clear presence around the town. For example, an individual used to go frequently to the shoe shop, engage in various rituals, and then depart, but always seemed to be treated with great respect and sensitivity by the staff. Another place would simply give ice creams to people with autism if they were not able to use money. These observations of the kindness shown by individuals link directly to the importance of Cuan as a place which happened to have developed a major initiative to support people with autism and learning disabilities more generally. This began with initiatives by local people who had autistic children. But then, thanks to the sheer level of volunteering and fundraising, it ended up with the establishment of an exemplary institutional response that subsequently became part of the national infrastructure funded by the state.

It is hard not to conclude that partly this is driven by the conscious attempt to repudiate a history where the institution that claimed moral authority, the Catholic Church, had been responsible for some of the worst sequestering of the victims of ill-fortune. The final feature of the contemporary attitude is the way in which the institutions that are responsible for assisting people with autism reject general solutions for autistic people as a category and instead work hard to create personal life plans for each individual, as far as possible through continual consultation with those individuals. The result is not just positive but exemplary. Whether this degree of compassion is a legacy of Catholic concern for suffering or more a result of the repudiation of Catholic sequestering is a question best left for discussion by the population. But, either way, the considerable evidence for compassion is an important constituent of the underlying claim for Cuan as an appropriate site for considering what we mean by the good enough life, where the term 'good' implicates virtue.

The material presented in the previous chapter provides a further test, however, to any such claim to virtue. Are all areas of Cuan being treated equally? The entire project of this book starts from the initial observation that there could hardly be a closer identification between Cuan and its residents. The geographical basis for their self-identification as a middle-class town between the more proletarian and the posh becomes appropriate for the self-designation as reasonable and unpretentious. But if this is the self-characterization of Cuan, what happens when the Vartry Estate doesn't fit this description and yet lies there in the very centre of Cuan as a locality? At one time, there would have been a clear discrepancy and the Vartry Estate would have to have been seen as excluded. But not today. People from the estate such as Alice or Fintan, introduced in the previous chapter, were amongst the original tenants but are now fully representative of the population presented in this ethnography as completely embedded within the politics of the CCA or other voluntary associations, sports, and other activities. This ethnography itself fully included the Vartry Estate, where several of my closest friends and informants live.

As was the case with the family, the argument is not that Cuan could be an exemplar of the ideal situation described by Rawls, but rather that we can discern a direction of travel towards Rawls. There may remain individuals in Cuan who try to ignore the presence of the Vartry Estate and make an effort to not even walk through there. But this feels vestigial. The clear trajectory is towards its general incorporation as an integral part of the town. Today, the issue of exclusion no longer applies to the estate as a whole but rather to those remaining households that are regarded as the 'pockets' – the households commonly described using the terminology of 'dysfunctionality'. This is not a term that an anthropologist would be comfortable with, but it is the one that is commonly used locally. On analogy with Rawls, it could be said that these 'pockets' occupy the category once filled by the whole Vartry Estate, namely what he describes as the 'least advantaged representative man', which has a key role in his discussion of justice as fairness. There might have been other candidates, such as ethnic minorities. But in practice Cuan contains a highly distorted sample of migrants, based on those who have enough resources to be able to rent or buy property in the town, which renders them much less suited to this role.

If we then imagine the pockets as the 'least advantaged representative man', what does this suggest about a Rawls-based assessment of Cuan? First, it confirms that Cuan would stand much closer to the ideas of the contracturalists than the utilitarians. Most people's actions and sentiments implied a similar concern that no one should become advantaged in a manner that rendered others, such as those on the Vartry Estate, thereby less advantaged. Similarly extrapolating from their behaviour and comments suggests that they regard it as fine for some people to do better in sports or business or leadership as dependent upon their abilities, as long as the 'least advantaged representative man' benefits from rather than is exploited by this success. Their acknowledgement of a sense of a contractual responsibility is evident in the sheer scale of their support for initiatives concerning issues such as youth depression and suicide. The money that was raised was specifically targeted to help fourteen youths suffering from depression who mostly came from families regarded as dysfunctional within the Vartry Estate. As reported in the previous chapter, the professional they hired seemed exemplary in her sensitivity and commitment. Almost all voluntary activity is evaluated by its contribution to those who most require support, whether the frail elderly, the autistic, or the low-income single mother.

Cuan is generally liberal in the European rather than the US sense. People usually did not blame the 'pockets' for their misfortune, or suggest that their condition was somehow their own fault. They mostly understood the causes, including the way children's lives were being stymied at this very early age, as derived from historical conditions, including poverty, alcoholism, and abuse that had come down the generations. They viewed inequalities as historical and structural rather than as a moral judgement on the household. At the same time, they tended to be reformist rather than radical. They argued that there was no quick fix based on intervention. Fintan, for example, managed through considerable effort to establish a special community centre for the Vartry Estate but the kids from the 'pockets' were never going to use it. On the other hand, what could be done should be done. Many of these retirees had worked in education and the health system, often in policy related to the most difficult of their clients. They could discuss in some detail how best to be helpful. For example, people tried to help parents rather than replace them, backing off when not wanted, but being there when help was sought. Their refusal of radical solutions was not because they lacked radical aspirations. They felt this approach was justified by their professional experience, which had taught them that welfare was more often improved by reform rather than by radicalism. This may or may not be correct, but it was a genuine belief. Radical solutions also tended to be based on considerable state intervention.

As many of the retirees had worked for the state, they were cautious about such involvement.

Seeing themselves as realists produced several conundrums, however. They assumed there would also be individuals or even families that disdained hard work, community involvement, or citizens' duties. They neither romanticized misfortune nor implied that one should ignore the degree to which people failed to perform what others would have seen as their responsibilities as parents or citizens without good reason. There may be structural and historical reasons why someone seemed to be an inept father, but they could still be regarded as inept. Mostly, these retirees were well aware of examples such as a mother of a child with physical or learning disabilities who was in some sense or other unable to cope. They rejected a meritocracy that ignores the degree to which people regarded as dysfunctional may be so by reasons of historical and current misfortune. There was more ambiguity around a family that was deemed dysfunctional because of alcohol, drugs, gambling, or criminality. This did not involve excluding such families in their overarching sense of justice as fairness. Where plausible, they tried to regard present vice as the legacy of prior family dysfunctionality. But this was balanced by the desire to respect the agency of individuals. Granting people respect for their individual agency means that one is also free to condemn them to the degree that they have used such agency as they possess in ways that should be both condemned and punished under the law. These retirees believed that inexcusable vice also exists in the world and should be acknowledged rather than always attributed to an historical cause. They knew these two positions were contradictory, implying that one both should and should not impute blame. But they believed moral assessments should contain elements of both. The problem was how to determine the appropriate balance. One of the impressive features of these retirees in such conversations was their ready admission of doubt and an ability to change their minds as a result of listening to others sitting around the table.

In general, then, the retirees of Cuan echo Rawls in not supporting an absolute equality of outcome. It was regarded as fair that some people through effort or ability were more successful than others. Some people merited these differential rewards. Nor did they view the working class or the impoverished as more authentic than themselves or than the middle class, a somewhat condescending attitude that pervades much of academia. They defended what they considered their realism, as opposed to their radicalism, on the grounds that they were thereby not being condescending or naïve, but simply more committed to improving welfare based on their cumulative experience rather than being praised for their political stance. A reader might consider these as self-serving beliefs, but they were genuinely held. Of course, there were research participants with a wide spectrum of views who have not been included here within a highly generalized presentation of a generic called Cuan. Much of the evidence came from conversations as well as participant observation; often a comment made about something they had read in the morning's newspaper rather than formal discussion. These descriptions always imply terms such as 'typical' or 'mostly'.

In summary, the ethnography suggested that people in Cuan saw themselves above all as reasonable. This was something affirmed through the rejection of what they characterized as more extreme left-wing and right-wing views. This is a sense of the reasonable that can be compared with the use of the term 'reason' by Rawls. These arguments suggest that Cuan as a community is following a similar trajectory to the family. Whatever the origins of this population, they have shifted towards a set of values that aligns quite well with many Rawlsian principles. They generally manifest a contractual responsibility that derives from the common identity of being a resident of Cuan.

Rawls and Citizenship

Following this segmentary logic, having considered Rawls in relation to the family and then to Cuan itself, the next step upwards would be to consider the attitude of people in Cuan to being Irish citizens and then perhaps citizens of the world. One of the most common ways in which they assert an espousal of basic principles of justice extending beyond their boundaries was that they seemed to go out of their way to ensure that everyone was fully aware of their personal positive appraisal of migrants. They used this example to assert their differences from the less liberal views that might persist within other Irish communities. Within Cuan itself, it was certainly possible to find far more negative and stridently racist views regarding migrants. There were those on the Vartry Estate who had made very clear their opposition to the use of the estate's community centre to assist migrants. At the same time, one of the most contentious teachers of English at the centre lived close by as a tenant on the estate. The degree to which people had a very different attitude towards migrants who were fellow Catholics from Eastern Europe as against migrants from Africa could be called racist, but was clearly an extension of the overall principle of contractual obligation being correlated with the degree of identification. High property prices meant that there were very few Black migrants in Cuan, but the ones whom I came to know well personally (e.g. both my neighbours) had a very positive view of their experience of living within the town. They would have seen themselves as having been included within the larger contractual relation that came from now being residents of Cuan. People in Cuan were well aware that migrants were relatively sparse as a result of high property prices and that their liberal attitudes came with few costs or responsibilities. Indeed, they wondered out loud whether their views would have been different in other circumstance.

The previous paragraph implies a kind of informal contractual relationship to all those who live within Cuan, be they from the estate or migrants. But the basis for all formally contractual identity remains nationalism. The inclusion of the people of the Vartry Estate, but also of these migrants, is premised on their being equally Irish citizens. Having in many cases worked for the state prior to retirement, these retirees tended to accept citizenship as the fundamental contract that rendered a person equal. Equality before the law came irrespective of birth. They did not expect to extend the same level of welfare provision to someone living in another state, only once those persons had become accredited citizens. After all, most of them were themselves blow-ins. As in the discussion of the family and then of Cuan, this version of nationalism and its degree of alignment with Rawls may be quite recent. A generation or two previously, most people would have been far more stridently nationalist in the anti-colonial struggle but not necessarily as aligned with the state as a system of government. Irish terms such as *cute hoor* reflect a recent past where those who found ways to cheat or escape the obligations of citizenship were to some degree admired for their creativity in evading taxes or finding informal, often illegal, ways of business dealing. Commonality was more an extension of kinship to those one had a more personal relation to than a sense of contractual obligation to the wider, more abstract unity of the state. As Fintan

O'Toole's book reveals,[33] it was not long ago that the state itself had been led by one such *cute hoor* in the figure of Charles Haughey.

Once again, things had changed dramatically. The historical shock constituted by evidence for sexual abuse by priests, the scandal of the Magdalene laundries, and the shenanigans associated with the likes of Haughey had cumulatively resulted in a more vociferous and aware surveillance of the state itself as something to be constantly judged as to whether its behaviour was just and fair. The persistence of centrist governments, largely free of ideology, meant that they were mainly judged on their actions in areas such as environmentalism, housing, and health. The recent rise of popularity for Sinn Féin had more to do with its opposition to failed health and housing policies than to its historical commitments. All of this means that the state itself is now also expected to play the good citizen along generally Rawlsian lines based on justice as fairness. The about-turn from the prior respect for the *cute hoor* to a sense of close alignment between the responsibilities of the individual and the responsibilities of the state was fully manifest during the Covid pandemic, the response to which required new restrictions on personal behaviour. The people of Cuan outdid each other in their incorporation of compliance with state rules as a personal responsibility. There were several memes circulating on Facebook that made fun of the degree to which everyone was watching out to ensure that everyone else was fully compliant with rules around social distancing, mask wearing, and similar restraints. Everyone became an extension of the Garda. A large proportion of Cuan households joined the Facebook group 'Cuan Against Coronavirus' to organize their response, including helping those who were negatively affected by the restriction. But also, as these retirees put it, they frequently 'gave out' against anyone who failed to comply with state restrictions.

A second example of the way people are developing a relationship between their identity as Irish citizens and the ideals of justice as fairness may be found within the very appropriately named Fair Deal Scheme.[34] This provides a concrete and explicit legislative manifestation of what the state itself seems to regard as justice as fairness. The starting point is the recognition that life and death are not naturally fair, but neither has been the individual's life course. Clearly, in a welfare state, the state has some responsibility in dealing with the cost of ill-health, but then so does the individual. One person may live in relatively good health and die having made little by way of financial claim either on their own assets or the state. But another may have a long-term illness or dementia which requires a very considerable expenditure in care, including the salaries of the carers or specialist care homes. Life and health are not intrinsically fair.

Rawlsian principles might suggest that while the bulk of the consequential expenses of care might be borne by the state through general taxation, it would also seem 'fair' for the individual to contribute if their life course, or possibly their inheritance, has led them to be relatively advantaged. The Fair Deal Scheme was constructed to decide what proportion of an individual's assets should be taken to pay towards their care before the state takes on the rest of that expenditure, assuming that they come to rely upon public health care. The rules at the time of my ethnography (2018) were that an individual has to use a proportion of their overall assets (apart from an initial €36,000) to pay towards their nursing home costs before the state will pay the rest. Most people I discussed the Fair Deal Scheme with had some grumblings. Not surprisingly, people suggested changes that would reflect their personal interests. But most did approve of the general principles behind the scheme. As a politically centrist population, people in Cuan supported redistribution to the degree that it corresponded to this same sense of 'fairness'. The 'fair deal' provision was not especially radical. It could hardly be called a socialist policy as it still left quite a bit of an individual's assets untouched. But it did provide a material expression of the general principle that a wealthier individual should be expected to pay more towards care before the state became involved. The ethnography suggested that the political policy of the Fair Deal Scheme was successful to the degree to which it corresponded with the Irish colloquial term of *fair play* – a term one could hear used almost daily. By contrast, the lack of a national health service was generally regarded as a considerable failing in the Irish state and an example where the state had not as yet developed sufficiently in the direction of justice and fairness.

Between Irish citizenship and global citizenship, an important new component is the growing sense of European identity. As stalwarts of the EU, the Irish seem quite easily to have extended expectations about commonality and mutuality to the rest of Europe. As many of them take holidays or even have property elsewhere in Europe, this is not just theoretical but rather a sense that they themselves participate in this wider European citizenship. A fondly repeated statement was the observation that, thanks to Brexit, Dublin has become the largest English-speaking town within the EU. With regard to the still wider world, the charitable activities that a few of this population engaged in probably do contain an element of contractual obligations that some individuals feel to humanity as a whole. Only a few people in Cuan are involved, but listening to their experiences suggested an important difference from charitable practices encountered elsewhere. These individuals seemed to have a more personal engagement, as in teaching or volunteering, resulting in a less top-down quality than other philanthropic gestures, and this may be reflected in the positive opinions often held about Irish people more generally that can be heard when travelling abroad. Rather than just giving money to the developing world, they had opted to actually go out in person and try to use their skills to assist people on a face-to-face basis. These days, when the term 'stereotype' has lost its moorings in relation to essentialism and racism, being used for almost any kind of generalization, anthropologists are often mistakenly accused of perpetuating stereotypes when mostly they are very careful to differentiate empirical generalizations from essentialism and instead investigate the causative conditions that account for that generalization. As it happens, there is quite a positive global stereotype of Irish egalitarian bonhomie and fun that puts people at ease and is opposed to the potentially hierarchical consequence of philanthropic actions. Excuse me if I reproduce the 'stereotype'.

Conclusion

Although no doubt working at a much inferior level, it was intended that the exercise carried out in this chapter should follow from and extend the work of Rawls. The treatment is also beholden to exemplary philosophy such as Nussbaum's *Frontiers of Justice* and Sen's *The Idea of Justice*, as well as their work on gender equality and many other topics, because they are thoroughly engaged in the problem of how to apply justice and fairness to the complexities of our contemporary world. As in the previous pairings, the idea was to juxtapose the normative aim of a philosophical approach as to how life should ideally be lived with the normative mechanism observed through ethnography that explains the consensual practices of an existing society. This allows the chapter to be presented both as an extension of Rawls, employing his transcendental approach as a yardstick for judgement of Cuan, and simultaneously as an extension of the critique of Rawls. The outcome was a portrait of these retirees as a generation who have moved closer to the ideals presented by Rawls of justice and fairness, irrespective of any comparison to other societies.

A critical social scientist has grounds to highlight many problematic issues that remain. It is possible to unearth tragedy and suffering in Cuan. These and their causes should be foregrounded rather than swept under the carpet. What happens to people in the households that others regard as its dysfunctional 'pockets'? What are the consequences of the amount of cocaine in circulation and the degree to which this is either unknown or ignored? What changes in our perception of Cuan when we examine the levels of depression and incidence of suicide? How are migrants treated and discussed? The first conclusion was that all of these problematic issues could nevertheless be incorporated into an adjudication of Cuan based on Rawls, because the ethnography demonstrated that everyone is included within an imagined contractual relationship that comes from being a resident within the town. Although they are ignored at some levels, when it comes to the practice of welfare, both the CCA and the people in Cuan more generally who are concerned to reduce youth suicide direct their attention to the most difficult families of the Vartry Estate. The ethnography also showed that in practice people on the estate were clearly regarded as equal representatives of Cuan, and have been included as such within this ethnography.

While the chapter has shown several ways in which Cuan has evolved into greater accordance with Rawls, this is not intended to be sufficient. There remain important criticisms of his approach. One of the reasons for the emphasis on bingo, as opposed to bridge, in the previous chapter was that it served to highlight the meritocratic elements that are central to Rawls. The problem with meritocracy, even when it takes many factors into account as intended by Rawls, is that, as Michael Young[35] and more recently Michael Sandel[36] have pointed out, it still enshrines the kind of inequalities and subsequent resentments that books such as *The Spirit Level* found to be invidious in themselves. Once again, a good enough society may have a long way to go before it can be called the good society.

I would acknowledge that my praise of Cuan has a foundation in certain precedents. For many years, I tried to encourage political debate in my academic teaching that focused on post-war social democratic Scandinavian welfare states. I was aware that these governments had been involved in awful things such as eugenics and that their egalitarian welfare policies overreached when children were taken into welfare as a result of relatively slight parental misdemeanours, because bureaucratic concerns overtrumped sensitivity to specific situations.[37] I nevertheless made them a common point of reference in teaching because it seemed important also to acknowledge that whatever was bad about such governments, they were probably better than any other government in the history of humanity. Furthermore, for many decades, these were both the most affluent and the most ethically progressive states in the world. This should have taught us another lesson: that being the world's most successful economies did not require adopting US-style competitive capitalism. Social democratic capitalism arose from contractual arrangements that included consumers and trade unions as well as businesses. What mattered for teaching purposes was that these states had actually existed for quite extensive periods.

The praise of these Scandinavian states would then be balanced by attention to historical structural inequalities that were clearly demonstrated by social scientists such as Immanuel Wallerstein,[38] who revealed the degree to which the affluence of certain states had been built upon a rapacious colonial exploitation of other states. The most laudable contemporary societies are also those that are trying to consider how to rebalance the unequal economic rewards that we have inherited. There are those that acknowledge the pittance that was traditionally paid for raw materials, which explains why some countries became relatively wealthy and others remained poor. There are also societies that further remonstrate about, for example, how that same global inequality is currently being reproduced when the low-salaried employment required by the digital world, in fields such as content moderation, is exported to the Global South.[39] Yet Cuan has a place in such consideration. One of the core questions for this volume has been whether the aspirations of migrants from such regions who want to settle in places such as Cuan are well founded.

At the level of the state, Ireland is also no utopia. It hosts vast servers that work for international IT corporations which are hardly a model for positive climate change and responsibility to the world at large. The Irish government was for a long time one of the nations most opposed to attempts in Europe and beyond to advance a minimal tax regime on corporations, because this would undermine a low taxation policy that over several decades has served the Irish well, but certainly not benefited the wider world. Ireland has finally agreed to acquiesce in higher taxation only because of global pressure.[40] It is questionable how far the Irish state's economic policies have lowered class and other structural inequalities. In terms of welfare, perhaps the most problematic failure has been the failure to create a national health service. As a result, there is a health apartheid with considerable reliance on private health insurance, and long waiting times for operations for those who can't afford this.[41] In housing, most people in Cuan felt that the government was far too lax in allowing builders to slip out of commitments to public housing, which meant that for many people even getting a residence in a place such as the Vartry Estate was impossible. The fact that it was the people of Cuan who had raised the money to help alleviate youth depression and suicide was partly testimony to the failure of the state to provide the requisite resources.[42] At the same time, while writing this book, I am living in a country, the UK, lurching between Boris Johnson and still worse. It is a country whose systematic and gratuitous cruelty to asylum seekers escaping from wars, rape, and torture is heart-breaking,[43] making you wish we could be more like Ireland in many respects.

This chapter stands out from others in that while the adjudication of Cuan often includes a comparative element, usually for an anthropologist this is a regional comparison, whereas in this chapter it has been largely an exercise in historical comparison. The central argument is that the retirees of Cuan represent a generation who have followed a trajectory that brings them ever closer to the ideals outlined by Rawls compared to the time of their birth. The contemporary family of Cuan could hardly be more different than the historical Irish family as represented by anthropologists of the past. The chapter also features the quite extreme contrast between the public and supportive presence of autism in the community and the historical sequestering of people seen as abnormal or undesirable in Irish history. Cuan itself has evolved a more contractual self-perception that includes a very active involvement in developing the welfare of its population, increasingly incorporating the Vartry Estate. On every measure, Cuan has become more 'Rawlsian'.

The context for such a progressive trajectory certainly includes the good fortune of Cuan. While its residents are amongst the most liberal and left-leaning within contemporary Ireland, people in Cuan often commented that their values had not yet been tested by any particular crisis[44] or problems that would tell us how deep or shallow these sensibilities have become. They wondered aloud how they would respond to ethical challenges that were significantly counter to their self-interest. But the degree to which they acknowledged and thought about such questions would mitigate against any accusation of complacency. Their good fortune is no more their fault than others are responsible for their poor fortune. What matters is the way the retirees of Cuan have responded to their privileged position, making them a suitable candidate for this consideration of philosophers such as Rawls, who would otherwise tend to operate mostly within theoretically envisaged ideal situations.

— Chapter 7 —

THE BODY AND SPORTS

I do watch quite a lot of Premier League football, but in general I would say that two topics that interest me very little are sports and the body. I am not alone: academics often do not give sports their due. There is a very large and at first sight apparently very comprehensive textbook on the sociology of Ireland.[1] Yet in over 600 pages and sixteen chapters there is scant mention of sports. At the same time, reading the newspapers circulating in Cuan, whether local or national, sports generally take up more space than any other topic, including politics. I have no idea how to measure such things accurately, but it seemed that the single most commonly discussed topic amongst people in Cuan generally was again sports.

If an anthropologist is as good as their word and through sensitive attention allows the population they are living amongst to determine what matters to them, rather than simply trying to project their own interests upon that population, then it would seem that the largest section in this book really ought to be about sports. I regard that as a challenge, because while I would acknowledge that this is what I ought to do, it mainly makes me appreciate that I really don't understand how and why sports and the body can be quite as prominent as they appear to be in Cuan. Even more difficult would be to say what we learn from that observation. But those are the tasks that, despite personal misgivings, were set for this and the following chapter. The evidence and the discussion will start with sports and then turn to the body more generally.

First, to map the presence of sports. Cuan has a population of a mere 11,000. Yet even if we discount by far the largest component of sports, which are sports for children, and just focus on the adults, we find organizations or groups dedicated to cricket, motorcycling, karate, golf, sea swimming, rowing, kitesurfing, hockey, cycling, rugby, football, tennis, sailing, volleyball, badminton, walking, boxing, bowling, athletics, and squash. In addition, there is the towering presence of the GAA, or Gaelic Athletics Association, which organizes the Irish sports of hurling for boys and camogie for girls, as well as Gaelic football. When it comes to young people's sports, the numbers involved are prodigious. The GAA fields seventy-three Cuan teams (yes, seventy-three). I am less sure about other sports, but overall there seemed to be at least fifteen rugby teams, twenty-five football teams, and twenty-one cricket teams.

Watching the rowing races is also rather impressive in terms of the numbers involved, especially considering that this club was only formed in 2012. It may not get anyone particularly fit, but betting on the horses and on a few other sports also sustains a couple of shops. When it comes to watching sports in pubs, it is probably rugby that dominates over football and the GAA, and for a bar in one pub the attraction always seemed to be horse racing. English Premier League football is an important part of general conversation, and one teacher complained that he could feel excluded if he didn't profess to supporting one of the Premier League teams. As a result, it feels like even to consider sports is exhausting, let alone playing them.

The club house of the GAA has a good-sized bar, as do the rugby club and the sailing club. Both they and the cricket club frequently host a range of events. Most sports have an active associated social scene often including a Christmas meal and intermittent fundraising events such as a pub quiz or raffle. For example, my weekly ukulele group took place within the GAA building, but so do weddings and funerals, while in a nearby town the GAA hosts a ceilidh. The association makes an important contribution to parental life through organizing summer camps lasting up to six weeks, often a significant break for parents. It is proudly amateur, and many parents become involved in tasks ranging from coaching to making sandwiches, and likely get roped into some aspect of fundraising. On several occasions, people described a particular sport as 'cliquey', including those of the GAA, worlds you were either in or not. But this always seemed to be people who had not joined. Almost invariably, the actual members would protest that they were in no way exclusive, and several noted that they had expected the so-and-so club to be cliquey, until they joined and found that it wasn't.

THE BODY AND SPORTS

For the purposes of this book, the single most important observation is the relationship between the sheer extent of these sports and the exorbitant love people have for Cuan itself, since by far the most common reason people give for why they enjoy living in the town, and even more why they see it as the perfect place to bring up their children, is this extensive array of sports. More than anything else, this is seen as something Cuan stands for, and the foundation for the good enough life. Most young people seemed to want to try out a range of sports, often driving their parents spare because of the logistical difficulties that this involved, while older adults tended to focus on the particular sport with which by then they had a more cultivated relationship. Then there were sports associated with ageing: golf and bowls. Not surprisingly, since Cuan is coastal, there is an emphasis on water sports such as sailing, sea swimming, and rowing. Fishing, meanwhile, is more usually seen as a business or leisure activity than a sport.

There are many ways in which the dominance of sports becomes clear. For example, at the annual St Patrick's Day parade, most of the floats were not related to the various schools, as would be typical for analogous parades in other regions or countries. The event was dominated, instead, by floats and processions representing the many sporting clubs. The Cuan community centre has no bar or even a place to have a cup of coffee. It is mainly the host to a gym and various sports such as badminton, so that what is called the community centre is mainly in practice a sports centre, though next to it is another complex that hosts the theatre and activities for senior citizens. Having observed that newspapers and conversations are dominated by sports, there is, then, plenty of additional evidence to suggest that this is an accurate reflection of the life of Cuan.

Most of the Cuan sports are competitive and feature teams playing against other towns through local leagues. There was a time when Cuan was known for its hardy inhabitants. I heard people from Dublin saying that they 'are all Vikings up there', which historically may have some truth to it. The sea swimming in midwinter would be one overt expression of this claim. But it is probably an attribute in decline given that most residents today are blow-ins and the town is equally proud of its sophistication. The most competitive sports, such as those of the GAA, recruit children aged around five or six and suggest that unless they start young, they are unlikely to thrive when it comes to the later team competitions. As people age, they remain involved in competitive sports mainly through coaching and then possibly administration. Some of these sports, such as hockey, were developed by the local community association, others go back generations, including cricket and the sports of the GAA. There are also major races, including cycling and motorbike races, that either pass through Cuan or finish in the town, and these can represent important well-attended annual local events. Historically, there had also been horse racing in Cuan. As noted in the introduction, the lack of a swimming pool was always mentioned alongside the absence of a hotel and cinema as the three bricks that were not yet in the Cuan wall.

The centrality of sports to people's identity has also become highly visible through the latest sartorial trends. As noted in chapter 3, so much clothing today is interchangeable between sports and everyday life. One of the most popular forms of shoe is called a trainer, although it seems often to consist of a training in choosing fashionable footwear. It is easy to spot the lycra-infused shiny materials that have become integrated into leggings and tops. Many of the more favoured brands are formally sports brands. Since most people, certainly most young people in Cuan, are impressively lithe, they, along with their clothing, present themselves as ever ready to burst into sports. They are walking, but that could be merely an interlude in jogging, or they are dressed such that they could be on their way to the gym or yoga class. Clothes have thereby become the overt everyday expression of the way sport is now foundational to everyday life.

Cuan is not especially favoured when it comes to sporting prowess. Its teams are usually middling in terms of wider Irish leagues, but occasionally someone from Cuan will be in a national team, in which case the town itself becomes their support. Almost the only notices that could be seen on the monument in the middle of town from time to time were those wishing success to a local individual in some forthcoming national or international game. The *Cuan News*, which was generally exemplary in its sensitivity to what actually mattered to people in the town, would include articles on a similar theme. It also had an impressive ability to find an excuse to congratulate children who were perhaps not especially accomplished, but had made some minor contribution to a sport, so that it was intention and effort that were praised, not just success. An article might feature someone with autism who ran a half-marathon, or report on how during the pandemic people cycled an impressive distance by going round in circles. Cuan is not particularly impressive for its display of team flags compared to other towns in Ireland. The town is within Dublin County, so, depending upon the league or sport, people can support Cuan, Dublin, or Irish teams. Yet listening to everyday conversation, the emphasis is more on how sports are good for children, rather than the potential for either nationalism or local identity that can be expressed through trying to win a competition. The fact that most adults in Cuan were not born there may also have dissipated the focus upon the immediate locality. Historically, sport in Cuan had been centred on rivalry with a specific nearby town, but that has faded. Cuan people tend to wear general sportswear rather than a specific team sports shirt.

The sports where cost is most likely to be an issue are golf and sailing, with consequential connotations of status. But sailing in Cuan took a strong stance against any kind of class distinction. As noted in chapter 3, the sailing club insisted upon not being called a yachting club. Golf is, then, the sole sport that would have traditionally attracted those who saw themselves as having a higher status in the community, such as doctors or some business people. I was told that there used to be around a €4,000 joining fee for the golf club, though, thanks to the recession and the lack of younger players, this had to come down to more like €1,200, plus perhaps €300 for the golf clubs and other equipment. Although some of its practitioners claim otherwise, golf is still regarded as a sport with at least some pretensions to status. One keen golfer commented:

> Golf is strongly associated with business because there is a feeling that it's an excellent way of getting a sense of somebody you might be doing business with. For example, how they handle disappointment, how competitive they are, whether they might cheat. Four rounds on the golf course is worth ten interviews in assessing a person for the job. Nothing else can give you that sense of their suitability for business in such a short time. The other sports don't have an equivalent.

There was a time when rugby also had quite specific class and political connotations that set it aside, a legacy of its original association with the private school sector. But most people think that time has passed. Rugby has quite a passionate following and the club is an important site for social drinking. There are retired people in Cuan who follow the Irish rugby team to international venues such as Japan. Perhaps more surprising is the hold of cricket in this part of Ireland (mainly along the east coast), a sport that seems to be thriving in Cuan with several teams and does not appear to have suffered from its links to the British. The political implications of the GAA are, however, more complex and need to be discussed in their own right.

The GAA

While Irish nationalism has many supports, ranging from the Catholic Church to its distinctive musical and literary traditions, its language and history, there are grounds for seeing the GAA as having become the most important of all. The Independence story usually starts with the foundation of Irish nationalism in opposition to the British. As noted in the introduction, the legacy of de Valera, who dominated Irish politics from the 1920s until the 1960s, left every settlement in Ireland resting upon strict Catholic foundations. But even prior to his influence, the GGA was another powerful force that had developed from the 1880s. As a result, the GAA and the Church were jointly regarded as the Irish heart of wherever one lived. The two bastions were strongly aligned. All GAA clubs were defined by the boundaries of the parish – that is, the units of the church – and both were deeply involved with the schools.

When the retirees were young, the political attention would have been on the role of the Church, given its control over education. What has changed, however, is that the authority of the Church has drastically declined, but not the centrality of the GAA. Irish language is known in Cuan but not used in everyday life, while the GAA with its seventy-three teams is an inescapable presence. The sports of hurling, camogie, and Gaelic football, fostered by the GAA, exist nowhere other than in Ireland and the Irish diaspora. One of the slight kinks in the story of Irish nationalism is that de Valera was quite fond of rugby. More generally, though, the GAA managed, at least for a period, to cast a pale over all other sports as being in some way less Gaelic.

The great icon of the GAA is Croke Park in Dublin, with a capacity of 82,000 and a historical legacy that includes the 'Bloody

Sunday' massacre of 1920, when the British forces opened fire on spectators during the Independence struggle. It is also used for concerts, boxing contests, and was the site of the Papal visit in 2018. More than any religious or political monument, Croke Park feels like the very heart of Ireland itself, and this was reflected in local Cuan sentiment when talking about going there for an event. There is, then, great significance in the way the relationship has changed between both Croke Park and the GAA and all other sports in Ireland. Almost everyone can tell of earlier periods when to be involved in any sport other than the GAA risked accusations of some kind of betrayal, and certainly the players could not have a boot in both camps. Until the 1970s, there was a formal rule that members who played or attended football, rugby, or cricket would be banned from the GAA. Playing another sport could feel analogous to being 'read from the altar': that is, not that much short of being excommunicated by the Catholic Church, which in those days was the price for having attended a Protestant church service.

By contrast, people in Cuan today speak with pride about how sports have become ecumenical. Recently, when a Cuan football team did unusually well in the league and it was felt the quality of their pitch was unsuited to this suddenly exalted status, they were allowed to use the rugby pitch for the match. Wearing a rugby shirt at the GAA was no longer a provocation. Croke Park finally allowed both football and rugby to use its hallowed grounds in 2007. The GAA has adapted to and thereby enshrined contemporary Irish liberal values. It is a place that now helps to integrate new migrants rather than test their 'Irishness'. The political ethos has switched almost entirely to embrace this ecumenical potential in sports. In discussing community developments, today it is the degree to which sports in Cuan collaborate and support each other that helps them appeal to local and central government for sports funding.

The importance of the GAA for Irish identity also lies in its ubiquity. Every settlement would be expected to have its own GAA club, and one of the reasons Cuan is seen as such an ideal town for sports is that it has its GAA club and some of the GAA sports fields located near the centre of town rather than, as in many other places, on the periphery. If you were migrating from your natal site to a new part of Ireland, the obvious way of integrating into this new region would be through joining the local GAA. Having seventy-three teams and the involvement of the parents of those young players also suggests a high level of participatory citizenship. Building the new GAA club house took eight years, including all the requisite fundraising with its endless raffles and sponsorships. These days, older adults can continue to support the club through assisting with ever more complex issues around insurance and data protection. In all these ways, the GAA represents a huge act of community development. As an expression of Irish values, it is perhaps the GGA sports whose commitment to amateurism are most overtly ideological. Other sports may be amateur, but this feature is discussed far more often when people are talking about the GAA, alongside its other ideals of being egalitarian and inclusive.[2]

This is not necessarily that simple an ethos, given that the GAA is based on fierce competition and the honing of skill from such an early age. The competitive element has, then, to be complemented by other activities. It seems appropriate that, given the importance of raffles to almost every community activity in Cuan, the GAA raffle easily dominates all others as a public event. Raffles are purely a matter of luck, as opposed to skill, so they help to balance the way the sport itself tries to simultaneously exclude chance in favour of skill. Another subtle way this wider aura operates is the feeling that in the GAA it is all about the sports, which prevents the entry of other interests. By contrast, drinking at the rugby club or the sailing club is seen as something of value in its own right, with potential connotations of status.

Yet, for all that has been described above, what is seen as special about Cuan is precisely that it probably depends less on the GAA than do many other towns, thanks to the sheer plethora of sports on offer. When people describe Cuan as heaven, implying that it is different to or better than other towns, what matters is the degree to which sports such as sailing or rugby or cricket have such a central place and attract passionate attachment for so many. People would more likely call Cuan a rugby town than a GAA town. Cricket is also prominent and chaired by someone from the Vartry Estate. At this point they are all just Cuan sports, and what matters is that the extent and variety of sports mean that almost anyone has a good chance of finding their niche. In conclusion, I never heard anyone say that Cuan was special because its GAA was special. The huge complex that is the GAA is rather what made Cuan typically Irish. It was the vast range of sport overall that made Cuan special.[3]

Age and Sport

From the perspective of an individual child, sport can become a major player in their daily life. One girl described how Monday was cricket and swimming, Tuesday was camogie, Wednesday was more cricket, Thursday was Gaelic football, Friday was athletics and tennis, Saturday was for matches, and Sunday was hockey. She may have had days off school, but there were no days off sport. The discussion I was overhearing with her parents was about how to find a space for sailing, because she felt this was something she was missing out on. For the parents, this might translate into incessant demands to be driven here or there and an overload of child-supporting WhatsApp groups as well as the ever-present threat that one would be 'press-ganged' into fundraising and making sandwiches, or, if they were able, into refereeing and coaching. As blow-ins, this child's parents had been particularly impressed with the camaraderie between the various sports in Cuan, as opposed to the rivalry over children between the different sports that they had experienced elsewhere. Other children focused on just one sport from quite early on: as one child put it to her mother when asked about sport, 'Hockey, hockey, always hockey.' The modern liberal ethos is, however, sympathetic to that quotient of children who either don't like sports or can't find a sport that they have any aptitude for. The impressive range of theatre, craft, ballet, music, computer coding, and other pursuits ensures that the focus on sports is not exclusionary and is complemented by other activities in creating this sense of Cuan as an ideal place to bring up children.

For older adults, there may be continued involvement in playing the sports they enjoyed while children. But more important is their involvement as supporters, managers, and trainers. Sport at this point becomes more part of the general social life of Cuan. The relationship between sport and alcohol is complex.[4] The culture of sports in Ireland is heavily entwined with drinking. The sports clubs rival the pubs as places for convivial drinking, and in turn the pubs are as likely as the sports clubs to be a site for watching sports. Rugby is probably the sport most closely associated with drinking (other than perhaps betting on horses) and the pubs advertise their coverage of rugby more than any other sport. Following sports can have quite a major role in adult lives: not just ferrying around their kids, but also making the commitment as supporters to go to away games, including in some cases international games in which Ireland is playing.

While the key to the centrality of sports in Cuan is the emphasis on their availability to children, importantly, once people retire, they again have more time for sports. Since older people are, however, less agile, there are few sports that are specifically associated with them. The two exceptions are golf, which typically is associated with people in their sixties, and bowls, which largely involves people in their seventies. The golf club has around 800 members, but not all are local and only about 120 are really active. Bowls is perhaps the only sport that has no pretensions to involving younger people. There are about eighty members who pay annual fees of around €160. It acts as perhaps the final example of Cuan-based competitive and team sports in that it can be enjoyed until one is very frail. The bowls club also has a club house, which in turn hosts the historical society, another group mainly patronized by older people. The active ageing group has an indoor bowls facility which may include people even beyond their eighties.

Another activity that continues until late in life, partly because it can be enjoyed at such a range of levels, is walking. This varied from casual walking for experiencing the countryside to the 'power walking' along the beach that people very visibly engaged in every day, including those in their sixties and beyond. The Cuan walking club is very hardcore. I paid to join it but I never once went on one of their longer walks since it turned out that I didn't have the right trousers and other specialist gear that they insisted upon. Golf also advertised itself on the basis that a round meant a walk of at least 9 km. The one health fitness smartphone app that had become significant in terms of the proportion of people who actually used it was the step-counting app, which had established the ideal of 10k steps per day. Step-counting apps often featured in everyday conversation for people at any age. The importance of maintaining walking as a kind of minimum or default commitment to keeping active was also strongly associated with having a dog that required walking at least twice a day.

Another sport that turned out to be especially impressive when it came to the association with older people was cycling, although sailing was also something many people in Cuan felt able to remain fully involved with in their seventies. Clara, aged seventy-two, and her husband, Conor, aged seventy-six, went out cycling almost every

Tuesday, Thursday, Saturday, and Sunday and would often complete around 40 km. She had been cycling for thirty-eight years. Mostly, she went with the local cycling group. She liked the way there were periods in which you were on your own enjoying the scenery and your own thoughts, but then, when you felt like it, you could cycle alongside someone and have a chat. At her age, there were some circuits where the club went 'very strong and very fast. I can't go with them. They do all the hard stuff and I'm not going with my tongue hanging out. Oh, God, it's a turn-off.' But these were exceptional and mostly she still felt fully involved. They went on an annual holiday around May/June, and no surprise that this was always a cycling holiday.

It is not just that keeping fit helps to keep you alive; it has a very explicit connotation of virtue and also status. One of the most referenced groups in Cuan are the sea swimmers, who go out without a wetsuit right through the winter. Failure to keep to the good path of physical activities has consequences. People who put on weight, other than for reasons of ill-health, are viewed as couch potatoes and are generally regarded as morally inferior. The 'fallen woman' today is not the one who is indulgent in her sexual promiscuity, but rather the one who sits alone in her own home after work, or in retirement, and takes daily comfort in three large glasses of wine. She may be heavily involved in watching sports on daytime TV, but this is seen as the path to social isolation and perhaps depression.

By contrast, there were older people for whom the onset of ill-health was a catalyst for an almost frenetic return to sports. One woman on recovery from cancer decided to dedicate herself to a re-engagement with sports. As she put it, 'I thought, every day that I feel well I'm going to make the best of it. It gives you a bit of a "Oh, my God." Do something before it's too late, kind of thing.' She had done four marathons, including the Dublin City marathon. She joined the cycling club, went swimming, and took part in the triathlon. Both these examples – the couch potato and the post-cancer sports enthusiast – link sports as a topic to the more general issue of how people treat and cultivate their bodies.

The Body

A previous chapter argued that the people of Cuan are not particularly materialistic. But if such a word existed, they could certainly be described as 'corporealistic'. Gráinne was sixty-three, tall and slim, with long black hair; she wore well-fitted clothes that suited her. She retired at the age of sixty-one from being a personal assistant in a college. She never enjoyed her work or felt she was particularly suited to it, but she hoped she would finally be able to enjoy a more fulfilling life on retirement. She was well known, well respected, and communally minded, helping to do the publicity for the GAA. Her main ambition at this point was walking the Camino pilgrimage route in northern Spain from one end to the other. So far, she had only done bits. She wasn't in the town sea swimming group, but she went swimming in the sea quite regularly and considered me a total wimp because I wouldn't. She also wanted to re-engage with drawing, something she enjoyed prior to going back to work, after having her children. Perhaps, she might now extend this to pottery. She was reading the Elena Ferrante quartet and we shared the love. She listened to science podcasts by Stephen Hawking, but she also always lit candles when she went into a church. As she put it, 'When you're praying, you have to say thanks when you get it. And I am aware that I am grateful to whoever is looking after me, because I've asked for something and I got it. I don't know ...'

Gráinne felt she should be spending more time and effort in keeping fit. She thought that she was using her car too much, though she regularly walked to the shops. The previous Christmas, her son had bought her a bicycle, so she was cycling around Cuan a fair bit. As with many women, keeping fit was also about fending off a decline in her appearance. One of her problems was the way clothing signifies age.

> From a personal point of view I find it difficult to dress at all, because I don't want to dress like mutton dressed as lamb. I want to look young, but my shape is different from even a thirty-year-old. I'm a different shape. But I want to wear the same clothes that they wear. But I wish they wouldn't cut it in at the waist. I wish they would give me the same thing for women. And if you shop in the shop that says women's sizes, it tends to be a bit more expensive.

For Gráinne, keeping fit was

> very, very important, because I don't want to gain weight. I physically don't want to change. I want to stay as fit, I want to look the same.

I want to feel the same as I always have. I want to look forty when I am sixty, but I don't want to look sixty when I am eighty. I want to look forty when I am eighty. My vision of myself: I don't want to look old and infirm. My mother is eighty-eight and she is not the most active person in the world, but she can walk down to the shops and she can drive. She is brilliant for her age and she has a great outlook. But, at the same time, she kind of behaves elderly in that when she goes for a little walk, she'll take a big long rest, and if you ask her to do something, she will say. 'Oh no, I was in town yesterday, I'm not doing anything today.' And she doesn't push herself enough. She definitely doesn't walk enough. So even though I admire my mother and she's very agile, I still want to push those boundaries out a bit. It's not just that I don't want to be a burden to other people, I don't want to be a burden to myself either. I always want to be able to get on a plane and walk the Camino, and I want to be able to carry my own luggage.

This last phrase about carrying your own luggage is key to why she favoured the Camino pilgrimage in northern Spain in particular. The linear Camino trail is incompatible with a suitcase unless someone is driving with that case to the next stop. Walking the Camino is about carrying all you need in your rucksack. As Gráinne put it, 'One change, 4 kilos and the heaviest thing is the wash bag. And you've no make-up, you've a comb or a hairbrush, your soap and shampoo and that's it, suntan lotion. That's what you go with.' It is not just that the Camino is strenuous; it is that it requires stamina. 'You walk from 6 in the morning till 12 and in that six hours you might walk 25–30 km.' During this time, she would not be thinking about spirituality, but rather about her feet or the beauty of the landscape, while chatting to passers-by and wondering what the next hostel would be like.

Gráinne had strong liberal views and didn't want to fall into the trap of blaming people who put on weight; the reason could be diabetes. She demurred at my suggestion that keeping fit brought social kudos, but this might have been because she didn't want to flatter herself. She was not keen on competitive sports, and found that her glasses flew off her face in tennis, but she went to Irish dancing weekly and saw this as very physically demanding. She also did Zumba classes at the community centre, which she saw as good aerobic exercise with good music. The problem was that so few men went to dance-related activities and she hated it when she saw two women dancing together.

For Gráinne, as likely for many women in Cuan, this re-focus upon the preservation and enjoyment of her own life was seen not as narcissistic selfishness, but rather as a final awakening from the way she had sacrificed herself over the years. Feminism had been a big influence. As Gráinne noted,

> I didn't realize when I was minding my children and complaining that I had no income and complaining that no one ever paid me to do this. Nobody appreciated what I was doing, and I kind of equated that with salary. And I have come to realize, which I didn't, that I spent my life wiping arse for the world. Now when I look back, I can have quite a creative life and the time to do it in. My mother constantly said to me, 'Don't fritter these years away. You'll never get them back,' and I wish I had had more wisdom then.

In short, in making one own life, one's life purpose is mainly about gaining self-confidence in one's own aims. Not to value activities because they are well paid or well regarded, but because they are personally fulfilling. This is only partial. Gráinne would probably never be reconciled to the future decline in her appearance, but she had come through poverty and some severe traumas in her life and found that the collective values around keeping fit accorded closely with her own determination to live as well as she could, for as long as she could.

This extended story of an individual is justified because Gráinne represents typicality in Cuan, not eccentricity. Her values and arguments are normative and reflect a common trajectory around coming to understand one's own life as craft, which implies an artisanal approach to one's own body and health. Yet Gráinne and all those like her are equally given to helping the community and are highly sociable. You can't help bumping into similar people at the café or theatre, or once a week in a particular pub, where they might be meeting with a group, perhaps relatives or friends. All of this suggests a need to consider the complex issue of what we mean by the self.[5] There may be a self that is selfish and narcissistic, at the expense of concern for others. But people such as Gráinne look after themselves more in the spirit of a civic or social responsibility. The sentiment constantly expressed by retired people is that they don't want to become a burden to others because they have failed to look after themselves. This is expanded to include working hard to look good for others, even though in truth a failure in this regard wouldn't burden anyone else in particular.[6]

The issue is complicated analytically because it aligns closely with government campaigns around keeping a healthy body. Our fieldwork followed the launch of the 'Healthy Ireland Framework',[7] a government-led initiative which aims to enhance the population's health. Critics have seen this as an expression of neo-liberal attempts by the government to save money in health costs by assigning more responsibility to the individual. Most people are quite cynical about government initiatives and see the health sector under the increasing pressure of targets based largely on saving money. This may be partly true, but there are good reasons for both encouraging and supporting people in what are clearly their own genuine aspirations. Movements that seem close to US-style entrepreneurial attitudes such as 'Successful Ageing' are generally rejected, however much they are supported by government.[8] Healthy Ireland, by contrast, did seem well aligned with popular sentiment.

Unlike sports, which were barely mentioned in my book with Pauline Garvey, these concerns with health were discussed there in some detail.[9] The key points can be quickly summarized. One chapter tries to explain why complementary health has such a huge presence in Cuan. It may well employ nearly as many people as bio-medical health. Conventional health services tend to be directed either to physical problems, for which one presents a specific complaint to a doctor, or to mental health problems, for which one might be referred to a psychiatrist. As people age, however, their experience of ill-health becomes increasingly holistic. The problem with their stomach seems to be related to a more general sense of stress that also seems to have some vague link to the tightness in the shoulder and muscles that is causing them pain. When they go to a holistic health practitioner, it may not matter too much whether the overt claim is to help them through homeopathy or reflexology. What matters is that instead of ten minutes with a doctor discussing a symptom in isolation, they may have an hour with someone who agrees that the physical issues and social circumstances that they experience as stress are indeed all related and should be considered together. These holistic practices do not separate out treating the physical body from the way the psychologist talks through all the wider issues faced by the patient. From the patient's perspective, such extended discussions are considered to have a cathartic benefit in themselves. As people age, they are more likely to have this sense of co-morbidity. As a result, alternative therapies become increasingly appealing to this relatively affluent segment of the population. The evidence lies in the high level of employment in this sector.[10]

In turn, the flourishing of complementary health connects to the pharmacies, which sell sometimes quite expensive alternative treatments. Then there are herbalists, who have taken on the style of a professional medical consultation and a general interest in a rather vague notion of a spirituality that people feel is lacking in their lives, even if they don't want to spend a whole lot of time cultivating it. All of this leads to the current growth of 'wellness' as a craft. Wellness doesn't necessarily rest upon any specific belief system, any more than going to church these days depends upon actual faith. Even the Men's Shed uses the term 'well-being' in two of its four proclaimed aims. It is not hard to find people in Cuan who are fervent believers in some version of these various spiritual or physical routes to wellness. Some would be coming to these arenas from a largely middle-class rejection of bio-medical assertions around health.[11] To conclude, the success of complementary health had almost nothing to do with direct efficacy. It could 'work' irrespective of whether a Chinese herb or a cranial massage did anything bio-medical at all.

The idea of wellness brings together this arena of complementary health with the considerable presence of physical activities represented by the triumvirate of Pilates, Tai Chi, and Yoga. There are seven venues within Cuan that provide these to the public. While some Yoga teachers offer just a session or two a week, one of them had previously grown to up to forty classes a week, all within Cuan. In addition, physiotherapy, Weight Watchers, nutritional advice, massage therapy, 'whole health design', and various other services account for the scale of this sector. It probably helps that the Irish health insurance companies, presumably as a response to competition, now cover a certain amount of complementary health. From the perspective of the users, these services are often seen as simply alternative approaches to the same basic goal. The fact that Yoga is closely aligned to Hinduism while Pilates derives from a German tradition of gymnastics becomes inconsequential. They are anyway reconfigured to fit the requirements of Cuan. For example, Tai Chi has come to occupy a niche for somewhat older people who find Yoga and Pilates too strenuous.

The period of fieldwork coincided with peak 'mindfulness',[12] which had proliferated into almost everything that was being studied. Mindfulness was being employed for restoring calm in a primary school right through to events for the elderly, though in the former case it was partly a re-labelling of prior activities. For example, giving naughty children colouring to do was seen as mindfulness, in as much as it made them focus upon an activity that might assist in relieving stress. Mindfulness seemed to represent a corporealization of the mind itself. Instead of focusing upon processes of thinking or the problems that a person might be facing, the effect of mindfulness, as a contemporary fashion, was to bring all such issues back to the body. A mindfulness session consisted primarily of focusing in turn on different parts of the body precisely in order to keep the brain from dwelling on anything else. Much of it consisted of a focus on one's own breathing. I confess, I always experienced mindfulness as excruciatingly boring and pointless, but the good people of Cuan clearly felt otherwise. A similar rapprochement between mind and body was evident in the way many retired people, who might still consider going to the gym or undertaking other exercises designed to keep fit, were also taking up various examples of 'brain training', as noted in the discussion of bridge. The concept of brain training depends entirely upon analogy with these body-centric notions of fitness and applying them to the mind, making the body increasingly the dominant idiom for thinking about the mind itself.

Three brief examples can characterize the range of these bodily pursuits. That all three involve women reflects the situation in Cuan, where almost everyone involved in this sector is female, although Yoga was originally introduced by a man. Cathy worked in accountancy, but the death of her mother proved a turning point, and her interest in what she called natural energy had helped her emerge from her mourning. It was something she felt she had a personal aptitude for, in that it worked for the people to whom she administered this treatment. She had trained for a weekend a month for ten months and had been practising in Cuan for two years. She felt people in Cuan carried a lot of 'baggage', reinforced by the daily problems one heard on the news and the difficulty in keeping up with the high expectations in this community. Her treatment, based on working with a group of people sitting in a circle, sometimes shaded into general meditation, using sound for relaxation as well as providing a collective forum in which people felt safe to discuss their problems. She saw an affinity with the growing range of spiritually orientated alternative treatments, whether it was people using Tibetan balls or crystals or shamanistic ritual. She was happy to work in conjunction with psychotherapists, though more sceptical of what she saw as the hierarchical, authoritarian world of bio-medicine, as became clear in her hostility to hormone replacement therapy when we were discussing menopause. As with many complementary therapists, she had stories of how she had combated a personal illness and had surprised the medics by doing so successfully using her own approach to treatment.

Lilian was brought to Cuan as a baby and was fully immersed in the town's sports as a child. She worked in the airport, but she was made redundant during the financial crisis, at which point she decided to change her life. In this case, the catalyst was meeting a Tai Chi master while on holiday who later came to Cuan to conduct some sessions with her. After returning home from some more intensive specialist training in Malaysia, she decided to set herself up as a Tai Chi teacher. The income was not quite enough to live on, but sufficed in combination with her husband's salary. She had various explanations for why she favoured Tai Chi over Yoga or Pilates, but appreciated that people in Cuan saw it as part of a range and found that which was most suited to their needs. Like many others, she felt frustrated by what she regarded as the lack of even an attempt at understanding complementary health when it came to trying to discuss what she did with people working in bio-medicine.

Finally, Denise had been working for fifteen years in Cuan as a professional acupuncturist and provider of Chinese Traditional Medicine, though at times she also learnt about everything from aromatherapy to reflexology and mindfulness. She specialized in issues of fertility and gynaecology and was clearly interested in my research on menopause.[13] She discussed at length the various ways her treatments related to hormonal systems in women. She appreciated that her field included people she would regard as charlatans and was careful to procure what she regarded as effective herbs from reliable sources. She followed the trends that came with digital devices such as the app Headspace for mindfulness or the popularity of period tracking apps, whether used in relation to contraception or when trying to become pregnant. Alongside all the other complementary health practitioners I interviewed, she presented the Cuan scene as friendly and eclectic, with everyone positively recommending other alternatives, if they might be helpful, and being clear that they avoided competition or disparaging each other's treatments. There was an underlying inference that this also represented a more female style of non-competitive health engagement. When these people talked about bio-medicine, they tended to assume that doctors were male, even though this was decreasingly the case.

To put all this in context, for every person in Cuan who is sympathetic to and utilizes complementary health, there will be another who regards them as crackpots and idiots, who must have slept through those elementary science lessons at school that would have explained to them why only bio-medicine, which has been rigorously tested and is constantly researching for better evidence, can be trusted when it comes to something as important as one's health and body. I spoke to several people who regarded complementary health as an essentially evil influence responsible for the deaths of those who took this path during serious illnesses rather than the medical treatments that might have saved them. Most people avoid both extremes and try to maintain some respect for both bio-medical and complementary treatments. This is clearly reflected in the stock of the local pharmacies. People from the Vartry Estate may not be able to afford the more expensive private treatments and medicines, but the days when complementary health was an exclusive middle-class concern seem to have passed.

One of the main points made in my book with Pauline Garvey was that several of these activities could just as well have been practised individually. It is easy to find a Yoga or dance class video on YouTube, and during the Covid lockdown that is what most people had to use. It is perfectly possible to go walking by oneself. Yet the fieldwork showed that, where they could, people chose to undertake these exercises in the company of others. In a case such as the gym, it can be argued that few people could afford to buy the equipment individually and so needed to come into the public arena. But when it comes to activities such as walking or mindfulness, this would not be the case. After a few lessons, there is probably not a whole lot of instruction that could not be acquired independently when it comes to an activity such as Yoga. The fact that people go to these classes indefinitely confirms the other evidence that a focus on one's own body is regarded as a social and communal task to be carried out alongside others, rather than as a private activity. It is yet another public demonstration of one's virtue in taking responsibility for the maintenance of one's health, in contrast to the isolated wine-guzzling couch potato.

History and Conclusions

This chapter has juxtaposed two facets of Cuan life that seem to represent two sides of the same coin: a focus on the body is essential for sport. Yet in one way they are remarkably different. The emphasis on sports has a long history, with the GAA pre-dating other facets of the nationalism that was entrenched as state policy by de Valera. By contrast, not very long ago, people in their sixties and seventies were associated with pubs and rocking chairs, not Yoga and gyms. To understand the contemporary meaning of such activities, it is important to reflect at least briefly on these vastly different trajectories.

Sport has been discussed in this chapter, in its own right, but it appears in other chapters because of its importance in bonding people to Cuan. As just noted, what makes Cuan special is not the GAA but the sheer numbers of alternative sports. Sports can have an important role in the development of post-colonial nationalism even when the sport came through colonialism. C.L.R. James' classic book about cricket in the West Indies and its role in the formation of post-colonial identity comes to mind.[14] At the same time, Ireland is unusual in that it is the sports that are only played by the Irish that have maintained their dominant position in fostering Irish national identity through the GAA, which is a clear contrast with most other colonized nations.

In the case of Cuan, this bonding was particularly important since it pertained not just to an original community of identity, but rather to a town that mainly consists of blow-ins. Today, the blow-ins are if anything more fervent in their belief that Cuan is the best place to live, especially for bringing up children. The following chapter will show how sports have come to be seen as the bastion of virtue that fortifies children against the temptations of evil. This is something that accords well with middle-class parents' ideals for their children and the constant fear that their children might otherwise fall down the precipices of cocaine, crime, and alcoholism. Modern ecumenical sports fit the liberal ethos of Cuan as a place that has a niche for every child as an individual. While this ethos is very different from that which linked the GAA and the Church a century ago, there is clear continuity in this relationship between sport and virtue and thereby the good enough life.

The much more recent development is the radical transformation in the conception and practices associated with the sustainability of the body, which have thereby brought the body itself into alignment with these projects of virtue. The practice of Yoga arrived in Cuan in the 1980s, assisted by the rather remarkable retained attachment that older people often mentioned in regard to their formative experiences during the 1970s. This was a period when quite a high proportion of these retirees flirted with hippie ideals and lifestyles. They still commonly reference those experiences as the origins of an alternative spirituality to that of the Catholic Church. But the sheer scale and extent of wellness has mostly developed in the last twenty years. The associated practices and treatment are often quite costly, and it is the relative affluence of these retired people that allows them to participate. Their contemporary relationship to health is entirely different from what they recall through oral histories. They regard their ancestors as essentially passive when it came to the body and health. Their parents would have seen ill-health as a problem to be delivered to the lap of the local doctor, who was assumed to have all the relevant expertise. The relationship with the doctor was historically viewed as a close one, sometimes inherited from prior generations. The ideal was encapsulated in the home visit of a figure who, like the priest, seemed almost an appendage to the family. The doctor would then do their best, and if this failed, that was fate and the organic truth of mortality.

Today, the situation could hardly be more different. In a separate paper, I have written about the impact of Googling for health information.[15] I show how this use of the search engine has become a regular pursuit, but one that people frequently hide from their doctors, because they know that the medical authorities regard it as mainly a nuisance. In my book with Pauline Garvey, we report on how this is just one of the ways in which men, in particular, may lie to or avoid their doctors.[16] At the same time, the medical profession has become far more distanced and strained, with many doctors leaving the profession because of the stress involved in practising medicine in Ireland. Many research participants now talk of doctors in complaining terms, saying that they only have only ten minutes to discuss a single problem and the doctor is making notes on their computer for much of the time. Partly this discourse may have become a means for justifying to themselves and others the considerable resources they now devote to complementary health. It is complementary health that now incorporates the general idea of wellness with an additional spiritual inflection, and becomes also an ethic of personal responsibility for one's health.

To conclude, the emphasis on wellness might be recent and that on sports might have far more historical depth, but the latter may well have rendered fertile the fields for the blossoming of the former. One of the points that arose from the discussion of sport is that older people now strive to maintain their relationship to sometimes quite energetic sports, such as cycling or extensive walks exemplified by the Camino pilgrimage, but then they also relax into more leisured golf and finally bowls. People believe that keeping fit, watching their diet, brain training, and countless other active interventions may stave off certain ailments, and where illnesses can't be avoided, for instance many cancers, they can at least help to make the treatments more effective. Health has been integrated into retired people's attitude to life as a form of artisanal craft, sculpting the best body they can manage at any given age, not only externally in appearance but also internally in terms of health. As with all the topics being discussed in this volume, the retirees perceive this growing emphasis upon the self and the body as a social activity rather than a turn towards individualism. Often it is even seen as a civic duty that prevents them from being a burden to their family or the state. This collective orientation in turn makes their concerns more akin to the quintessential social activity of Cuan: sports.

Chapter 8

THE ORIGINS OF PHILOSOPHY IN SPORT

Through most of the chapters of this book, the primary contrast drawn between aspects of the Western philosophical tradition and Cuan derives from the relative abstraction of philosophy compared to learning from the complex, compromised, and messy world of life as lived. Philosophy tends to the speculative and the theoretical. Philosophical schools such as the Stoics saw the reproduction of philosophy as facilitated by a life of contemplation rather than engagement. But the birth of Western philosophy could not have been more different from this characterization, and the place where this becomes clearest is in the relationship between ancient philosophy and sport. This chapter will therefore explore some of the parallels between what was described in the previous chapter as the role of sports in contemporary Cuan and the scholarship around the birth of Western philosophy itself, which, as it turns out, arose in large part from and through sports.

The evidence for the central role of sport in classical Greece spans from the huge significance attributed to events such as the Olympic Games to the role of the gymnasium for young men in fifth-century BCE Athens, which formed the backdrop to many of the early philosophical dialogues. Everyday life in fifth-century BCE Athens seems to be just as directed towards sports and the body as everyday life in twenty-first-century Cuan, although in ancient Athens the phrase 'everyday life' should be imagined as including cosmology and religion. In reading a playwright such as Aristophanes, it is hard to separate out fields such as religion, sport, and philosophy, as they are all part of the backdrop to his comedies. Still earlier, during the period of Homer's *Iliad*, we find sports competitions as an important part of funerary rituals, while the perfection of the body was already linked to the transcendent perfection of the gods. Philosophy came into existence as one part of a triangle formed alongside sport and religion.

This chapter is indebted to various publications by Heather Reid, who provides a very helpful guide to the common and intertwined origins of sport and philosophy.[1] She in turn uses the scholarship of Stephen Miller in his account of classical Greek athletes.[2] Sport and philosophy grew from the same point of origin in the Greek concept of *aretē*,[3] the quality of excellence that results in good actions. As with some other terms that became central to philosophical thinking, this focus on excellence was part of the everyday language of the time. Sport and education together transform excellence from a property that is given, as in the assumed qualities of an aristocracy, to something that can be cultivated and trained irrespective of social status. Even in Homeric times, athletic ability could confirm a person's worthiness and closeness to divinity, as, for example, in the case of Achilles. Odysseus, on returning home, demonstrates his nobility through an archery contest rather than just his guile.

The Olympic Games, founded in 776 BCE, established the ideal of an impartial contest under the auspices of a religious sanctuary. The profound consequences of sport in classical times are exemplified by the way the Olympic Games established the principle of *isonomia* – that is, equality under the law – and how this influenced the subsequent development of democracy.[4] The nudity that Miller shows as fundamental to the portrayal of athletes in sculpture and on vases was an expression of the ideal that people should compete in a spirit of pure equality stripped of status and any other attributes of difference, including clothes. This absolute equality expressed in nudity was the principle that helped in turn establish an absolute equality of citizens within democracy. This suggests that it was not that sports reflected a philosophy, but rather that core ideals, around which both philosophy and democracy developed in classical Greece over the following two centuries, were initially derived from sports.

The close relationship between sport and philosophy in ancient Greece is mediated by the third part of this triangle: religion. The Olympic Games were viewed as an essentially religious event dedicated to Zeus, and the five days of the games were the occasion of many sacrificial and other religious activities. To go to the games was a form of pilgrimage. The athletes tried to secure their victory as much through prayer and their pledges to the gods if they were successful as through physical training. The very act of taking part was viewed as a form of religious devotion, since victory was a test of that individual whose body and strength had most pleased the gods. On return to their home towns, the victors were treated as demi-gods themselves. Equally important is the way they represent a transcendent identity. Mostly, we think of this period in terms of the relentless fighting between Athens and Sparta, alongside almost constant fighting between the other *poleis* – a legacy of Thucydides amongst others. Yet at the Olympic Games there is an annual holiday from fighting, as all came together in a higher cause funded by their respective *polis*. The Olympic Games is the event through which the wider Hellenic identity is proclaimed, prior to the bonding that came through the common cause of fighting against the Persian invaders. Finally, the Olympics represented equal subservience to the consensual rules of the game, as opposed to the arbitrary imposition of rules by tyrants. Miller notes that athletes are most commonly depicted in Attic vase painting during the period of democracy[5] and Reid provides still more parallels between democracy and sports.[6]

By the time we come to the key era of fifth-century BCE Athens, there are constant references to the gymnasium as the place where young men developed their physical training. But these were equally the site where they received education more generally. The desire to educate the young was crucial to the birth of philosophy,[7] as both physical and intellectual development were recognized as essential to the formation of character. This is where young men would learn to be good citizens and good soldiers. Socrates and the other nascent philosophers tended to hang around the gymnasia, which is the context for the later accusation levelled at Socrates that he corrupted the Athenian youth. Reid notes how Alcibiades tied ribbons around the head of Socrates, a notoriously ugly man, to emphasize a beauty that corresponded to that of the victorious athlete.[8]

Plato went so far as to found an important gymnasium, the original *academy*, which espoused this idea that *aretē* had to be developed by training, including physical training – a goal made very explicit in the *Republic*.[9] This may lead semantically to our idea of the academic, though we seem to have lost the bit about physical training. Aristotle in his *Rhetoric* praised the creation of *kalokagathia*: literally beautiful goodness, as achieved by the beauty of pentathletes.[10] This is a concept which Reid argues is understood as the balance between athletic and humanistic training found in the gymnasium. The ideal of the good life is also expressed in the way happiness is achieved through physical activity. The athlete trained to the point of reliable performance. They also learned that what is good and beautiful applies equally to moral and civic virtue. The athletic and the moral were connected virtues that could then equally be appraised as beautiful, coming together, for example, in the courage of the soldier or the beauty of justice, all of which could be integrated into the teachings of the gymnasia united by the trope of virtue.

As noted, Socrates (470–399 BCE) spent much of his time in the public gymnasia, especially the Lyceum. Reid draws many parallels here between the wrestling schools and the way he conducts his dialogues. She writes:

> At *Philebus* 41b Socrates says: 'So let us get ready like athletes to form a line of attack around this problem.' In *Cratylus* (421d) he says that 'once we're in the competition, we're allowed no excuses'. In *Euthydemus*, the argument is compared to a ball game (277b) and wrestling match (277d, 278b, 288a). Meanwhile, the conversation in *Protagoras* resembles a heavyweight bout, complete with boxing blows (339e), umpires (336c, 338b) and talk of conceding victory – all followed by an enthusiastic and partisan audience (336e, 339e). The *Theaetetus* practically equates philosophical dialogue with wrestling. Here Socrates is compared to Antaeus, a mythological athlete who lived in a cave and forced passers-by to wrestle him, ultimately defeating them all.[11]

Reid argues further that Socrates' concept of *agon* strips the contestants from worldly rank and attachment, to examine only the qualities of the soul in a form analogous to the nude athletes of the time. She suggests that Socrates' own preference was for sparring rather than boxing.[12]

The early philosophical dialogues are framed as contests. Even if Socrates always beats his opponents with ease, they were still trying their best to win this competition through more incisive and persuasive arguments. Socrates is trying to overcome the sophists, renowned for their ability to argue from any side, with his own form of dialogue through *agon*. As with sport, there is also an ideal of mutual improvement. This is achieved partly through the way Socrates transforms the competitive nature of wrestling into an inner struggle to know oneself, where one competes with oneself against one's own ignorance, but also against the false pretence of omniscience.[13] But while Reid emphasizes the pursuit of virtue, what also comes across clearly in Socrates is the element of play in these sports. Socrates has a good deal of fun through his dialogues and his overcoming of the sophists. An occasion such as the symposium, associated with drinking and often clever and impressive *hetaira* – women who participated in the symposia in various ways – was intended to be as enjoyable as possible. In conclusion, Socrates was a philosopher who fully understood the principle of good *craic*, which is fundamental to Irish sociality, life purpose, and indeed sport.

All of this is evidence that at the time of Socrates, philosophy was itself a form of sport and had developed many of its primary features in emulation of sport. This was one facet of the way Socrates sought to create his philosophy of virtue from within everyday life. Pierre Hadot shows how this gradually changed: first, when Plato creates a separate environment within which to teach young people the values they might need to enter into politics; and then when Aristotle goes further in creating a more sequestered environment within which to think about the nature of the world, which then becomes the primary mode for philosophy as a discipline.[14] Compared to Socrates, the philosophy that Aristotle developed was no fun at all. It was the beginning of that absolutely serious philosophy that we later find in Kant and Heidegger, where intellectual pursuits are elevated to become both separate from and far above the mere physical cultivation of sporting life, or the enjoyment of *craic*. Aristotle and later philosophers might therefore perhaps be understood as 'spoil-sports'.

Irish Sports

There is no evidence in Cuan for the kind of abstracted philosophical discourse that stems from Aristotle. People talk about what matters in their lives and the various ethical dilemmas that they constantly confront but in the context of messy everyday life and politics. Cuan dialogues have something in common with Socrates in that they are usually held in the spirit of friendly discussion and argument, often accompanied by drinks, very possibly also after helping with or watching a sport. As described in chapter 5, Cuan dialogue is often in the spirit of banter incorporating competitive insults, which are often directed at taking down any kind of pretension or claims that threaten the fundamental equality between those taking part. As in the time of Socrates, the most important place for the development of ideas and virtue, of the principles of *aretē* Irish style, is through sports themselves and the role they play in the cultivation of character, identity, morality, and sociality. The key sites in Cuan, such as the community centre (which, as previously noted, is almost entirely a sports centre) and the GAA sports centre, are the Irish gymnasiums, and they stand for the town as a democratic and egalitarian *polis*.

The comparison between the role of sports in classical Athens and in Cuan seems apt since the evidence provided in the previous chapter indicated the extent to which the body and sports have become ever more integral, not just to everyday life, but also to the aspirations and morality of Cuan society. The sheer plethora of sports available to young people was a crucial element in people's description of Cuan itself as 'heaven' – the ideal place for one's child to grow up in. People did not discuss philosophy, but they would certainly consider the principles of excellence and virtue through their discussion of the latest rugby, soccer, or hurling match. If anything, then, the proper analogy is between Cuan and pre-Socratic Greece. As in that period, in Cuan, philosophy has to be extrapolated from everyday life, and one of the key fields in which it may be found are in the practices that pertain to the body and sports.

An examination of these relationships can commence from the way sports in Cuan contribute to the wider ideals of morality and virtue, initially in alignment with religion, but increasingly displacing religion as the foundation for such concerns.[15] The introduction to this book documents the birth of Cuan within theocratic Ireland, where almost everything was practised under the control of the Church, including a highly constrained moral ethos that disciplined the body and especially sex. The underlying authority of the Church came from its alignment with post-Independence nationalism, within which its primary ally was the GAA. Every Irish community had at its heart two establishments: the church and the GAA sports centre. While Catholicism is found in many countries, the GAA is exclusively Irish, giving it a particular value in the development of Irish nationalism. As argued in the previous chapter, the razing of the Church, at least with regard to its ability to command most of the population, left the GAA standing alone and supreme as the central icon of Irish settlements.

There are many reasons why the Church and the GAA had been so closely aligned. If parents are thinking of sports when they describe Cuan as heaven, the reason may well be the role or sports in securing what they regard as the salvation of their children. Youths are often viewed as growing into teenage life confused and conflicted by two opposed temptations perched on their respective shoulders and whispering their blandishments into their ears. On one shoulder is the devil tempting them into binge drinking, cocaine, crime, and other misdemeanours. On the other shoulder is perched the attraction of sports as the place in which to bond with and impress one's peers and as a path to fulfilment. The two are in direct competition since if a child is going to impress their GAA team at ten o'clock on a Saturday morning, they can't really get totally wasted the night before. The role of sport in keeping children away from drugs and excessive drinking continued the tradition of *mens sana in corpore sano* ('a healthy mind in a healthy body'). Another common expression was about sports keeping children 'off the streets'. The psychotherapists described young people with drug addiction who had said that they wished they had stayed within the regime of sports, which might have prevented their subsequent struggle with drugs by giving them a focus. Of course, there were binge drinkers and cocaine addicts within sports, but mostly sports could plausibly appear to be the potential salvation of the young and this had become central to their appeal to the middle classes' more ascetic claims to virtue. In Cuan, just as in classical Athens, sport is viewed as character building. As described in the previous chapter, parents subject themselves to a frenetic round of activity, even though both may be in full-time work, to make sure their children can participate in as many sports as possible. The schools provide education, but it's the parents who take responsibility for ensuring sport's capacity to complement education as the other essential component in bringing up their children in the right way.

All of this helps us to understand how first the GAA and then ecumenical sports managed to take on a mantle that the Church could no longer wear. Even if older people retain their affection for religiosity, it is now very rare for young people to have the slightest interest in religion post-communion, and especially not once they are teenagers. Sporting heroes and heroines provide ideal icons based on real people whom one could imagine oneself becoming, making them far more effective today than what the young regard as a bunch of wooden saints. Sports, then, ground youths' increased concern with identity, as much as with morality.

Imagine identity as a segmentary system in which each level incorporates the level beneath it. At the lowest level, the child identifies with their school's class team. This is easily subsumed at the next level when they come as a group to cheer for their school team or later a college team. This in turn is subsumed by support for Cuan sporting teams, whether at the GAA or in the many other sports available to them. In practice, parents do more of the supporting from the side-lines, but mainly because the children themselves are too busy actually playing. In turn, support for Cuan is subsumed by county teams, and finally the exuberant support for Irish rugby, football, and other such national sports teams alongside the nationalism connoted by the GAA, representing exclusively Irish sports. Each one of these is a clear-cut delineated level which may play a major role in helping a young person know who they are in terms of identity.

There are many ways in which sport can be a virtuous practice. Playing games means learning to abide by rule-based activities more generally. The team element helps develop social bonding, especially in a sport where it is the team's collective ability rather than individual prowess that secures the victory. For a sport to be sporting requires the mutuality expressed by the hospitality extended to the opposition team after the game. Finally, sports often involve lessons in strategy that are not merely physical. A rather different appeal of sports lies in contingency. I enjoy Premier League football partly because of the number of times a lowly placed team still manages to win against a top team. The excitement in sport comes from not being sure about the outcome. Alasdair MacIntyre in *After Virtue* praises the unlikely figure of Machiavelli in his analysis of virtue, because Machiavelli insisted on the central role of Fortuna.[16] MacIntyre is showing how a philosophy of virtue that fails to acknowledge the central role of contingency just doesn't work.

This contingency derives in some measure from other very different possible outcomes from playing sports. Sports can easily succumb to the creation of hierarchies that demean and diminish the less sporty. Competition can lead to an inflation of the victorious ego. Sports are often associated with heavy drinking. There is evidence from Ireland that involvement in team sports may also lead males to engage in online gambling.[17] Competition can lead to far more problematic enmity between regions and nations, as found in the fighting between rival fans, and sometimes even to war. Sport can lead to obsessive concern resulting in the neglect of other worthwhile pursuits. Since all these vices are the other side of its virtues, they demonstrate this role of contingency not only in who is going to win a game, but also in considering the consequences of sport. The close relationship between spectator drinking and sport is, then, not a contradiction but a contribution to this quality of sport. Contingency as Fortuna can become an integral part of what makes sports attractive. It is an uncertainty of their moral status as well as their outcome that allows people to experience them as a bit more 'edgy', not just boring old virtue.

There is nothing new in this. Sports have always fluctuated between purity and decadence. Occasionally, key moments can be observed within the constant shifting between these poles. For example, at the 416 BCE Olympic Games, Alcibiades extravagantly sponsored three teams and his celebration of victory was one of the great blow-out parties of ancient times.[18] If Alcibiades thereby contributed to the decline of the Olympic Games, which he was clearly exploiting for personal political advantage, his (possibly romantic) association with Socrates led to the ultimately fatal accusation that the latter had corrupted the youth of Athens. These tensions and contradictions have been taken up in the wider anthropology of sports.[19] What anthropologists tend to add is sensitivity to the way they are worked out in many different cultural settings: for example, how sports bring together what otherwise are seen as contradictions, such as fun and seriousness, or individualism and the collective.

One important shift evident in Cuan has been the increasing emphasis on sport and the body amongst older people. This is without precedent simply because the population itself is unprecedented. It is the growth in life expectancy and the possibility of nearly three decades of retirement that explains this shift towards a new craft: the artisanal cultivation and maintenance of the body. For the retirees of Cuan, the direction of travel is not from sports and the body to the philosophy of the good life, but the other way around. Having found the good enough life, through developments in practices rather than through contemplation, there is then every incentive to extend life itself as much as possible. This is achieved mainly through careful attention to personal health and fitness, because everything else they desire rather depends on still existing. This accounts for the proliferation of walking groups, Yoga classes, Pilates sessions, and healthy eating – all part of the drive for personal sustainability. These older people are frequently found sea swimming or sailing or playing badminton, tennis, or golf, because a life that is purposeful tends to lead them back to sports and personal sustainability.

To summarize: for young people in Cuan, formal education and training in academic issues are the role of school, complemented by involvement in sports. This is a situation not so different from the way in which in classical Athens these two were united in the gymnasium. While in ancient times this led to an increasingly abstracted philosophy, in Cuan what we think of as philosophical has still to be extrapolated from embedded activities, the most prominent amongst which are sports. In the case of older people in Cuan, the trajectory is rather different. While there is no evidence for people becoming deeply philosophical as they age, they are increasingly concerned with life purpose and deciding what to do with retirement. This then leads to a continued engagement in sport and the sustaining of the body. But the result is the same for the young and the not so young. Philosophy, or at least the values and virtues with which philosophy is concerned, has remained in Cuan an embodied pursuit.

Why Not Yoga?

As anthropologists have recently noted, it is quite surprising how little overlap there has been between the study of health and that of sport, given the degree to which these are seen as overlapping terrains for most people.[20] This was part of the incentive to combine the two topics in the previous chapter. Once again, classical Greece reveals a comparable holistic concern. The authors who contributed to the Hippocratic tradition clearly felt the fit body was an important element in health more generally. They would have approved of diet and exercise as creating a body that is both good looking and healthy, much as is common in public culture today.[21]

In order to consider this relationship, I was tempted to shift from the strictly Western philosophical tradition to consider whether the second part of the previous chapter could be subject to a similar study. The obvious activity to focus on was Yoga, given its sheer prevalence within Cuan and its position as iconic for various wellbeing practices that are now common for people of all ages. The popularity of Yoga today derives from a South Asian tradition with its own holistic ideal of metaphysical and physical fitness. Yoga developed first as a cosmological tradition, rather than a medical system, and was later associated with nationalism rather than wellbeing. Could the origins of Yoga therefore be related to the place of the body in contemporary Cuan? This enquiry soon led to a realization that Yoga seems to have developed out of a wider tantric branch of ancient Hindu philosophy that was concerned with training the body in pursuit of various spiritual purposes. The trouble is that, at least according to Geoffrey Samuel, the primary trajectory that created Yoga derives from a series of practices connected with the Nath tradition, which focused on sexual rituals such as the consumption of the mixed sexual secretions of a male and female. As Samuel notes:

> The principal *hatha yoga* text, the *Hathayogapradipika*, is an explicitly Nath text directed towards the classic Nath internal yogic and sexual practices. Given the extremely negative views of Tantra and its sexual and magical practices which prevailed in middle-class India in the late nineteenth and twentieth centuries, and still largely prevail today, this was an embarrassing heritage. Much effort was given by people such as Swami Vivekananda into reconstructing yoga, generally in terms of a selective Vedantic reading of Patañjali's *Yogasūtra*. ... The effort was largely successful, and many modern Western practitioners of yoga for health and relaxation have little or no knowledge of its original function as a preparation for the internal sexual practices of the Nath tradition.[22]

At this point, I rather felt that any attempt to draw analogies between the origins of Yoga and the contemporary practice of Yoga in Cuan might not make me especially popular amongst the latter, whose views on this topic might be rather closer to contemporary middle-class Indians. I will therefore leave any further excavation of these roots and routes to others.

Conclusion

One of the first observations in writing up these topics was the discrepancy between the place of sports in life and in academic discourse. Why do newspapers have more content devoted to sport than to politics? Why is sport the most common topic in general conversation? How did sport become the core to why people love Cuan, and what they most prize in the town? One explanation turns out to be the way people in Cuan imagine sport as the mechanism through which the young will be inculcated into local ideals of the virtuous life that will protect them from moral decay. Sport is where values are developed through practices – values which relate to many other aspects of life, including the relationship between the individual and the wider community and between egalitarianism and meritocracy. If the original question of philosophy was what constituted the good life, then for the good enough people of Cuan, sports have a major part to play in the answer.

This becomes much more plausible when one considers that philosophy itself arose as an emanation of sport. It wasn't just that Socrates and the sophists spent their time in the gymnasia, but that the model for philosophical dialogue was itself contested debate as an example of sport: besting one's opponent as in wrestling, but through discourse. This was the tradition that was largely left behind when Aristotle, rather than Socrates, became the dominant subsequent model for how one does philosophy. The same point extends to the later discussion of health and the body. The corporealistic population of Cuan think about the world through bodily practices, which may include walks in the countryside rather than competitive sport, or ideas about how to maintain health through diet. An important route into seeing how they construct their system of values is the way they discuss the alternative epistemologies behind bio-medicine as science, or complementary health as spirituality. Philosophy was only absent in Cuan if one failed to recognize a situation analogous to that which existed at the time of Socrates. This was a situation whereby one could develop moral practices, ideals about the good life and about society, through their physical engagement with the world rather than through an abstract intellectual exercise that, thanks to the influence of subsequent Western philosophy, increasingly defined itself as a form of superiority to the merely physical. The lesson from Cuan in this and several other chapters is that philosophy extrapolated from everyday practice may be just as profound as philosophy developed as abstracted writing. If one of the conclusions of this book is that Cuan is rather more akin to the *polis* of classical Greece than might ever have been anticipated, then sports have played a major role in substantiating this analogy.

Chapter 9

CREATING COMMUNITY

Historical Cuan

This chapter will start with a brief description of the history of Cuan. But that might be misleading in that its primary purpose is to show how contemporary Cuan is not a result of that early history. As the chapter unfolds, the emphasis will be increasingly on the way in which the modern community has been constructed largely by more recent migrants. It will examine the factors behind their extraordinary success in creating Cuan and what we can learn from their achievements.

Cuan was for a period an important fishing village, but this peaked in the eighteenth century.[1] A mid-nineteenth-century estimate suggests that around 400 of the 2,300 inhabitants were fishermen. By the 1880s, fishing had declined and been replaced by trade in potatoes, herring, coal, and stone from local quarries. In turn, this trade had largely ended by the 1940s. There was a trickle of factory work, but very limited. The surrounding area is fertile, but was dominated by rapacious English landowners. More recently, as noted in the introduction, Cuan became a seaside tourist destination and entertainment centre with extensive provision for tourists, including well-known ballrooms from 1947 and a cinema from 1948. It seems to have been a very lively town for three months in the summer, but with nothing much going on the rest of the year. Tourism declined drastically from the 1970s, when people started going abroad for holidays, and today there is almost nowhere to stay in the town other than via Airbnb. There are records of pubs from 1618, with fifteen recorded in the early nineteenth century. There was secondary school education from 1875, but this only really expanded with free schooling from 1966. The first train service began in 1844 and the first bus service was in 1926.

Chapter 5 discussed the building of two social housing estates. The first was situated outside the main village in the 1950s and then a more extensive estate followed in the 1960s. Cuan was radically transformed through the development of much more extensive private housing, especially after 1973, with successive major estate building which gradually increased the population from 2,300 to its present 11,000. Around 60 per cent of those living on these early new private estates were from or worked in Dublin. Despite these developments, it was noted in the introduction that if in Dublin, or elsewhere in Ireland, you make mention of Cuan, it is viewed as an off-the-beaten-track, undistinguished place that people know little about and that doesn't feature in tourist guides. There remain a good number of restaurants serving the town and hinterland, but several pubs have recently closed down, either as part of general trends, such as the shift to cafés, or as a result of Covid and the expenses of the hospitality trade. There are now a mere six pubs. Much of the local employment today is in services, including health and education, with a strong emphasis on care work. A good proportion of the businesses in Cuan are locally owned.

If Cuan was until recently a village, what was traditional village life like in Ireland? The answer is not at all clear, whether we rely on oral history testimony, fiction, or earlier work by anthropologists. A tempting and impressive portrait, though set in Northern Ireland, might be the magisterial presentation by Henry Glassie in *Passing the Time in Ballymenone*.[2] What this book celebrates above all is the richness of oral culture, the songs, stories, and conversation that permeate everyday life. In Glassie's book, community is based on a fundamental unit of neighbourliness as opposed to individualism, though neighbourly relations are held in balance with the need to follow particular interests and not everyone lives up to the ideals.

At the other end of the spectrum lie several works described in previous chapters, such as Nancy Scheper-Hughes' book *Saints, Scholars and Schizophrenics*, whose negative depiction of traditional Irish families caused some controversy. I can only attest to my ethnography. I did not live anywhere else in Ireland or in Ireland's past. I have, however, spent many years living in small rural communities in other parts of the world such as India and Trinidad. In general, I have been more struck by the long-standing quarrels and petty jealousies in neighbourly relations found in small communities, though often alongside the way such communities cooperate and come together for crises or rituals. I believe that the constant evaluation and surveillance that come with living in a small village together with the relative lack of opportunities have historically been important reasons why young people so readily abandoned rural life in many regions of the world. The bucolic romance of the rural and the past is mostly a construction of urban authors.

A similar division can be found within Irish literature. This is replete with plays that seem close to Glassie's positive portrait, especially as they are often set in pubs where people are able to tell these extended stories and celebrate this facility in oral culture that is well suited to play writing. Such plays may also depict relentless struggles over a piece of land[3] or the memory of a slight. Chapter 5 mentioned the notoriety of Brinsley MacNamara's book *The Valley of the Squinting Windows*, which became infamous for bursting this romantic bubble around rural life with its dystopian portrayal of a traditional community. The 2022 film *The Banshees of Inisherin* provides another useful corrective to the romantic portrait, especially of the Irish islands, that was evident in earlier anthropology and remains a popular sentiment.

The oral histories of research participants in Cuan indicate a similar asymmetry. The dominant portrayal is close to this more romantic image of a village whose foundations lay in family and the Church. It is portrayed as a time when people felt no need to lock their doors at night and would come together for any kind of ritual, such as a funeral, or the recurrent crises represented by people lost at sea. Generally, people play down any tension between Catholic and Protestant families and do not bring up the divisions of the civil war. It is very rare for people to expose memories of ancient quarrels. One older man told of a grandmother who hated another Cuan family so much that she said she would cut off any child that married into it. (After she died, her daughter did marry into that family.) He described the old town square as a good example of 'the valley of the squinting windows'. Still today there is a legacy of the time when the village was dominated by certain older families. For example, when a pub reopened after refurbishment, its success was assured because of its strong links to one of these established families who owned and ran it and could thereby guarantee a sufficient clientele. Many clearly enjoy the constant companionship and sociality of never being able to go for a walk without meeting a relative or neighbour of old. Less obvious were a few people who had moved out to the new estates at the edge of town in their retirement to escape the very same experiences and were thankful for the peace and lack of attention this had brought them.

It was still a slight shock meeting Ciara, quite late on in this fieldwork. By that stage, I had more or less concluded that the distinction between blow-ins and locally born, while essential for explaining how things had developed historically, wasn't particularly important in understanding contemporary Cuan. Ciara, especially because she was only in her early thirties, demonstrated, however, that this conclusion was premature. She was every inch indigenous Cuan. She couldn't go out into the street without getting into conversation with others from those original families. She knew all the gossip and the importance of 'not knowing' all the stuff that would have disrupted lives if acknowledged, such as regretted affairs. The pub owner came over and made a big joke of the fact that she was drinking a 'glass' and not a pint, something that she claimed you would never normally see of someone from her particular family. She told many stories about growing up in Cuan, when so many people had seemed to be sort of family, like the great 'aunt' who never married but everyone went to as teenagers since she was so accepting and could talk dirty for Ireland.

Ciara could provide a whole slew of negatives and positives that come from being old Cuan. Blow-ins could never really have quite the great *craic* that she experienced, and in the end great *craic* is the measure of how life should be. This was because with families you overlooked the foibles and sins; getting drunk and snogging the wrong person would be 'forgotten'. Old Cuan people still had that anti-establishment or 'getting away with it' spirit that fostered good *craic*, while the blow-ins were all a bit too 'goody two shoes'. Within old Cuan, there was always someone to call on in need, a sense that people had 'got your back'. But at the same time, whenever Ciara saw two people taking a walk along the seashore together, she couldn't quite stop herself worrying that they were talking about her. She also felt that there were strong elements of fear and guilt that were the legacy of prior religiosity. And then, of course, there were one or two people she was not on speaking terms with and hadn't been for years. For Ciara, everything going on in town, including the success or failure of businesses, could be explained if you knew the true ins and outs of the people involved. She had friends or family in every sport. For her, *Cuan News* was not the fortnightly magazine with this title but a nickname for that woman who knew all the gossip.

The Arrival of the Blow-Ins

Whatever the views and experiences of the Cuan-born, they represent a village that had been a mere 2,300. The majority population today are the blow-ins who have come in waves since the 1970s and whose experiences are crucial to understanding contemporary Cuan. Some living in the oldest estates find it quite strange to reflect back on when they first arrived and recall that coming to live in the town actually felt a bit like going abroad. One Dubliner told how the catalyst was when several friends moved to Australia. He had felt that if people were going that distance, then he might as well move as far as Cuan because 'at least it's still in Ireland'. One man who came in the 1950s claimed at that time he felt there was a distinct accent different from Dublin. Eamon, like many others, came from Dublin in the 1970s simply because that was how far you needed to go to find affordable housing. Noel recalls moving in as one of the first blow-ins early in that decade by putting a £10 deposit on a house. Many had rather fortuitous reasons to be there. One came because his wife's brother-in-law was an architect involved in the new housing. Another was looking for opportunities to become a hairdresser. Michael recalls that 'we ended up here quite by accident. We looked at three different houses and both the location and the house design we preferred Cuan, and once we got here I think we kind of realized that it really was a nice place to settle and never regretted it.' The most common expression was that at the time Cuan was simply 'off the beaten track', which was something confirmed by the look that their friends in Dublin gave them when they admitted that they had bought a place in the town.

Eamon recalled that the car journey around the coast to Cuan seemed long and winding. His wife, Katherine, hated the place at first. They didn't really know people, which meant there was little support for her as a new mother of three children compared to living in Dublin, where she had family and established friends. Katherine's only outing was to walk twice a day by the sea. She remembers the people of Cuan as being quite unfriendly to the blow-ins, whom they regarded as pretentious. She tells a story of going to the grocery and asking for yoghurt, to be met by the loud riposte: 'This woman wants yoghurt. What the hell is yoghurt?' A common expression used about the blow-ins was that they were 'the people on the hill who were also on the pill'.

Noel recalled being at an event and someone saying, 'Blow-in! Speak when you are spoken to.' He tried to join the golf club but gave up because of the amount of local politics involved. This attitude has not entirely disappeared. As noted in chapter 1, there was a major controversy over trees on pavements. At the time, a friend from one of the original Cuan families insisted that those making a fuss couldn't really be from Cuan itself; these green activists, for whom he clearly had little time, had to be blow-ins. Things were made especially difficult for one man who had moved to Cuan from a nearby town with which there was an established historical rivalry, as he was ostracized for a considerable period. The isolation of the early blow-ins had its recompense, however. One of them noted how the indigenous population all seemed to be related to each other, so they couldn't move without being accosted by a cousin.

Historically, most children in Cuan were expected to leave school at fourteen and find work in fishing or agriculture, or perhaps become nuns or priests: one traditional fate of surplus children in Ireland. But expectations were rapidly changing, especially for the children of these blow-ins, but also for a cadre of blow-in women who already had been strongly influenced by nascent feminism and tried to become the first women on the board of various institutions. They might also have been sporting mini-skirts to local disapproval. But then Cuan itself was modernizing. It was during the 1970s that people saw a shift to central heating and the last houses were finally getting their indoor toilets that could then match the standards of the new housing where the blow-ins were settling.

There was, however, an entirely other side to this migration. The people discussed so far who came to Cuan for either fortuitous or economic reasons were in fact probably the minority of the blow-ins, at least with respect to the earlier settlement of the 1970s. For the majority, there was one dominant reason why they had decided to come to Cuan. This was the legacy of the town's period as a holiday destination for several decades, mainly in the first half of the twentieth century. This was a time when it had attracted the best bands and had the best dance floors. The tourism was based on quite a peculiar tradition. Many of the older homes in Cuan had a reasonably large garden space. During the summer months, as noted in chapter 5, the residents would rent out their own houses to these tourists and live in a much smaller home built within their own gardens. In the active retirement group, people reminisced about that time when the conversations were all about whether they had managed to find a summer tenant yet.

From the perspective of the Dubliners, this worked well, since quite often they would rent such accommodation for their family while the working man would visit mainly on weekends or short periods through the summer. This meant there would be a large number of children with strong and fond memories of their time spent in Cuan associated with holidays. One reminisced about the wonderful springy dance floor. Another recalled how Cuan was especially good because where she lived in Dublin it was not safe on the main road and they were not allowed out much to play, whereas when they came to Cuan she felt completely free.

The result was a generation for whom Cuan was an idyll, representing the best of memories. By the 1970s, Cuan was no longer a tourist destination but the generation who had stayed there were now grown up and wanted to buy their own homes. Their memory of Cuan as an ideal location is likely to have played a major role in their decision to settle there. For some, as in the case quoted above, the initial experience of Cuan was very likely quite disappointing and not at all as they had hoped. But their past experiences might well have helped galvanize the blow-ins in their commitment to then transform Cuan into the location they had always hoped it would be. Indeed, what emerged from the ethnography and oral history was that this is exactly what they succeeded in doing.

The Emergence of Community

The oral history of the blow-ins probably exaggerates the conservatism of the indigenous population, who may already have seen themselves as amongst the most progressive regions in Ireland. After all, Cuan was a holiday resort, with its vibrant music scene making it likely to have been one of the more modern and cosmopolitan villages well before the blow-ins arrived. While clearly there was some distancing from the blow-ins, others, such as the estate agents, were doing very well out of this transformation and were active in support of change. They and others saw how this was leading to a general commercial uplift and joined hands with the blow-ins in helping transform the town. Nevertheless, almost everyone agrees that much of the energy and commitment to the subsequent transformation of Cuan came from the blow-ins.

They also agree that there was a key moment at which pretty much everything changed. This was the event that allowed the blow-ins to effectively bond as an incipient community and which then built the momentum that led to their active engagement in creating the contemporary and beloved Cuan of today. Eamon, already referred to, was a key figure in this. At the time, Cuan already had a drama association supported by a local priest. One of the new features was an interest in musicals. But nothing had been attempted that was remotely of the scale of their 1979 production of *Guys and Dolls*.[4]

For whatever reason, the production of *Guys and Dolls* was the catalyst that crystallized the blow-in community. By the time one included all the people sewing costumes or helping to make props, organizing the tickets and advertising the show, the production had brought in hundreds of people. The cast itself was nearly a hundred-strong. The memories of working together, of queuing together, or simply of enjoying this enormously successful production took on the proportions of legend. Even forty years later, an event celebrating the anniversary of the show, held by the history society at the bowls club, had a kind of electrifying effect on those who were present; they ran out of chairs for this event. After the success of the musical, a particularly zealous blow-in who had moved to Cuan in 1970 took a lead in raising funds, as a result of which the CCA centre was built in the early 1980s.

It is perhaps not surprising that blow-ins dominate most activities, given that they would be the numerical majority, but there was more to it than that. Blow-ins took the lead in almost everything that speaks to the idea of Cuan itself as a community. They would run the fortnightly *Cuan News*, be mainly responsible for running the CCA, present papers in the Cuan Historical Society. In short, they turned Cuan from simply the place you happen to be born and live in into a self-designated and self-conscious community deluged in the self-praise of its inhabitants. Still today they take a lead, for example, in finding ways to integrate the latest migrants at the newest Brittas

Estate into the activities already established in Cuan, just as they did for the previous waves of blow-ins.

The primary reason for this was most likely that the creation of Cuan was something the blow-ins needed far more than the indigenous population. Institutions such as the CCA are a self-conscious and deliberate construction based around an abstracted concept called *community*. The Cuan that had previously existed hadn't needed to construct community, because family and Church were simply taken for granted as the fabric of life. By contrast, the incoming community were sundered both from family and the network of friendship that comes from school and neighbourhood. They were also more secular, or at least less bound to the Cuan Church. As just noted, many of them had come with the legacy of their holiday experiences that led them to see Cuan as idyllic. But this was no longer a holiday; it was everyday life. If they wanted Cuan to be all that they had imagined, then they had to actively create a town that would live up to this image.

This would never have worked, however, if there had remained a separation between the prior village and the blow-ins. But in contemporary Cuan the two work together very well. The secret as to how that was achieved is best understood if we scale up an observation made in the introduction to this book about what happens when two strangers meet. They first seek to find the people they know in common, at which point they are comfortable in their own relationship. This helps explain the unexpected finding that many blow-ins research and present papers to the local history society even though they have no ancestors in Cuan.

Today, in many affluent regions, one finds some kind of local history society. Commonly, there is considerable interest in older history and local archaeology, in artefacts and remains. While such papers have been presented, the overwhelming emphasis during the Cuan historical society's regular talks is on relatively recent history, including oral history. This is still, however, a time prior to the arrival of the blow-ins. A meeting of the historical society would include both blow-ins and those with long-resident families in Cuan. When a blow-in gave a talk, they would invariably mention someone who had been living in Cuan in the 1920s or 1940s. That would then elicit comments from people present who actually knew, or whose parents knew, that individual. Once this pattern is established, that they are talking about someone in common, then there is no longer a barrier between blow-in and locally born. What works for two strangers meeting also works collectively.

How Community Operates

The traditional heart of the community had been the Catholic Church. For many people, that role is relegated to events such as Christmas, first communion, and funerals. But there remain those older people for whom almost everything they understand as community comes through the Church. They regularly attend mass, following which they may have tea in the church itself, or join one of a series of smaller groups who then meet up at the town cafés and stay the entire morning. They sing in choirs, compose the parish bulletin, and keep the church spotless. They think in terms of grace, sin, and confession and whether the person they are talking to is Catholic. But looking around during a service reveals most of them to be older or indeed elderly.

Outside of the Church, the organization that stands *primus inter pares* (apart from the previously discussed sports associations) is Tidy Towns. As described in chapter 3, Tidy Towns feels like the heart of voluntary activities. Its success has become one of the various virtuous circles that help maintain this community development. As was previously noted, this has only been bolstered further by its increasing association with environmentalism. Other relevant institutions include the library, with its computer courses. There is also a very active Citizens Advice Bureau where several of the research participants volunteer. The charitable sector includes meals-on-wheels, St Vincent de Paul, the Samaritans, and a very popular charity shop where people frequently meet, equally as helpers or customers. There is a very helpful newsflash sponsored by the CCA that goes out to most households by email on an almost daily basis. The fortnightly *Cuan News*, which almost everyone reads and discusses, seems to hit just the right notes by focusing upon the low-key achievements that everyone can associate with, such as children's activities, someone's pet dog, or celebrating a hundredth birthday, as well as the rather remarkable litany of very impressive achievements in publishing, music, and other activities in which Cuan seems to punch above its weight.

An important new player in all of this is Facebook. A mere decade before this fieldwork, Facebook was derided by older people as a narcissistic site for teenagers to post selfies on. I was strongly criticized by both the BBC and *The Economist*[5] when I suggested in 2013 that Facebook was no longer cool for young people.[6] By 2018, however, it had become clear to everyone that young people had largely migrated to other platforms. Instead, Facebook had become something altogether different. It was now thriving, for example, as the face of the Cuan community. The most active Facebook groups included, not surprisingly, Tidy Towns, but also the CCA and *Cuan News*. Practically every sports and arts group in Cuan had a presence on Facebook. The young may have largely deserted Facebook but, as noted above, Cuan boasts some of the best-established Instagram influencers in Ireland – yet one more reason for young people to associate with and be impressed by the town they come from. The role of Facebook was further enhanced during Covid when, as mentioned in chapter 6, within a remarkably short time thousands joined the newly established 'Cuan Against Coronavirus' Facebook group, which then became an important resource for the organization of volunteers to help those particularly affected by the crisis if they were shielding or needed help to obtain their groceries.

If it was a musical that galvanized the sense of community for the early blow-ins, then, for the latest influx of blow-ins on the Brittas Estate, the sense of a collective is being formed through the Brittas Estate Facebook group. Since the properties on the estate are almost identical, the Facebook group is an ideal place for asking questions about how the functions of the house operate, or when something infrastructural can't be found or goes wrong. It is the place where people report lost property. Rather as neighbours a century ago would have come round for a cup of sugar, Facebook is the place where someone might ask to borrow a garden tool they only need once every couple of years. The group even organized a community-level Christmas collection for the postman. The importance of Facebook was also evident in that it was already turning into the site of local community anxieties: for example, people 'giving out' about the youths who seemed to be hanging around in the local playground and were assumed to have come from the Vartry Estate rather than the Brittas Estate.

A key aspect of community is the establishment of routine. It is because someone goes every week to the active retirement group to play bingo, to the church for mass, to the café for coffee with the same group of friends, to the breast-feeding group, to the Spanish- or

Irish-language practice group, to the Men's Shed, or to countless other groups, that ensures that they will see other people with sufficient frequency for proper friendships to develop. A second important element, at least in Cuan, seems to be the strong integration and involvement of local businesses. One hairdresser helps organize the community support amongst Cuan businesses. An estate agent may run the walking group. The local chamber of commerce works closely with the CCA in making decisions. The person who founded the local bookshop would also be in local book discussion groups. One pub is closely associated with the lifeboat volunteers, another with the local betting shops, and others with various sports and hosting weekly music sessions. The supermarkets have notice boards for community activities and are prominent in all forms of sponsorship. As a result of all this activity, Cuan businesses are seen not as distant capitalist enterprises but rather as places that might employ your children when they are teenagers and whose owners might live on the same street.

Another feature that closely bonds commerce to the town is the ubiquity of raffles. It seems impossible to hold any event in Cuan without a raffle. As suggested in chapter 7, by introducing this element of luck, raffles also contribute to the insistent egalitarianism of the town. But there is also an expectation that the raffle prizes will be sponsored by local commerce, which must receive a prodigious number of requests for such sponsorship and seem to at least try to respond positively to most of them. An important element is also the way the town keeps a wary eye on the encroachment of big business. The CCA has always tried to favour local owner entrepreneurship and protect it from outside business interests. At one point it helped thwart an attempt to buy Cuan harbour and there are conflicting reports about its relationship to attempts by big supermarkets, other than the one already present, to be established there. Finally, campaigners sought to establish a 'no-fry zone' when a fast-food chain tried to open an outlet too close to a local school.

Maria

Mostly, blow-ins came either from Dublin or from a rural background. Maria was born on a farm in central Ireland. As a child, she was busy bringing food to the farmhands or clearing up after meals. There was no electricity and an outdoor toilet. Many of her recollections evoke the portrayal of the Ireland found in classic anthropological studies such as that by Arensberg and Kimball,[7] in that it was fully accepted that one son would inherit the farm and so the rest of the siblings needed to find some other occupation. Although there was a strong emphasis upon education, Maria's early interest in art was discouraged in favour of training for a 'proper job' such as shorthand typing. Her subsequent clerical work gave her some financial independence. Then, in the mid-1960s, she married a trainee accountant, which meant that by law she had to give up her own job. Following this, she had four children as well as several miscarriages. The children, who were born in Dublin, have been highly successful in their respective careers, with one of them living close by in Cuan and the others in England and the US.

The couple knew Cuan from renting a house there every summer, where Maria stayed with the children while her husband mainly commuted from Dublin. So, when the new estates were created from 1973, they initially considered moving to one of these. Instead, however, they purchased one of the older houses with a large garden, which turned out to be the perfect family home. Maria already had some connections thanks to her holidays, and with her children transferred to Cuan schools, plus participation in church activities, she soon knew plenty of people in the town. She was heavily involved in the production of *Guys and Dolls* and is still close friends with someone she first met in the queue for the auditions. As with so many others, she saw this as a pivotal moment for blow-ins such as herself. She also did voluntary clerical work that helped in the initial formation of the CCA. Subsequently, this evolved into her being present on the board of management of both a school and a local arts centre. By now, she was free to follow her original interest in the arts, to the extent that she decided to open her own art gallery in the town, largely on borrowed money. Her paintings were the exact right sort for creating the greeting cards that could be sold in her art shop or later at local cafés. For many years, she also ran a kind of arts club where those with similar interests could meet and discuss their work.

Now at the age of eighty, Maria had no problem transferring those interests to Instagram, where she followed a good number of Irish artists and posted her own work. Otherwise, she supported her children's involvement in various sports and continued to be involved in a minor capacity with the Church. She knew that, while three of her children seemed settled abroad, they were always talking about getting a place in Cuan, because the entire family retained that idea of the town as idyllic. As is often the case, it was work that kept the children from coming back, and having been very successful in their careers, it was hard for them to move from their metropolitan locations abroad.[8]

While there is much about Maria's life that characterizes the blow-ins, it is worth juxtaposing her story with that of Alice, who was introduced in chapter 5. Alice was born in the original Cuan social housing estate, later moving into the Vartry Estate, where she was equally involved in community activities. Some of these, such as the Christmas savings club which she ran, were specific to the Vartry Estate. But there were others, such as supporting the local school or Tidy Towns, where Cuan-born Alice and farm-born Maria could easily have found themselves working together for the common cause of Cuan.

Why Cuan Works: Geography and History

A book comparing an ethnography with philosophical accounts of the good life required its subjects to be positive about their life, but perhaps not as besotted with Cuan itself as was indicated in the introduction to this volume. This section will suggest that some of the reasons for this adulation are specific to Cuan and to good fortune. This is why the book is careful to apply these arguments only to Cuan and not make assumptions about other places, even within Ireland. This does not diminish the importance of Cuan as an example of what is possible, given the right conditions. Other towns have their own histories and circumstances that may also have worked in their favour and from which other lessons might be drawn.

The first of these more fortuitous factors comes from the influence of geography on history. The seaside location of Cuan accounts for its success as a holiday destination and the subsequent idyllic impression left on many of the blow-ins. Geographical factors also ensure that Cuan will probably not expand much beyond its present size, so long-term planners are looking to other towns for future growth. This spatial constraint favours Cuan as an 'organic' community, in that its size is natural to its geography. Eleven thousand is not such a small population, but is a size such that people feel they know most other people in the town, even if they clearly don't.[9] It is not quite big enough to attract most of the larger retail chains, which is why most businesses are local, with the benefits just discussed. Yet it is large enough to have spawned this extraordinarily comprehensive range of sports and other facilities and opportunities, especially for children. It can also host a decent-sized St Patrick's Day parade and a few minor festivals in which it can take pride. As previously noted, the central position of the GAA and some sports fields also help. For the later teens, however, Cuan becomes far too small and mostly they spend at least a period of time away before returning to have children.

Oral histories suggested that it was significant that the blow-ins did not come all at once, but in a series of waves based on each major building project. As a result, Cuan never felt overwhelmed by its migrants. Rather, each wave would settle and have children. They then naturally bonded with established residents through involvement in children's activities, especially at school and in sports: for example, helping each other with the transport or through volunteer sports coaching. There is currently a significant new wave based on the extensive Brittas Estate, still being built today, but this is fifty years from the first estate that attracted blow-ins. A recently returned individual noted, 'Now I love to see all the new blood coming into the town.' Each wave has regenerated the advantages and energies represented by these migrants. In some other parts of the world, migrants who have been discriminated against assert local identity by being opposed to the next wave of migrants. But the blow-ins of Cuan were always more self-confident and had a benign attitude to the further waves of blow-ins, helping them benefit from their own previous experience. Furthermore, the blow-ins were always predominantly Irish. There is evidence that around a third of those settling into the Brittas Estate are descendants of people from Cuan.[10] They might not have expected to be able to afford to live in Cuan, but can just about manage a mortgage on the newest estate, which is furthest from the town centre.

Just as new waves of people helped reinvigorate community, so did new causes. The initial CCA was focused on developing Cuan's physical infrastructure. Later waves took up progressive projects such as tackling inequalities. Most recently, there has been an evident shift towards environmental and sustainable goals. Just as the momentum starts to fall away as goals are fulfilled, new challenges bring new energy to local initiatives. Similarly, the CCA would have originally drawn from people with higher education and visions of community, while now it includes more people with professional expertise, since currently the key problems concern dealing with bureaucracy and red tape.

The result is this clear positive feeling of community. The most quoted examples of everyone in the town coming together related to tragedies at sea – when people were lost or drowned. That such events were still possible created a strong sense of a town united in effort or grief. But this percolated down to much smaller collective concerns: for example, when people had been subject to house-breakings. The community came together not only to support those whose private space had been violated, but also to assert that the culprits probably came from another town. The Vartry Estate might have been an important caveat to this glorification of the town, but mostly people simply ignored it when they were thinking about Cuan as a locality. Their image of Cuan would be dominated by the older, more characterful section along the seafront, which pre-dates the estates, rather than glancing backwards to either Vartry or Brittas.

Cuan's Virtuous Relationship to the State

A quality of Cuan society described in chapter 1 was the general lack of interest in power: the fact no one wants to be the chair of anything and that they only undertake these roles as good citizens when it is their turn to do so. The two individuals who subsequently became prominent politicians were conviction politicians who wanted to 'do something'. But how does this individual and micro-politics relate to the power of the Irish state? To achieve almost any public task involves larger networks and lobbying for the funding required for, say, a children's play area or a better water supply. Then there are all the regulations that have to be agreed upon for a new voluntary development around sustainability or for helping people in need.

A member of the local regional council was usually present at the weekly Men's Shed, giving advice on dealing with bureaucratic requirements: for example, when applying for government grants. Another was present when the active ageing committee tried to formulate a scheme to help elderly people reach the local hospital or care homes since there are none within Cuan. Observing the details in such interactions revealed the way Cuan benefits from another 'virtuous circle', based on the mutual benefit that accrues to both sides of negotiations with the state. The regional councils and the state are involved in hundreds of such interactions with each and every local community. Often these can be quite frustrating, since to be successful a project requires an effective local organization that may not exist. In such cases, even a willingness to invest and support resulted in little by way of positive results. Some populations probably retain that older respect in Ireland for the clever rogue who thwarts the state. There are those skilled in making money off the state by using fake litigious claims which prise financial benefits and damage the government's ability to be locally involved for fear of such litigation. By contrast, people in Cuan, many of whom have previously worked for the state in some capacity, tend to side with the state and complain that insurance companies and government give in too easily to such claims so as to avoid the costs of court proceedings, which 'only encourages them'.

All of this meant that state and local authorities knew from experience that if they agreed funding for a Cuan initiative or needed to implement a government directive in a locality, then they would find a corresponding group in the town who were easy to work with, often one including individuals who had professional experience within government itself and knew how to couch requests in the right phrases and talk the talk of community development. Furthermore, they had genuine networks and support within Cuan such that they met their deadlines and ensured high-quality results. For example, Fiona had previously held an important position in local government and was now chair of one of Cuan's voluntary associations. She saw the problem as the sheer number of progressive initiatives, many of which didn't know of each other. This provided her with a clear goal of 'joining the dots', which she did very effectively. Not just the local dots, however; she was helping to ensure the state's health services collaborated better with the transport services. But then this is just the sort of thing she used to do when working for the regional council. Her other main concern was to develop techniques for consulting local people that were more genuine than just getting people to tick boxes. Not every older person wants to discuss a five-year plan, but given the right tea and biscuits they might.

The presence of people such as Fiona meant that when the regional council was presenting itself to the higher state authorities, it could point to its Cuan endeavours as examples of its successes, to show how well its money had been invested. While other places were seen as a source of endless complaints, Cuan was often the source of its compliments. Cuan had become the poster child for local state investment. There would be occasional rows, over charges for rubbish bins, or water supply, but at a far lower rate than in most other communities. In turn, people in Cuan knew how to leverage this reputation to raise funds and government support more easily than a less affluent town with less active and professional leadership. This was the virtuous circle of a largely middle-class professional location. As a result, Cuan was almost certainly differentially supported compared to a less well-resourced town. This could be legitimated through appeal to a meritocratic ethos. Cuan argued that the town deserved to be supported because it had acted as good citizens should. From this perspective, being even better supported was 'fair'.

The Tensions

What was remarkable was the sheer lack of counter-examples to this consensual idyll. Everywhere else I have conducted ethnography, it is soon evident that diving beneath even the most placid surface reveals constant factions, frictions, and historical disputes. The best evidence for the paucity of these in Cuan was that it always seemed to be the same two disputes that were recalled historically and mentioned many times over. Neither was particularly severe. One was a dispute as to the direction that the local theatrical group should take in respect to the kinds of play and performances they should put on. The other was a dispute over a planned re-routing of the local traffic through a one-way system with implications for various spaces, parking restrictions, and fees. Somehow these two had become almost legendary in the history of Cuan. Perhaps because they were the only examples.

There were of course periodic complaints about some services, such as the water supply or sanitation, but these would bond rather than sever the community. Only one internal dispute occurred during the fieldwork itself: the issue over tree roots becoming an impediment to mobility vehicles that was discussed in chapter 1. As noted there, the CCA was its usual effective self in defusing the situation, ensuring widespread and transparent consultancy. Quite soon the emphasis was redirected to questions of how to make requisite changes in the most environmentally acceptable manner, since ultimately environmental activists were also concerned with mobility vehicles and the elderly.

Conclusion

The core question addressed by this chapter is a simple one: how was Cuan created as a community? It started with the point made by one of the earliest interviewees that the people born in Cuan hadn't required a community since they mostly socialized within families and through the Church. Between the large number of children and family intermarriage, what mattered was kin rather than an abstraction called community. Hilda recalled growing up as one of nine in Cuan. All her siblings went to the same Cuan school and tended to stick together. Many still lived within half a mile of each other and the Church dominated any public activity that Hilda attended. The identification with Cuan as a town came largely from rivalry with the other localities around it, expressed in competitive sports. Others associated Cuan more with the benefits of dance halls and the incoming tourists.

None of this was true for the blow-ins. They arrived from the 1970s almost entirely as couples planning to have children, which meant that they were committing to a nuclear family but without the support of an extended family. As 'the people on the hill who were also on the pill', they tended to be more secular and more invested in modern developments. They had often worked in government, had experienced higher levels of education, and were familiar with the more overt politics of Dublin, all of which would have fostered a concept of community in its more abstract and idealized guise.

Community was therefore something the blow-ins both needed and wanted, and not surprisingly it was the blow-ins who did most of the heavy lifting when it came to building Cuan as a contemporary community. For example, Mona, a shop assistant, had come from a more traditional rural area to settle in Cuan. She was actually very surprised that she knew far more people in Cuan than in her old village. On reflection, she realized that this was precisely because family had been sufficient in her natal village, while in Cuan she had had to develop all those networks that ensured her children were fully integrated. This chapter has provided a long list of reasons, some quite specific, others more general, for how and why this town became such a successful community.

It was hard to resist the constant repetition of Cuan-love that is felt by most people who live in Cuan today, and this book shows just how much I failed. In any case, anthropologists tend to readily associate with their fieldsites. But they also feel obliged to recount the problematic and divisive aspects of society. The village in India where I conducted my Ph.D. was riven by hierarchy and exploitation. The young people I spoke to in small rural settlements in Trinidad couldn't wait to leave the place they associated with spite and vengefulness from quarrels that went back generations, and the claustrophobia of everyone knowing everything about you. My study of English hospice patients revealed the traditional animosity to neighbours and the loneliness that resulted from the protection of domestic privacy. So far from a romance of the indigenous or of long-term continuity, these previous studies had revealed the extent to which historical poverty rarely produces community. Mostly, it creates the necessity of economic interdependence, which is then resented. In Cuan, by contrast, the networks were those that people had chosen, not the mere juxtaposition of neighbours, in the same way that friendship was supplanting kinship as the preferred mode of sociality. Above all, community in Cuan was the product of its migrants. Cuan was not an inheritance, but something that people could view as their own labour. This is not just a challenge to the way anthropologists and most people tend to think about authentic community as historical. As the next chapter will show, it also provides an unusual perspective on at least one highly influential philosopher.

— Chapter 10 —

PLACING HEIDEGGER

Heidegger

The last chapter brings us back to the starting point of the entire enterprise: an appreciation of Cuan's sheer love of Cuan; the palpable joy of place that precipitated this enquiry into the good enough life. It turns out that this phenomenon is quite recent and derives not from indigeneity, but mainly from the work of migrants attempting to realize their abstract ideal of community. It may seem an odd choice to juxtapose this discussion about the creation of a place next to the German philosopher Martin Heidegger (1889–1976), whose principal work has the title *Being and Time*,[1] not being and space. This seemed appropriate, however, because the incorporation of Heidegger's work into social science has been dominated by a secondary element to his writing. Issues of space and place are fundamental to the impressive and sustained work of philosophically inflected writing by British cultural geographers such as David Harvey.[2] I spent much of my university years skiving off from lectures I was supposed to be going to and instead attending those in cultural geography, because the level of discussion was inspiring and exciting. An often-cited contribution was Heidegger's concept of dwelling. In anthropology, too, there are influential discussions of Heidegger by Tim Ingold and others concerned with dwelling.[3] This, then, sounded like an ideal point of juxtaposition. However, as this chapter will show, this did not prove possible, at least with regard to the discussion of Heidegger's principal work. But if instead attention shifts to some of his later essays, then a critique can be deployed to consider the implications of this ethnography.

Why might Heidegger's thoughts on place matter for the findings of the ethnography? This chapter has a specific political aim. The current dehumanizing of migrants and asylum seekers found in contemporary UK politics is appalling. There has been a continual ratcheting up of an unbelievable level of gratuitous cruelty to people who have often fled from oppression, rape, poverty, and war. This is repeatedly legitimated by reference to nativist populist politics, which are often seen as the most effective mode for achieving electoral success by right-wing politicians. After completing the ethnography in Cuan, it seemed that the achievements of the blow-ins could support a critique of common and popular assumptions about the relationship between authenticity, indigeneity, and place. The initial aim of this chapter was therefore to use the example of Cuan to counter, not just a philosophical tradition, but also the political exploitation of those ideas to justify some of the most barbarous treatments of human beings both historically and today. It therefore matters a great deal to show that effective community can be the positive creation of migrants rather than something inherited by an indigenous population.

This led to the second reason for focusing upon Heidegger. The extensive discussions within cultural geography had led me to believe that Heidegger had made a significant contribution to a more formal philosophical underpinning of the German concept of *Heimat*. These discussions also suggested that this represented a clear alignment between Heidegger's formal philosophy and his own private and public political stance. *Heimat* stands for the idea and the ideal of a deep historical relationship between a people and their homeland, one that unfolds over centuries to produce a profound and authentic relationship between the two. It is generally held that this belief in *Heimat* was one of the foundations for the rise of National Socialism and the Nazi affirmation of the German *Völkisch* movement as creating a superior form of humanity to those regarded as rootless, most particularly the Jews.

Initially, there seemed to be clear grounds for associating Heidegger with this *Heimat* tradition, since there can be no doubt that he was firmly attached to many of the principles and politics of National Socialism. In a book concerned with Heidegger's failures with regard to 'the Jewish Question', Berel Lang provides a litany of quotations and actions that demonstrate his stance.[4] These range from a positive reference Heidegger wrote for a potential staff member at his university who he hoped would act as a bastion against 'Jewification',[5] to his affirmation of the *Volk* that 'Only from the Germans can world historical mediation come – provided that they find and defend what is German'[6] and that 'The Fatherland is Being itself, which from the ground up carries and ordains the history of a Volk as one that exists: the historicity of its history.'[7] The relatively recent publication of the Black Notebooks,[8] a set of thirty-four notebooks Heidegger wrote over forty years, has further eradicated any doubt about his allegiance. It appears that, to the degree to which Heidegger distanced himself from the Nazi Party, this was because its wider idealization of the *Volk* tradition had become based on a national or universal rather than a local conceptualization. By contrast, Heidegger was fond of using examples based on the traditional rural German peasantry – examples which depend on a sense of immediacy in locality rather than this Nazi abstraction of *Volk* as ideology. In short, Heidegger was perhaps more wedded to *Heimat* than was the Nazi Party.[9]

There was therefore every reason to expect an alignment between these personal beliefs and a philosophy that constantly places emphasis upon the *being-in*, the *being-there*, and various versions of being *situated*. A careful analysis of Heidegger's philosophical writings by Jeff Malpas demonstrates that topology (the relationship between places) is as central to his philosophy as is temporality. *Being and Time* could then also have been called *Being and Place*. Yet what Heidegger actually meant by such terms turns out to be something rather different. Malpas specifically repudiates the critical comments by cultural geographers such as David Harvey and Doreen Massey, who have taken his political allegiances to be expressed in his formal philosophy, suggesting that these are a misunderstanding of Heidegger.[10]

I am inclined to agree with Malpas. Despite my desire to neatly fit Heidegger into this emblem of the values and ideas that I had intended to critique, a more careful reading of *Being and Time* suggested this book could not serve such a purpose. Instead, it seemed that a more honest approach to Heidegger would be to link his work back to a section of this book's introduction devoted to the discussion of Kant. It is more plausible to suggest that *Being and Time* is principally directed, as is so much else in philosophy, to an argument with Kant's transcendental philosophy and other forms of post-Cartesian ideas concerning the fundamental nature of being. To reprise some of the discussion of Kant in the introduction, the appeal of Kant within philosophy was that he demonstrated that there was a requirement for philosophy to engage in a deeper level of enquiry based on that which had to be *a priori* before we even come to the nature of reason. This is typical of a core philosophical tradition that is constantly trying to excavate beneath what is seen as the superficiality of whatever we regard as apparent, and to demonstrate their archaeological prowess in finding a still more foundational level.

What Heidegger sets out to do, then, is to return us to an earlier starting point than the conscious 'I' associated with the writings of Descartes. As with Kant, he wants to go back not only into the traditions of metaphysics and the transcendent, but still further. This is why these critical readings of *Being and Time* as an intentional justification for a sense of place in the spirit of *Heimat* are mistaken. If Kant understood space as *a priori* with respect to reason, then Heidegger asserts what he calls Dasein or Being, as that being in the world that comes before any form of objectification. As Hubert Dreyfus shows, Heidegger is trying to reveal to us a state of being that is prior to consciousness, intentionality, or practical activity.[11] Dasein is that primordial sense that there is a capacity for orientation based on concern with that in which being will be situated. It is prior to engagement with any actual space. It is this state of concernfulness with the world that will then subsequently lead us, in the sense of give us a reason, to make sense of our world through aspects of consciousness such as spatial orientation. But Heidegger is concerned with something earlier and more latent. First, we have to appreciate Dasein as the ultimate pre-cognitive *a priori*. Heidegger is concerned with the conditions of sense-making that *prefigure* any discussion of place. A positive way of interpreting this argument about concernfulness is to view Heidegger as trying to ensure that our care for the world is primary, and needs to be asserted before, and protected from, the kind of objectification found in theory and in science.

In *Being and Time*, Heidegger tries to develop a language of spatiality that is irreducible to our more conventional understanding of space.[12] I am sure my summary oversimplifies, but in my reading, it seemed that Heidegger is arguing that Being (Dasein) is a primordial but constant process that is based on our acceptance of our already being situated in the world, but prior to any actual engagement that would thereby objectify that world. Before we are practically engaged in the world, we recognize that the things around us are of interest to us because of their potential, their readiness to hand. The hammer is a thing we use, but prior to that it is a potential that will be perceived to be part of our imagination of being engaged in the world. Even this imagination is already too far towards objectification, the state that Heidegger is trying to avoid. Prior to this sense of things as 'ready to hand' is an awareness that the world is situated prior to us being situated. As Heidegger explains in a later work concerning technology,[13] the possibility of nature – as in the seed's potential to germinate – is part of the interconnectedness into which we as human beings are thrown. Initially, we are aware that we exist as already situated within this interconnected world, but it is an understanding of this latency that is key. In the same way that we may have a conceptual awareness of the implications of seeing something prior to actually seeing it, we also have an orientation that is not yet of a conceptual form. So, prior to making specific things, the objects of our concern are ready to hand. We first have a sense of the essence of concernfulness itself as a latent but essential preparedness to be concerned about these objects.

In Heidegger, despite discussion of us being already thrown into the world, there is his constant desire to go beneath and before. It is as though if we can describe something, we are already too far in the direction towards that thing for this to be an example of Dasein. It is only in that which is hinted at and problematized through the development of a terminology invented so as not to be merely the language we already understand that we can glean this essence. Since everyday language is already in close embrace of our alienated world, a world now redolent of technology, science, capitalism, and an overweening state, Heidegger must invent an unsullied language to discuss this primordial and more authentic condition.

To convey his idea of latency or the possibility of space prior to the experience of space, a key concept is that of de-severance. To be situated is to demolish the distance implied by any concerned orientation to the world. There is thereby an implication that we are making things more proximate in the sense of severing the distance of unconcern, what Heidegger calls circumspectual concern.[14] As Heidegger states, 'In Dasein there lies an essential tendency towards closeness.'[15] So we are clearly prepared to be concerned as an orientation to the world in which we are situated. But by using his own, rather than conventional, terminology, Heidegger tries to ensure that this use of the idea of proximity is not ever to be confused with everyday spatial proximity. He wants to make sure that the idea of distance he is discussing is not conflated with anything we would normally understand as distance in space. Proximity is not the de-severance of actual spatial distance. He notes that 'If Dasein, in its concern, brings something close by, this does not signify that it fixes something at a spatial position.'[16] 'Dasein is never present-at-hand in space.'[17] Dasein is a primordial condition that is about the essence or latency expressed by this idea of having concern, in that potentially something may matter to us prior to any actual manifestation of such concern.[18]

Being lies in the possibility and necessity of having care in respect to the world in which we are situated. Being comes prior to knowing, but it is still a presence rather than a theoretical apprehension. It is something pre-theoretical, in that Dasein is prior to what we normally imply when we use the word 'being'. Once being is an entity, it is no longer Dasein. Terms such as *prior* or *pre-* sound like references to temporality, but *Being and Time* is equally concerned to distance these concepts from merely apparent or conventional ideas of temporality. They are closer to the term *a priori* as used by Kant. This is not time as we know it and must be distanced from merely apparent time, just as we are now distanced from merely apparent or conventional space. Only in this manner, Heidegger argues, can he reveal a world that is free from the forces unleashed by industry and capitalism that have created the objectified world that we currently experience.

I am not a philosopher and certainly no expert on Heidegger. I have laid out my reading – almost certainly a misreading – of *Being and Time* principally to explain why I felt unable to employ that book in the way cultural geographers and others have used it, to critique Heidegger's political stance or stance on anything at all. As Pierre Bourdieu has suggested in an analogous critique of Heidegger,[19] the philosopher's emphasis upon considering the pre-ontological[20] conditions that make an enquiry into humanity possible obviates any actual contribution to our understanding of actual humanity.[21] As soon as we are engaged in anything we recognize as the world of time and space, we have parted company with Heidegger's Dasein. I can see why philosophers and others are interested in this speculative endeavour to find the pre-ontological. But personally, I simply don't believe this latent state exists other than in and through the language created by Heidegger. Therefore, despite Heidegger's prominence, *Being and Time* could not be used to find a correspondence with life as lived.

There are, fortunately, other later post-war essays by Heidegger that are more conducive to the task of engaging with Cuan.[22] Essays that focus more on technology and dwelling.[23] One much-cited essay of Heidegger's, probably because it is rather more grounded in exemplification, is called 'Building, Dwelling, Thinking'.[24] The essay asked what we mean by the German term translated as dwelling and how much deeper this might be than simply the idea of inhabiting a building. It suggests dwelling is more like an intrinsic condition of being human and also a desired condition of being spared from harm and at peace, free to be present. Much of the essay extends from a metaphorical discussion of the way a bridge creates its own landscape joining the banks and gathering together the features that turn this into a location. Heidegger argues that space is not a sort of measurement, but something akin to what the bridge is doing. So, a proper building is not just a place within which we reside, but it should be a structure of living or being in the world, expressed as this possibility of dwelling. What this has in common with his earlier work is Heidegger's striving to ensure that dwelling is never reduced to mere space. It is holistic, even spiritual, derived from the heart and then the hand.

The context for the essay is a wider argument about the drive for more housing after the Second World War. Heidegger is suggesting that merely building more houses is insufficient because the deeper problem is that we have lost the capacity for dwelling. He then provides one of his examples that give licence to proceed with this chapter's critique, because the essay exposes his nostalgia for some romantic past to set against the technocratic present, the same anti-objectivizing ethos that clearly influenced Adorno and Horkheimer's *Dialectic of Enlightenment*.[25] His model of the kind of building that can evoke dwelling, as he would wish it to be, is that of the traditional peasant farmhouse of the Black Forest. This brought together landscape, weather, the legacy of generations, and the spiritual: all necessary components of what Heidegger means by dwelling; that which makes the peasants authentic as opposed to the 'moderns' of twentieth-century Germany. While it was suggested that *Being and Time* is concerned with core issues of philosophy and therefore not really as engaged with politics in the manner suggested by some critics of Heidegger, these later essays do speak to Heidegger's alignment with the ancient German concept of *Heimat* (though necessarily that of the Nazis, since these ideas developed at a later period) and certainly link the authenticity of a people – a *Volk* – to their historical experience of dwelling.

Heidegger and Cuan

In the conclusion to this book, it will be argued that, in stark contrast to Heidegger, Hegel saw objectification not as a curse, but as an essential component of the process that makes dwelling possible. Dwelling, as opposed to merely living in a place, should be regarded as the product of objectification not of history. This is why we have so much more to learn about dwelling from Cuan than from Heidegger. The case of Cuan as described in the previous chapter could not be more different from Heidegger's romantic nostalgia for the German peasant. Dwelling did not come to Cuan as a given of history or indeed of being. The blow-ins consciously created Cuan as the manifestation of reason in the form of their prior idea and ideal of an ethical community. Like Hegel, they fully embraced objectification as a positive; deliberately and systematically creating community as a manifestation of their prior objective. They have nothing in common with the Black Forest peasants, who are assumed to inherit their condition as a given of history. As Karl Marx would equally have appreciated, Cuan is meaningful to the blow-ins because they not only created it through their labour, but they can also thereby see themselves in it and understand through it who they have become. Ironically, Heidegger's nostalgia may be viewed itself as much a product of industrialization as any factory. Nostalgia for a condition held to have existed prior to modern forms of objectification has itself become a mass-produced image that functions within a highly ideological critique of the contemporary – a critique that owes quite a bit to Heidegger.

This romantic ideal of pre-industrial holism, from which we are now sundered, has many versions. The German concept of *Heimat* is one of the most fully developed and linked to the concept of the population as *Volk*.[26] But it was by no means confined to Germany. During the nineteenth and twentieth centuries, the appeal of *Heimat* was especially strong because vast political movements were drawing on conservative politics, as people become anxious about the impact of modernization and change. Similar ideals and movements arose in some places through other versions of fascism, but more often as resurrections of (often invented) ancient roots and cosmologies. Ireland itself took part in this movement. Local and equivalent versions of the Germanic ideal of the *Volk* arose at that time partly because there were many clear parallels between the history of Germany and of Ireland. As Shane Nagle shows, 'Historians in both contexts proceeded from a sense of their nation as possessing a fractured past, a belated or arrested development, a past of historical weakness vis-à-vis its powerful neighbours, the absence of a nation state since the Middle Ages or even earlier and manifesting serious religious and regional heterogeneities.'[27] All of this provided ample reason to develop an assertive ideal of Irish Celtic culture and identity, given its political realization by de Valera through the politics of the newly independent Ireland, including an extremely close relationship to the Catholic Church, which exercised what Tom Inglis called a 'moral monopoly'.[28] In short, the Irish state first constructed itself in a movement analogous to the spirit of *Heimat*. It was only through the radical repudiation of this ideology and its association with the Church that people in Cuan were able to forge an alternative objectification that brought them so much closer to the good enough life.

Most of the research participants acknowledged that this triumphant achievement, represented by Cuan as the ideal place of dwelling, this heaven on earth, was principally the work of blow-ins, and not necessarily just Irish blow-ins. Being on the eastern coast, Cuan has been strongly influenced by people migrating from the UK, often without any Irish ancestry. These have now been supplemented by migrants from other countries, especially from Eastern Europe, who identify with Irish Catholicism and are sometimes now the stalwarts of the local Catholic churches; they could also blend in especially easily because they were white and middle class. During the ethnography, there were named and acknowledged individuals seen as contributing to the maintenance of Cuan as a successful community who had been born abroad. Both they and the blow-ins benefited from, and had an interest in, promoting the more cosmopolitan liberal outlook that is now characteristic of the wider Cuan population. This includes a very positive embrace of European identity that followed from Ireland becoming part of the EU, which enabled a reduction in the historical linkages with the UK and indeed with Irish tradition, thereby providing a broader sense of identity than post-Independence nationalism.

Historically, there have been many societies with *Heimat*-like qualities and others that were entirely different. If we return to the classical world, the Greek *polis* had its clear commitments to exclusivity and roots. Most of the people who lived within the *polis* would not have been citizens; more than half the population were women or slaves. You were Spartan or Athenian by descent. From 450 BCE, being Athenian depended upon descent from two Athenian citizens, making this effectively an endogamous society.[29] A large vote was required to make any exceptions. The *polis* was, then, analogous to *Heimat* societies to the degree that culture was viewed as a biological inheritance. This is remarkably different from the formation of the Roman Empire, which was replete with stories of how people who started as barbarians or slaves reached the heights of authority. Officially, the Roman Empire also had restrictions, at least to becoming full citizens. But the granting of successive grades of citizenship to outsiders became part of the policy of Romanization that allowed the Empire to expand and flourish. This meant that the Empire itself was increasingly the product of its blow-ins – a trend made official by the Edict of Caracalla in 212 CE.[30] Although many references have been made in this book that equate Cuan with the *polis*, in this respect it had far more in common with the Roman Empire. In conclusion, there are many ways in which people create place and associate with place. This can be just as successfully sustained by the incorporation of migrants as by an insistence on endogamy and internal reproduction.

These are important issues here as much for anthropology as for philosophy. Anthropology began with the study of small-scale communities where culture was viewed almost axiomatically as the product of long-term presence. Anthropologists can also romanticize indigeneity and, given their field's colonial history, many of them have felt a subsequent moral and political imperative to defend populations regarded as indigenous. More problematically, anthropologists are cited in defence of opposition to *cultural appropriation*, as though culture itself can be viewed as an inherited possession. Gradually, however, over the twentieth century, anthropologists started to appreciate that many of the societies they study are in fact of relatively recent development or have resulted from the integration of several different historical sources. They also began to suspect that their own prejudices masked a dynamic history of migration, change, and reconstruction.

My own work as an anthropologist has been dominated, first, by the study of consumption and, later, by an interest in the consequences of digital technology. Both these topics required a growing appreciation that culture is often *a posteriori* rather than *a priori*. As digital technologies spread across the world, they fragment and take on local aspects. Their authenticity is established through their subsequent appropriation by populations, not because they arose from those populations. One of the key publications I was recently involved in is called *How the World Changed Social Media*.[31] Note that we didn't call the book 'how social media changed the world'. What makes the smartphone smart is the ways in which it is transformed by users through creative deployment, adding apps and content. For the same reason, I tend not to align with the contemporary critique of cultural appropriation, preferring the stance of Paul Gilroy,[32] who favours an authenticity that comes from the dynamics of fusion and hybridity – from routes rather than roots.[33] All culture is hybrid. Therefore anthropology as much as philosophy gains from observing and learning how Cuan was created by its blow-ins and our capacity both to create worlds anew and then to regard them as equally authentic as historical worlds. This is also reflected in the wider liberalism of Irish society. People in Cuan would often relate with some pride, bringing it constantly into conversation, that the current Taoiseach was a gay man whose father came from India. Ultimately, then, the project of objectification exemplified in the way the blow-ins helped create Cuan is the perfect repudiation of any assumption that identity is only determined by ancestry.

A Caveat

Being and Time is a dense and difficult work with many alternative interpretations to the one provided in this chapter. I fully acknowledge that many others have found inspiration from Heidegger's writings. There are appeals to poetry and an ethos of care that may be seen as far from the dense prose of his primary work. Karsten Harries has argued that through the mysticism, nostalgia, and poetics, there are aspects of Heidegger's essay on dwelling that can remain an inspiration for architects.[34] The anthropologist Tim Ingold, who also has a much more sustained relationship to Heidegger's work than I can claim, reflects on the possibilities of a more positive juxtaposition that is achieved through focusing on Heidegger's insistence upon dwelling as an activity that precedes building, rather than involving merely inhabiting a building. He does this partly through his own reading of the same late essay by Heidegger on dwelling that I have critiqued. What he takes from Heidegger is the idea that 'dwelling in the world, in short, is tantamount to the ongoing temporal interweaving of our lives with one another and with the manifold constituents of our environment'.[35] This may well be a proper and helpful interpretation of that essay. Yet it still seemed important to acknowledge how the ethnography gives this argument a still more radical twist, by showing that this process is much less beholden to the prior construction of the environment by ancestors than we might have imagined. Contrary to Heidegger, I believe the path should be through objectification rather than through its avoidance.

Chapter 11

ENGAGING WITH THE WORLD

To pre-empt the chapter that will follow this one, there has been a tendency throughout the history of philosophy towards a certain disengagement from the world. There has been a natural inclination for philosophers to value what they do and extol what is essentially an exercise of the mind. Philosophy can thereby become the promotion of contemplation at the expense of a more physical engagement with and sensual experience of the world. Chapter 12 will illustrate this tendency through a discussion of the Stoics and Epicurus, but prior to that this chapter will provide evidence for a stark alternative represented by Cuan: a cosmology based on valuing a physical, sensual, and expanding engagement over that of abstract contemplation. How should we view that preference? Is there some way that this desire for increased engagement could be regarded as analogous to, or equivalent to, philosophy? Or are these two irreconcilable ways of being in the world? The first half of this chapter will examine the evidence for my research participants' relationship to just one activity, that of travel, followed by a brief introduction to their involvement in social activities. To beg some patience, this chapter is largely descriptive, and the more ambitious attempt to argue for the relationship between the evidence presented here and philosophy will unfold over the following two chapters.

Where Next?

As part of the slightly more formal interviews that comprised part of the ethnography, there was a question, put in various versions, asking mostly retired people what they still wanted from their lives. What was quite startling was that although the topic had not been implied or asked about as part of these questions, most people just took it for granted that asking about what more you want to do with the rest of your life was essentially a question about travel – where did they still want to visit. This was quite unexpected, but it goes to the heart of the arguments and evidence of this chapter, so I will elaborate on their answers.

A typical response came from Robert, in his seventies:

> I've done practically everything I want to do. ... I've been involved in the rugby clubs over in England. I went to Australia and New Zealand, I haven't been to South Africa. I might like to go to South America. I've been to Mexico, Cuba. I've been to New York and I've been to Boston.

Suzanne, in her sixties, wanted to go to Uruguay, Canada, and Australia, and if she had the money, she would buy a place in Spain. Patricia, again in her sixties, noted, 'Yeah, I definitely still want to travel. I enjoy travelling. Particularly I enjoy train journeys. The train journeys in India are quite the experience.' Clara, another woman in her sixties, simply stated, 'I don't really have aspirations, except places to go.' Similarly, Lilian, in her eighties, said she would still like to travel. 'If I had more money. Can't think of anything in particular. In the past ... I probably wanted to go on holiday a bit more.'

Closely linked to this emphasis upon travel is the concept of the 'bucket list', an expression which several people used explicitly, even if some noted that they disliked the term. The idea of a bucket list is matched by many popular books with titles such as *Fifty Places to See before You Die*. These bucket lists are dominated by travel, though they can include other ambitions, ranging from pop bands you want to see before you die or popular culture clichés such as swimming with dolphins. People do act on these. Sarah told of a visit to Sorrento in Italy that was determined by its presence on the bucket list she had made with her husband. She recalled that just before he died,

> I came in one day and he was on the computer and he said, 'Right, I've done it.' 'What have you done?' 'I've booked a holiday to Sorrento.' I had been leaving a brochure open every day. I never thought he'd take the hint. We had a lovely time and he had a lovely time.

The poignancy arose precisely from the fact that this was an ambition fulfilled just before her husband died.

In trying to explain cultural phenomena derived from ethnographic fieldwork, it is relatively rare that there is a single or simple factor that can be identified as the 'cause'. More commonly, there are a series of factors that start to align with and reinforce each other such that in aggregate they seem to account for that unexpected finding. This seems to be a case in point. The first factor facilitating local travel is that Irish people over the age of sixty-six are entitled to a pass for free travel on any transport in Ireland. This is a real boon that many take advantage of. Frances, in her seventies, noted that,

> I travel a bit more with my free pass. I want to visit Belfast to see the Titanic exhibition. I'll do that next week. My brother-in-law spends his time using free travel. I think it's an abuse in a sense. I know [I can use it] if I have time to go somewhere, but I wouldn't spend all day going up and down from Cork.

This implies that there are now some people who make very frequent use of this free travel. The active retirement group, described in chapter 5 and consisting mainly of older women who play bingo weekly, have a couple of outings a year by coach to other parts of Ireland and they may arrange something like a tea dance at that destination. Wealthier families may also holiday locally, and since they can afford boats, they may prefer to sail around the Irish coast or to Scotland, or perhaps simply along the River Shannon.

Another reason why people in Cuan might be particularly attracted to travel may derive from historical factors. After all, it was holidaying that had been the primary reason why many of my research participants came to Cuan in the first place. This may have left a legacy in this foregrounding of holidays. Another common reason for travel abroad was to visit family, since a high proportion of people in Cuan have relatives living abroad. A typical example might be this comment from Chris, also in his seventies: 'The only time I really did long-distance travel was to Australia. That was six years ago. Because our daughter and her husband and kids were out there.' Brian, in his seventies, noted, 'I've been most places. The only continent I've not been to is Australia. I have cousins there, maybe I should go. But when you fly as far as Singapore and realize you're only half-way there ... .' Oonagh, again in her seventies, mainly visited a property owned by her retired sister in the Costa del Sol, where she could stay in a self-contained flat and see her sister's children and grandchildren, several of whom were now fluent in Spanish. Sometimes the family connection was historical. Lilian wanted to go to Sri Lanka because her mother was buried there, while Suzanne wanted to go to Uruguay since her husband's great grandmother went there after they were married. Ireland is a small country on the periphery of Europe, with a history of emigration and a massive diaspora, and going abroad for work was a historical commonplace. These may be amongst the reasons why foreign travel is regarded as relatively mundane.

The contrasting justification for going abroad is to fully escape from family and other responsibilities. Once you are abroad, no one can ask you to baby-sit. If one factor dominates over all others, it is simply getting away from the Irish climate to somewhere warm. The weather factor would be behind the observation of Maria, in her eighties, that 'I probably wouldn't mind living in northern Spain for maybe six months or a year.' This is the core reason there was such a dramatic shift from Cuan itself being a holiday destination when people could afford to take holidays in Spain from the 1970s. With that kind of package holiday, people rarely cared much about the hinterlands; it was the sunbathing on the beach and playing cards around the swimming pool that they craved. Holidays may also be devoted to health and fitness, as in a walking holiday, with the Camino de Santiago as a prime example discussed in detail in my book with Pauline Garvey.[1] A walking holiday may also have a wider aesthetic appeal: for example, going to New England to see the autumn leaves, or experiencing the *sakura* (cherry blossom) season in Japan.

Different regions of the world represented different values. The main contrast was between an orientation to Europe as against a desire to visit places regarded as exotic, or the sites of the Irish diaspora such as Australia, the UK, or the US. The emphasis on Europe will certainly have been influenced by the rapid and recent shift towards the idea that Irish people are now themselves fully European, viewed as integral to, rather than replacing, the sense of being Irish. As described in chapter 1, this comes as a welcome movement away from the previous understanding of being Irish as within the compass of the erstwhile colonial power of the UK. It is unlikely to be a coincidence that within this sense of gratitude to what they have gained in becoming part of Europe, they end up wanting to spend their surplus money on having a 'little place in' – or at least visiting – the most familiar Western European countries, such as France and Spain.

In contrast was another of those unexpected and striking findings: how commonly this particular age group retained strong memories around 'Eastern' mysticism and music that was a key influence in the 1970s, even if they had not themselves been hippies. This seemed to have carried through right into their seventies. It reflected back to a period in their youth when going abroad meant looking for experiences of a transcendental kind. Some still retained the idea of going somewhere exotic to 'find themselves'. Barbara, in her sixties, was clear that it was only when travelling that she found out who she really was. This was because it was the only time when she felt she was free to be authentic, to be herself. As she put it, 'The only thing I'd crack up without is travel. Travel is me.' When her parents sold their property, she bought a flat in Spain, where she spent twelve weeks during the winter. Her next ambition was to go to St Petersburg, but also she would go back 'in a heartbeat' to Latin America. Travelling brought out something in her that was repressed at home. Barbara continued:

> I wouldn't dream of getting into the front of a taxi in Ireland. I'm nervous in all taxis in Ireland, especially Dublin. But I got into taxis in Buenos Aires on my own. Not a care in the world, not a bother, just dunno. I don't know what it is.

A related perspective comes from some people's conception of having lost authenticity. One woman had many stories about her experiences with shamans in Bolivia, or her time in Alaska, while others said they might return to India. They saw travel not as escapism to some fantasy, but rather as a search for the authenticity that they felt had been lost in Ireland, but which they projected onto the people they visited, who were regarded as in some ways pre-modern and therefore in touch with an original spirituality. A very different version of this search, which will not be reprised here since it is discussed in detail in my book with Pauline Garvey,[2] is the growing interest in pilgrimage. While some sites, such as Medjugorje in Bosnia, are mainly visited by devout Catholics, the main rise in pilgrimage, whether to Lough Derg in Ireland or the Camino in northern Spain, is a more secular ideal of getting in touch with a sort of generic spirituality.

This desire to find oneself abroad then split into two very different agendas, although there were those who managed to partake in both. The first was to own a property abroad. One couple had 'a little place in France' where they lived for three months of each year. In describing their life there, they stressed the degree to which they could be very different people. For example, they had no television in their French home, while they did have one in Cuan. In France, they went swimming quite a bit, but not in Cuan. There was also that greater sense of freedom 'where we can get away and have our own time, do our own thing'. They painted in their French home, they gardened, they relaxed, they cooked good food for themselves, accompanied by good wine. They enjoyed the context, which was a very small hamlet. If they went there in winter, only two of the thirteen other houses would be occupied. Within Cuan, they sometimes met up with other people who had a place in France, and this seemed also to be true of families who had a property in Spain. Their common possessions became a source of social bonding back within Cuan.

There were, however, quite a few people who would reject this option of a settled residence. Maria recalled,

> Generally speaking, we wouldn't go on holidays to the same place twice. We'd be looking for somewhere new. What sometimes surprises me is that people go back to the same place. There's people that go to Tenerife and that's all they do, go to Tenerife, so that kind of interests me or amuses me.

Of course, disparaging someone's possession of a property abroad could be interpreted as sour grapes, but listening to several such examples suggested a genuine difference in the route towards the use of holidays as fulfilment. Both are attempts to extend the experiences of life, but one concentrates more on extending who one can be, while the other is more focused upon extending what one has been able to experience. The former will also emphasize relaxation, while the later may be concerned to balance the life of a retired person with a continued sense of adventure.

A third version of enjoying time abroad was the preference for cruises, for which a common justification was that the cruise had a more social component. The cruise ship was a place where one met new friends and the adventure was at least as much in whom one might meet as what one might see, which was no surprise given the wider emphasis on sociality in Cuan. On the other hand, given the intense sociality of Cuan, some people went away precisely in order not to meet with people, new or otherwise. The cruise ship could be a compromise as one would only be meeting new people, while for the couple with their place in France, escape was achieved through meeting no one at all.

All these examples relate to the wider alignment between choice of vacations and the expression of wider values. These are also evident from the way people talk about their holidays on their return. This is a population that generally loves anecdotes suggesting that rather than a superficial 'beach and cocktails' holiday, they had achieved some encounter with authenticity. It doesn't have to be shamans and the indigenous (although there are examples of both). They may talk about how they developed a relationship to proper French cooking, or watched elderly men play board games on a Greek island. In some cases, travel is linked directly to more philanthropic concerns, including two individuals who travelled periodically to engage in charitable work. For them, it was important not only that they should see the struggles of the world, but also that they should use that vantage point to be involved in some way or other. In the case of Patricia, this had resulted in the development of some of her strongest personal friendships with a family in India.

Another issue that shows the complexities and contradictions involved in travel brings us back to the discussion of the 'satiable society', and the relationship to materialism. Many of these research participants had surplus money. They did not need or desire more material goods, while, as chapter 3 showed, they gained more status by disengagement from commodities as they generally ascribed to a green and sustainable ethos. Spending on holidays was a way of using money without accumulation. Also, Edmond, in his fifties, put it, 'I don't want things, but I want experiences. I want to travel and freedom for stuff like that. I don't want a flash new kitchen.' Even if they were not wealthy, travel had become a life priority. As Georgia noted, 'We went up on a cruise this year, we actually put money aside. Another thing I wanted to say to you, my husband thought cruises are very expensive but I wanted to do something different. I wouldn't go next year, but I would go again.'

Her sentiment brings out a further crucial piece of evidence with regard to the dominance of travel. This emerged from a quite different question also commonly asked during formal interviews: a question about how people decided when exactly to retire. It became clear that many people would continue in jobs they would rather have given up until they felt they had enough money for regular holidays and travel during retirement, which meant this had become a priority in envisaging future expenditure. Aspirations around travel were also evident for Lucy, a research participant, from the Vartry Estate, who, now in her fifties, had lived her entire life in relative poverty, and was currently working part-time washing up in a café. For her it was simply a wonder that she and her husband could now afford to go abroad so easily. Indeed, she was almost affronted at herself that she had barely set foot in Europe, and this was something she felt she now needed to do and greatly looked forward to.

There was also the sheer frequency of travel. Chapter 3 laid out the expectations of a taxi driver in terms of yearly travel, including Las Vegas and Aintree. To afford all this, he worked his taxi incredibly hard, often only sleeping a few hours each day or night. Mostly, the people from the Vartry Estate shared similar aspirations to the rest of Cuan, if at a more affordable level. When Rebecca, in her early sixties, said she went abroad around three times a year, she described this as 'not much'. Maria, who had been recently been to Portugal, to Greece with the drama society, and also to Russia, said this showed that she and her husband were 'moderately adventurous travellers'.

When people meet in public, one of the most common conversations is about where they have been on holiday. For example, when we sit around at the Men's Shed waiting for the meeting to formally start, men will give hints as to best modes of transport, or places to stay. At first, I assumed that this kind of conversation might be a way of demonstrating public status and conveying affluence. After a while, however, it became clear why this was mistaken. As a couple of people noted explicitly, in a situation where almost everyone can afford to travel, describing one's holidays doesn't really impress anyone. Instead, these conversations are regarded as a positive social concern to share advice and experiences which may help other people decide whether they would like to embark on the same trip and how best to accomplish it. Consistent with the arguments of the satiable society, the competitive element is much more likely to be conveyed through examples of thrift and declarations of how little one spends. This was exemplified by sixty-three-year-old Gráinne, whom we met in chapter 7. She noted:

Personally I think it's brilliant to go off with a rucksack and stay in a hostel. In Barcelona, I stayed in a very cheap pensione and did a cycle tour around the town. Walked down to the beach and found a free concert in the church and in the three days we got a great sight of Barcelona. This girl told me that she went to a five-star hotel down by the beach and saw that part of the city, went down to the sauna, had five-star hotel life, and I think went out once or twice. I feel sorry for people who think they need to bring a suitcase on holiday and stay in the five-star hotel to bring their wardrobe. I worked with a girl who was going to the Canaries. She had a trunk, she had an outfit and shoes for every day of the week. What kind of holiday is that?

Clearly, travel was an expression of her anti-materialism, not her affluence. It resonated with the way values and status have changed over recent years for many in Cuan. People will more often talk about the ways they saved money, than how they spent money, on holidays.

Travel as expansive culture is also related to the general theme of education. I was expecting to hear many more examples of formal education as a goal at this life stage, with retired people involved in taking online free university courses (MOOC) (partly because I have been involved in creating two of these). Once again, I was wrong, in that, while there were individuals who had followed this path, continued education was much less of a priority in retirement than I had anticipated. But one reason for my mistake may be that I had misunderstood the meaning of education. After a while, it became evident that many of these retirees saw education more as means than as a goal. A further degree course made sense in their forties or fifties for learning skills that they would then use, as in writing, music, or art. But by far the most common reason to be on a course at this later age was for language learning, with, for example, two dedicated Spanish courses available in Cuan, and this education was precisely in order to enhance their travelling. This was the same reason why older people had the Duolingo language learning app on their smartphones.

The sheer scale of this topic reflects the context of an extended period of relatively healthy life. But that is not indefinite. It will eventually be followed by a shift towards the shrinkage of such experiences that come with frailty as it affects people in their eighties and nineties. Terry, in his eighties, noted that,

While I am to some degree a 'home bird', ideally, I would like to be able to afford to do more travelling. As against this, I find that holidays can involve quite a lot of hassle these days, particularly when air travel is involved – so perhaps this deprivation is not such a major disadvantage. I find that nowadays I need far less in the way of entertainment and am quite happy to go for a walk or read a book.

Patricia remarked on what was quite a frequent dilemma for people in Cuan, given the very large number who had dogs. 'Yeah, I still love to travel. I have to balance that with that I love that dog on the couch and when I go travelling I have to put her into a kennels and I don't want her to spend her life in the kennels.' Even though she wasn't frail, Leah, in her early eighties, noted,

> I don't want to travel. I feel it sounds awful. I feel I have everything I need in my head. I have always moved too much. There was rarely a year I was in the same place. Rarely two years. I moved far too much. It's enough, yeah. It's not admirable, I'm sure. Everybody's going to see wonderful things and my daughter's a great traveller.

The slightly apologetic tone conveys her sense that this goes against the norm. It was common, however, for people to feel that they had already travelled extensively and that any further desire to travel could be incorporated into the idea of a satiable society. With the exception of Lucy, mentioned above, who because of poverty had barely started on this route, almost all the others who have appeared in this discussion will have had the benefits of extensive travel in various forms by the time they are frail and unable to continue. At this point, they may feel that their inability to do much more travelling is 'fair enough': that they have achieved a decent proportion of any bucket list and can now rest and explore the experiences closer to hand, feeling that this quest is now largely satiated.

This is consistent with the discussion of the satiable society. People in Cuan view the consumption of the world in the same spirit as the consumption of goods. They refuse to regard these travel ambitions as infinite or insatiable, even though they contain an inherent logic that might have made them so, since there are always more places to visit. The value of travel seems more often evidence that they have not got stuck in a rut with no ambition as to how they might continue to broaden their experience and engagement with the world. It is a bulwark against the accusation that their lives can no longer be expansive. They rarely feel that they 'need' to go to some particular place as an essential prerequisite to having had a life worth living. Instead, travel is conceived as something that it is likely to be sufficiently accomplished as part of a good enough life. A fly in this balmy view is the environmental impact of travel. The fact that this was not mentioned suggests that it represented a contradiction that people preferred not to see, in much the same way that they often didn't see the inequality represented by the Vartry Estate. Along with most populations, people in Cuan resolve moral contradictions at times by keeping them apart within separate discourses and practices.

Finally, there is the phenomenon of 'sort of' travel. While no one particularly mentioned travel programmes on TV, there was a strong affection for David Attenborough's nature programmes, which allow us all to travel to a proximity with non-human life that would be impossible otherwise. These programmes relate to a well-established reason for travelling, which ranges from actual bird watching to imagining that one might go on safari. Many of the core experiences that promote travel find a new compensation through easy access to analogous TV. This is an obvious boon both to those now too frail to travel and to most people in Cuan who will never have the kind of money required for a safari.

At the start of this discussion, it was suggested that there is no one single reason that should be extracted as the 'cause' of this emphasis upon travel. It is rather the mutual reinforcement of so many different reasons ranging from the weather, to values, to history, to finding another dimension to the self, that make the case. I will cede the final word to Michael, in his sixties, who joined up several of these justifications:

> If they have the discretionary money to spend, then someone says, I just had a holiday in Vietnam and Cambodia and you really have to go. Then there are so many places: South America, South Africa, China. They like to understand cultures that are totally different, their histories, their lifestyles. You try to get some sense of ordinary life. They also feel if they want to go there they'd better go now, because in five years' time I mightn't have the health to do it.

The Social World

The following chapter will attempt to render this evidence for why people focus upon travel, and the way they discuss it, into something amounting to a Cuan cosmology. This, however, requires a demonstration that, so far from being consigned to just travel, there are elements in these discussions that apply to much of the rest of these Cuan residents' lives as expressions of fundamental values. Further examples will also be provided in the next chapter. For the remainder of this chapter, the discussion will return to the way people expand their horizons from within Cuan, and not just by travel, but through embarking on a wide variety of social activities and then sharing information to facilitate others in the same aspirations. A presentation of these social activities represents another area of overlap with the content of the previous book written with Pauline Garvey.[3] There, the intention was to show how individuals exemplify that book's sub-title of *When Life Becomes Craft*, while the emphasis within the present volume has been on the social as opposed to the individual nature of these pursuits. The classic 'portrait of the artist' is that of an individual pursuing their craft in their studio. But most painting in Cuan is carried out within groups attached to specific art classes. Often the exhibitions displayed in, for example, a café will be based on the collective output of one year of that art class, rather than highlighting the work of one individual.

In the interest of balance, the ethnography also looked to find at least some areas that could be regarded as more focused on the individual. It seemed likely that religion would be one domain that might foster an orientation towards more individual introspection. But the Church is primarily a collective and community institution, and both the parish priest and a prominent member of the Protestant clergy commented on the difficulty in finding anyone in Cuan who wanted to discuss religious ideas or philosophical notions *per se* as a contemplative activity. They both saw this as a matter of regret, and the Protestant leader, in particular, had made several attempts to initiate such discussions, with very limited success. In an entirely different mode, most people will spend some time just watching TV or going on the internet alone or with their family. But here, as in many parts of the world, there has been a social taming of the media. The ever-increasing choice of programmes, when people now have Sky and Netflix and Amazon Prime alongside terrestrial stations, might have led to fragmentation. But, as noted in chapter 4, there will be the key TV series that everyone is talking about, which at the time of fieldwork included *Game of Thrones*, but also various BBC dramas. They have become the 'fillers' in social discourse when people run out of other things to talk about. Both these examples helped confirm the overall generalization around the constant emphasis on the social rather than the individual or contemplative approach to life in Cuan.

These observations came to the fore towards the end of the ethnography. The ASSA project[4] was committed to trying to use our findings in each of our respective fieldsites to construct projects that would directly enhance the welfare of populations we had been living amongst, partly to show our gratitude to our research participants for their forbearance of our presence and partly because these had become people we cared about and hoped to be of some value to.[5] Following from these conclusions, Pauline Garvey and I decided to develop a project called *social prescribing* as a practical intervention. The idea of social prescribing is that the medical prescription of drugs for conditions such as depression might be reduced if individuals were provided with an alternative 'prescription' of some social activity.[6] Our aim was to develop a comprehensive listing of such activities and supply these to local psychotherapists, doctors, and so on, who might find this useful. In the event, our initiative was curtailed by the Covid pandemic, but in preparation I identified within Cuan over seventy activities to choose from, ranging from computer courses and badminton to Pilates, silk embroidery, therapeutic scrapbooking, a Catholic charismatic group, and a group that played whist. Pauline carried out the equivalent search in her Dublin fieldsite. Many of these groups develop informally and other people in Cuan are not necessarily aware that they exist, which was precisely the point of our initiative.

The people we expected to be helped by this social prescribing were relatively few, while the sheer plethora of activities that had been located represented the degree to which most people were already socially engaged and expanding their range of hobbies and pursuits. For the typical retiree of Cuan, the single most important substance that is being carefully shaped in order to craft the good enough life is time. In my book with Pauline, we explored the way people create weekly routines.[7] How Tuesday is marked as different from Thursday, when the former features a Yoga class and the latter classes for Irish dancing. In that book, I provided detailed accounts of several such activities, including a Cuan ukulele class and the Cuan Men's Shed, while Pauline wrote portraits of activities including a walking group and a craft and coffee group organized by the local church. Since these are already published, what follows here is just a brief summary of three pursuits: two pub-based and one based outdoors.

Three Activities
It would surprise no one to suggest that the pub holds a key position within an Irish town. But while in England pubs are generally just a place to eat and drink with friends, the pubs in Cuan hosted a wide range of other activities, quite apart from what could be considered attenuated versions of the traditional storytelling described by Glassie for Northern Ireland.[8] Several pubs hosted weekly musical sessions. One I attended as part of the audience to accomplished players. But the other was just a bunch of people, including myself, who gathered informally but regularly. There were usually between six and ten of us, mostly older men, meeting fortnightly from around 9.00 p.m. to 11.00 p.m. Typically, each individual would perform around four times in turn and consume two pints of Guinness. One man was very quiet and almost never contributed to the banter but played extremely impressive and elaborated instrumental guitar versions of well-known songs. By contrast, another man, known for his fine acting, sang without any instrument and commonly took the lead in relation to banter. There were two regular female participants but one of them never played. One contributor seemed to always begin with a little apology as to whether he was going to remember the song or that maybe he had a cold. Another had memorized almost the entire back catalogue of Leonard Cohen, whose songs almost always featured in his repertoire. A third contributor impressed because of the range of different instruments he would perform on: for example, joining together two tin whistles, which he could play simultaneously but in harmony with each other. Perhaps 40 per cent of the songs had an Irish connection, either through their content or through the composer, the most popular being songs that related to the struggle for Irish Independence. The rest were mainly classic pop songs such as Ralph McTell's 'Streets of London', or comic songs. The overall impression was that there was something about the style of the contributions that reflected the personality of the performer. For example, the actor threw back his head and sang with

great gusto, or there was a wry smile on the face of the performer of Leonard Cohen songs that made one feel a natural affinity between him and his selections. Every performance was followed by applause and congratulatory comments. In about half the contributions, others would start to add background instrumentals after the first few bars.

Although Ireland was quite impoverished when most of these retirees were born, there were high literacy rates (90 per cent by 1911), as evident in the extensive literature that seems to pour out from Ireland annually and is reflected in the number of authors in Cuan, as well as in the two creative writing groups. The group I sometimes attended had each contributor in turn present a poem or prose work for critical comment. The film I made about Bob, the butcher-turned-poet, demonstrates how people can enter into such creative writing irrespective of their background and work.[9] Still more common were informal book reading clubs.[10] The one I joined met twice a month in a pub, at 8.00 p.m., and consisted of up to a dozen women and two men including myself, mostly in their sixties and seventies. As with all such clubs, the role of chair and secretary was seen as a conscientious duty and undertaken in turn. For each meeting, somebody would have previously volunteered to read a short story and another person a poem. The voice was generally modest with the emphasis on having selected a story that carried poignancy, irony, sometimes tragedy, and commonly humour, mostly with some Irish connection.

Although we were based in a pub, the actual drinking was minimal. There was no attempt to reach consensus about books. If anything, people enjoyed the play of contrasting opinions and expected everyone to stick to the integrity of their own reading. It was fine to dismiss a book as boring or poorly composed immediately after someone else clearly regarded it as lyrical and engaging. Equally, one person might feel free to talk for a good five minutes, including reading an extract or two from the book, but if another felt they didn't have much to say, they were happy to utter just a couple of sentences and pass on to the next person. There was no status in erudition or greater knowledge. Books varied from popular writers of the bestselling variety to more literary works. For example, we read Mike McCormack's *Solar Bones*, a quite experimental (and rather good) recent Irish novel that features not a single full stop. But we could follow that with a popular crime thriller. What was consensual was the general liberal ethos that often emerged through discussing a book about the Holocaust or that expressed sympathy for migrants. There were also occasional additional activities, such as visiting the Titanic exhibition in Belfast for Christmas.

A final example of community activities aligns with earlier discussions about the contemporary significance of environmentalism and sustainability. The Cuan allotments are a relatively recent acquisition and still somewhat fragile in that they depend on land granted from the regional council.[11] But they were an immediate success, growing within five years to over 250 rented lots. The Men's Shed had its own allotment, and several other research participants served on the allotment committee. Since much of what is grown needs to be eaten soon after harvesting, there is an obvious incentive to share one's own bounty and be recompensed in turn by the bounty of others. The allotment also included several migrants from Eastern Europe, who had developed a series of polytunnels that looked more like a commercial enterprise. Grandparents hoped that children would enjoy coming for at least an occasional foray and the allotments were an obvious site for relaxed chatting and sociality.[12]

A typical conversation with an allotment owner revealed what they grew in different years: raspberries, strawberries, blackcurrants, redcurrants, Swiss chard, rhubarb, mint, parsley, beetroot, lettuce, dwarf beans, garlic, and onions. A fisherman from the Vartry Estate had developed a campaign to stop the council just dumping the seaweed when they cleared the beaches and instead have it used as fertilizer for the allotments. The allotment area was more or less equally divided between the land that was fully organic and the rest. There were also collective ventures being developed such as chickens and a piggery.

Sharing a High-Quality Life
These descriptions of three activities need to be read in the context of having identified more than seventy different kinds of social activity in Cuan. To complete the evidence provided by this chapter, a final topic brings together the sociality that develops during these kinds of activity with the previous discussions of travel. It's an important additional observation since such discussions act as the mortar that binds many such examples into the wall from which Cuan is built. What matters more than the quantity of activities that can be found in the town is the quality of those activities. Many of these retired people have a phobia around wasting time, but this isn't just about

having something to do; it is about making sure that what they are doing is worthwhile.

As a result, in Cuan, one of the best presents one individual can give to another is the ability to raise the quality of their time. To let them know about things they are likely to find either enjoyable or fulfilling, or ideally both. These typically include suggestions and advice based on the books you have recently read, the TV series you are following, an especially scenic coastal walk, a new restaurant worth going to, or perhaps today a useful smartphone app. Both of you are presumed to have experienced a wide range of activities, entertainments, and travel, and the conversation is aimed as much at protecting people from spending their time on something you felt was tedious or poor quality as it is about personal recommendation. (Don't bother going to this play. I walked out at the interval.) This constant social exchange has three consequences. First, it helps everyone towards a higher quality and quantity of collective use of time, avoiding lower-quality occupations. Second, it contributes to greater consensual normativity, though, as noted in the book reading group, this can include contrasting views. And, third, it helps people to value their personal relations with others who share their tastes or who are simply a reliable source of these gifts.

Not surprisingly, information about holidays was one of the most common subjects of such gifting. (If you liked the Canaries for winter escapes, have you also thought of the Azores?) Travel is an expensive commitment of money and time, and it was important to avoid choices that might prove disappointing judging by the previous experiences of a friend or relative. Conversations could add depth to travel. (When in Malta, don't miss a visit to this historical town or that lovely church, and as background there is this book about the history of the Knights of Malta, local cuisine, or the birds one might see.) Then there is merely pointing out that this resort faces away from the local sunsets, while an alternative hotel gives a much a better view. After attending the sailing club and historical society talks over sixteen months, it became clear just how impressive these retirees could be when it came to detailed research. A two-week vacation could mean just sitting on a beach, but for this retired population it was more likely to require reading about the history and people of Sicily, visiting a classic temple, and assiduous trawling through the comments on TripAdvisor to find the best-rated arancini, cannoli, and caponata. But it likely began with making notes based on a conversation with another Cuan resident about their prior trip to Sicily.

Conclusion

This chapter has been largely descriptive, and the justification for including this amount of detail may not be clear, prior to its deployment within the following two chapters. Features that will be highlighted include the way people balance ideals of breadth and depth in achieving the good enough life, using the description found within this chapter of how people choose their holidays. The same evidence will also provide the foundation for a much broader investigation into the ways these retirees strive to remain engaged with the wider world: a continual desire to come to know more of the globe in person and through sensual experiences. Whether through the breadth of finding new places to visit or the depth of coming to master a local cuisine, both are testimony to an expansive vision of what life should still be for. The topic was complemented by the other half of the chapter, which concerned people's continued engagement with activities within Cuan, which tallied with their commitment to remain socially engaged, since these activities were almost inevitably carried out with others, even if the reason to do so did not emanate from the nature of the activity itself.

The problem for this chapter, and for several of the ethnographic chapters, is the difficulty in taking these examples seriously. Who cares about how people discuss their choice of holidays – so what? Fortunately, there are grounds for seeing the juxtaposition between these discussions and philosophical debate as more than an affectation of this author. As noted at the beginning of the chapter, these accounts regarding travel were not a reply to questions about holidays. They were a response to an explicit question about life purpose, what people still wanted from life at this stage. The anthropologist is merely taking seriously the lead given by these retirees as research participants within an ethnography. There seems to be something more profound going on here, and the task is to work out what that is and why.

Chapter 12

THE STOICS AND EPICURUS

This book compares an ethnography of the good enough life with some philosophical enquiries into the good life that began even before fifth-century BCE Athens. It has therefore made reference to classical philosophers such as Socrates and Aristotle. But with regard to moral philosophy, the two schools that came to subsequently dominate the classical and Hellenistic periods stand in stark contrast, at least to those Socratic dialogues that seem to have been less influenced by Plato, and which were found to use many sporting analogies. One of these schools, the Stoics, has bequeathed us a considerable literature, while the other, associated with Epicurus, is known mainly from a few fragments and letters[1] alongside the secondary writings of Lucretius.[2] It is generally assumed that the differences between them are highly significant. But when set against the approach to life purpose extrapolated from the ethnography, these differences will appear as relatively slight. This chapter will first examine the more negative aspects of these schools of philosophy in the way they seem to espouse a withdrawal from life and object to what they regarded as unnecessary pleasures. This then provides for a marked contrast which allows us to see more clearly how the expansive pursuits of pleasure by the retirees of Cuan and their use of reason for the purposes of pleasure can be equated with an alternative cosmology. The term 'cosmology' is employed here not to mean ideas about the cosmos, but rather a system of foundational values, outside of religion, that help us map out the cultural propensities, or habitus (see below), that are typical of a population.

The Stoics

During the recent Covid pandemic, it was said that sales of the *Meditations* by Marcus Aurelius soared.³ The attraction to his example of Stoic philosophy makes sense, as lockdown enforced just such a shift from engagement with the wider world into a more isolationist mode that may well have led people to spend more time in contemplation. But Marcus Aurelius takes this to an extraordinary degree, especially in the knowledge of what we otherwise know about the author. As a historical figure, he could hardly have been more engaged with the world. The Roman emperor from 161–80 CE and a major figure even prior to that, he was involved in a series of wars, was constantly embroiled in politics, and made key decisions effectively directing the world's greatest empire of that time, including the increased persecution of the early Christians. Indeed, the *Meditations* was probably written while he was on a military campaign. Yet this book comes close to suggesting that life might have been better through the consistent avoidance of all such experiences. The likely reason for this discrepancy was that the *Meditations* was constructed as a quite separate exercise in philosophical writing, a practice that had become common amongst the Roman elite, perhaps influenced by the Greek Stoic Epictetus.

The *Meditations* of Marcus Aurelius suggests someone fully involved in the contemplation of their inner self and challenging themselves to develop a purer soul through the medium of normative aphorisms. It asserts that everything good comes from withdrawal and relative unconcern with the external world. For example, Marcus Aurelius states, 'Inquire of thyself as soon as thou wakest from sleep, whether it will make any difference to thee, if another does what is just and right. It will make no difference';⁴ or 'Consider thyself to be dead, and to have completed thy life up to the present time; and live according to nature the remainder that is allowed thee';⁵ or '[A]ll things soon pass away and become a mere tale, and complete oblivion soon buries them'.⁶ In short, there is a strong emphasis on the pointlessness of trying to achieve anything, or really giving much concern to the world. Self-limitation is construed as a way to come to terms with the contingency of the world and the vulnerability of everything that we might value. While this seems to give comfort to some, I find Marcus Aurelius to be one of the most depressing of all philosophers. When you consider who he was and then what he wrote, there could be no more eloquent exemplification of the complete separation between life and some forms of philosophy. There seems very little here to be gleaned about how to actually rule an empire, which is a great pity, since while this is a topic we might not want to emulate, the lessons learnt from such an intelligent and introspective Roman emperor could have been fascinating.[7]

Occasionally, people in Cuan, too, may look for something akin to this retreat from the world, but that retreat is intended as an escape from the hurly-burly, mainly to appreciate the beauty that is near to hand, the holidays discussed in the previous chapter, the love of a garden or landscape, or spending time with one's grandchildren. They seek to replace one kind of experience with another. This does not, however, correspond to the exhortations of Marcus Aurelius, for whom the only real retreat is back into contemplation, closing the door as tightly as possible to the world outside. The distinction from how people in Cuan imagine withdrawal from the world – which seems to have had its equivalent amongst the Romans – is made quite explicit when he states:

> [M]en seek retreats for themselves, houses in the country, seashores, and mountains; and thou too art want to desire such things very much. But this is altogether a mark of the most common sort of men, for it is in thy power whenever thou shalt choose to retire into thyself. For nowhere either with more quiet or more freedom from trouble does a man retire than into his own soul, particularly when he has within himself such thoughts that by looking into them he is immediately in perfect tranquillity; and I affirm the tranquillity is nothing else than the good ordering of the mind.[8]

Marcus Aurelius has certainly nailed Cuan here, where people mostly do want a nice and quiet little place on the seashore or in sight of mountains. Clearly nothing will do for the tranquillity of his soul other than philosophy itself, understood as an internal contemplation, though one that is clearly amenable to being written about, as in the *Meditations*. For the Stoic, everything that people in Cuan hope to achieve, such as an appreciation of the world, its loveliness and its variety, experienced through their devotion to walking along the coast, which is perhaps their single favourite activity, is to be

THE STOICS AND EPICURUS

shunned as something contingent and vulnerable, unlike the abiding value of philosophy.

Such indifference to the world is at the heart of Stoic philosophy. One of its best-known adherents was the slightly earlier Seneca (1 BCE–65 CE), who, while not an emperor, was tutor to one, unfortunately, in this case, the rather less exemplary Nero. Seneca would be equally opposed to the Cuan ideal of life as the accumulation of pleasant and fulfilling experiences, because the overwhelming emphasis is on protection against the hurtful events of fortune. Adversity is almost preferred since it provides the fundamental training in inuring oneself to life's vicissitudes. Several of Seneca's letters are attempts to 'console' people largely by implying that too much grief is itself a kind of self-indulgence and inimical to a Stoical outlook: for example, 'Little importance is to be attached to external things, and they cannot possess great influence in either direction: the wise man is neither raised up by prosperity nor cast down by adversity.'[9] As with Marcus Aurelius, there is an almost pre-romantic ideal of death as the release from earthly woes: 'Death is a release from all pains, and a boundary beyond which our sufferings cannot go: it returns us to that state of peacefulness in which we lay before we were born.'[10] As an ethnographer hoping to give respect to people's worldly desires and aspirations, it is hard to find much value in a philosophical approach that implies we might have been better off if we had not actually been born in the first place.

These philosophers were not necessarily characteristic of their own world either. One of the best portrayals of life in classical Greece and the more general attitudes to consumption can be found in James Davidson's book *Courtesans and Fishcakes*.[11] Davidson provides considerable detail of the refined pleasures cultivated by the ancient Greeks. For ancient Rome, we are indebted to Juvenal for his portrayal of the rather excessive and indulgent pleasures that may well help account for the more extreme Stoic reaction.[12]

The one form of experience the Stoics did seem to care about was the manner of death itself. If there was an event that seems to have become the defining moment for the birth of the classical philosophical tradition, it was surely the death of Socrates, the significance of which was that, although Socrates had been condemned by his *polis* to death, he could easily have escaped and gone into exile. Instead, he took the enactment of his suicide as the opportunity to make this into the culmination of his philosophical endeavours. So, too, Seneca seemed to almost look forward to his own suicide, as emblematic of his ability to both seize control over his own fate and fulfil the constant rhetoric around the significance of death in his own actions. At least you could say this Stoic was true to his word. The Stoics held no monopoly over Roman philosophy. Cicero, for example, has many helpful and practical suggestions regarding topics ranging from friendship to becoming elderly, perhaps precisely because he and some of his contemporaries were fully involved with statesmanship, economic activities, and making their philosophy an aspect of their engagement with the world.

The idea of a final stage in life dedicated to reflective contemplation remains common practice in South Asia. When I lived in a village in India studying for my Ph.D., on any morning one might see mendicants asking for alms to support such a life. There may even be a common legacy. There was constant exchange between the classical and South Asian worlds of antiquity. Alexander the Great met sages through his conquest of North-West India. Megasthenes wrote a book about India, having been an ambassador there.[13] Christians had their own monastic version of detachment and withdrawal, including the more extreme anchorites, though these aspirations were never quite as fundamental to Christianity as to Hinduism, and perhaps especially to Buddhism. One of the fun ways of getting to grips with this antipathy between Buddhism and sensual experience is through reading the novel *Zorba the Greek*.[14] All of this matters because while philosophers discussed the virtues of such withdrawal from worldly affairs, historically it has been mainly religions that have manifested this goal.

Epicurus

At first glance, it might seem that there was a welcome alternative to Stoicism in the school of Epicurus. We are often told that these two schools were in strident conflict over the place of pleasure in life. Certainly, the Stoics had absolutely nothing good to say about pleasure itself. For Seneca, ironically, the only allowable pleasure is in despising pleasure, as in 'he is the one who takes pleasure in his own resources and wishes for no joys greater than his own heart. Would he not be justified in matching these joys against the petty and worthless and transitory sensations of that thing, the body: That day a man triumphs over pleasure, he will triumph over pain.'[15]

The contemporary connotations of the word 'Epicurean', as hedonism, imply quite the opposite relation to experience and all that might be gained from worldly engagements. There certainly are some positives to the outlook associated with the limited writings that have come down to us from Epicurus himself, who lived from 341 BCE to 270 BCE.[16] For example, we know that he was unusual amongst classical philosophers in welcoming women and servants to live within the gardens where their philosophical discourses were developed. There is also at least one important alignment between Cuan and Epicurus, or more precisely Lucretius, since it is the latter's work that has actually come down to us, to become the main source of what we take to be the philosophy of Epicurus. The Irish went through a period of radical secularization, while Lucretius is the prime example of an essentially secular philosophy within the classical period, one that refused to subject humanity to issues of guilt and sin or punishment from gods. There are sections in Lucretius that feel close to the secularism that followed the decline of Catholic influence upon the Irish. A helpful guide to the consequences of Lucretius's extraordinary poem *The Nature of Things* (*De Rerum Natura*)[17] is to be found in Stephen Greenblatt's excellent book *The Swerve*.[18] Greenblatt argues that the Renaissance developed as an early enlightenment partly because of the radical alternative to Christian theocracy, which could be conceptualized partly thanks to the rediscovery of Lucretius in that period.

The problem is that while there may be many profound differences between the Stoics and Epicurus, these become less clear for the discussions most relevant to the previous chapter. Surprisingly, it is in the relationship to pleasure that the differences are not quite as they are usually portrayed. Unlike the Stoics, Epicurus is prepared to say things like 'No pleasure is a bad thing in itself'[19] or that '[P]leasure is the starting point and goal of living blessedly.'[20] But examined more closely, there is nothing in common between Epicurus and the contemporary term Epicurean. While for Epicurus, with his secular cosmology, desire takes its place within the core to life purpose, the only pleasures that are thereby validated are the satisfactions of desires for what we genuinely need. Hegel in his lectures on the history of philosophy[21] makes this same point by quoting Seneca's approval of Epicurus, as in: '[T]he teachings of

Epicurus are holy and upright, and, if examined closely, rigorous; for his well-known doctrine of pleasure is reduced to small and slender proportions, and the rule that we prescribe for virtue he prescribes for pleasure.'[22] Epicurus doesn't valorize suffering as a kind of toughening up in the manner of the Stoics. Yet, as Heather Reid argues,

> Roman Epicureans cultivated pleasure through discipline rather than indulgence. In this sense, their philosophy displays its Socratic ancestry, but Epicureanism differs from classical Greek ethics in that it aims for independence from rather than engagement with society (*autarkeia*) and embraces peace of mind (*ataraxia*) rather than struggle for excellence.[23]

Understood from this perspective, Epicurus is really not much closer to Cuan than are the Stoics.

What both classical schools have in common is the attempt to deliver people from their fear of death. As Epicurus helpfully points out, the dead don't have a problem with being dead. Yet it's hard to find in the fragments of his writing any aspirations to pleasure much beyond its ability to escape pain. Food and drink are welcome to the degree they take away hunger and thirst, but this certainly doesn't lead to an appreciation of the banquet or of cuisine. This so-called philosopher of pleasure was known to have lived mainly on bread and water with occasional indulgences consisting of a pot of cheese and some wine. Epicurus was essentially at one with the Stoics in that the main point of life was to avoid suffering, and since a deeper involvement with life was the source of such suffering, it was best avoided. As he put it, 'The purest security is that which comes from a quiet life and withdrawal from the many.'[24] Epicurus suggests that even pleasure that caused no pain should be shunned if it required much by way of effort to obtain.[25] As with several fellow philosophers, he assumed that greater reliance on the intellect would result in a retreat from any wider desire for pleasure. The main positive of Epicurus was that he was a bit less infatuated by such an individualistic internal contemplation. Rather, he was famous for his cultivation of friendship and, as previously noted, his attempt to free humanity from superstition. But there seems to be nothing at all in the writings of Epicurus that supports the subsequent attachment of the term hedonism to his name.

Yet even these small concessions to an embracing of the sensual world proved too much for the moralist in Kant, who wrote in the *Critique of Practical Reason*:

> He [Epicurus] differed from the Stoics chiefly in making this pleasure the motive, which they very rightly refused to do. For, on the one hand, the virtuous Epicurus, like many well-intentioned men of this day who do not reflect deeply enough on their principles, fell into the error of presupposing the virtuous disposition in the persons for whom he wished to provide the springs to virtue.[26]

Why should this rather slight shift towards pleasure as the primary and positive mode for avoiding pain be a source of moral confusion for Kant? It is because acting from pleasure is categorically different from acting from duty, and virtue is a matter of the latter. Moral people don't do the right thing because it feels good, but because it is just, or otherwise morally requisite. They may even find it positively uncomfortable having to do it, as when we speak up against a bully, knowing that we are going to suffer for it. For Kant, you must keep your eye on doing the right thing if you want to be moral. What you feel about it is beside the point.[27]

How, then, did Epicurus give rise to Epicurean? Following Greenblatt's account of the impact made by the rediscovery of Lucretius, it seems that this discrepancy between what Epicurus actually stood for and his later reputation as a hedonist arose because, for the Christianity of that time, the most heinous crime was the genuine secularism of Lucretius, who portrayed a world made from atoms in which the gods had little interest. By tarring Epicurus with the brush of hedonism, they found a way to also condemn these more fundamental arguments for a secular perspective. This propaganda campaign against Epicurus seems to have remained in place till now.

These schools of philosophy have had an enduring influence, often through the aphorisms they preferred as a mode of exhortation. As it happens, one of my research participants in Cuan, James, quoted Epicurus during an interview to the effect that a person should be at peace with themselves, have good friends, and not expect too much from life. I knew James reasonably well and felt that this was something that had made an impression upon him in devising his own life of retirement. It should also be acknowledged that the

THE STOICS AND EPICURUS

Stoics and Epicurus are just two schools within classical philosophy. An approach to the good life based on Cicero, for example, would be very different and a good deal more congenial.[28] Cicero could perhaps have been a candidate for the philosophy of the good enough life. Even Marcus Aurelius includes some discussion on how to work well with others. To appreciate why my account has nevertheless focused entirely upon the negative aspects of the Stoics and Epicurus, we need to return to the juxtaposition with Cuan.

Cuan and the World

If classical and later figures, such as Kant, pitch philosophy as an examination of what makes sense rationally, in opposition to acting unthinkingly in the pursuit of pleasure, then the people of Cuan have again achieved something surprisingly important. The detailed discussion of how people in the town choose their holidays was also an account of how they bring the faculty of reason itself to the task of expanding, refining, and absorbing the pursuit of pleasure as an explicit goal of life. So far from placing pleasure in opposition to reason, the retirees of Cuan generally assume that one of the principal and best uses of reason is for creating a pleasurable and fulfilling life, rather than assuming there is some kind of antipathy between reason and pleasure. I have undoubtedly missed some of the subtlety in both Kant's and classical moral philosophy, but it certainly seemed as though the way people in Cuan approach pleasure, through the application of considerable thoughtfulness and their criteria of reasonable pleasure, appears very different from the way certain philosophical schools imagine that people generally seek to pursue all sorts of pleasures that cannot be regarded as the fulfilment of necessary desires.

The final set of observations prior to the conclusion of the previous chapter concerned the degree to which people research holidays and seek the advice and experience of others in that task. As described there, Cuan provides a kind of conversational TripAdvisor that is an important component of general discussion. The earlier detailed discussion of travel demonstrated that there are usually a great many factors involved, and the application of reason is primarily to sort through, prioritize, and then reach a balanced view as to where exactly people should travel to and what they should do there.

Finally, there was the realization of just how important holidays have become to people in Cuan, evidence for which came from the examples of those who postponed retirement specifically until they had sufficient money to afford the holidays they planned.

This prioritizing of holidays is a helpfully explicit example of a much wider cosmology based on the project of maximizing our experience of the world, in contrast to the exhortation to retreat from the world found in Stoic philosophy. The cosmology of Cuan is not just different from these philosophers, it is radically different, essentially the diametric opposite approach to life purpose. Life in Cuan should not ever be reduced to mere contemplation, but should directly employ contemplation in order to enhance sensual experience, such as enjoying nature on a long walk. The idealized site of contemplation is the Camino pilgrimage trail in Spain, but descriptions of walking the Camino are always replete with stories about whom one meets on the way and the combination of strenuous walking with wine and sociality at the various hostels. My research participants may also contemplate death, if not to the same degree as the Stoics. But if Stoic philosophers seem on occasion to use the trope of death to make life itself seem rather pointless, these retirees, who mostly enjoy decades of retirement before that eventual demise, see death as the grounds for making the most of the life they have while they still have it. Their previous belief in the afterlife combined with the Catholic emphasis on sin and guilt that dominated their youth had suppressed the goal of life as lived, through the combined promise of heaven and the threat of hell that would follow after death. Once these burdens had been lifted, they could be replaced by an enthusiastic re-focusing on the possibilities of the present and future life on earth.

Thanks to this generational emancipation, most of my research participants now believe that, other things being equal and to the degree to which they can afford this, the foundational desire is to see as much, experience as much, and above all enjoy as much of life as one can. Happiness is not the avoidance of pain and the fear of death. It is a quality to be savoured in its own right. The crucial difference from the philosophers is that pleasure is associated not with necessary pleasure, but just as much with unnecessary pleasure, making pleasure and joy goals of life and criteria for achieving the good enough life. The possibilities vouchsafed by this expansive vision are very suited to present circumstance, because these retirees' lives have coincided with a constantly expanding universe. Each of the key technologies that have arisen during their lives has created an ever-larger world. Television and then the internet have vastly expanded their knowledge of the world, as have science and improvements in education, while cheaper flights have given them the opportunity to visit more of that world. Smartphone apps can help them find their way in a foreign city, translate menus, and give background information on everything they encounter. All of this is assisted by the rise of affluence, such that they can afford more education, more travel, and online exploration. When not on holiday, sensual enjoyment is avowed in the exhortation towards good *craic* as the local term for the best of times. *Craic* is not a means to an end; reason is employed for plans whose aim is to secure the ambience that hopefully will be suffused with good *craic*.

There is no inevitability that an expanding universe will lead to an expansionist cosmology. This is not the place for any extensive discussion, but it is very likely that this same exposure to the vastness of our world has had the opposite effect on many other populations. There are various versions of contemporary xenophobia, reactionism, and populist localism that reflect the experience of being intimidated by this exposure. Fascism was surely at least in part a repudiation of the threat of cosmopolitanism, as can be seen in its destructive reaction to the avant-garde arts and its appeal to a pseudo-historical ideal of the authenticity of the original *Volk*. It may well be that much of the rise of contemporary right-wing politics today represents an updated wave of similar repudiation of the still more powerful cosmopolitanism that has grown since the 1930s. Cosmopolitanism, being comfortable with difference, may be associated with elites, who can easily come across as intimidating to the more fearful. There are quite specific factors outlined in previous chapters around education, work, affluence, and freedom that can explain why people in Cuan, by contrast, have opted to become exemplary cosmopolitans, rather than to retreat from that possibility into these more populist and xenophobic views.

One of the main capacities that makes this cosmopolitanism work for people in Cuan is their employment of reason. They are well aware of the obvious threat of being lost in an ever-expanding universe. You can't possibly see everywhere or experience everything, and the desire to do so could have led, if not to anti-cosmopolitan xenophobia, then instead to a new superficiality that privileges breadth over depth. This is a very commonly assumed result of the mass consumer society. The great German sociologist Georg Simmel was especially eloquent in showing how the urban experience, in particular, could reduce a population to shallow loneliness in the crowd, and how the individual could become overstretched by trying to have too many consumer experiences and as a result have no significant relationship to anything in particular. All of this was thanks to the incessant nature of an expanded modern life and the relentless blandishments of consumer capitalism.[29] In chapter 4, it was argued that Adorno and Horkheimer took it for granted that the mere common people, unlike themselves, had already succumbed to pure superficiality in the face of mass culture that was being promoted through the world of entertainment. To be honest, even my research participants are as prone as any other group to denigrate tourists, other than themselves, for the latter's assumed superficial encounters with the world.

This is another reason why the evidence around the selection of holidays is so important to the arguments of this chapter. The best way of incorporating an expanding universe to produce a positive incorporation of greater knowledge and experience and ameliorate this possibility of mere superficiality is precisely through the careful employment of reason in the task of balancing breadth and depth. Once again, Cuan demonstrates, contrary to Adorno and so many other philosophers, that ordinary people have this capacity to a degree that we just never seem to sufficiently respect. Even if they haven't read Aristotle, my research participants combine this maximizing and expansionist approach to the world with a measured strategy of how to keep things in balance, and what they might thereby accomplish in terms of the depth of their subsequent relationships to people, to things, and to places.

Listening carefully to these discussions about holidays reveals these internal negotiations. My research participants know full well that if they go every year to their summer apartment in the Algarve, they may not then get to Patagonia or see the *sakura* (cherry blossom) season in Japan. But this is not seen as some ultimate choice between breadth or depth *per se*. My informants seemed to believe that balancing breadth and depth can give them the best of both worlds. The depth corresponds to the gains of returning to the 'little place' they have invested in in France, where they have established a good relation to the local boulangerie and patisserie; or to the commitment to multiple return visits to northern Spain linking up walks on the

Camino de Santiago pilgrimage trail until they have completed the entire distance. It is also fine to not go abroad every year but return instead to the beauty of nearby Connemara with its mix of red and purple fuchsias set against yellow gorse. This may allow them to save for the occasional extravagance of their visit to Bali or Iceland. They plot life as a musical score in which the high and bass notes gain their resonance through contrast. Recall the example from chapter 3 of the taxi driver, with less income, balancing visits to the horse races at Aintree with annual trips to Las Vegas.

This ability of these retirees to control their desires and aspirations, rather than be controlled by them, which was highlighted in chapter 3 on the satiable society, is also evident in the way this older population finally become elderly. At this point, the balance between breadth and depth is also a means for accepting the gradual curtailments that come with fraility. When you know you are never going to go diving in the Galapagos Islands, then you are grateful for the abundance of nature programmes on the TV. When you can't afford to travel abroad at all, you are grateful that travel in Ireland is now free for the elderly. If you are housebound and frail, then instead of looking for the new, you reconcile to that which was comfortable from the past. You are also more prepared to acquiesce in giving up whole areas of interest in favour of a few that help you to relax often from intermittent experience of pain and frailty, the hip replacement operations, or chemotherapy. You might re-watch past episodes of *Poirot* or *Father Ted*, or the football games of the 1970s, or listen to that old Toscanini version of a symphony, or traditional Irish folk sessions, all happily interrupted by WhatsApp images of grandchildren. This is the time to prioritize feeling as comfortable as possible, under increasingly difficult circumstances. People understand the maxim of growing old gracefully and gratefully, if also inevitably fearfully. But there may be decades of surprising, retained agility and expansion prior to narrowing down to the few key relationships and the inability to do more than these things, even if one wanted to. The memories of where you did go and what you did get up to when you could, meanwhile, help reconcile the self to its current limitations. Overall, these retirees might tend to agree with Martha Nussbaum and Saul Levmore in noting the importance, when ageing, of also growing 'more comfortable with one's own skin'.[30]

It might seem pretentious to claim any philosophical value to such discussions of mere holidays. But this seems warranted when we extrapolate from these observations and see how a similar logic to the crafting of life in retirement is found in many other activities. This balance between depth and breadth is also the key to the relationships people build through activities within Cuan. First, there is the appeal of breadth: the choices provided by the more than seventy activities located in order to develop a project of social prescribing. Retired people will happily start the new year with a resolution to take up photography more seriously, volunteer for the Citizen's Advice Bureau, learn more about wine, or improve their skills on the tin whistle. Equally, there is no end to the possibility of depth: adding to their knowledge of coastal birdlife, the history of Ireland during the Second World War, or the art of origami. They take up their painting, ukulele playing, walking, acting, bridge, or singing without much expectation of reaching any professional standard. They would like to be good enough to play their ukulele as entertainment in a home for the elderly, but that is generally good enough. The pursuit of excellence is moderated by the place of sociality as the *a priori* to life. They don't really want to bore others with tales of their extensive knowledge, skills, and achievements, nor to intimidate them. They simply don't want to show off, partly because, as previous chapters have revealed, there is real quality to Irish insult and invective that brings people down if ever they should appear to be talking from a greater height than oneself. If that is the stick, the carrot is the pleasure that other people gain when knowledge is shared as an egalitarian gift, rather than a claim to status. A modest sharing of helpful tips. Once again, the superior commitment to sociality underlies the deployment of reason in finding the appropriate balance between breadth and depth.

The Cosmology of Cuan

To consolidate the argument so far: the evidence from the previous chapter for how people choose holidays, develop social activities, and share their knowledge is starting to emerge as a set of more abstract principles: the use of reason, the balance of breadth and depth, and an expansionist commitment to embrace the world. In order to take all this one stage further and suggest that this is also evidence for something we could call the cosmology of Cuan, we need to extrapolate from these discussions to incorporate many more aspects of these people's lives. Two examples now follow, deliberately taken from quite different parts of life. The first is an exploration of the consequences of feminism, particularly for men. The second concerns the use of smartphones.

Traditional gender roles often severely constrained what people could do in life. When these older men were younger, they had been socialized into growing up specifically as 'men'. Consequently, they often had limited experience of cooking and many of the more mundane aspects of parenting, such as nappy changing and waiting on benches at the playground. Thanks to feminism, now, at least to a degree, universally espoused by the inhabitants of Cuan, it has become common for retired men in the town to take on these activities. While this could have been an affectation, I did not find men boasting about their new involvement in childcare or cooking, which is something I have certainly encountered elsewhere. Rather, they constantly talked about how much they had 'missed out' as a result of their lack of involvement in parenting the first time around.

An example described in chapter 1 was their involvement in grandparenting. It was far more likely to be women who were wary about losing the freedoms of retirement through over-committing to grandchild care, while men were more likely to enthuse about those same commitments. Both attitudes were formed out of their contrasting experience of parenting: the hard labour of women, in many senses, and the lack of involvement for men. Feminism had thereby opened up a world for the potential colonization by males of that they had previously been excluded from, even if the initial cause was the historical prevalence of male privilege. The point, though, is that this represents much the same underlying expansionist cosmology evident from the selection of holidays. Here was a world of very sensual experience (nappy changing) that they had previously been cut off from, that they could now enter into, and so they did.

An example would be men's greater involvement in the more domestic aspects of cooking such as jam making. A man discussing the berries he was growing at his allotment talked about this at length:

> The kids they said my standard was improving after a while. I've baked bread, made jams, things I never did before. I pick blackberries, made lovely blackberry and apple jam, and I made batches last week. I make nice rhubarb and ginger jam from my own rhubarb. And

the blackberry is dead easy to make. It sets just at the time it says it sets, 210 degrees centigrade. The kids sent me on two courses: a breadmaking course and they sent me on a one-pot cooking course, one-pot meals.

These are generalizations. It was possible to meet the gender-shifting bore: a man who would not stop talking about his prowess at jam making or Lego. This was a performance that naturally infuriated a whole lot of women who had previously been doing exactly the same tasks without any expectation of subsequent bragging rights. But this was rare. It's not that men practised a conscious self-effacement, but rather that, as in this quote, they were starting to associate the technologies and practicalities involved with genuine interest.

The other side of the feminist coin would need to be a female sense of equality in respect to both work, leadership, and other activities. These retired women certainly seemed to exude confidence and mainly talked of gender inequality as their past rather than present experience, although they also pointed out areas which remained unequal, as in the ethnographic evidence that men still often burdened women with the dominant role of caring for dying parents, or parents with dementia. On the other hand, women were more at ease in developing social networks, a strongly gendered difference that came to the fore in retirement. Recognition of this legacy and men's relative lack of expertise was the ethos behind the Men's Shed, which seemed to be a highly successful venture directed towards addressing this problem. Men bonded over carrying out physical labour that improved the appearance of the town, and the Men's Shed also encouraged them to develop an interest in areas such as cooking and gardening.

A very different example that also builds upon discussion within previous chapters, but now can be reconsidered as evidence for this wider cosmology, was the way these older people responded to the expansion of their universe represented by the smartphone: the official subject of my research project. Those older people with sufficient self-confidence swiftly took for granted twenty new possibilities granted by their smartphones to the extent that they could no longer really imagine being without them. Of course, they would now check an app to see if the bus was coming, check-in at the airport using their phone screen, buy something online, record a noticeboard about a forthcoming play using the 'perpetual opportunism' provided by the smartphone camera, which was now always with them, or be constantly looking at their WhatsApp family group. Such things had become commonplace within 'the blink of an eye'. This was the culmination of their gradual colonization of the internet itself as perhaps the single most obvious example of the way our universe has expanded in recent decades. There were more things to know about, to look up, and to do, or in some cases to simply recover, as streaming music made up for those LPs of favoured bands that had been lost many years ago.

As always, these retirees would find a way to turn this into expanded sociality. A woman in her sixties could be up till 3.00 a.m. chasing down new relatives through ancestry.com. A year later, those newly discovered American relatives might also come to visit. At this point, those same smartphones made arrangements to meet up with the visitors locally so much easier. A mere decade after berating young people's use of smartphones as evidence for anti-social narcissism, epitomized by the selfie, seventy-year-olds could be seen as equally adept at taking out their own smartphones a hundred times a day, because, so far from being anti-social, these were devices with an extraordinary capacity for increasing sociality. In addition, the search engines on those smartphones gave them a seemingly infinite capacity to look things up, such that their enjoyment of many TV series was interrupted because they were desperate to remember where they had seen that actor before.

Considering these four very different examples together – holidays, social activities, feminism, and the smartphone – may now be sufficient for an argument that they are all equally manifestations of the same deeper expansionist cosmology. Together they equate to what anthropologists, following Bourdieu,[31] call a habitus. A habitus is the structural propensity to view everything through a common lens. This could be a religious faith or include a commitment to always be polite, and is assumed to have been inculcated as a taken for granted habit during childhood. Yet in this case habitus clearly did not arise from early socialization. In several projects that I have undertaken as an ethnographer, the evidence suggests that, contrary to popular approaches, such as psychoanalysis, the primary determinants of the dominant social structures we bring to bear on life, may not develop at six months or at six years, but often at the age of twenty-six and sometimes at sixty. The expansionist cosmology of Cuan is coming into bloom at the point of retirement.

In Cuan, retirement means ending the constraints of salaried occupation, not retirement from life. These exceptionally free people deploy that freedom to grow themselves, through more and enjoyable experiences of life. In common parlance, the pursuit of pleasure tends to be associated with the young. It helps us to rethink the importance of pleasure if instead it is reconsidered as a goal for older people, because it then becomes harder to simply denigrate the pursuit of unnecessary pleasure, as philosophers and others are wont to do. It is also harder to oppose pleasure to reason. Instead, we can re-cast reason as the instrument people use for sculpting time, allowing them to prioritize between looking after grandchildren and pursuing a number of social activities in the company of new friends or people they love, alongside taking breaks, visiting new places or enjoying Cuan itself.

It is also now possible to add to this mix the evidence from chapter 3 about the satiable society. The people of Cuan continually upgraded to better computers and then smartphones until upgrades just didn't seem worth the cost. They then stopped upgrading, even though there was no let-up in the advertising industry's attempts to retain that habit. They live in a consumer society but now balance the capacities of consumption with the moral virtues of environmentalist decluttering. The idea that mass consumption is necessarily individualizing is firmly repudiated once we think about these older people as consumers. The capacity that enables the satiated society is the same quality of reason. To be satiated is to consolidate the benefits of one pursuit, following which they may or may not take interest in some other new and attractive hobby or venture.

This expansion of often instrumental action, rather than contemplation, represents a very different approach to mid-life than the one presumed and advocated by the philosopher Kieran Setiya. In his recent book, Setiya views mid-life as a time for moving towards less teleological aims, which follows the general advocacy within Western philosophy for older age to be an appropriate time for greater contemplation.[32] This is a very reasonable and, in many ways, admirable sentiment. It is, however, not at all the approach of Cuan. Some of these retirees may think that they are prone to some philosophizing after a few drinks, but the key to this is usually the drinking. Serious philosophy would almost certainly have killed the vibe of good *craic*. Fortunately, any philosophical pretensions based on drinking are easily forgotten by the morning. One might have expected that as the sheer weight of Catholic sin had lifted off their shoulders, this generation would have developed a more hedonistic phase. But perhaps in repudiation of another massive burden, that of historical alcoholism, the drinking of people in Cuan today is relatively sober compared to the past. Today, they drink within reason.

Conclusion

For the strongest rejoinder to my portrayal of these classical and Hellenistic philosophers, Martha Nussbaum elaborates on the therapeutic value of Epicurean and especially Stoic philosophy, outlining their many positive contributions and stressing an affinity with Cicero, rather than the contrast I have drawn.[33] The defence of my emphasis upon the more negative interpretation of these texts is that such a stark contrast emerged primarily from the direct juxtaposition with Cuan. The limitations of philosophical traditions whose emphasis is ultimately on freedom from suffering become more apparent when we consider the possibility of the expansive and sensual relation to the world found amongst the retirees of Cuan. The critical contribution of the perspective from Cuan is that it permits us to respect the ability of ordinary people to embrace an expansive and engaged approach to life purpose without necessarily falling into excess. The problem with so much philosophical writing is the lack of respect for the moral capacities that can be discerned within everyday life. Yet we know from James Davidson's more 'ethnographic' portrayal of everyday life and consumption in classical Greece that people at that time also were constantly engaged in a careful consideration of how to enjoy pleasure.[34] What was the right way to drink, eat (especially fish), and have sex that would bring pleasure, but avoid excess, through exercising self-control. Aristotle first develops the idea of habitus, but there was already a habitus that helps to explain Aristotle.

There is also a long-term and perhaps rather damaging legacy that comes from the Stoics and afflicts our contemporary society. It may well be that one of the main reasons much of the environmentalist movement has been less successful than it obviously needs to be right now is that it makes the future look dreary. When environmentalists focus upon giving up certain pleasures associated with over-consumption and once again make asceticism the virtue that secures the good life, then green activists sometimes seem to echo the Stoic tendency to almost celebrate what we cannot or should not buy and enjoy. As the anthropologist Richard Wilk has argued, we might do a good deal better in furthering the environmentalist cause by showing how reducing carbon emissions and over-consumption need not make the future less fun and pleasurable.[35]

There is no harm whatsoever in sugaring the environmentalist pill by focusing as much on the many routes to pleasure and joy that might continue to grow as part of our expanding universe of entertainment, which is relatively light on energy consumption. The good news is that we have recently seen a significant break from the historical linkage between economic growth and higher carbon emissions. Today, it is the most affluent economies that are starting to lower those emissions. This exposes the problematic moralizing that may have stymied adherence to climate goals. Instead, it allows us to focus upon lowering harmful emissions as the ultimate goal in its own right. We no longer need to use environmentalism as a justification for ascetic oppositions to economic development[36] – a view which may well be in part a legacy of the Stoics.[37] So, far from diminishing the fight against climate change, stripping away a parasitic asceticism should help make it more effective. Furthermore, as an anthropologist who has spent years studying poverty, I am entirely, if quite unfashionably, in favour of even more rapid economic development, as long as this does not cause such environmental damage. Apart from avoiding climate catastrophe, the single most important contemporary goal should be the elimination of poverty, which requires this ever more rapid economic development, concentrated in those parts of the world which have been tragically neglected.

The previous chapters suggest that the residents of Cuan have quite a clear idea of virtue. But they never fetishize this in the manner of the Stoics and some other classical philosophy. They see no reason to assume that virtue is the sole route to happiness, when every day they can see the contribution of pleasure to happiness. The Stoic philosophers had no empirical base for their railings against pleasure. Most likely it was rather the greater likelihood of suffering and tragedy during those historical periods that explains the popularity of Stoic ideals during the Roman Empire, which perhaps should make us more sympathetic to their views. Cicero may have approvingly cited the Stoics but was himself neither Stoic nor hedonist. Cicero was always a better guide to life. The good enough life should be about the simultaneous development of virtue and happiness, not the suppression of one on behalf of the other. There are many reasons for regarding fun and joy as intrinsically virtuous and taking this as one more lesson gained from the ethnography. It is what many people think Epicurus said, even if he didn't.

To return to Cuan, this was an older population, and these retirees were well aware that their time on earth was coming to an end. Mostly, they did not flinch from such knowledge, though undoubtedly they found it depressing. Again and again, they stated that what they feared most was dementia rather than death, a sentiment with which Epicurus might well have approved. Any theoretical or religious assumption that, without a strong belief in the afterlife, humanity would see death as evidence for the pointlessness of life turns out to be entirely mistaken. The retirees were drinking Guinness, not the apricot cocktails of the French Left Bank. Beckett may have been Irish, but these retirees were not Beckett. Many of them were already experiencing a wide variety of frailties that limited what they could now do. Some could no longer drive or drink and some men were surprisingly open about 'other stuff' they could no longer do or enjoy. On the whole, they gave things up with good grace and a measured sense of whether the gain of further experiences was still worth the effort. They could just about manage that extra holiday, but honestly when you thought about the flight and the packing and all the other paraphernalia, it was just no longer worth the creaking joints and breathlessness.

A great support at this time was precisely the amount that had by then been accomplished. People in their eighties were quite explicit about having travelled enough, seen enough, and tried out enough activities or cuisines. The satiable society is supported by the satiated individual who is blessed by the knowledge that life has been worth it. As against the Stoic pre-emptive self-limitation in the face of possible failure that suggests you might as well not have been alive in the first place, the retirees of Cuan come to death knowing that they have had as fulfilling a life as the world can offer them, or at least if they haven't, it hasn't been for the lack of trying.

CONCLUSION
Hegel, Anthropology and Philosophy

Hegel

The aim of this conclusion is to develop a reconciliation between the writings of some philosophers concerning the good life and what has been extrapolated as the good enough life from the everyday lives of mostly retired people in Cuan. The figure chosen to serve this purpose is the German philosopher Georg Wilhelm Friedrich Hegel (1770–1831). This conclusion will propose a reading of Hegel that allows us to expand and deepen our understanding of Cuan. Hegel wrote on many topics and here I will only focus on certain limited facets of his oeuvre that appear most relevant. What Hegel brings to the appreciation of Cuan is an understanding of how its residents' active agency in the social creation of their community not only became the source of their good enough lives and their love for their town, but also created them as the people I was privileged to come to know through this ethnography. At the same time, perhaps the example of Cuan illustrates what Hegel hoped to convey through his concept of self-actualization: a term that refers to rational social action, not individual pursuit. The same caveat applies to this as to other chapters. What follows is a personal reading of a philosopher whose writing can be extremely difficult. But ultimately this book is not about trying to assert a correct reading of any philosopher. It is about trying to use my limited interpretation of philosophers to good effect through applying what has been thereby gleaned to reach a deeper comprehension of the ethnography.

Initially, Hegel will be inspected through the prism of a book called *Hegel's Ethical Thought* by Allen Wood. Wood starts by

CONCLUSION

admitting that most of Hegel's work should be regarded as a failure, especially his attempt to supplant conventional logic with a system of what he called speculative logic. Wood doesn't particularly dwell on this, but, reading Hegel, one can't escape a feeling of massive hubris around someone who clearly felt that their own writing in *The Phenomenology of Spirit*[1] represented the end point of both philosophy and history as the moment in which both of these finally came to understand their own true nature. Wood, following the work of Charles Taylor,[2] argues that while Hegel wrote as though his social and ethical discussion rested on the foundation of his vast logical system, it was really the other way around. One can safely abandon these projects of grand narrative and still retain a respect for Hegel's contribution to the fields of ethics and the study of society.[3]

An attraction of Hegel in looking for a correspondence with this ethnography is that, in contrast to so much philosophy, he is less centred on the individual. Hegel's concept of *Sittlichkeit* or ethical life is derived from our involvement in the wider world, a world he considers in three successive layers: the family, civil society, and the state. Especially helpful is the treatment of civil society since most of this book concerns an analogous level. The town of Cuan is more than the family and less than Ireland, but is the source and subject of most of the activities described here.[4] For Hegel, an emphasis on civil society does not represent the suppression of the individual, because it is only through the medium of civil society and the state that the individual can achieve the goal of an ethical life.[5] Indeed, he is critical of civil society because it is too individualistic. At a still more basic level, it is the family as a communal unit that helps people reconcile individualism with social membership at an emotional level.[6] Furthermore, again unlike several of the philosophers previously discussed, Hegel saw all of this as situated historically. Ethics must be related to the circumstances of the time and not merely equate with some universal human nature hovering above our messy engagements with the day-to-day world. As with Hegel, my research participants understood that their desire to become effective ethical members of society needed to be expressed through institutions, not just as a personal stance. Their actions were not simply customary, derived as a legacy from their past. They were an emanation of consciousness, in that these retirees knew what they were doing – another facet of societal self-creation that was an important component of ethical action for Hegel.

CONCLUSION

Hegel espouses a route to freedom accomplished through conscious engagement with the construction of this ethical world: '[M]y duties as a member of the rational social order do not really constrain me, but instead liberate me.'[7] An individual in Cuan may well have found that it was through becoming an active citizen that they were able to manifest and experience the associated freedoms discussed in chapter 2. They had created a town with endless opportunities to put on a play, take pride in Tidy Towns, help develop sports, meet for a book reading group, and above all to become good people who could effectively support the welfare of others. These freedoms are not freedoms from coercion. They are capacities that exist only thanks to the collective construction of social activities and institutions. These also include the ability to conduct politics with a small p: that is, being actively involved in political action that had an immediate impact upon their own small town. They were creating freedom they could taste in the Cuan air. As described in this volume, while respecting a wider pluralism, Cuan institutions tended to be normative and consensual, negotiated through debate and compromise, to allow for the collective development of practical projects that manifestly improved the welfare of the town.

The retirees of Cuan, as also Hegel, are, then, far removed from the highly individualistic ethics of contemporary liberalism, and the colloquial meaning of the word 'freedom'. Both, in their own way, might regard the concept of a 'free individual' as a contradiction in terms. Freedom is not especially associated with individual choice. A contrast may be drawn with the US, viewed as a place that fetishizes individual choice, even to the level of ordering meals in a restaurant from a menu that always have to be altered in some way to express individual choice. That is not the way of Cuan, where people gain freedom only by dissolving their individuality within the relationships, ethics, and organizations that give them the capacity to be free. An important difference from Hegel is that typically people in Cuan would not have regarded their engagement with family as representing a lower level than engagement with civil society and the state. For them, the family remained paramount. But then the family is another arena through which relationships make individuals, more than the other way around. Social relationships for Hegel, for Cuan, and for anthropology are *a priori*, thereby confirming the initial response to Kant in the introduction to this volume.

CONCLUSION

Objectification
To take these arguments further requires moving on from Wood, who mainly focuses on Hegel's last work, *Philosophy of Right*,[8] and turning to Hegel's most extensive volume, *Phenomenology of Spirit*, the book that is also properly accused of being saturated with hubris. I am recapitulating here an argument I first made in 1987 in a book called *Material Culture and Mass Consumption*. The first part of that book comprised an examination of the term 'objectification'. In colloquial conversation, when we discuss the world around us, we generally take a person or institution as given. We talk about what the person does, or what the institution does. For Hegel, by contrast, the person or institution must always be regarded as a process of becoming. When a person acts, those acts may in turn change who that person is. One of the tasks of *Phenomenology of Spirit* is to describe these processes.

Most people would have come across a version of Hegel's ideas on objectification through the writing of Karl Marx. In his early Paris manuscripts, Marx starts from a Hegelian perspective.[9] Humanity isn't simply a given. Human beings make themselves through labour. We grow or manufacture, and through this creation of a world external to ourselves, through these acts of self-alienation, we create not just new capacities but also a kind of mirror that reflects back on us who we are. We can recognize ourselves in this world because we created it as an external version of ourselves. Unfortunately, under conditions of capitalism, we are sundered from this appreciation of the world as something we have created and through which we might grow. The world we created has become instead the private property of others and thereby excludes us from what should by rights be an aspect of ourselves.

The original Hegelian version of objectification sees this process to completion rather than placing the emphasis on the forces that prevent this. An example would be the institution of law.[10] At first, we may experience the law both as a constraint and as oppressive. Why should I obey this imposition on my freedom created by others? But later we may come to appreciate that law is not – at least in principle – an opposition to our freedom but the very institution that allows for the possibility of being free. Free to develop ourselves without being suppressed by others. As soon as we are threatened or cheated, we hope that *our* law will be there to protect us. If the law fails in this and takes the side of the oppressor, then we feel this is not acting as the law should. It is not really the law, but something that has been twisted to betray its very purpose. This sequence implies that we, too, have a conception of a proper law that would and should be ours. We have come to see how law might aspire to be an embodiment of reason, even if right now it feels like it has been turned into merely a tool for securing the enrichment of lawyers. The very reasoning that first led us to see the law as oppression may also provide for us a confirmation of the nature of 'real' law, a potential project of reason created in the pursuit of our common welfare.

In a similar fashion Hegel considers how other institutions, such as the family, civil society, and the state, could also be conceived of as projects of reason, even if the current representatives of those institutions fail to accord with that ideal. Hegel considers the discrepancy between this ideal of reason embodied in institutions and the way institutions come to betray that logic of reason. A problem with this approach is that it may have led him to give more credit to contemporary institutions, such as the Prussian state, as embodying reason than was warranted. Today, we are more inclined to focus on how far actual institutions have slipped towards becoming instruments of present oppression, rather than of our potential liberation. But this same condemnation confirms our ideal of normative reason, what we think the state or the family should be, against which the present institutions are judged, often by us.

These are all examples of what Hegel meant by the concept of objectification. It refers to the entire process: the process that began with self-alienation. Something has been created, such as the law, family relations, or the state, which feels oppressive and which at first we may not identify with. Gradually, we realize that these are facets of the world that resonate with and ideally express our own capacity for reason. We come to identify with them as our family or as citizens. The person we consider ourselves to be is a product of parenting and education, and we take our turn in creating and changing the world around us. When derived from Hegel, the term 'objectification' becomes a positive assertion of how we create ourselves in creating the world around us. Yet this term is far more commonly employed today for something that is looked at in horror by other philosophers. For Heidegger, Dasein cannot exist alongside modern Cartesian and scientific objectification. For Adorno, and now colloquially for most people, becoming subject to objectification is a term seen through the lens of Marxist studies. This is because of the way Marx inherited but then transformed Hegel's concept of objectification. Marx retreats from the process of objectification as a completed process and focuses almost entirely on the various ways in which this is sundered by capitalism.[11] The term 'objectification' is then redeployed to describe this rupture through the unholy triumvirate of fetishism, alienation, and reification. In modern parlance, objectification is further reduced to a term for the reduction of our humanity to a mere object-like status. It is very hard today to consider something called self-alienation and imagine this as a positive and necessary stage through which we become ourselves. The negative turn is very clear in works such as *Dialectic of Enlightenment* and Adorno's wider writings on reification. In different ways, these philosophers spent their lives trying to rescue society from objectification. But this may be because they had a narrower or particular view of objectification itself when compared to the expansive concept that Hegel was trying to expound.

The arguments of this conclusion depend on returning to the Hegelian meaning of this term: objectification as the requisite process by which people are constructed through their engagement with the world. Fortunately, there is much in the premise of anthropology that comes close. For most anthropologists, there are no human beings who can be considered as prior to objectification, because there are no pre-cultural people.[12] Contemporary anthropology has hopefully by now repudiated its original primitivism, which implied that some people are more cultural than others. For anthropologists, we really are all already thrown into the world as the product of the cultural values into which we are socialized. We observe how people come to identify with culture and then appropriate the possibilities of further objectification by their actions in the world and the consequences for the way they are thereby changed. Anthropology becomes the study of objectification. The difference from Hegel is that most anthropologists do not usually associate culture and institutions with any abstract presumption of reason, seeing them more as historically contingent and often arbitrary.

Freedom
Once we recognize that cultural processes are forms of objectification, then the discussions around freedom in chapters 1 and 2 make more sense. Over the last century, many societies have undergone a period of relative emancipation, especially for groups

historically more oppressed than today, such as women or LGBTQ+ people. Thanks to education and science, we are aware of a much larger world. In our lifetimes, we have witnessed the addition of a vast expanse of online worlds that simply did not exist when many of us were born. It does not follow, however, that these historical processes have made everyone freer. As noted in the previous chapter, the sociologist Georg Simmel discussed the contradictory nature of an expansion of culture,[13] which can oppress us if we are unable to follow Hegel's sequence of objectification and negate the initial sense of alienation by identifying with this expansion of the world as potential. Anthropologists are often involved with indigenous societies, such as in Australia, with their own cultural traditions who consider themselves to have been diminished rather than expanded by exposure to the vast worlds that now surround and infest them. Many people experience some kind of curtailment. There is a bigger world out there, but it does not seem to be their world.

It is therefore not simply the expansion of possibilities that makes people free. What has been described are conditions tantamount to remaining within a situation of self-alienation. Something more has to happen to achieve objectification. That something is a process of active engagement in the creation, or at least consumption, of those expanded capacities. Cuan helps us to see how, at least for some people in certain circumstances, this remains possible. The inhabitants of Cuan do not just buy smartphones; they delete and add apps, change settings, and add content. What is produced is the specific smartphone they have created, which can become an extension of their interests and character, but also add capacities that make them more than they had been prior to their possession of smartphones. The same applies to their involvement in community associations or sports. It is only when they themselves are active in creating this expanding world, or at least can see themselves reflected within it, that the world in turn expands them. To return to the example of law, thanks to their positive identification with civil society, these retirees even outdid the Garda in monitoring compliance to Covid restrictions. They believed that it was only through the rigorous, collective, and consensual application of law that they could become free – in this case from Covid.

Hegel insisted that objectification should also be the incremental growth of a conscious and self-conscious process. The blow-ins knew what they were doing in creating Cuan as a community. At the stage of retirement, they have lived through their own history and learnt from it. The very opposite of Heidegger's Black Forest peasant, they had repudiated their own past and in consciousness created and embraced their present and, as far as they could, the future for their children. Reading Fintan O'Toole's account *We Don't Know Ourselves* alongside this ethnography leads to the diametric opposite conclusion to the title of his book. Compared to any other population I had worked with, these Irish people *do* know themselves, precisely because they have now lived the lives so excellently described by O'Toole. They had experienced that period of rampant conspicuous consumption, which is why they can now become the satiable society. They often personally experienced the problems of being born in very large families economically dependent upon their neighbours. Some had folk memories of *The Valley of the Squinting Windows*, where social comparison was odious rather than supportive. If the rise in affluence had started to develop the patina of complacency, this had been scrubbed clean by the scouring of recent and deep recession.

Hegel thereby provides us with a more profound understanding of what has been described through the ethnography. This book has been about objectification: the process by which a population can obtain freedom through constructing themselves and gaining the self-confidence to use that expanded world, with its systems of education, science, arts, and travel, to become more than they could otherwise have been. This may not yet be a common condition; it may sadly be quite exceptional. A tragedy of the world is the degree to which we live in a period of extraordinary expansion, online and offline, yet this is as likely to have become oppressive as liberating. But it is therefore of considerable importance to remind ourselves that, given the right circumstance, it is possible to become free to develop the good enough life.

Pluralism
Further evidence of the value of Hegel's writing in bringing philosophy into better alignment with actual social trajectories, such as portrayed through this ethnography, can be found in the work of philosophers who took their inspiration from Hegel. For a period, these ideas came together under the title of communitarianism.[14] This movement had more respect for the potential of anthropology because it had a clear commitment to pluralism. It recognized that although philosophers are increasingly concerned with universal goals, such as human

rights, in order to apply these principles, we need to acknowledge that there may be multiple versions of the good life.[15]

In considering pluralism in more detail, the communitarian movement, as also Martha Nussbaum and Amartya Sen, was concerned, for example, with the relationship between Eastern versions of the good life as against Western, trying to avoid a Western imperialism that ignored models of the good life developed in countries such as China and India.[16] Philosophers such as Charles Taylor wondered whether there were more general points about the good life that might be derived from what these various versions have in common.[17] As they become more concerned with such specifics of policy and practice, as opposed to more abstract reasoning, there also comes a blurring of the boundary between philosophy and other disciplines. Is Sen an economist or a philosopher? Was Amitai Etzioni, a contemporary exponent of these communitarian ideas, a sociologist or a philosopher?

Following from Hegel, these philosophers are also more directly concerned with institutions such as the family and civil society, and concepts of the good life that are not reduced to the liberal individual.[18] Figures such as Etzioni became involved in trying to map a path towards the good community,[19] akin to Cuan but with reference to wider issues such as the reach of the welfare state and the role of voluntary organizations – comparing, for example, the imagined community of people who think of themselves as connected, as against a community of common locality that actually meet together. This is a discussion which chimes with questions as to how far the success of Cuan lies in its geography, or how far devotion to the private family becomes the idiom through which people develop their wider involvements as citizens.[20] Such discussions bring these philosophers into familiar arguments of policy and politics.

A Reasonable Polis
My research participants may not have read Hegel, but they used their new capacities and knowledge to embrace the expanding world and make it their world. Furthermore, the way they accomplished this provides another facet of their behaviour whose profundity might be better appreciated when re-imagined in the light of Hegelian philosophy. For Hegel, our engagement and expansion are through institutions that embody reason. So where, then, is this core role of

reason found within the ethnography? In practice, the criteria that ordinary people, who are not philosophers, tend to use to evaluate reason is encapsulated by the related term 'reasonable'.[21] How much should the CCA reasonably interfere with what Cuan citizens want to do? What would be a reasonable division between care for family and care for climate change? What actions deserve the widely used Irish expression of 'fair play'? While they rarely invoke reason as an abstraction, people in Cuan constantly invoke terms that equate with reasonable.

There are considerable benefits to a consideration of the term 'reasonable' as opposed to the more abstract term 'reason'. Almost every condition that we face has elements of the contradictory. The smartphone has simultaneous negative and positive possibilities; so does parenting. We hardly ever encounter reason, but we constantly confront situations which demand an assessment of what is reasonable. Hegel constructed an abstract philosophy around reason but was deeply involved in complex discussions around topics such as civil society, which can be more easily aligned with the projection of reasonableness in trying to balance its harms and benefits. The people of Cuan typically see the fulfilment of happiness through their alignment with social and institutional forces that they identify with to the degree to which these forces are regarded as reasonable. The reasonable provides the basis for the normative. In the case of Cuan, this meant being aligned with the social expectations of one's peers, whether through participating in a Men's Shed, or an art course, volunteering to help autistic children, or helping generate good *craic* in a pub. The same approach to balance can be seen in how my research participants weigh up their relationship to people, things, and the world. Is it better to have many friends or deeper friendships? It is their answer to the fundamental question posed by the ancient Greeks with respect to *eudaimonia*: how should we balance our pursuit of virtue and of happiness such that the former contributes to the latter?

An extended example was presented in the previous chapter through exploring how people choose their holidays through trying to balance the rewards of depth and breadth, now recast as coming to a reasonable outcome through the application of reason. Once identified as such, these principles can be discovered in multiple examples found in every previous chapter, ranging from which and how many sports their children should join, to whether they need any new clothes, to how much time they should give to a community initiative.

Caveats
Does all this depend on a rather overly positive view of Cuan; a kind of presentist version of nostalgia? Returning to Cuan after completing a draft of this book with a desire to be more sceptical, I was defeated. There were just too many new examples of this town/ *polis* in action. The new open orchards that are being planted, where everyone will be free to pick their own fruit. The quantity and quality of planted flowers on the verges around the trees. The subsequent success of active politicians, who I could personally attest came to politics as an altruistic vocation, evident from my conversations with them before they had been voted in. Still more sensitive approaches to autism and the egalitarianism of their poetry festival. None of this means that a good enough life corresponds to the good life. There remains the evidence presented in chapter 5 of how many people can still ignore the state housing that lies at the core of Cuan, reflecting the degree of inequality that remains within the town. There is evidence also for depression, the degree of drug use, and the number of psychotherapists and others who are required to help heal the experience of traumas, whose causes include the pressure on young people that Cuan's own vision of success imposes upon them. The plight of young people wanting to move out of their parents' homes also raises the question of whether this 'golden generation' will be the last as well as the first. There is a growing concern with the problem of inequality in the distribution of life's burdens between the generations.

It should also have been clear that not everyone in Cuan has been included within the ethnography. There were those people described as the 'pockets' in chapter 5, who are an integral part of Cuan but share few of my generalizations about the rest of the town. They were, however, contrasted with other people living on the Vartry Estate, who have been included in this portrait of Cuan as they have been a major source for this study. The people of Cuan are not all middle class, though this is the direction of travel. This is also a book about a largely retired population rather than of Cuan as a whole. The term Cuan itself is obviously a generalization. Each individual would be in some ways exceptional. They had very different backgrounds in terms of former employment, the absence or presence of savings and private pensions. Those living on the Vartry Estate rarely enjoyed the same levels of affluence as others.

Important strands of Greek philosophy developed the idea of the democratic *polis* and the ideal of the good life as the *eudaimonia* discussed and described by the first philosophers. But the reality was highly exclusive, based on only privileged male citizens. By contrast to such a Greek *polis*, Cuan is highly inclusive. The town works very hard to ensure the provision of full access, whether to the elderly or to the autistic. The integration of the Vartry Estate has been much slower than it should but is incrementally developing. So even if this falls far short of the good life, because we can and should go a good deal further, Cuan confirms the direction of travel, and right now we could do with some pointers.

My research participants generally knew that life was better and happier at this juncture than it had ever been. Indeed, one of the most common discussions overheard was about whether their current happiness depended upon their previous experience. This took the form of worrying about the next generation. If these retirees had avoided simplistic nostalgia and were able to appreciate their advantages because they themselves had lived through experiences of struggle and often poverty, would the new generation, born into relative affluence, be thereby unable to appreciate their good fortune and be less able to act upon it? Was a background in poverty somehow yet one more advantage that older people had compared with the young? I had this conversation several times during the ethnography. My interlocutors didn't know the answer to that question and neither do I. I have, however, previously worked with young people in other regions and found them far more mature and impressive than common discourses and the media would suggest. What can be said is that merely by commonly debating such a question in such an explicit manner, these retirees tell us how much they have understood about who they are and the factors behind their good enough lives.

Anthropology and Philosophy

From its inception, central strands of philosophy have attempted to delineate the nature of the good life. Yet there has been no equivalent attempt to find an analogous definition of the ideal good life from this study of Cuan. The people of Cuan are not scholastic philosophers and have generally no interest in such a task. I, too, have no ambition to be an academic philosopher. Cuan constitutes a single case study in which almost everything about people's lives and values was found to be contingent upon their history and circumstance. This represents both the possibilities and the limitations of ethnography. The considerable advantage of ethnography is that it is not speculative. It is an encounter with an existing population that can be observed, demonstrating a version of the good enough life achieved by at least one population. On the other hand, every ethnographic chapter includes a detailed account of the background history and factors that help explain what was observed: for example, the precise distance between Cuan and Dublin and the type of employment in which most of these retirees had spent their lives. How important is the size of this town/*polis*? Could we imagine similar outcomes in a place that was much smaller or much larger?[22] Is size the key to a balance between what Ferdinand Tönnies called *Gemeinschaft* and *Gesellschaft* or what Émile Durkheim called mechanical and organic solidarity?[23] There are so many contingent variables. No other population is the result of this particular history or combination of factors. This book has been specifically about Cuan. I hardly set foot outside the town, so I cannot even affirm how Irish they are.

Mostly, anthropologists develop their wider claims out of such ethnographic particularism, through comparative studies rather than through philosophy. Only comparative studies can answer the question just posed in relation to Tönnies and Durkheim as to the impact of size. For anthropologists to go straight to philosophy is a kind of cheating, since we tend to grant philosophers a level of universalism that would obviate the more patient set of steps through comparison that ensures we keep hold of the value of the particular that comes with ethnography.

For example, the ASSA project, which provided the funding and rationale for this ethnography, also resulted in our book *The Global Smartphone*.[24] Each of the ten simultaneous ethnographies that contributed to that volume is shown to provide a different perspective on what it means to age, the purpose of retirement, and the potential of smartphones. *The Global Smartphone* includes a general statement about the smartphone being more a place within which we now live, 'the transportal home', rather than simply being a phone. This is then followed by a discussion on how that generalization means very different things for a migrant with family in several locations,

CONCLUSION

or for a young person unable to afford any other home, as well as the different meanings of home between a Japanese fieldsite and a Ugandan fieldsite. The present volume is, by contrast, not a typical ethnographic monograph. Situating the ethnography in relation to philosophy has resulted in the addition of extensive normative discussions and moral arguments conventionally eschewed in traditional ethnographic monographs in favour of clearly presenting the values of the research participants. My holistic ideal of trying to study whatever is there – in this case, sports, holidays, and bingo – rather than mainly focusing on the research topic may be seen as rather dated by other anthropologists. The contemporary emphasis would be more on my own presuppositions (the current clunky academic term is 'positionality'), which inform my outlook when studying others, and acknowledging the critique that has arisen from important developments in decolonial perspectives.[25]

This book has tried not to blur the boundaries between anthropology and philosophy but rather to juxtapose them as quite different disciplines, each with its own integrity and goals. The initial idea was that the juxtaposition of chapters might provide a yardstick which would allow the ethnography to be measured against philosophy and vice versa. In retrospect, perhaps the only pairings that followed this plan are the present conclusion's use of Hegel and chapter 6 on Rawls. A different, but hopefully positive, outcome arose through the juxtaposition of Socrates in chapter 8 with chapter 7 on sports. Re-examining the birth of philosophy was of considerable assistance in helping to acknowledge the profundity of sports in the life of Cuan. Other pairings brought out qualities of Cuan through a more negative appraisal of the relevant philosophy. Chapter 4 on Western Marxism consisted mainly of a critique of the rather condescending and elitist nature of *Dialectic of Enlightenment*. The capacity of these retirees to develop an anti-materialist stance, while living within neo-liberal capitalism, was used to repudiate assumptions made in philosophy and social science as to the relationship between economy and social values. The discussion of the Stoics and Epicurus in chapter 12 was also largely critical, in order to accentuate the radical difference between a search for the good life based on a retreat from sensual experience into contemplation, as opposed to an expansive cosmology that seeks to experience as much of sensual life as can reasonably be assimilated prior to the extinction of death.

CONCLUSION

In other cases, the attempt at juxtaposition proved rather frustrating. Significant philosophers of freedom, such as Sartre and Berlin (chapter 2), were concerned with issues of ontology and politics that proved hard to equate with the extraordinary shifts in the experience of freedom found within this single generation of retirees in Cuan. Fortunately, Nussbaum and Sen then provided exemplary work on how to relate philosophy and universal principles to the specific conditions and struggles of contemporary populations, without being reduced to mere cultural relativism. In the case of Heidegger (chapter 10), the original intention was to relate his philosophy to the German concept of *Heimat*, in order to contest a common assumption about the relationship between origins and authenticity. Although this was partially achieved in relation to a later essay by Heidegger, my limited understanding of *Being and Time* suggested that he was too engaged with a specific philosophical trajectory to be exploited as any kind of yardstick held against an extant population.

Common themes found across various philosophical writings that might appear inimical to anthropology included the emphasis on the relationship between individuals and the universal for philosophers such as Kant and Rawls, and the excavation of a pre-ontological and other-worldly semantics, found in Heidegger, that is difficult to square with ethnographic studies. There is also the tendency to asceticism and to idealize the life of the philosopher most clearly enunciated by the Stoics. It is, however, very easy to name philosophers who would not accord with such generalizations. Whatever Maurice Merleau-Ponty might be accused of, it would not include ignoring the body as the vehicle of experience.[26] A major fault in this book is that it has only considered some philosophers and schools within what is itself the highly problematic category of 'Western' philosophy. I dearly wish that I had the knowledge and background for a wider encounter, but I do not.

There are an equal number of arguments that would demonstrate the weakness or limitations of anthropology as against philosophy. It is very rare for anthropologists to even attempt the intense scholarly and consistent lines of reasoning that are expected within professional philosophy. If anything, contemporary anthropologists prefer to sidle up to literary figures who do not represent such exacting standards of argument, but instead valorize our more general descriptive powers of exemplification. Anthropologists are excellent at observing and explicating the normative practices of the peoples whom we have

CONCLUSION

studied, but do not usually try to create the detailed discussion of the normative as a speculative philosophical endeavour by which we might all judge ourselves, with the associated complex caveats and considerations of consequence. Anthropologists obviously tend to the particular, as characterized by ethnography. As Susan Neiman has argued, there are many ways in which philosophy has developed inspirational ideals and moral clarity well beyond the playbook of anthropology.[27]

It was noted in the introduction to this volume that this book is hardly alone in examining the relationship between philosophy and anthropology. A very different example of this relationship would be found, for example, in a recent book by Veena Das.[28] The introduction also acknowledged the way many philosophers have argued from their side for some kind of juxtaposition with social science. Particularly influential was the book *After Virtue* by Alasdair MacIntyre, which cleared a pathway along which we might proceed.[29] MacIntyre argues that all moral theory implicates a sociology in as much as it implies its application to some social setting.[30] Along with Charles Taylor, he saw the possibility that different cultural traditions might at least respect each other and consider what they have in common.[31] This would bring philosophy closer to the comparative anthropological project. MacIntyre argues that the project of a universal moral philosophy based on a single idea of reason must fail. Instead, we have to recognize a plurality of moral arguments that are always taken in large measure from cultural traditions such as Christianity or historical ideals of honour. He was clearly influenced by the structural anthropology of Mary Douglas and the sociology of Erving Goffman in recognizing the arbitrary nature of many cultural rules, while noting how within philosophy Nietzsche provided a similar and earlier acknowledgement of the arbitrary.[32]

Yet in several respects the conclusions of this book do not follow the expectations of MacIntyre in *After Virtue*. In philosophy and in much of anthropology, an opposition is commonly drawn between collective and inherited cultural tradition as opposed to the creativity of active individual agency and choice. Yet in Cuan the creation of *eudaimonia* accords with neither of these. It is a thoroughly social and cultural process, based on considerable normativity and consensus, rather than distinctive individual choice, which appears mainly as eccentricity or atypicality. The most influential approaches to morality and freedom in recent anthropology, such as those by

CONCLUSION

Laidlaw, Mattingly, Robbins,[33] and others, differ from more traditional anthropological writing in that they become more like the philosophers in their emphasis on the moral dilemmas and decisions of individuals. In this, they provide a welcome corrective to the often over-generalized treatment of peoples in earlier anthropological work.[34] This book, by contrast, is almost entirely a discourse about a collective termed either Cuan or its retirees. It is a collective that does not require us to take the concept of a society to a meta level in the manner of Durkheim. Cuan is, rather, an empirical collective. The ethnography encountered a relatively consensual population who could be observed creating and maintaining their own normativity, which underpins the way they have been represented here. The principal reason for choosing to emphasize the general and the typical is that understanding the creation of a town/*polis* as the foundation for a good enough life is quite different from a study of how individuals make ethical choices.

A further difference is that the creation of Cuan was not based on inherited tradition, as emphasized by MacIntyre and many social scientists. Its creators were far more influenced by their repudiation of their past, whether it was the values of Catholicism or consumerism.[35] The previous chapters focused on how, mainly as blow-ins, these people undertook to forge Cuan itself, as an entirely different place from historical Cuan, based on their imported vision of community, which was something they, rather than the indigenous population, required. The term 'forgery' is eloquent here because it simultaneously expresses the artificial nature of this endeavour, its malleability, and also its final and brilliant authenticity. It captures the movement from forging banknotes to forging steel. Mostly, then, *eudaimonia* is a result of the collective creation of culture as community.

The main purpose of this concluding chapter was, then, to turn the whole thing around, to use Hegel's concept of objectification to shift the story from how this population made Cuan to how their labour in creating Cuan in turn made them into this population. Appropriately, the final conclusion has merely reiterated what I was being told from day one of my stay in Cuan. My research participants had been trying to explain to me the very same thing. The idea of writing this book came from the initial observation that people in Cuan don't talk about the personal happiness that they have created, or about their own individual virtues. Instead, they talk incessantly about Cuan as

CONCLUSION

the best place they could possibly live in. What seemed initially a rather 'over the top' affirmation of how lucky and how blessed they were to be living in Cuan became the catalyst around which this project crystallized. Cuan is as much the source and presumption of *eudaimonia* as was the *polis* in classical Greece, except for the latter the *polis* was the given context, while this book has explored how people made a town that made them.

Finally

A reader of a draft of this manuscript, herself from Cuan, commented as follows: 'In the chapters I read everything you say is correct, but I found it too "picture perfect". Cuan is great but not that great and not without problems. And so are its inhabitants.' There again, I have presented Cuan as a modest population who would be expected to baulk at being so explicitly praised. The deep structural inequalities, problems with drug use and depression, as described in chapter 5, give sufficient reason why Cuan is not presented as a candidate for the ideal society. The term 'good enough' has been used throughout this book to stress the anthropological criterion of comparison. The point is not how good Cuan is but how difficult it would be to find an existing contemporary society that is demonstrably better. On analogy with the term 'good enough mother' used in psychology, it is also intended to show respect for the compromises and achievements that are accomplished through the struggles of ordinary life. This makes for a very different goal than the philosophical consideration of the good life as a speculative ideal.

As mentioned in the introduction to this book, most of my previous ethnographic experiences have been with populations characterized by life in struggle. My first ethnography, undertaken for my Ph.D., was based in an Indian village riven by poverty and oppression, with no access to modern medicine. Later I was involved in projects concerned with poverty in Jamaica,[36] with migrant women in the UK from the Philippines trying to mother their left-behind children,[37] and, more recently, with people in a hospice who had a terminal diagnosis.[38] But anthropology is tasked with understanding humanity as a whole. Research engaged with suffering and poverty should be balanced by encounters that help us understand what populations have managed to become when blessed by more fortunate historical circumstances.

CONCLUSION

A book of praise is nevertheless an unusual endeavour within contemporary social science. This one was written during a period of so much suffering, whether in Sudan, Myanmar, or the current invasion of Ukraine by Russia. The participants in this study were an example of that mostly middle-class, reasonably affluent, quiet, suburban (in the sense of neither metropolitan nor rural) society that tens of millions of people are trying to reach and to emulate. Hopefully, one day in the future, the attainment of these conditions may not require migration. If regions in Africa, South and East Asia, and Latin America are enabled to reduce poverty, Cuan might then become still more relevant to the imagination of a feasible good enough life. Sadly, that day does not seem at all close. If anything, circumstances seem set to decline rather than improve. This does not just relate to the increase in global inequality. Locally, many younger people in Cuan, unable to afford their own homes, would certainly not feel they had been adequately represented by this generic portrait of Cuan. Millennials are unlikely to have the same advantages as their parents.

It is, however, neither complacent nor naïve to extol the humanity and virtue in a population. This study was based not on the presumption that Cuan is typical or a sign of the future, but rather on the fact that Cuan has been possible. The book has argued that a flawed but existing population might teach us things about whom we might strive to be that an ideal, but speculative, model could not. And perhaps this is something that we really need at this justifiably pessimistic historical moment: to recognize that Cuan can only exist because of a relatively privileged and affluent condition, but equally that there are plenty of privileged and affluent populations who are nothing like Cuan. We surely want to continue a discussion about the good life that started in the fifth century BCE but remains as important as ever. This requires both philosophical contributions to what ideally the good life could be and ethnographic evidence for what varieties of the relatively good enough life already exist.

NOTES

Introduction: Cuan and Kant

1 Here and elsewhere I have followed the gender bias of the original texts, but only with reference to those writings.
2 Plato, *Euthydemus* 282a, in *The Dialogues of Plato: Volume 2*, trans. B. Jowett, London: Sphere Books, 1970, p. 147.
3 Aristotle, *The Nicomachean Ethics*, trans. J.A.K. Thomson with H. Tredennick, London: Penguin, 2004.
4 The results published jointly as P. Garvey and D. Miller, *Ageing with Smartphones in Ireland: When Life Becomes Craft*, London: UCL Press, 2021.
5 D.W. Winnicott, *Babies and Their Mothers*, New York: Addison Wesley, 1987.
6 X. Wang, *Social Media in Industrial China*, London: UCL Press, 2016.
7 Equally important are ethnographic accounts of how people who regard themselves as the 'left-behinds' of modernity manage to extract what good they can from otherwise extremely difficult circumstance: for example, B. Knauf, 'Finding the Good: Reactive Modernity amongst the Gebusi, in the Pacific and Elsewhere', *The Australian Journal of Anthropology* 30 (2019): 84–103.
8 D. Miller, *The Comfort of People*, Cambridge: Polity, 2017.
9 D. Miller, *Social Media in an English Village*, London: UCL Press, 2016.
10 Ibid.
11 Ø. Rabbås, E. Emilsson, H. Fossheim, and M. Tuominen (eds), *The Quest for the Good Life: Ancient Philosophers on Happiness*, Oxford: Oxford University Press, 2015.
12 H. Walker and I. Kavedžija (eds), *Values of Happiness: Toward an Anthropology of Purpose in Life*, Chicago: Hau Books, 2016.
13 For example, A. Jiménez Corsín (ed.), *Culture and Well-Being:*

Anthropological Approaches to Freedom and Political Ethics, London: Pluto, 2008; I. Kavedžija, *Making Meaningful Lives: Tales from an Aging Japan*, Philadelphia: University of Pennsylvania Press, 2019; M. Lambek, 'Value and Virtue', *Anthropological Theory* 8(2) (2008): 133–57; J. Robbins, 'Beyond the Suffering Subject: Toward an Anthropology of the Good', *Journal of the Royal Anthropological Institute* 19(3) (2013): 447–62. There is a flourishing concern with the anthropology of ethics and morality: for example, M. Lambek, V. Das, D. Fassin, and W. Keane, *Four Lectures on Ethics*, Chicago: HAU Books, 2015; or J. Zigon, *Morality: An Anthropological Perspective*, Oxford: Berg, 2008. These studies often focus upon the location of ethics: for example, D. Henig, A. Strhan, and J. Robbins (eds), *Where is the Good in the World?* New York: Berghahn, 2022. Such locations might be within interactions (e.g. W. Keane, *Ethical Life: Its Natural and Social Histories*, Princeton: Princeton University Press, 2016), in the everyday (e.g. M. Lambek, ed., *Ordinary Ethics: Anthropology, Language, and Action*, New York: Fordham University Press, 2010), or in the various exemplars of ethics (e.g. J. Robbins, 'Where in the World are Values? Exemplarity and Moral Motivation', in C. Mattingly, R. Dyring, M. Louw, and T. Wentzer (eds), *Moral Engines: Exploring the Ethical Drives in Human Life*, London: Berghahn, 2018, pp. 155–73). By contrast, this volume attempts to understand why Cuan itself is seen as the ideal site for the good life, with as much concern for happiness as for virtue.

14 A book that could be described as an extended essay on the relationship between anthropology and philosophy, as opposed to this volume's emphasis upon the relationship between an ethnography and philosophy, would be J. Laidlaw, *The Subject of Virtue*, Cambridge: Cambridge University Press, 2014. There are also many works of anthropology and ethnography that see themselves as in dialogue with particular philosophical approaches, such as V. Das, *Textures of the Ordinary: Doing Anthropology after Wittgenstein*, New York: Fordham University Press, 2020. For a more general discussion about the relationship between anthropology and moral philosophy, see C. Mattingly, R. Dyring, M. Louw, and T. Wentzer (eds), *Moral Engines: Exploring the Ethical Drives in Human Life*, London: Berghahn, 2018.

15 A. MacIntyre, *After Virtue: A Study in Moral Theory*, 3rd edn, Notre Dame, IN: University of Notre Dame Press, 2007 [1981].

16 F. Mckay, 'Eudaimonia and Culture: The Anthropology of Virtue', In J. Vitterso (ed.), *Handbook of Eudaimonic Well-Being*, Cham: Springer, 2016, pp. 409–26.

17 T. Widlock, 'Virtue', in D. Fassin (ed.), *A Companion to Moral Anthropology*, Oxford: John Wiley and Sons, 2012, pp. 186–203.

18 M. Nussbaum and A. Sen (eds), *The Quality of Life*, Oxford: Clarendon Press, 1993.
19 See note 4 above.
20 Much within the following sections overlaps, for obvious reasons, with the introduction to Garvey and Miller, *Ageing with Smartphones in Ireland*. Pauline Garvey should be fully credited as the co-author of those sections.
21 F. O'Toole, *We Don't Know Ourselves: A Personal History of Ireland since 1958*, London: Head of Zeus, 2021.
22 P. Share, H. Tovey, and M.P. Corcoran, *A Sociology of Ireland*, Dublin: Gill & Macmillan, 2007.
23 One example is the Global Irish Civic Forum, which encourages the Irish diaspora abroad to come to Dublin to discuss their work and engage with government. See https://www.dfa.ie/global-irish/support-overseas/global-irish-civic-forum/.
24 T. Inglis, *Moral Monopoly: The Rise and Fall of the Catholic Church in Modern Ireland*, 2nd edn, Dublin: University College Dublin Press, 1998. This can be seen in the 1937 Irish Free State Constitution, which 'endeavours to ensure that mothers shall not be obliged by economic necessity to engage in labour to the neglect of their duties in the home' (Article 41, Paragraph 2). For further discussion, see C. Wills, 'Women, Domesticity and the Family: Recent Feminist Work in Irish Cultural Studies', *Cultural Studies* 15(1): 33–57.
25 T. Inglis, *Global Ireland: Same Difference*, New York: Routledge, 2007.
26 M. Keenan, 'Sexual Abuse and the Catholic Church', in T. Inglis (ed.), *Are the Irish Different?*, Manchester: Manchester University Press, 2014, pp. 99–110.
27 E. Drążkiewicz et al., 'Repealing Ireland's Eighth Amendment: Abortion Rights and Democracy Today', *Social Anthropology* 28(3): 1–25.
28 D. Hakim and D. Dalby, 'Ireland Votes to Approve Gay Marriage, Putting Country in Vanguard', *The New York Times*, 23 May 2015.
29 Unemployment benefits are the third highest of the OECD jointly with Iceland, and pensions are relatively generous at €243 per week (2021), compared to the UK, where they are £159. Some of this is explained by the high cost of living in Ireland compared to other countries in the EU.
30 S. O'Riain, *The Rise and Fall of Ireland's Celtic Tiger: Liberalism, Boom and Bust*, Cambridge: Cambridge University Press, 2014.
31 For more details of the 2013 initiative to encourage the Irish diaspora to visit Ireland, see https://www.discoverireland.ie/The-Gathering-Ireland.
32 F. Murphy, 'Austerity Ireland, the New Thrift Culture and Sustainable Consumption', *Journal of Business Anthropology* 6(2): 158–74.
33 J. Garry, N. Hardman, and D. Payne, *Irish Social and Political Attitudes*, Liverpool: Liverpool University Press, 2006.

34 H. Forsberg and V. Timonen, 'The Future of the Family as Envisioned by Young Adults in Ireland', *Journal of Youth Studies* 21(6): 765–79.
35 Most of the trends described above are typically interpreted as aspects of growing individualism: see J. Gray, R. Geraghty, and D. Ralph, *Family Rhythms: The Changing Textures of Family Life in Ireland*, Manchester: Manchester University Press, 2016, p. 101. Inglis (*Global Ireland*) documents key changes during the late twentieth century in Irish society, from being dominated by Catholicism to a liberal-individualist consumer culture, emphasizing the influence of the media and the market.
36 L. Connolly, 'Introduction' and 'Locating "the Irish Family"': Towards Plurality of Family Forms?', in L. Connolly (ed.), *The 'Irish' Family*, London: Routledge, 2015, pp. 1–9 and pp. 10–38 respectively.
37 Gray et al., *Family Rhythms*.
38 Connolly, 'Locating "the Irish Family"'.
39 S. Arber and V. Timonen (eds), *Contemporary Grandparenting: Changing Family Relationships in Global Contexts*, Bristol: Policy Press, 2012; Forsberg and Timonen, 'The Future of the Family'; Gray et al., *Family Rhythms*.
40 For a more detailed discussion, see D. Miller, 'Brexit and the Decolonization of Ireland', *HAU: Journal of Ethnographic Theory* 10(2) (2020): 356–60.
41 M. Norris, *Property, Family and the Irish Welfare State*, Cham: Springer, 2016; M. Norris, 'Davis Now Lectures: Unmaking Home: Making Homes for Shelter or for Investment?', RTE.IE, 4 February 2020: https://www.rte.ie/culture/2020/0131/1112298-davis-now-lectures-making-homes-for-shelter-or-for-investment/.
42 M. Hickman, 'Thinking about Ireland and the Irish Diaspora', in T. Inglis (ed.), *Are the Irish Different?*, Manchester: Manchester University Press, pp. 133–44.
43 O'Toole, *We Don't Know Ourselves*, p. 567.
44 Cuan seems in some ways comparable to the pastoral ideal and its positive connotations for parenting expressed by the inhabitants of Ratoath in M. Corcoran, '"God's Golden Acre for Children": Pastoralism and Sense of Place in New Suburban Communities', *Urban Studies* 47(12) (2010): 2537–54.
45 Literally shared a tradition of training in that Pauline Garvey had at one time been my Ph.D. student. Positionality might, however, be of very considerable consequence in other cases. For an example, see another of the ASSA monographs: C. Hawkins, *Ageing with Smartphones in Urban Uganda*, London: UCL Press, forthcoming.
46 D. Miller, *Material Culture and Mass Consumption*, Oxford: Blackwell, 1987.

47 I. Kant, *Critique of Pure Reason*, ed. and trans. P. Guyer and A.W. Wood, Cambridge: Cambridge University Press, 1998 [1781].
48 I. Kant, *Critique of Practical Reason*, ed. and trans. M. Gregor, Cambridge: Cambridge University Press, 2015 [1788].
49 I. Kant, *Fundamental Principles of the Metaphysics of Morals*, trans. T.K. Abbott, Project Gutenberg, 2002 [1785]: https://www.gutenberg.org/ebooks/5682.
50 Kant notes in the third section of his *Fundamental Principles of the Metaphysics of Morals* that 'Freedom must be presupposed as a Property of the Will of all Rational Beings'. See also Kant's preface to *Critique of Practical Reason*.
51 Though Kant does allow for nuance depending upon context. See S. Neiman, *Moral Clarity*, Princeton: Princeton University Press, 2009, p. 214.
52 Lambek has pointed out that anthropology would have difficulty assuming ethics as essentially a study of reason, and would be better served by Aristotle's emphasis on ethics as exemplified by action. See M. Lambek, 'Introduction', in M. Lambek (ed.), *Ordinary Ethics: Anthropology, Language, and Action*, New York: Fordham University Press, 2010, pp. 1–36 (p. 14).
53 M. White, 'The Virtues of a Kantian Economics', in J.A. Baker and M.D. White (eds), *Economics and the Virtues: Building a New Moral Foundation*, Oxford: Oxford University Press, 2016, pp. 94–115.
54 J. Otteson, 'Kantian Individualism and Political Libertarianism', *Independent Review* 13(3) (2009): 389–409.
55 D. Miller, *Tales from Facebook*, Cambridge: Polity, 2011, pp. 111–21.
56 M. Strathern, *After Nature*, Cambridge: Cambridge University Press, 1992.
57 A. Macfarlane, *The Origins of English Individualism*, Oxford: Blackwell, 1979.
58 D. Miller et al., *How the World Changed Social Media*, London: UCL Press, 2016.
59 Miller, *Social Media in an English Village*.
60 Published as *The Comfort of People* (see note 8 above).
61 A problem marvellously portrayed in the recent film *The Banshees of Inisherin* by director Martin McDonagh.
62 For an interesting alternative discussion of these parallels and differences between Kant and the way anthropology, but also Durkheim, insist upon an *a priori* sociality, see M. Holbraad, 'The Contingency of Concepts', in P. Charbonnier, G. Salmon, and P. Skafish (eds), *Comparative Metaphysics*, London: Rowman & Littlefield, pp. 131–56.
63 For a parallel philosophical critique, see I. Hacking, *The Social*

Construction of What?, Cambridge, MA: Harvard University Press, 1999.
64. M. Klein, *Envy and Gratitude and Other Works*, London: Delacorte Press, 1975.
65. This is hardly the first book to suggest that such empirical studies of society can become the complement to philosophy, a point that goes back at least as far as Durkheim's 1909 essay 'The Contribution of Sociology to Psychology and Philosophy', in É. Durkheim, *The Rules of Sociological Method*, trans. W.D. Halls, New York: The Free Press, 1982, pp. 236–40.
66. Issues discussed in considerable detail by the anthropologists noted above who work on issues of ethics, responsibility, and choice.
67. C. Mackenzie, 'Relational Autonomy, Normative Authority and Perfectionism', *Journal of Social Philosophy* 39(4) (2008): 512–33; C. Mackenzie, 'Three Dimensions of Autonomy: A Relational Analysis', in A. Veltman and M. Piper (eds), *Autonomy, Oppression and Gender*, Oxford: Oxford University Press, 2014, pp. 15–41; C. Mackenzie and N. Stoljar (eds), *Relational Autonomy: Feminist Perspectives on Autonomy, Agency, and the Social Self*, New York: Oxford University Press, 2000.
68. These contributions of Kant's moral philosophy are summarized in Neiman, *Moral Clarity*, pp. 93–110, 151–62.
69. The concept of cultural relativism and the term 'culture' are often critiqued within anthropology itself but they remain a presumption underlying most anthropological practice. See, for example, L. Abu-Lughod, 'Do Muslim Women Really Need Saving? Anthropological Reflections on Cultural Relativism and Its Others', *American Anthropologist* 104(3) (2002): 783–90.

Chapter 1 An Exceptionally Free Society
1. Garvey and Miller, *Ageing with Smartphones in Ireland*.
2. O'Toole, *We Don't Know Ourselves*, pp. 158–73.
3. Garvey and Miller, *Ageing with Smartphones in Ireland*, p. 183.
4. Inglis, *Moral Monopoly*; Inglis, *Global Ireland*.
5. M. Duque, *Ageing with Smartphones in Urban Brazil: A Work in Progress*, London: UCL Press, 2022.
6. Details of these activities can be found in Garvey and Miller, *Ageing with Smartphones in Ireland*, chapter 3.
7. D. Miller and P. Garvey, 'Grandparenting as the Resolution of Kinship as Experience', *Journal of the Royal Anthropological Institute* 28(3) (2022): 975–92.
8. For Irish grandparenting more generally, see R. Geraghty, J. Gray, and D. Ralph, 'One of the Best Members of the Family: Continuity and Change in Young Children's Relationships with Their Grandparents',

in L. Connolly (ed.), *The Irish Family*, London: Routledge, 2015, pp. 124–39; M. Share and L. Kerrins, 'The Role of Grandparents in Childcare in Ireland: Towards a Research Agenda', *Irish Journal of Applied Social Studies* 9(1) (2009): 33–47; M. Ward and C. McGarrigle, 'The Contribution of Older Adults to Their Families and Communities', Dublin: TILDA, 2018 (https://tilda.tcd.ie/publications/reports/pdf/w3-key-findings-report/Chapter%202.pdf).

9 D. Miller, 'The Ideology of Friendship in the Era of Facebook', *Hau: Journal of Ethnographic Theory* 7(1) (2017): 377–95.

10 P. Higgs and C. Gilleard, *Rethinking Old Age: Theorising the Fourth Age*, London: Macmillan International Higher Education, 2015.

11 Drążkiewicz et al., 'Repealing Ireland's Eighth Amendment'.

12 For this point more generally, see Hickman, 'Thinking about Ireland and the Irish Diaspora'.

13 For an extended version of this argument, see Miller, 'Brexit and the Decolonization of Ireland'.

14 R. Wilkinson and K. Pickett, *The Spirit Level*, London: Penguin, 2009.

15 Personal communication from David Whyte. See also D. Whyte, 'Viral Intimacy and Catholic Nationalist Political Economy: COVID-19 and the Community Response in Rural Ireland', *Anthropology in Action* 27(3) (2021): 39–43. Also E. Devereux, 'The Lonely Furrow: Muintir Na Tire and Irish Community Development 1931–1991', *Community Development Journal* 28(1) (1993): 45–54.

16 R. Breen, D. Hannan, D. Rottman, and C. Whelan, *Understanding Ireland: State, Class and Development in the Republic of Ireland*, Basingstoke: Palgrave Macmillan, 1990, p. 6.

17 A. Koster and K. Garde, 'Sexual Desire and Menopausal Development: A Prospective Study of Danish Women Born in 1936', *Maturitas* 16(1) (1993): 49–60. For a counter-argument, see Duque, *Ageing with Smartphones in Urban Brazil*, pp. 181–207.

18 For a sense of the complexity of Irish post-colonial identity, see, amongst many discussions, M. Free and C. Scully, 'The Run of Ourselves: Shame, Guilt and Confession in Post-Celtic Tiger Irish Media', *International Journal of Cultural Studies* 21(3) (2018): 308–24; S. Howe, *Ireland and Empire: Colonial Legacies in Irish History and Culture*, Oxford: Oxford University Press, 2000; D. Kiberd, *Inventing Ireland: The Literature of the Modern Nation*, Cambridge, MA: Harvard University Press, 1995; G. Moane, 'A Psychological Analysis of Colonialism in an Irish Context', *Irish Journal of Psychology* 15 (1994): 250–65.

19 T. Scharf, V. Timonen, C. Conlon, and G. Carney, *Changing Generations: Findings from New Research on Intergenerational Relations in Ireland*, Trinity College Dublin and National University of Ireland Galway, April 2013: http://www.tara.tcd.ie/handle/2262/75620.

Chapter 2 Philosophers of Freedom

1. J.-P. Sartre, *Being and Nothingness: An Essay in Phenomenological Ontology*, trans. S. Richmond, London: Routledge, 2020 [1943].
2. S. Bakewell, *At the Existentialist Café: Freedom Being and Apricot Cocktails*, London: Chatto & Windus, 2016.
3. Sartre, *Being and Nothingness*, pp. 482–92.
4. J.-P. Sartre, *Anti-Semite and Jew*, trans. G.J. Becker, New York: Schocken, 1995 [1946].
5. J.-P. Sartre, *Critique of Dialectical Reason: Volume 1: Theory of Practical Ensembles*, trans. A. Sheridan-Smith, London: Verso, 2004 [1960]; *Critique of Dialectical Reason: Volume 2: The Intelligibility of History*, trans. Q. Hoare, London: Verso, 2006 [1985].
6. J.-P. Sartre, *Nausea*, trans. R. Baldick, London: Penguin, 2000 [1938].
7. I. Berlin, *Four Essays on Liberty*, Oxford: Oxford University Press, 1969.
8. I. Berlin, *Liberty*, Oxford: Oxford University Press, 2003.
9. I. Berlin, *Freedom and Its Betrayal: Six Enemies of Human Liberty*, London: Chatto & Windus, 2002.
10. Ibid., pp. 74–104.
11. An exemplary case of positive freedom, taken from communist China, is found in W. Hinton, *Fanshen: A Documentary of Revolution in a Chinese Village*, New York: Monthly Review Press, 1966.
12. A.W. Wood, *Hegel's Ethical Thought*, Cambridge: Cambridge University Press, 1990, pp. 41–2.
13. M. Nussbaum, 'Nature, Function, and Capability: Aristotle on Political Distribution', Working Paper 31, Helsinki: World Institute for Development Economic Research of the United Nations University, 1987.
14. Aristotle, *The Politics*, trans. T.A. Sinclair, London: Penguin, 1962, pp. 255–98.
15. Ibid., p. 5.
16. Ibid., p. 7.
17. M. Nussbaum, *Women and Human Development: The Capabilities Approach*, Cambridge: Cambridge University Press, 2000, pp. 11–13.
18. A. Sen, *Development as Freedom*, Oxford: Oxford University Press, 1999.
19. Ibid., p. 17.
20. M. Nussbaum, *Frontiers of Justice: Disability, Nationality, Species Membership*, Cambridge, MA: Harvard University Press, 2006, pp. 75–81.
21. Nussbaum, *Women and Human Development*.
22. Sen, *Development as Freedom*, pp. 189–203; Nussbaum, *Women and Human Development*.
23. É. Durkheim, *Suicide: A Study in Sociology*, trans. J.A. Spaulding and G. Simpson, New York: Free Press, 1979 [1897].

24 S. Marks, 'Durkheim's Theory of Anomie', *American Journal of Sociology* 80(2) (1994): 329–63.
25 Miller, 'The Ideology of Friendship in the Era of Facebook'.
26 E. Norbeck and H. Befu, 'Informal Fictive Kinship in Japan', *American Anthropologist* 60(1) (1958): 102–17.
27 A. Sen, *The Idea of Justice*, London: Penguin, 2010.

Chapter 3 The First Satiable Society
1 T. Veblen, *A Theory of the Leisure Class*, London: George Allen & Unwin, 1970 [1899].
2 J.K. Galbraith, *The New Industrial State*, Boston: Houghton Mifflin, 1967.
3 C. Campbell, *The Romantic Ethic and the Spirit of Modern Consumerism*, Oxford: Basil Blackwell, 1987.
4 P. Bourdieu, *Distinction: A Social Critique of the Judgement of Taste*, trans. R. Nice, London: Routledge & Kegan Paul, 1984 [1979].
5 M. Douglas and B. Isherwood, *The World of Goods*, London: Allen Lane, 1979.
6 M. Sahlins, *Culture and Practical Reason*, Chicago: University of Chicago Press, 1976.
7 D. Miller and S. Woodward, *Blue Jeans: The Art of the Ordinary*, Berkeley: University of California Press, 2012.
8 Words by Mick McConnell.
9 Garvey and Miller, *Ageing with Smartphones in Ireland*, pp. 156–78.
10 For environmentalism in Ireland, see L. Leonard, *The Environmental Movement in Ireland*, New York: Springer, 2007; H. Tovey, *Environmentalism in Ireland: Movement and Activists*, Dublin: Institute of Public Administration, 2007.
11 https://www.tidytowns.ie/about-us/history/.
12 There is some evidence more generally in Ireland for the correlation between higher social class and level of education, on the one hand, and environmental concern, on the other: see B. Motherway, M. Kelly, P. Faughnan, and H. Tovey, *Trends in Irish Environmental Attitudes between 1993 and 2002: First Report of National Survey Data*, Dublin: Environmental Protection Agency, 2003, pp. 48–54.
13 G. Simmel, *The Philosophy of Money*, trans. T. Bottomore and D. Frisby, London: Routledge & Kegan Paul, 1989 [1907].
14 https://dogsfirst.ie/holisitic-vets-in-ireland/.
15 K. Thomas, *Man and the Natural World*, London: Penguin, 1983.
16 Or now BeReal. If you are young enough, then TikTok is *so* last year.
17 D. Miller et al., *The Global Smartphone: Beyond a Youth Technology*, London: UCL Press, 2021.
18 Ibid., pp. 135–56.

Chapter 4 Philosophers and Consumerism

1. D. Horowitz, *The Morality of Spending: Attitudes towards the Consumer Society in America, 1875–1940*, Chicago: Ivan R. Dee, 1992; *The Anxieties of Affluence: Critiques of American Consumer Society, 1939–1979*, Cambridge, MA: University of Massachusetts Press, 2004; *Consuming Pleasures: Intellectuals and Popular Culture in the Postwar World*, Philadelphia: University of Pennsylvania Press, 2012.
2. O. Gurova, 'Ideology of Consumption in Soviet Union: From Asceticism to the Legitimating of Consumer Goods', *Anthropology of East Europe Review* 24(2) (2006): 91–8.
3. For a summary of the influence of the Frankfurt School on anthropology, see C. Lynteris, 'The Frankfurt School, Critical Theory and Anthropology', in M. Candea (ed.), *Schools and Styles of Anthropological Theory*, London: Routledge, 2018, pp. 159–72.
4. T. Adorno and M. Horkheimer, *Dialectic of Enlightenment*, trans. J. Cumming, London: Verso, 1977 [1944].
5. I would not claim to understand Adorno and Horkheimer's use of the term 'dialectic' as well as a professional philosopher would. But outside of the convolutions of their rather impenetrable theory, which includes concepts such as 'determinate negation', the gist of their text includes a consistent critique of the consumers of mass culture, which is what I have chosen to discuss.
6. Adorno and Horkheimer, *Dialectic of Enlightenment*, p. 6.
7. The authors believed that all these contradictions could be justified within the theoretical structures they had developed. But we are not obliged to accept this.
8. Galbraith, *The New Industrial State*.
9. Adorno and Horkheimer, *Dialectic of Enlightenment*, p. 120.
10. Ibid., p. 159.
11. Ibid., p. 134.
12. Ibid., p. 136.
13. Ibid., p. 128.
14. Bourdieu, *Distinction*, pp. 11–18.
15. W.F. Haug, *Critique of Commodity Aesthetics: Appearance, Sexuality and Advertising in Capitalist Society*, trans. R. Bock, Cambridge: Polity, 1986 [1971].
16. J. Baudrillard, *For a Critique of the Political Economy of the Sign*, trans. C. Levin, St Louis, MO: Telos Press, 1981 [1972]. See also *The Mirror of Production*, trans. M. Poster, St Louis, MO: Telos Press, 1981 [1973].
17. H. Marcuse, *One-Dimensional Man*, London: Routledge & Kegan Paul, 1964.
18. C. Lasch, *The Culture of Narcissism*, New York: W.W. Norton, 1979.
19. Miller, *Material Culture and Mass Consumption*.

20 D. Miller, *A Theory of Shopping*, Cambridge: Polity, 1998.
21 R. Wiggershaus, *The Frankfurt School: Its History, Theories, and Political Significance*, Cambridge, MA: MIT Press, 1995.
22 D. Ferris (ed.), *The Cambridge Companion to Walter Benjamin*, Cambridge: Cambridge University Press, 2004.
23 W. Benjamin, 'The Work of Art in the Age of Mechanical Reproduction', in *Illuminations: Essays and Reflections*, ed. H. Arendt, trans. H. Zohn, New York: Schocken Books, 1969, pp. 166–95.
24 W. Benjamin, *The Arcades Project*, trans. H. Eiland and K. McLaughlin, Cambridge, MA: Belknap Press, 1999.
25 W. Benjamin, 'Unpacking My Library: A Talk about Book Collecting', in *Illuminations: Essays and Reflections*, ed. H. Arendt, trans. H. Zohn, New York: Schocken Books, 1969, pp. 1–11.
26 Ibid., p. 2.
27 Ibid., p. 4.
28 Ibid., pp. 4–6.
29 Ibid., pp. 6–7.
30 Adorno and Horkheimer, *Dialectic of Enlightenment*, p. 124.
31 My favourites from last year were Self Esteem and Wolf Alice.
32 O'Toole, *We Don't Know Ourselves*, pp. 105–13.
33 Baudrillard, *For a Critique of the Political Economy of the Sign*.
34 Readers of Shoshana Zuboff's writing on 'surveillance capitalism' might consider my observations naïve, arguing that if something seems to be free, it is because you are now the commodity in the form of data. But the evidence was consistent with other studies I have carried out where most people seemed much less concerned with privacy than critics might assume. Targeted advertising reveals the work of surveillance, but is regarded as a minor irritant compensated for by improvements in the ability of the phone to predict usage. In their own lives, surveillance is often seen as the other side of the coin to care. In short, an argument that people ought to protest against these incursions and extractions is not evidence that they do. In any case, much of this is not contrary to arguments for surveillance capitalism, which mainly occurs in the backstage of business. The fact that most people don't even see surveillance as much of a threat could itself be grist to Zuboff's mill. See S. Zuboff, *The Age of Surveillance Capitalism: The Fight for a Human Future at the New Frontier of Power*, London: Profile Books, 2019. Also D. Miller, 'Care and Surveillance – The Good Citizens of COVID-19', in S. Abram, L. Lambert, and J. Robinson (eds), *How to Live through a Pandemic*, London: Routledge, 2023.
35 T. Piketty, *Capital in the Twenty-First Century*, Cambridge, MA: Harvard University Press, 2014.
36 One more example of our common life trajectory, though you are not

obliged to imagine the author with shoulder-length hair in floral shirts, beads, and very flared trousers.
37 K. Soper, *Post-Growth Living: For an Alternative Hedonism*, London: Verso Books, 2020. For the potential contribution of the citizen consumer to the good life, see also K. Soper, 'Re-thinking the "Good Life"', *Journal of Consumer Culture* 72(2) (2007): 205–29.
38 As reported in different ways for all the various fieldsites in Miller et al., *The Global Smartphone*.
39 Miller et al., *The Global Smartphone*, pp. 227–39.
40 For example, R. Braidotti, *The Posthuman*, Cambridge: Polity, 2013.
41 For a powerful argument in this direction, see R. Miller, *The Triumph of Prometheus: The Rise and Fall of Animal Experimentation*, Oxford: Oxford University Press, 2023. Full disclosure – Richard Miller is my brother.
42 For an anthropological discussion, see A. Smart and J. Smart, *Posthumanism: Anthropological Insights*, Toronto: University of Toronto Press, 2017. Also L. Kopnina, 'Anthropocentrism and Post-Humanism', *International Encyclopaedia of Anthropology*, Oxford: Wiley, 2019: https://doi.org/10.1002/9781118924396.wbiea2387.
43 D. Haraway, 'The Companion Species Manifesto: Dogs, People and Significant Otherness', in *Manifestly Haraway*, Minneapolis: University of Minnesota Press, 2016, pp. 91–198.
44 N. Charles, 'Post-Human Families? Dog–Human Relations in the Domestic Sphere', *Sociological Research Online* 21(3) (2016). Also see N. Charles and C. Davies, 'My Family and Other Animals: Pets as Kin', *Sociological Research Online* 13(5) (2017). This work suggests a compromise position between anthropomorphism and post-humanism. Also E. Power, 'Furry Families: Making a Human–Dog Family through Home', *Social and Cultural Geography* 9(5) (2008): 535–55; Thomas, *Man and the Natural World*.
45 See D. Miller and J. Sinanan, *Webcam*, Cambridge: Polity, 2014, pp. 4–20, for a more detailed account of these ideas.
46 T. Ahlins, *Calling Family: Digital Technologies and the Making of Transnational Care Collectives*, New Brunswick, NJ: Rutgers University Press, 2023.
47 For example, P. Descola and G. Palsson (eds), *Nature and Society: Anthropological Perspectives*, London: Routledge, 1996.

Chapter 5 Inequality, Drugs, and Depression
1 The topic of inequality is much discussed in Ireland. This includes the consequences of the major recession that followed the collapse of the Celtic Tiger, for which see M. Savage, T. Callan, B. Brain, and B. Colgan, *The Great Recession, Austerity and Inequality: Evidence*

from Ireland, Dublin: Economic and Social Research Institute Working Paper 499 (2015): https://www.econstor.eu/bitstream/10419/129395/1/823265064.pdf. Most common were discussions around more specific topics such as housing inequalities: for example, R. Grotti, H. Russell, É. Fahey, and B. Maître, 'Discrimination and Inequality in Housing in Ireland', Dublin: Economic and Social Research Institute, 2018: https://www.esri.ie/publications/discrimination-and-inequality-in-housing-in-ireland; and S. Burke, *Irish Apartheid: Healthcare Inequality in Ireland*, Dublin: New Island, 2009.

2 For a more general guide to contemporary inequalities in Ireland, see the frequent publications of the Economic and Social Research Institute, Dublin.

3 See https://www.youtube.com/watch?v=7EJUVkcpXB4&t=11s.

4 'Fucking' rather than 'fecking' tells you he was born in England.

5 On the other hand, there is evidence that intergenerational poverty is increasing in Ireland as also in Europe more generally. See D. Curristan, B. Maître, and H. Russell, *Intergenerational Poverty in Ireland*, Dublin: Economic and Social Research Institute, 2020.

6 C. Ryan, 'The Power of Bingo during COVID-19', 25 May 2020: http://somatosphere.net/2020/bingo.html/.

7 For other writings about bingo, see K. King, 'Neutralizing Marginally Deviant Behavior: Bingo Players and Superstition', *Journal of Gambling Studies* 6(1) (1990): 43–61 and J.-C. Moubarac, N.W. Shead, and J. Derevensky, 'Bingo Playing and Problem Gambling: A Review of Our Current Knowledge', *Journal of Gambling Studies* 24 (2010): 164–84.

8 D. Scott and G.C. Godbey, 'An Analysis of Adult Play Groups: Social versus Serious Participation in Contract Bridge', *Leisure Studies* 14(1) (1992): 47–67. See also T. Brkljačić, L. Lučić, and I. Sučić, ' 'Well-Being, Motives and Experiences in Live and Online Game Settings: Case of Contract Bridge', *International Journal of Gaming and Computer-Mediated Simulations* 9(4) (2017): 19–43.

9 M. Young, *The Rise of the Meritocracy*, London: Thames & Hudson, 1958.

10 By contrast, African migrants were an important component in a nearby town. More generally, see M. Maguire and F. Murphy, *Integration in Ireland: The Everyday Lives of African Migrants*, Manchester: Manchester University Press, 2015.

11 M. Gilmartin and B. Migge, 'European Migrants in Ireland: Pathways to Integration', *International Journal of Health Services* 22(3) (2015): 459–82.

12 Thanks also to Maria A., who gave me considerable help in contacting migrants and supporting my project.

13 A. Mauger, 'A Great Race of Drinkers? Irish Interpretations of Alcoholism and Drinking Stereotypes, 1945–1975', *Medical History* 65(1) (2010): 70–89; E. Malcolm, *'Ireland Sober, Ireland Free': Drink and Temperance in Nineteenth-Century Ireland*, Syracuse, NY: Syracuse University Press, 1986.
14 For the association of cocaine with masculinity and higher status, see C. Darcy, 'Making the Invisible Visible: Masculinities and Men's Illicit Recreational Drug Use', *Irish Journal of Sociology* 26(1) (2018): 5–24.
15 M. Keyes, *Rachel's Holiday*, London: Michael Joseph, 1998.
16 For a recent summary, see A. Doyle et al., *Drugnet Ireland* 82 (2022): https://www.drugsandalcohol.ie/37086/1/Drugnet_Ireland_Issue_82.pdf. This suggests that the evidence from Cuan is consistent with Ireland more generally: a marked decrease in the use of alcohol by young people (pp. 10–13) but an increase in the use of cocaine, which is high by European standards (pp. 18–20). For other discussions see D. Bellerose et al., *Trends in Treated Problem Cocaine Use in Ireland, 2002 to 2007*, Dublin: Health Research Board, 2011: https://www.lenus.ie/bitstream/handle/10147/84034/HRB_Trend_Series_6.pdf?sequence=1; P. Maycock, 'Cocaine Use In Ireland: An Exploratory Study', in R. Moran et al., *A Collection of Papers on Drug Issues in Ireland*, Dublin: Health Research Board, 2021, pp. 80–152.
17 M. Foucault, *The History of Sexuality: Volume 1: An Introduction*, trans. R. Hurley, London: Allen Lane, 1979 [1976].
18 N. Scheper-Hughes, *Saints, Scholars and Schizophenics*, Berkeley: University of California Press, 1979.
19 A high incidence is suggested by https://www.irishtimes.com/news/social-affairs/young-irish-women-suffer-highest-levels-of-depression-in-europe-1.3947527 and https://ec.europa.eu/eurostat/web/products-eurostat-news/-/EDN-20181010-1.
20 https://www.darknessintolight.ie/.
21 For example, J. Bowlby, *Attachment: Volume 1: Attachment and Loss*, 2nd edn, New York: Basic Books, 1969.
22 For example, Winnicott, *Babies and Their Mothers*.
23 D. Miller, 'The Tragic Dénouement of English Sociality', *Cultural Anthropology* 30(2) (2015): 336–57. See also E. Cockayne, *Cheek by Jowl: A History of Neighbours*, London: Vintage Books, 2012.
24 B. MacNamara, *The Valley of the Squinting Windows*, Dublin: Maunsel and Company, 1918.
25 See P. Stafford (ed.), *The Global Age-Friendly Community Movement*, New York: Berghahn Books, 2019.
26 Except me, since I really can't sing. When it was my turn, I would recite song lyrics or poetry.

Chapter 6 Justice as Fairness

1. J. Rawls, *A Theory of Justice*, Cambridge, MA: Harvard University Press, 1999 [1971].
2. C.F.A. Marmoy, 'The "Auto-Icon" of Jeremy Bentham at University College, London', *Medical History* 2(2) (1958): 77–86.
3. H. Sidgwick, *The Methods of Ethics*, New York: Macmillan and Co., 1907 [1874].
4. Rawls, *A Theory of Justice*, p. 87.
5. Ibid., p. 64.
6. Ibid., p. 234.
7. Ibid., p. 237.
8. A. Nove, *The Economics of Feasible Socialism*, London: Routledge, 1983.
9. An argument for an ethnographic/anthropological approach to justice *per se*. See S. Brandtstädter, 'Rising from the Ordinary: Virtue, the Justice Motif and Moral Change', *Anthropological Theory* 21(2) (2021): 180–205.
10. Rawls, *A Theory of Justice*, p. 53.
11. Ibid., p. 63.
12. Rawls' text subsumes women within the generic male.
13. Piketty, *Capital in the Twenty-First Century*.
14. Rawls, *A Theory of Justice*, pp. 124, 464–74.
15. Ibid., pp. 474–5.
16. G. Doppelt, 'Rawls' System of Justice: A Critique from the Left', *Noûs* 15(3) (1981): 259–307.
17. M.J. Sandel, *Liberalism and the Limits of Justice*, Cambridge: Cambridge University Press, 2012.
18. Nussbaum, *Frontiers of Justice*, p. 1.
19. Ibid., pp. 408–15.
20. Sen, *The Idea of Justice*, p. 7.
21. Ibid., pp. 102–5, 225–52, 299–304.
22. Ibid., pp. 155–73.
23. For example, J. Rawls, *Political Liberalism*, New York: Columbia University Press, 1993.
24. Rawls, *A Theory of Justice*, p. 480.
25. Miller, *A Theory of Shopping*.
26. Rawls, *A Theory of Justice*, p. 482.
27. Ibid., p. 483.
28. V. Munoz-Dardé, 'Rawls, Justice in the Family and Justice of the Family', *The Philosophical Quarterly* 48(192) (2003): 335–52.
29. C.M. Arensberg and S.T. Kimball, *Family and Community in Ireland*, Cambridge, MA: Harvard University Press, 1940.
30. See also Scheper-Hughes, *Saints, Scholars and Schizophrenics*.

31 Ibid.
32 S. Barry, *The Secret Scripture*, London: Faber & Faber, 2008.
33 O' Toole, *We Don't Know Ourselves*, pp. 351–6.
34 https://www2.hse.ie/services/fair-deal-scheme/about-the-fair-deal-scheme.html.
35 Young, *The Rise of the Meritocracy*.
36 M.J. Sandel, *The Tyranny of Merit: What's Become of the Common Good?*, London: Penguin, 2020.
37 For example, M. Rojas, *Sweden after the Swedish Model: From Tutorial State to Enabling State*, trans. R. Tanner and C. Edbrooke, Stockholm: Timbro, 2005.
38 I. Wallerstein, *World-Systems Analysis*, Durham, NC: Duke University Press, 2004.
39 M. Anwar and M. Graham, *The Digital Continent*, Oxford: Oxford University Press, 2022; M. Gray and S. Suri, *Ghost Work*, Boston: Houghton Mifflin Harcourt, 2019.
40 P. Sweeney, 'Ireland's Low Corporation Tax: The Case for Tax Coordination in the Union', *Transfer* 16(1) (2010): 55–69.
41 A. Brick and S. Connoll, 'Waiting Times for Publicly Funded Hospital Treatment: How Does Ireland Measure Up?', *The Economic and Social Review* 52(1) (2021): 41–52.
42 For an assessment of current inequality in Ireland compared to Europe more generally, see R. Sweeney and D. Storrie, *The State We Are In: Inequality in Ireland 2022*, May 2022: https://www.tasc.ie/assets/files/pdf/2205-4_tasc_inequality_in_ire_2022.pdf.
43 I am keenly aware of these stories as my partner is a volunteer at a drop-in centre for asylum seekers.
44 The recession following the Celtic Tiger did, however, leave deep scars mainly amongst the younger population of Cuan.

Chapter 7 The Body and Sports
1 H. Tovey and P. Share, *A Sociology of Ireland*, Dublin: Gill and Macmillan, 2007.
2 For a study of motivation in joining the GAA amongst contemporary youth in Dublin, see M. Lawler, C. Heary, G. Shorter, and E. Nixon, 'Peer and Parental Processes Predict Distinct Patterns of Physical Activity Participation among Adolescent Girls and Boys', *International Journal of Sport and Exercise Psychology* 20(2) (2022): 497–514.
3 For more on the GAA, see K. Liston, 'The GAA and the Sporting Irish', in T. Inglis (ed.), *Are the Irish Different?*, Manchester: Manchester University Press, 2014, pp. 199–210; W. Mandle, *The Gaelic Athletic Association and Irish Nationalist Politics, 1884–1924*, London: Christopher Helm and Dublin: Gill & Macmillan, 1987.

4 T. Collins and W. Vamplew, *Mud, Sweat and Beers*, Oxford: Berg, 2002.
5 See G.H. Mead, *Mind, Self and Society*, Chicago: University of Chicago Press, 2015 [1934].
6 A fine example of how people in Italy regard concern with their own style and appearance as a civic duty can be found in R. Nicolescu, *Social Media in Southeast Italy*, London: UCL Press, 2016.
7 *Healthy Ireland – A Framework for Improved Health and Wellbeing 2013–2025*, Dublin: Department of Health, 2013: https://www.drugsandalcohol.ie/19628/1/Healthy_Ireland_Framework.pdf.
8 The Irish are certainly not alone in their suspicions around the idea of 'Successful Ageing'. See S. Lamb (ed.), *Successful Aging as a Contemporary Obsession*, New Brunswick, NJ: Rutgers University Press, 2017.
9 Garvey and Miller, *Ageing with Smartphones in Ireland*, pp. 132–41.
10 For more general discussion, see J.A. Astin, 'Why Patients Use Alternative Medicine: Results of a National Study', *JAMA* 279(19) (1998): 1548–53.
11 Unlike other studies in Ireland, I rarely found people referencing traditional folk medicine in relation to these new forms of complementary health, though they may count as precedents. See R. Foley, 'Indigenous Narratives of Health: (Re)Placing Folk-Medicine within Irish Health Histories', *Journal of Medical Humanities* 36 (2015): 5–18; A. Murphy and C. Kelleher, 'Contemporary Health Practices in the Burren', *The Irish Journal of Psychology* 16(1) (1995): 38–51.
12 For anthropological attention to this phenomenon, see J. Cook and J. Cassaniti (eds), 'Mindfulness and Culture', *Anthropology Today* 38(2) (2022).
13 For details of which, see P. Garvey, D. Miller, and S. Mohammid, 'From Menopause to Hypertension: The Problem of Securing Engagement', in C. Hawkins, P. Awondo, and D. Miller (eds), *mHealth: An Anthropological Approach*, London: UCL Press, forthcoming.
14 C.L.R. James, *Beyond a Boundary*, London: Hutchinson, 1963. See also T. Fletcher, 'The Making of English Cricket Cultures: Empire, Globalization and (Post)colonialism', *Sport in Society*, 14(1) (2011): 17–36.
15 D. Miller, 'Dr Google will see you first', in C. Hawkins, P. Awondo, and D. Miller (eds), *mHealth: An Anthropological Approach*, London: UCL Press, forthcoming.
16 Garvey and Miller, *Ageing with Smartphones in Ireland*, pp. 139–41.

Chapter 8 The Origins of Philosophy in Sport
1 For example, H.L. Reid, *Introduction to the Philosophy of Sport*, Lanham, MD: Rowman & Littlefield, 2012.

2. S. Miller, *Ancient Greek Athletics*, New Haven: Yale University Press, 2004.
3. S. Miller, *Arete: Greek Sports from Ancient Sources*, Berkeley: University of California Press, 2012.
4. H.L. Reid, *Olympic Philosophy: The Ideas and Ideals behind the Ancient and Modern Olympic Games*, Sioux City, IA: Parnassos Press, 2020.
5. Miller, *Ancient Greek Athletics*, p. 284.
6. H.L. Reid, *Athletics and Philosophy in the Ancient World: Contests of Virtue*, London: Routledge, 2011.
7. P. Hadot, *What is Ancient Philosophy?*, trans. M. Chase, Cambridge, MA: Harvard University Press, 2002 [1995], p. 12.
8. H.L. Reid, 'Athletics and Philosophy in Ancient Greece and Rome: Contests of Virtue', *Sport, Ethics and Philosophy* 4(2) (2010): 109–234 (p. 119).
9. H.L. Reid, 'Sport and Moral Education in Plato's *Republic*', *Journal of the Philosophy of Sport* 34(2) (2007): 160–75.
10. H.L. Reid, 'Athletic Virtue and Aesthetic Values in Aristotle's Ethics', *Journal of the Philosophy of Sport* 47(1) (2020): 63–74.
11. Reid, 'Athletics and Philosophy in Ancient Greece and Rome', p. 158.
12. Ibid., p. 165.
13. Thanks to Jeremy David Bendik-Keymer for this point and this phrasing.
14. Hadot, *What is Ancient Philosophy?*
15. For a discussion of the relationship between sport and religion more generally as cosmology, see E. Bain-Selbo and D. Sapp, *Understanding Sports as a Religious Phenomenon*, London: Bloomsbury, 2016.
16. MacIntyre, *After Virtue*, p. 93.
17. B. Duggan and G.A. Mohan, 'Longitudinal Examination of Young People's Gambling Behaviours and Participation in Team Sports', *Journal of Gambling Studies* 39 (2023): 541–57.
18. Z. Papakonstantinou, 'Alciabiades in Olympia: Olympic Ideology, Sport and Social Conflict in Classical Athens', *Journal of Sport History* 30(2) (2003): 173–82.
19. N. Besnier, S. Brownwell, and T. Carter, *The Anthropology of Sport*, Berkeley: University of California Press, 2017. See also N. Besnier and S. Brownell, 'Sport, Modernity and the Body', *Annual Reviews of Anthropology* 41 (2012): 443–59.
20. Besnier et al., *The Anthropology of* Sport, pp. 71–4.
21. Ibid., pp. 74–6.
22. G. Samuel, *The Origins of Yoga and Tantra: Indic Religions to the Thirteenth Century*, Cambridge: Cambridge University Press, 2012, p. 336. See also E. de Michelis, *A History of Modern Yoga*, London: Continuum, 2004.

Chapter 9 Creating Community
1. There are no academic references in support of this historical discussion since they would compromise the use of Cuan as a pseudonym.

2 H. Glassie, *Passing the Time in Ballymenone*, Bloomington: Indiana University Press, 1982.
3 For example, J.B. Keane, *The Field*, Cork: Mercier Press, 1966.
4 The name of the production has been changed for reason of anonymity.
5 'Unfriending Mum and Dad – Fears That Teenagers Are Deserting Facebook Are Overblown', *The Economist*, 4 January 2014.
6 https://blogs.ucl.ac.uk/global-social-media/2013/11/24/what-will-we-learn-from-the-fall-of-facebook/.
7 For example, Arensberg and Kimball, *Family and Community in Ireland*.
8 A description of Maria's recent downsizing is given in Garvey and Miller, *Ageing with Smartphones in Ireland*, pp. 166–7.
9 It may also thereby correspond to the advantages said to accrue to living within a '15-minute city'. See A. Duany and R. Steuteville, 'Defining the 15-Minute City', *Public Square*, 8 February 2021: https://www.cnu.org/publicsquare/2021/02/08/defining-15-minute-city.
10 Information sourced from an interview with a person working for the main company that supplies mortgages to people moving into this estate.

Chapter 10 Placing Heidegger

1 M. Heidegger, *Being and Time*, trans. J. Macquarrie and E. Robinson, New York: Harper & Row, 1962 [1927].
2 For example, D. Harvey, *The Condition of Postmodernity*, Oxford: Blackwell, 1989. See also D. Massey, *Space, Place and Gender*, Minneapolis: University of Minneapolis Press, 1994.
3 T. Ingold, *The Perception of the Environment: Essays on Livelihood, Dwelling and Skill*, London: Routledge, 2000, pp. 185–6.
4 B. Lang, *Heidegger's Silence*, Ithaca, NY: Cornell University Press, 1996.
5 Ibid., p. 36.
6 Ibid., p. 41.
7 Ibid., p. 43.
8 A. Mitchell and P. Trawny, *Heidegger's Black Notebooks*, New York: Columbia University Press, 2017.
9 J. Malpas, *Heidegger's Topology: Being, Place, World*, Cambridge, MA: MIT Press, 2008, p. 23.
10 Ibid., pp. 18–20.
11 H. Dreyfus, *Being-in-the-World: A Commentary on Heidegger's Being and Time, Division 1*, Cambridge, MA: MIT Press, 1991, pp. 13–14, 49–50.
12 Heidegger, *Being and Time*, pp. 134–48 and 419.
13 M. Heidegger, *The Question Concerning Technology and Other Essays*, trans. W. Lovitt, New York: Garland, 1977.
14 Ibid., p. 142.

15 Ibid., p. 140. Italicized in the original.
16 Ibid., p. 142.
17 Ibid., p. 419.
18 Dreyfus, *Being-in-the-World*, pp. 128–33.
19 Bourdieu, P., *The Political Ontology of Martin Heidegger*, trans. P. Collier, Cambridge: Polity, 1991 [1988].
20 Pre-ontological in the sense that Dasein is the entity that does ontology. See J. Haugeland, *Dasein Disclosed*, Cambridge, MA: Harvard University Press, 2013, p. 83.
21 J. Weiner, 'Anthropology Contra Heidegger Part 1: Anthropology's Nihilism', *Critique of Anthropology* 12(1) (1992): 75–90.
22 Malpas (*Heidegger's Topology*, p. 20) dates such essays to the period after 1945.
23 Heidegger, *The Question Concerning Technology and Other Essays*.
24 M. Heidegger, 'Building Dwelling Thinking', in M. Heidegger, *Poetry, Language, Thought*, trans. A. Hofstadter, New York: Harper Perennial, 1971, pp. 143–59.
25 For all the antipathy between Adorno and Heidegger, they seem to have possessed a similar horror of objectification.
26 For a sense of the complexity of *Heimat* as a lived experience, see M. Svasek, 'Narratives of "Home" and "Homeland": The Symbolic Construction and Appropriation of the Sudeten German Heimat', *Identities* 9(4) (2002): 495–518.
27 S. Nagle, *Histories of Nationalism in Ireland and Germany: A Comparative Study from 1800 to 1932*, London: Bloomsbury, 2016, p. 152.
28 Ingles, *Moral Monopoly*.
29 J. Blok, *Citizenship in Classical Athens*, Cambridge: Cambridge University Press, 2017.
30 J. Gardner, *Being a Roman Citizen*, London: Routledge, 1993.
31 Miller et al., *How the World Changed Social Media*.
32 P. Gilroy, *The Black Atlantic*, London: Verso, 1993.
33 For the anthropological contribution to this distinction see J. Clifford, *Routes: Travel and Translation in the Late Twentieth Century*, Cambridge, MA: Harvard University Press, 1997.
34 K. Harries, *The Ethics of Architecture*, Cambridge, MA: MIT Press, 1997, pp. 152–78.
35 Ingold, *The Perception of the Environment*, p. 348.

Chapter 11 Engaging with the World
1 Garvey and Miller, *Ageing with Smartphones in Ireland*, pp. 198–202.
2 Ibid., pp. 196–200.
3 Ibid., pp. 50–73.

4 ASSA – The Anthropology of Smartphones and Smart Ageing – conducted by myself and a wider team between 2017 and 2022 with funding from the European Research Council. See https://www.ucl.ac.uk/anthropology/assa/.
5 All of the research projects within the ASSA team were tasked with creating practical health projects based on our research which would improve the health and welfare of the populations where we worked. Several of these have been taken up and are summarized in a forthcoming volume: C. Hawkins, P. Awondo, and D. Miller (eds), *mHealth: An Anthropological Approach*, London: UCL Press. In the case of Ireland, however, apart from our social prescribing project, we failed in a parallel project intended to improve communication about menopause. These are discussed in the forthcoming edited collection about mHealth. Despite having to more or less start again from scratch thanks to Covid, Pauline Garvey is hoping to resurrect the project on social prescribing in her fieldsite in Dublin.
6 H. Chatterjee, P. Camic, B Lockyer, and L. Thomson, 'Non-Clinical Community Interventions: A Systematised Review of Social Prescribing Schemes', *Arts & Health* 10(2) (2018): 97–123.
7 Garvey and Miller, *Ageing with Smartphones in Ireland*, pp. 50–73.
8 Glassie, *Passing the Time in Ballymenone*.
9 See chapter 5, note 3.
10 See also C. Craig, 'Reading Identity: American and Irish Women's Book Clubs, Culture, and Identity', *Irish Journal of Sociology* 27(2) (2019): 128–52.
11 For allotments in Dublin, see P. Kettle, 'Motivations for Investing in Allotment Gardening in Dublin: A Sociological Analysis', *Irish Journal of Sociology* 22(2) (2014): 30–63.
12 See also M. Corcoran and M. Hayes, 'Towards a Morphology of Public Space in Suburban Dublin', *Built Environment* 41(4) (2015): 519–37.

Chapter 12 The Stoics and Epicurus
1 B. Inwood and L. Gerson (ed. and trans.), *The Epicurus Reader*, Indianapolis: Hackett Publishing Company, 1994.
2 Lucretius, *The Nature of Things*, trans. A.E. Stallings, London: Penguin, 2007.
3 Marcus Aurelius, *Meditations*, London: Collins Classics, 2020.
4 Ibid., p. 104.
5 Ibid., p. 69.
6 Ibid., p. 31.
7 It is easier to make this critique of Marcus Aurelius in the light of a recent book by Gordon Brown: *Seven Ways to Change the World*, New York: Simon & Schuster, 2022. This is an exemplary case of what we

can learn from a senior politician reflecting upon their experience as a politician.
8 Marcus Aurelius, *Meditations*, p. 24.
9 Seneca, 'Consolation to Helvia', in *Dialogues and Essays*, trans. J. Davie, Oxford: Oxford University Press, 2007, pp. 163–87 (p. 166).
10 Seneca, 'Consolation to Marcia', in *Dialogues and Essays*, trans. J. Davie, Oxford: Oxford University Press, 2007, pp. 53–84 (p. 74).
11 J. Davidson, *Courtesans and Fishcakes: The Consuming Passions of Classical Athens*, London: Fontana Press, 1998.
12 Juvenal, *The Satires*, trans. N. Rudd, Oxford: Oxford University Press, 2008.
13 R. Stoneman, *Megasthenes' Indica: A New Translation of the Fragments with Commentary*, London: Routledge, 2021.
14 N. Kazantzakis, *Zorba the Greek*, trans. C. Wildman, London: Faber & Faber, 2008 [1946].
15 Seneca, 'On the Happy Life', in *Dialogues and Essays*, trans. J. Davie, Oxford: Oxford University Press, 2007, pp. 85–111 (p. 89).
16 Inwood and Gerson (ed. and trans.), *The Epicurus Reader*.
17 Lucretius, *The Nature of Things*.
18 S. Greenblatt, *The Swerve: How the Renaissance Began*, New York: Vintage Books, 2011.
19 Inwood and Gerson (ed. and trans.), *The Epicurus Reader*, p. 32.
20 Ibid., p. 30.
21 G.W.F. Hegel, *Lectures on the History of Philosophy: Vol. 2: Greek Philosophy*, ed. and trans. R.F. Brown, London: Routledge & Kegan Paul, 1955, pp. 302–4.
22 Seneca, 'On the Happy Life', p. 95.
23 Reid, 'Athletics and Philosophy in Ancient Greece and Rome', p. 196.
24 Inwood and Gerson (ed. and trans.), *The Epicurus Reader*, p. 33.
25 Ibid., p. 34.
26 Kant, I. 2015 *Critique of Practical Reason*. Cambridge: Cambridge University Press P94
27 This point and its phrasing is from Jeremy Bendik-Keymer
28 M. Cicero, *On the Good Life*, trans. M. Grant, London: Penguin, 1971.
29 G. Simmel, 'The Metropolis and Mental Life' (1903), in D. Levine (ed.), *Simmel: On Individuality and Social Forms*, Chicago: University of Chicago Press, 1971, pp. 324–39.
30 M. Nussbaum and S. Levmore, *Aging Thoughtfully: Conversations about Retirement, Romance, Wrinkles, and Regret*, Oxford: Oxford University Press, 2017, p. 1.
31 P. Bourdieu, *Outline of a Theory of Practice*, trans. R. Nice, Cambridge: Cambridge University Press, 1977 [1972].

32 K. Setiya, *Midlife*, Princeton: Princeton University Press, 2017.
33 M. Nussbaum, *The Therapy of Desire: Theory and Practice in Hellenistic Ethics*, Princeton: Princeton University Press, 1994.
34 Davidson, *Courtesans and Fishcakes*.
35 R. Wilk, 'Taking Fun Seriously in Envisioning Sustainable Consumption', *Consumption and Society* 1(2) (2022): 255–72.
36 'Climate Change: Green Light', *The Economist*, 12 November 2022, pp. 75–6.
37 Juvenal's *Satires* might be regarded as a kind of hyper-moralizing version of the Stoics.

Conclusion: Hegel, Anthropology, and Philosophy
1 G.W.F. Hegel, *Phenomenology of Spirit*, trans. A.V. Miller, Oxford: Oxford University Press, 1977 [1807].
2 C. Taylor, *Hegel*, Cambridge: Cambridge University Press, 1975.
3 Wood, *Hegel's Ethical Thought*, p. 6.
4 While civil society has been portrayed as strong in Cuan, there is evidence that it may be much weaker in its relationship to the state in other areas of Ireland. See M. Murphy, 'Civil Society in the Shadow of the Irish State', *Irish Journal of Sociology* 19(2) (2011): 170–87.
5 Hegel, too, was critical of civil society, its individualism, and its economic foundations, and saw the state as a more appropriate level for dealing with various problems. See D. Kolb, *The Critique of Modernity: Hegel, Heidegger and After*, Chicago: University of Chicago Press, 1986, pp. 20–37.
6 M. Hardimon, *Hegel's Social Philosophy*, Cambridge: Cambridge University Press, 1994, p. 182.
7 Wood, *Hegel's Ethical Thought*, p. 50.
8 G.W.F. Hegel, *Philosophy of Right*, trans. T.M. Knox, Oxford: Oxford University Press, 1942 [1820].
9 K. Marx, *Early Writings*, trans. R. Livingstone and R. Benton, Harmondsworth. Penguin, 1975.
10 Hegel was a strong supporter of the role of codified law. See Wood, *Hegel's Ethical Thought*, pp. 103–6.
11 See, for example, C. Arthur, 'Objectification and Alienation in Marx and Hegel', *Radical Philosophy* 30 (1982): 14–24; J. Hyppolite, *Studies on Marx and Hegel*, trans. J. O'Neill, London: Heinemann, 1969 [1955]; J. Torrance, *Estrangement, Alienation and Exploitation*, London: Macmillan, 1977.
12 See Miller, *Material Culture and Mass Consumption*, pp. 50–67, where I present this argument through a discussion of the anthropologist Nancy Munn. See N. Munn, *The Fame of Gawa*, Cambridge: Cambridge University Press, 1986.

13 G. Simmel, *The Conflict in Modern Culture and Other Essays*, ed. and trans. K.P. Etzkorn, New York: Teachers College Press, 1968.
14 https://plato.stanford.edu/entries/communitarianism/.
15 For example, Sandel, *Liberalism and the Limits of Justice*.
16 For example, M. Walzer, *Spheres of Justice*, Oxford: Blackwell, 1983. As previously noted, I regret my own ignorance of these alternatives. See also Nussbaum and Sen (eds), *The Quality of Life*.
17 C. Taylor, 'Conditions of an Unforced Consensus on Human Rights', in J.R. Bauer and D. Bell (eds), *The East Asian Challenge for Human Rights*, New York: Cambridge University Press, 1999, pp. 124–44.
18 Sandel, *Liberalism and the Limits of Justice*.
19 A. Etzioni, *The Spirit of Community*, New York: Crown Publishers, 1993.
20 See the discussion of Tönnies and Durkheim below.
21 For a discussion about the relationship between reason and reasonable, including the normative connotations of the latter, see Neiman, *Moral Clarity*, pp. 189–225.
22 See chapter 9, note 9 regarding the '15-minute city'.
23 For a debate between these two characterizations of society, see J. Aldous, É. Durkheim, and F. Tönnies, 'An Exchange between Durkheim and Tönnies on the Nature of Social Relations, with an Introduction by Joan Aldous', *American Journal of Sociology* 77(6) (1972): 1191–200.
24 Miller et al., *The Global Smartphone*.
25 For example, W. Mignolo, 'Epistemic Disobedience, Independent Thought and Decolonial Freedom', *Theory, Culture and Society* 26(7–8) (2009): 159–81; F. Nyamnjoh, 'Blinded by Sight: Divining the Future of Anthropology in Africa', *Africa Spectrum* 47(2–3) (2012): 63–92.
26 N. Crossley, 'Merleau-Ponty, the Elusive Body and Carnal Sociology', *Body and Society* 1(1) (1995): 43–63.
27 Neiman, *Moral Clarity*.
28 Das, *Textures of the Ordinary*.
29 MacIntyre, *After Virtue*, pp. 88–108. See also Mckay, 'Eudaimonia and Culture'.
30 MacIntyre, *After Virtue*, pp. 88–108.
31 Ibid., p. 276. See also Taylor, 'Conditions of an Unforced Consensus on Human Rights'.
32 A useful critique of MacIntyre from an anthropological perspective is provided by Laidlaw, *The Subject of Virtue*, pp. 55–77.
33 Robbins argues that an emphasis on the way people negotiate their ideas and practices of morality between contested systems of values lies somewhere between Durkheim's version of societal/normative determinacy and more contemporary individualistic approaches: see J. Robbins, 'Between Reproduction and Freedom: Morality, Value, and

Radical Cultural Change', *Ethnos* 72(3) (2007): 293–314. Mattingly has also defended an emphasis upon individual moral action as opposed to structuralist and post-structuralist opposition to this level of analysis: see, for example, C. Mattingly, 'Two Virtue Ethics and the Anthropology of Morality', *Anthropological Theory* 12(2) (2012): 161–84; T. Wentzer and C. Mattingly, 'Towards a New Humanism', *Hau: Journal of Ethnographic Theory* 8(1–2) (2018): 144–57. Ethnographic examples for these approaches include J. Laidlaw, *Riches and Renunciation: Religion, Economy, and Society among the Jains*, Oxford: Oxford University Press, 1995; and J. Robbins, *Becoming Sinners: Christianity and Moral Torment in a Papua New Guinea Society*, Berkeley: University of California Press, 2004.

34 Anthropologists have also been concerned to retain their differences from mainstream work in psychology. For an excellent discussion of the relationship between the anthropological discussion of individual ethical choices and approaches from the natural sciences, see Keane, *Ethical Life*.

35 For something closer to what MacIntyre seems to have had in mind, see the portrait of a Swiss farmer by Lambek, where evidence for a fulfilling life and subsequent happiness is founded on a conservative tradition, as being Swiss is an inherited gift rather than something achieved through active involvement in creating a new *polis*. M. Lambek, '*Le bonheur Suisse*, again', in H. Walker and I. Kavedžija (eds), *Values of Happiness: Toward an Anthropology of Purpose in Life*, Chicago: Hau Books, 2016, pp. 237–65.

36 H. Horst and D. Miller, *The Cell Phone*, Oxford: Berg, 2006.

37 M. Madianou and D. Miller, *Migration and New Media*, London: Routledge, 2012.

38 Miller, *The Comfort of People*.

REFERENCES

Abu-Lughod, L., 'Do Muslim Women Really Need Saving? Anthropological Reflections on Cultural Relativism and Its Others', *American Anthropologist* 104(3) (2002): 783–90.

Adorno, T., and M. Horkheimer, *Dialectic of Enlightenment*, trans. J. Cumming, London: Verso, 1977 [1944].

Ahlins, T., *Calling Family: Digital Technologies and the Making of Transnational Care Collectives*, New Brunswick, NJ: Rutgers University Press, 2023.

Aldous, J., É. Durkheim, and F. Tönnies, 'An Exchange between Durkheim and Tönnies on the Nature of Social Relations, with an Introduction by Joan Aldous', *American Journal of Sociology* 77(6) (1972): 1191–200.

Anwar, M., and M. Graham, *The Digital Continent*, Oxford: Oxford University Press, 2022.

Arber, S., and V. Timonen (eds), *Contemporary Grandparenting: Changing Family Relationships in Global Contexts*, Bristol: Policy Press, 2012.

Arensberg, C.M., and S.T. Kimball, *Family and Community in Ireland*, Cambridge, MA: Harvard University Press, 1940.

Aristotle, *The Nicomachean Ethics*, trans. J.A.K. Thomson with H. Tredennick, London: Penguin, 2004.

Aristotle, *The Politics*, trans. T.A. Sinclair, London: Penguin, 1962.

Arthur, C., 'Objectification and Alienation in Marx and Hegel', *Radical Philosophy* 30 (1982): 14–24.

Astin, J.A., 'Why Patients Use Alternative Medicine: Results of a National Study', *JAMA* 279(19) (1998): 1548–53.

REFERENCES

Bain-Selbo, E., and D. Sapp, *Understanding Sports as a Religious Phenomenon*, London: Bloomsbury, 2016.

Bakewell, S., *At the Existentialist Café: Freedom Being and Apricot Cocktails*, London: Chatto & Windus, 2016.

Barry, S., *The Secret Scripture*, London: Faber & Faber, 2008.

Baudrillard, J., *For a Critique of the Political Economy of the Sign*, trans. C. Levin, St Louis, MO: Telos Press, 1981 [1972].

Baudrillard, J., *The Mirror of Production*, trans. M. Poster, St Louis, MO: Telos Press, 1981 [1973].

Bellerose, D., et al., *Trends in Treated Problem Cocaine Use in Ireland, 2002 to 2007*, Dublin: Health Research Board, 2011: https://www.lenus.ie/bitstream/handle/10147/84034/HRB_Trend_Series_6.pdf?sequence=1.

Benjamin, W., *The Arcades Project*, trans. H. Eiland and K. McLaughlin, Cambridge, MA: Belknap Press, 1999.

Benjamin, W., 'Unpacking My Library: A Talk about Book Collecting', in *Illuminations: Essays and Reflections*, ed. H. Arendt, trans. H. Zohn, New York: Schocken Books, 1969, pp. 1–11.

Benjamin, W., 'The Work of Art in the Age of Mechanical Reproduction', in *Illuminations: Essays and Reflections*, ed. H. Arendt, trans. H. Zohn, New York: Schocken Books, 1969, pp. 166–95.

Berlin, I., *Four Essays on Liberty*, Oxford: Oxford University Press, 1969.

Berlin, I., *Freedom and Its Betrayal: Six Enemies of Human Liberty*, London: Chatto & Windus, 2002.

Berlin, I., *Liberty*, Oxford: Oxford University Press, 2003.

Besnier, N., and S. Brownell, 'Sport, Modernity and the Body', *Annual Reviews of Anthropology* 41 (2012): 443-59.

Besnier, N., S. Brownell, and T. Carter, *The Anthropology of Sport*, Berkeley: University of California Press, 2017.

Blok, J., *Citizenship in Classical Athens*, Cambridge: Cambridge University Press, 2017.

Bourdieu, P., *Distinction: A Social Critique of the Judgement of Taste*, trans. R. Nice, London: Routledge & Kegan Paul, 1984 [1979].

Bourdieu, P., *Outline of a Theory of Practice*, trans. R. Nice, Cambridge: Cambridge University Press, 1977 [1972].

Bourdieu, P., *The Political Ontology of Martin Heidegger*, trans. P. Collier, Cambridge: Polity, 1991 [1988].

Bowlby, J., *Attachment*, vol. 1: *Attachment and Loss*, 2nd edn, New York: Basic Books, 1969.

REFERENCES

Braidotti, R., *The Posthuman*, Cambridge: Polity, 2013.

Brandtstädter, S., 'Rising from the Ordinary: Virtue, the Justice Motif and Moral Change', *Anthropological Theory* 21(2) (2021): 180–205.

Breen, R., D. Hannan, D. Rottman, and C. Whelan, *Understanding Ireland: State, Class and Development in the Republic of Ireland*, Basingstoke: Palgrave Macmillan, 1990.

Brick, A., and S. Connoll, 'Waiting Times for Publicly Funded Hospital Treatment: How Does Ireland Measure Up?', *The Economic and Social Review* 52(1) (2021): 41–52.

Brkljačić, T., L. Lučić, and I. Sučić, 'Well-Being, Motives and Experiences in Live and Online Game Settings: Case of Contract Bridge', *International Journal of Gaming and Computer-Mediated Simulations* 9(4) (2017): 19–43.

Brown, G., *Seven Ways to Change the World*, New York: Simon & Schuster, 2022.

Burke, S., *Irish Apartheid: Healthcare Inequality in Ireland*, Dublin: New Island, 2009.

Campbell, C., *The Romantic Ethic and the Spirit of Modern Consumerism*, Oxford: Basil Blackwell, 1987.

Charles, N., 'Post-Human Families? Dog–Human Relations in the Domestic Sphere', *Sociological Research Online* 21(3) (2016).

Charles, N., and C. Davies, 'My Family and Other Animals: Pets as Kin', *Sociological Research Online* 13(5) (2017).

Chatterjee, H., P. Camic, B Lockyer, and L. Thomson, 'Non-Clinical Community Interventions: A Systematised Review of Social Prescribing Schemes', *Arts & Health* 10(2) (2018): 97–123.

Cicero, M., *On the Good Life*, trans. M. Grant, London: Penguin, 1971.

Clifford, J., *Routes: Travel and Translation in the Late Twentieth Century*, Cambridge, MA: Harvard University Press, 1997.

Cockayne, E., *Cheek by Jowl: A History of Neighbours*, London: Vintage Books, 2012.

Collins, T., and W. Vamplew, *Mud, Sweat and Beers*, Oxford: Berg, 2002.

Connolly, L., 'Introduction', in L. Connolly (ed.), *The 'Irish' Family*, London: Routledge, 2015, pp. 1–9.

Connolly, L., 'Locating "the Irish Family": Towards Plurality of Family Forms?', in L. Connolly (ed.), *The 'Irish' Family*, London: Routledge, 2015, pp. 10–38.

REFERENCES

Cook, J., and J. Cassaniti (eds), 'Mindfulness and Culture', *Anthropology Today* 38(2) (2022).

Corcoran, M., '"God's Golden Acre for Children": Pastoralism and Sense of Place in New Suburban Communities', *Urban Studies* 47(12) (2010): 2537–54.

Corcoran, M., and M. Hayes, 'Towards a Morphology of Public Space in Suburban Dublin', *Built Environment* 41(4) (2015): 519–37.

Craig, C., 'Reading Identity: American and Irish Women's Book Clubs, Culture, and Identity', *Irish Journal of Sociology* 27(2) (2019): 128–52.

Crossley, N., 'Merleau-Ponty, the Elusive Body and Carnal Sociology', *Body and Society* 1(1) (1995): 43–63.

Curristan, D., B. Maître, and H. Russell, *Intergenerational Poverty in Ireland*, Dublin: Economic and Social Research Institute, 2020.

Darcy, C., 'Making the Invisible Visible: Masculinities and Men's Illicit Recreational Drug Use', *Irish Journal of Sociology* 26(1) (2018): 5–24.

Das, V., *Textures of the Ordinary: Doing Anthropology after Wittgenstein*, New York: Fordham University Press, 2020.

Davidson, J., *Courtesans and Fishcakes: The Consuming Passions of Classical Athens*, London: Fontana Press, 1998.

de Michelis, E., *A History of Modern Yoga*, London: Continuum, 2004.

Descola, P., and G. Palsson (eds), *Nature and Society: Anthropological Perspectives*, London: Routledge, 1996.

Devereux, E., 'The Lonely Furrow: Muintir Na Tire and Irish Community Development 1931–1991', *Community Development Journal* 28(1) (1993): 45–54.

Doppelt, G., 'Rawls' System of Justice: A Critique from the Left', *Noûs* 15(3) (1981): 259–307.

Douglas, M., and B. Isherwood, *The World of Goods*, London: Allen Lane, 1979.

Doyle, A., et al., *Drugnet Ireland* 82 (2022): https://www.drugsandalcohol.ie/37086/1/Drugnet_Ireland_Issue_82.pdf.

Drążkiewicz, E., et al., 'Repealing Ireland's Eighth Amendment: Abortion Rights and Democracy Today', *Social Anthropology* 28(3): 1–25.

Dreyfus, H., *Being-in-the-World: A Commentary on Heidegger's Being and Time, Division 1*, Cambridge, MA: MIT Press, 1991.

REFERENCES

Duany, A., and R. Steuteville, 'Defining the 15-Minute City', *Public Square*, 8 February 2021: https://www.cnu.org/publicsquare/2021/02/08/defining-15-minute-city.

Duggan, B., and G.A. Mohan, 'Longitudinal Examination of Young People's Gambling Behaviours and Participation in Team Sports', *Journal of Gambling Studies* 39 (2023): 541–57.

Duque, M., *Ageing with Smartphones in Urban Brazil: A Work in Progress*, London: UCL Press, 2022.

Durkheim, É., 'The Contribution of Sociology to Psychology and Philosophy' (1909), in É. Durkheim, *The Rules of Sociological Method*, trans. W.D. Halls, New York: The Free Press, 1982, pp. 236–40.

Durkheim, É., *Suicide: A Study in Sociology*, trans. J.A. Spaulding and G. Simpson, New York: Free Press, 1979 [1897].

Etzioni, A., *The Spirit of Community*, New York: Crown Publishers, 1993.

Ferris, D. (ed.), *The Cambridge Companion to Walter Benjamin*, Cambridge: Cambridge University Press, 2004.

Fletcher, T., 'The Making of English Cricket Cultures: Empire, Globalization and (Post)colonialism', *Sport in Society* 14(1) (2011): 17–36.

Foley, R., 'Indigenous Narratives of Health: (Re)Placing Folk-Medicine within Irish Health Histories', *Journal of Medical Humanities* 36 (2015): 5–18.

Forsberg, H., and V. Timonen, 'The Future of the Family as Envisioned by Young Adults in Ireland', *Journal of Youth Studies* 21(6): 765–79.

Foucault, M., *The History of Sexuality: Volume 1: An Introduction*, trans. R. Hurley, London: Allen Lane, 1979 [1976].

Free, M., and C. Scully, 'The Run of Ourselves: Shame, Guilt and Confession in Post-Celtic Tiger Irish Media', *International Journal of Cultural Studies* 21(3) (2018): 308–24.

Galbraith, J.K., *The New Industrial State*, Boston: Houghton Mifflin, 1967.

Gardner, J., *Being a Roman Citizen*, London: Routledge, 1993.

Garry, J., N. Hardman, and D. Payne, *Irish Social and Political Attitudes*, Liverpool: Liverpool University Press, 2006.

Garvey, P., and D. Miller, *Ageing with Smartphones in Ireland: When Life Becomes Craft*, London: UCL Press, 2021.

Garvey, P., D. Miller, and S. Mohammid, 'From Menopause to

Hypertension: The Problem of Securing Engagement', in C. Hawkins, P. Awondo, and D. Miller (eds), *mHealth: An Anthropological Approach*, London: UCL Press, forthcoming.

Geraghty, R., J. Gray, and D. Ralph, 'One of the Best Members of the Family: Continuity and Change in Young Children's Relationships with Their Grandparents', in L. Connolly (ed.), *The 'Irish' Family*, London: Routledge, 2015, pp. 124–39.

Gilmartin, M., and B. Migge, 'European Migrants in Ireland: Pathways to Integration', *International Journal of Health Services* 22(3) (2015): 459–82.

Gilroy, P., *The Black Atlantic*, London: Verso, 1993.

Glassie, H., *Passing the Time in Ballymenone*, Bloomington: Indiana University Press, 1982.

Gray, J., R. Geraghty, and D. Ralph, *Family Rhythms: The Changing Textures of Family Life in Ireland*, Manchester: Manchester University Press, 2016.

Gray, M., and S. Suri, *Ghost Work*, Boston: Houghton Mifflin Harcourt, 2019.

Greenblatt, S., *The Swerve: How the Renaissance Began*, New York: Vintage Books, 2011.

Grotti, R., H. Russell, É. Fahey, and B. Maître, 'Discrimination and Inequality in Housing in Ireland', Dublin: Economic and Social Research Institute, 2018: https://www.esri.ie/publications/discrimination-and-inequality-in-housing-in-ireland.

Gurova, O., 'Ideology of Consumption in Soviet Union: From Asceticism to the Legitimating of Consumer Goods', *Anthropology of East Europe Review* 24(2) (2006): 91–8.

Hacking, I., *The Social Construction of What?*, Cambridge, MA: Harvard University Press, 1999.

Hadot, P., *What is Ancient Philosophy?*, trans. M. Chase, Cambridge, MA: Harvard University Press, 2002 [1995]

Hakim, D., and D. Dalby, 'Ireland Votes to Approve Gay Marriage, Putting Country in Vanguard', *The New York Times*, 23 May 2015.

Haraway, D., 'The Companion Species Manifesto: Dogs, People and Significant Otherness', in *Manifestly Haraway*, Minneapolis: University of Minnesota Press, 2016, pp. 91–198.

Hardimon, M., *Hegel's Social Philosophy*, Cambridge: Cambridge University Press, 1994.

Harries, K., *The Ethics of Architecture*, Cambridge, MA: MIT Press, 1997.

REFERENCES

Harvey, D., *The Condition of Postmodernity*, Oxford: Blackwell, 1989.

Haug, W.F., *Critique of Commodity Aesthetics: Appearance, Sexuality and Advertising in Capitalist Society*, trans. R. Bock, Cambridge: Polity, 1986 [1971].

Haugeland, J., *Dasein Disclosed*, Cambridge, MA: Harvard University Press, 2013.

Hawkins, C., *Ageing with Smartphones in Urban Uganda*, London: UCL Press, forthcoming.

Hawkins, C., P. Awondo, and D. Miller (eds), *mHealth: An Anthropological Approach*, London: UCL Press, forthcoming.

Hegel, G.W.F., *Lectures on the History of Philosophy*, vol. 2: *Greek Philosophy*, ed. and trans. R.F. Brown, London: Routledge & Kegan Paul, 1955.

Hegel, G.W.F., *Phenomenology of Spirit*, trans. A.V. Miller, Oxford: Oxford University Press, 1977 [1807].

Hegel, G.W.F., *Philosophy of Right*, trans. T.M. Knox, Oxford: Oxford University Press, 1942 [1820].

Heidegger, M., *Being and Time*, trans. J. Macquarrie and E. Robinson, New York: Harper & Row, 1962 [1927].

Heidegger, M., 'Building Dwelling Thinking', in M. Heidegger, *Poetry, Language, Thought*, trans. A. Hofstadter, New York: Harper Perennial, 1971, pp. 143–59.

Heidegger, M., *The Question Concerning Technology and Other Essays*, trans. W. Lovitt, New York: Garland, 1977.

Henig, D., A. Strhan, and J. Robbins (eds), *Where is the Good in the World?* New York: Berghahn, 2022.

Hickman, M., 'Thinking about Ireland and the Irish Diaspora', in Tom Inglis (ed.), *Are the Irish Different?*, Manchester: Manchester University Press, pp. 133–44.

Higgs, P., and C. Gilleard, *Rethinking Old Age: Theorising the Fourth Age*, London: Macmillan International Higher Education, 2015.

Hinton, W., *Fanshen: A Documentary of Revolution in a Chinese Village*, New York: Monthly Review Press, 1966.

Holbraad, M., 'The Contingency of Concepts', in P. Charbonnier, G. Salmon, and P. Skafish (eds), *Comparative Metaphysics*, London: Rowman & Littlefield, pp. 131–56.

Horowitz, D., *The Anxieties of Affluence: Critiques of American Consumer Society, 1939–1979*, Cambridge, MA: University of Massachusetts Press, 2004.

REFERENCES

Horowitz, D., *Consuming Pleasures: Intellectuals and Popular Culture in the Postwar World*, Philadelphia: University of Pennsylvania Press, 2012.

Horowitz, D., *The Morality of Spending: Attitudes towards the Consumer Society in America, 1875–1940*, Chicago: Ivan R. Dee, 1992.

Horst, H., and D. Miller, *The Cell Phone*, Oxford: Berg, 2006.

Howe, S., *Ireland and Empire: Colonial Legacies in Irish History and Culture*, Oxford: Oxford University Press, 2000.

Hyppolite, J., *Studies on Marx and Hegel*, trans. J. O'Neill, London: Heinemann, 1969 [1955].

Inglis, T., *Global Ireland: Same Difference*, New York: Routledge, 2007.

Inglis, T., *Moral Monopoly: The Rise and Fall of the Catholic Church in Modern Ireland*, 2nd edn, Dublin: University College Dublin Press, 1998.

Ingold, T., *The Perception of the Environment: Essays on Livelihood, Dwelling and Skill*, London: Routledge, 2000,

Inwood, B., and L. Gerson (ed. and trans.), *The Epicurus Reader*, Indianapolis: Hackett Publishing Company, 1994.

James, C.L.R., *Beyond a Boundary*, London: Hutchinson, 1963.

Jiménez Corsín, A. (ed.), *Culture and Well-Being: Anthropological Approaches to Freedom and Political Ethics*, London: Pluto, 2008.

Juvenal, *The Satires*, trans. N. Rudd, Oxford: Oxford University Press, 2008.

Kant, I., *Critique of Practical Reason*, ed. and trans. M. Gregor, Cambridge: Cambridge University Press, 2015 [1788].

Kant, I., *Critique of Pure Reason*, ed. and trans. P. Guyer and A.W. Wood, Cambridge: Cambridge University Press, 1998 [1781].

Kant, I., *Fundamental Principles of the Metaphysics of Morals*, trans. T.K. Abbott, Project Gutenberg, 2002 [1785]: https://www.gutenberg.org/ebooks/5682.

Kavedžija, I., *Making Meaningful Lives: Tales from an Aging Japan*, Philadelphia: University of Pennsylvania Press, 2019.

Kazantzakis, N., *Zorba the Greek*, trans. C. Wildman, London: Faber & Faber, 2008 [1946].

Keane, J.B., *The Field*, Cork: Mercier Press, 1966.

Keane, W., *Ethical Life: Its Natural and Social Histories*, Princeton: Princeton University Press, 2016

Keenan, M., 'Sexual Abuse and the Catholic Church', in T. Inglis (ed.), *Are the Irish Different?*, Manchester: Manchester University Press, 2014, pp. 99–110.

Kettle, P., 'Motivations for Investing in Allotment Gardening in Dublin: A Sociological Analysis', *Irish Journal of Sociology* 22(2) (2014): 30–63.

Keyes, M., *Rachel's Holiday*, London: Michael Joseph, 1998.

Kiberd, D., *Inventing Ireland: The Literature of the Modern Nation*, Cambridge, MA: Harvard University Press, 1995.

King, K., 'Neutralizing Marginally Deviant Behavior: Bingo Players and Superstition', *Journal of Gambling Studies* 6(1) (1990): 43–61.

Klein, M., *Envy and Gratitude and Other Works*, London: Delacorte Press, 1975.

Knauf, B., 'Finding the Good: Reactive Modernity amongst the Gebusi, in the Pacific and Elsewhere', *The Australian Journal of Anthropology* 30 (2019): 84–103.

Kolb, D., *The Critique of Modernity: Hegel, Heidegger and After*, Chicago: University of Chicago Press, 1986.

Kopnina, L., 'Anthropocentrism and Post-Humanism', *International Encyclopaedia of Anthropology*, Oxford: Wiley, 2019: https://doi.org/10.1002/9781118924396.wbiea2387.

Koster, A., and K. Garde, 'Sexual Desire and Menopausal Development: A Prospective Study of Danish Women Born in 1936', *Maturitas* 16(1) (1993): 49–60.

Laidlaw, J., *Riches and Renunciation: Religion, Economy, and Society among the Jains*, Oxford: Oxford University Press, 1995.

Laidlaw, J., *The Subject of Virtue*, Cambridge: Cambridge University Press, 2014.

Lamb, S. (ed.), *Successful Aging as a Contemporary Obsession*, New Brunswick, NJ: Rutgers University Press, 2017.

Lambek, M., '*Le bonheur Suisse*, again', in H. Walker and I. Kavedžija (eds), *Values of Happiness: Toward an Anthropology of Purpose in Life*, Chicago: Hau Books, 2016, pp. 237–65.

Lambek, M., 'Introduction', in M. Lambek (ed.), *Ordinary Ethics: Anthropology, Language, and Action*, New York: Fordham University Press, 2010, pp. 1–36.

Lambek, M. (ed.), *Ordinary Ethics: Anthropology, Language, and Action*, New York: Fordham University Press, 2010.

Lambek, M., 'Value and Virtue', *Anthropological Theory* 8(2) (2008): 133–57.

Lambek, M., V. Das, D. Fassin, and W. Keane, *Four Lectures on Ethics*, Chicago: HAU Books, 2015.

Lang, B., *Heidegger's Silence*, Ithaca, NY: Cornell University Press, 1996.

Lasch, C., *The Culture of Narcissism*, New York: W.W. Norton, 1979.

Lawler, M., C. Heary, G. Shorter, and E. Nixon, 'Peer and Parental Processes Predict Distinct Patterns of Physical Activity Participation among Adolescent Girls and Boys', *International Journal of Sport and Exercise Psychology* 20(2) (2022): 497–514.

Leonard, L., *The Environmental Movement in Ireland*, New York: Springer, 2007.

Liston, K., 'The GAA and the Sporting Irish', in T. Inglis (ed.), *Are the Irish Different?*, Manchester: Manchester University Press, 2014, pp. 199–210.

Lucretius, *The Nature of Things*, trans. A.E. Stallings, London: Penguin, 2007.

Lynteris, C., 'The Frankfurt School, Critical Theory and Anthropology', in M. Candea (ed.), *Schools and Styles of Anthropological Theory*, London: Routledge, 2018, pp. 159–72.

Macfarlane, A., *The Origins of English Individualism*, Oxford: Blackwell, 1979.

MacIntyre, A., *After Virtue: A Study in Moral Theory*, 3rd edn, Notre Dame, IN: University of Notre Dame Press, 2007 [1981].

Mackenzie, C., 'Relational Autonomy, Normative Authority and Perfectionism', *Journal of Social Philosophy* 39(4) (2008): 512–33.

Mackenzie, C., 'Three Dimensions of Autonomy: A Relational Analysis', in A. Veltman and M. Piper (eds), *Autonomy, Oppression and Gender*, Oxford: Oxford University Press, 2014, pp. 15–41.

Mackenzie, C., and N. Stoljar (eds), *Relational Autonomy: Feminist Perspectives on Autonomy, Agency, and the Social Self*, New York: Oxford University Press, 2000.

MacNamara, B., *The Valley of the Squinting Windows*, Dublin: Maunsel and Company, 1918.

Madianou, M., and D. Miller, *Migration and New Media*, London: Routledge, 2012.

Maguire, M., and F. Murphy, *Integration in Ireland: The Everyday Lives of African Migrants*, Manchester: Manchester University Press, 2015.

Malcolm, E., *'Ireland Sober, Ireland Free': Drink and Temperance *in Nineteenth-Century Ireland*, Syracuse, NY: Syracuse University Press, 1986.

Malpas, J., *Heidegger's Topology: Being, Place, World*, Cambridge, MA: MIT Press, 2008.

Mandle, W., *The Gaelic Athletic Association and Irish Nationalist Politics, 1884–1924*, London: Christopher Helm and Dublin: Gill & Macmillan, 1987.

Marcus Aurelius, *Meditations*, London: Collins Classics, 2020.

Marcuse, H., *One-Dimensional Man*, London: Routledge & Kegan Paul, 1964.

Marks, S., 'Durkheim's Theory of Anomie', *American Journal of Sociology* 80(2) (1994): 329–63.

Marmoy, C.F.A., 'The "Auto-Icon" of Jeremy Bentham at University College, London', *Medical History* 2(2) (1958): 77–86.

Marx, K., *Early Writings*, trans. R. Livingstone and R. Benton, Harmondsworth: Penguin, 1975.

Massey, D., *Space, Place and Gender*, Minneapolis: University of Minneapolis Press, 1994.

Mattingly, C., 'Two Virtue Ethics and the Anthropology of Morality', *Anthropological Theory* 12(2) (2012): 161–84.

Mattingly, C., R. Dyring, M. Louw, and T. Wentzer (eds), *Moral Engines: Exploring the Ethical Drives in Human Life*, London: Berghahn, 2018.

Mauger, A., 'A Great Race of Drinkers? Irish Interpretations of Alcoholism and Drinking Stereotypes, 1945–1975', *Medical History* 65(1) (2010): 70–89.

Maycock, P., 'Cocaine Use In Ireland: An Exploratory Study', in R. Moran et al., *A Collection of Papers on Drug Issues in Ireland*, Dublin: Health Research Board, 2021, pp. 80–152.

Mckay, F., 'Eudaimonia and Culture: The Anthropology of Virtue', In J. Vitterso (ed.), *Handbook of Eudaimonic Well-Being*, Cham: Springer, 2016, pp. 409–26.

Mead, G.H., *Mind, Self and Society*, Chicago: University of Chicago Press, 2015 [1934].

Mignolo, W., 'Epistemic Disobedience, Independent Thought and Decolonial Freedom', *Theory, Culture and Society* 26(7–8) (2009): 159–81.

Miller, D., 'Brexit and the Decolonization of Ireland', *HAU: Journal of Ethnographic Theory* 10(2) (2020): 356–60.

Miller, D., 'Care and Surveillance – The Good Citizens of COVID-19', in S. Abram, L. Lambert, and J. Robinson (eds), *How to Live through a Pandemic*, London: Routledge, 2023.

Miller, D., *The Comfort of People*, Cambridge: Polity, 2017.

Miller, D., 'Dr Google will see you first', in C. Hawkins, P. Awondo, and D. Miller (eds), *mHealth: An Anthropological Approach*, London: UCL Press, forthcoming.

Miller, D., 'The Ideology of Friendship in the Era of Facebook', *HAU: Journal of Ethnographic Theory* 7(1) (2017): 377–95.

Miller, D., *Material Culture and Mass Consumption*, Oxford: Blackwell, 1987.

Miller, D., *Social Media in an English Village*, London: UCL Press, 2016.

Miller, D., *Tales from Facebook*, Cambridge: Polity, 2011.

Miller, D., *A Theory of Shopping*, Cambridge: Polity, 1998.

Miller, D., 'The Tragic Dénouement of English Sociality', *Cultural Anthropology* 30(2) (2015): 336–57.

Miller, D., and P. Garvey, 'Grandparenting as the Resolution of Kinship as Experience', *Journal of the Royal Anthropological Institute* 28(3) (2022): 975–92.

Miller, D., and J. Sinanan, *Webcam*, Cambridge: Polity, 2014.

Miller, D., and S. Woodward, *Blue Jeans: The Art of the Ordinary*, Berkeley: University of California Press, 2012.

Miller, D., et al., *The Global Smartphone: Beyond a Youth Technology*, London: UCL Press, 2021.

Miller, D., et al., *How the World Changed Social Media*, London: UCL Press, 2016.

Miller, R., *The Triumph of Prometheus: The Rise and Fall of Animal Experimentation*, Oxford: Oxford University Press, 2023.

Miller, S., *Ancient Greek Athletics*, New Haven: Yale University Press, 2004.

Miller, S., *Arete: Greek Sports from Ancient Sources*, Berkeley: University of California Press, 2012.

Mitchell, A., and P. Trawny, *Heidegger's Black Notebooks*, New York: Columbia University Press, 2017.

Moane, G., 'A Psychological Analysis of Colonialism in an Irish Context', *Irish Journal of Psychology* 15 (1994): 250–65.

Motherway, B., M. Kelly, P. Faughnan, and H. Tovey, *Trends in Irish Environmental Attitudes between 1993 and 2002: First Report of National Survey Data*, Dublin: Environmental Protection Agency, 2003.

REFERENCES

Moubarac, J.-C., N.W. Shead, and J. Derevensky, 'Bingo Playing and Problem Gambling: A Review of Our Current Knowledge', *Journal of Gambling Studies* 24 (2010): 164–84.

Munn, N., *The Fame of Gawa*, Cambridge: Cambridge University Press, 1986.

Munoz-Dardé, V., 'Rawls, Justice in the Family and Justice of the Family', *The Philosophical Quarterly* 48(192) (2003): 335–52.

Murphy, A., and C. Kelleher, 'Contemporary Health Practices in the Burren', *The Irish Journal of Psychology* 16(1) (1995): 38–51.

Murphy, F., 'Austerity Ireland, the New Thrift Culture and Sustainable Consumption', *Journal of Business Anthropology* 6(2): 158–74.

Murphy, M., 'Civil Society in the Shadow of the Irish State', *Irish Journal of Sociology* 19(2) (2011): 170–87.

Nagle, S., *Histories of Nationalism in Ireland and Germany: A Comparative Study from 1800 to 1932*, London: Bloomsbury, 2016.

Neiman, S., *Moral Clarity*, Princeton: Princeton University Press, 2009.

Nicolescu, R., *Social Media in Southeast Italy*, London: UCL Press, 2016.

Norbeck, E., and H. Befu, 'Informal Fictive Kinship in Japan', *American Anthropologist* 60(1) (1958): 102–17.

Norris, M., 'Davis Now Lectures: Unmaking Home: Making Homes for Shelter or for Investment?', RTE.IE, 4 February 2020: https://www.rte.ie/culture/2020/0131/1112298-davis-now-lectures-making-homes-for-shelter-or-for-investment/.

Norris, M., *Property, Family and the Irish Welfare State*, Cham: Springer, 2016.

Nove, A., *The Economics of Feasible Socialism*, London: Routledge, 1983.

Nussbaum, M., *Frontiers of Justice: Disability, Nationality, Species Membership*, Cambridge, MA: Harvard University Press, 2006.

Nussbaum, M., 'Nature, Function, and Capability: Aristotle on Political Distribution', Working Paper 31, Helsinki: World Institute for Development Economic Research of the United Nations University, 1987.

Nussbaum, M., *The Therapy of Desire: Theory and Practice in Hellenistic Ethics*, Princeton: Princeton University Press, 1994.

Nussbaum, M., *Women and Human Development: The Capabilities Approach*, Cambridge: Cambridge University Press, 2000.

Nussbaum, M., and S. Levmore, *Aging Thoughtfully: Conversations about Retirement, Romance, Wrinkles, and Regret*, Oxford: Oxford University Press, 2017.

Nussbaum, M., and A. Sen (eds), *The Quality of Life*, Oxford: Clarendon Press, 1993.

Nyamnjoh, F., 'Blinded by Sight: Divining the Future of Anthropology in Africa', *Africa Spectrum* 47(2–3) (2012): 63–92.

O'Riain, S., *The Rise and Fall of Ireland's Celtic Tiger: Liberalism, Boom and Bust*, Cambridge: Cambridge University Press, 2014.

O'Toole, F., *We Don't Know Ourselves: A Personal History of Ireland since 1958*, London: Head of Zeus, 2021.

Otteson, J., 'Kantian Individualism and Political Libertarianism', *Independent Review* 13(3) (2009): 389–409.

Papakonstantinou, Z., 'Alciabiades in Olympia: Olympic Ideology, Sport and Social Conflict in Classical Athens', *Journal of Sport History* 30(2) (2003): 173–82.

Piketty, T., *Capital in the Twenty-First Century*, Cambridge, MA: Harvard University Press, 2014.

Plato, *Euthydemus* 282a, In *The Dialogues of Plato: Volume 2*, trans. B. Jowett, London: Sphere Books, 1970, p. 147.

Power, E., 'Furry Families: Making a Human–Dog Family through Home', *Social and Cultural Geography* 9(5) (2008): 535–55.

Rabbås, Ø., E. Emilsson, H. Fossheim, and M. Tuominen (eds), *The Quest for the Good Life: Ancient Philosophers on Happiness*, Oxford: Oxford University Press, 2015.

Rawls, J., *A Theory of Justice*, Cambridge, MA: Harvard University Press, 1999 [1971].

Rawls, J., *Political Liberalism*, New York: Columbia University Press, 1993.

Reid, H.L., 'Athletic Virtue and Aesthetic Values in Aristotle's Ethics', *Journal of the Philosophy of Sport* 47(1) (2020): 63–74.

Reid, H.L., 'Athletics and Philosophy in Ancient Greece and Rome: Contests of Virtue', *Sport, Ethics and Philosophy* 4(2) (2010): 109–234.

Reid, H.L., *Athletics and Philosophy in the Ancient World: Contests of Virtue*, London: Routledge, 2011.

Reid, H.L., *Introduction to the Philosophy of Sport*, Lanham, MD: Rowman & Littlefield, 2012.

Reid, H.L., *Olympic Philosophy: The Ideas and Ideals behind the Ancient and Modern Olympic Games*, Sioux City, IA: Parnassos Press, 2020.

REFERENCES

Reid, H.L., 'Sport and Moral Education in Plato's *Republic*', *Journal of the Philosophy of Sport* 34(2) (2007): 160–75.

Robbins, J., *Becoming Sinners: Christianity and Moral Torment in a Papua New Guinea Society*, Berkeley: University of California Press, 2004.

Robbins, J., 'Between Reproduction and Freedom: Morality, Value, and Radical Cultural Change', *Ethnos* 72(3) (2007): 293–314.

Robbins, J., 'Beyond the Suffering Subject: Toward an Anthropology of the Good', *Journal of the Royal Anthropological Institute* 19(3) (2013): 447–62.

Robbins, J., 'Where in the World are Values? Exemplarity and Moral Motivation', in C. Mattingly, R. Dyring, M. Louw, and T. Wentzer (eds), *Moral Engines: Exploring the Ethical Drives in Human Life*, London: Berghahn, 2018, pp. 155–73.

Rojas, M., *Sweden after the Swedish Model: From Tutorial State to Enabling State*, trans. R. Tanner and C. Edbrooke, Stockholm: Timbro, 2005.

Ryan, C., 'The Power of Bingo during COVID-19', 25 May 2020: http://somatosphere.net/2020/bingo.html/.

Sahlins, M., *Culture and Practical Reason*, Chicago: University of Chicago Press, 1976.

Samuel, G., *The Origins of Yoga and Tantra: Indic Religions to the Thirteenth Century*, Cambridge: Cambridge University Press, 2012.

Sandel, M.J., *Liberalism and the Limits of Justice*, Cambridge: Cambridge University Press, 2012.

Sandel, M.J., *The Tyranny of Merit: What's Become of the Common Good?*, London: Penguin, 2020.

Sartre, J.-P., *Anti-Semite and Jew*, trans. G.J. Becker, New York: Schocken, 1995 [1946].

Sartre, J.-P., *Being and Nothingness: An Essay in Phenomenological Ontology*, trans. S. Richmond, London: Routledge, 2020 [1943].

Sartre, J.-P., *Critique of Dialectical Reason: Volume 1: Theory of Practical Ensembles*, trans. A. Sheridan-Smith, London: Verso, 2004 [1960].

Sartre, J.-P., *Critique of Dialectical Reason: Volume 2: The Intelligibility of History*, trans. Q. Hoare, London: Verso, 2006 [1985].

Sartre, J.-P., *Nausea*, trans. R. Baldick, London: Penguin, 2000 [1938].

REFERENCES

Savage, M., T. Callan, B. Brain, and B. Colgan, *The Great Recession, Austerity and Inequality: Evidence from Ireland*, Dublin: Economic and Social Research Institute Working Paper 499 (2015): https://www.econstor.eu/bitstream/10419/129395/1/823265064.pdf.

Scharf, T., V. Timonen, C. Conlon, and G. Carney, *Changing Generations: Findings from New Research on Intergenerational Relations in Ireland*, Trinity College Dublin and National University of Ireland Galway, April 2013: http://www.tara.tcd.ie/handle/2262/75620.

Scheper-Hughes, N., *Saints, Scholars and Schizophenics*, Berkeley: University of California Press, 1979.

Scott, D., and G.C. Godbey, 'An Analysis of Adult Play Groups: Social versus Serious Participation in Contract Bridge', *Leisure Studies* 14(1) (1992): 47–67.

Sen, A., *Development as Freedom*, Oxford: Oxford University Press, 1999.

Sen, A., *The Idea of Justice*, London: Penguin, 2010.

Seneca, 'Consolation to Helvia', in *Dialogues and Essays*, trans. J. Davie, Oxford: Oxford University Press, 2007, pp. 163–87.

Seneca, 'Consolation to Marcia', in *Dialogues and Essays*, trans. J. Davie, Oxford: Oxford University Press, 2007, pp. 53–84.

Seneca, 'On the Happy Life', in *Dialogues and Essays*, trans. J. Davie, Oxford: Oxford University Press, 2007, pp. 85–111.

Setiya, K., *Midlife*, Princeton: Princeton University Press, 2017.

Share, M., and L. Kerrins, 'The Role of Grandparents in Childcare in Ireland: Towards a Research Agenda', *Irish Journal of Applied Social Studies* 9(1) (2009): 33–47.

Share, P., H. Tovey, and M.P. Corcoran, *A Sociology of Ireland*, Dublin: Gill & Macmillan, 2007.

Sidgwick, H., *The Methods of Ethics*, New York: Macmillan and Co., 1907 [1874].

Simmel, G., *The Conflict in Modern Culture and Other Essays*, ed. and trans. K.P. Etzkorn, New York: Teachers College Press, 1968.

Simmel, G., 'The Metropolis and Mental Life' (1903), in D. Levine (ed.), *Simmel: On Individuality and Social Forms*, Chicago: University of Chicago Press, 1971, pp. 324–39.

Simmel, G., *The Philosophy of Money*, trans. T. Bottomore and D. Frisby, London: Routledge & Kegan Paul, 1989 [1907].

Smart, A., and J. Smart, *Posthumanism: Anthropological Insights*, Toronto: University of Toronto Press, 2017.

Soper, K., *Post-Growth Living: For an Alternative Hedonism*, London: Verso Books, 2020.

Soper, K., 'Re-thinking the "Good Life"', *Journal of Consumer Culture* 72(2) (2007): 205–29.

Stafford, P. (ed.), *The Global Age-Friendly Community Movement*, New York: Berghahn Books, 2019.

Stoneman, R., *Megasthenes' Indica: A New Translation of the Fragments with Commentary*, London: Routledge, 2021.

Strathern, M., *After Nature*, Cambridge: Cambridge University Press, 1992.

Svasek, M., 'Narratives of "Home" and "Homeland": The Symbolic Construction and Appropriation of the Sudeten German Heimat', *Identities* 9(4) (2002): 495–518.

Sweeney, P., 'Ireland's Low Corporation Tax: The Case for Tax Coordination in the Union', *Transfer* 16(1) (2010): 55–69.

Sweeney, R., and D. Storrie, *The State We Are In: Inequality in Ireland 2022*, May 2022: https://www.tasc.ie/assets/files/pdf/2205-4_tasc_inequality_in_ire_2022.pdf.

Taylor, C., 'Conditions of an Unforced Consensus on Human Rights', in J.R. Bauer and D. Bell (eds), *The East Asian Challenge for Human Rights*, New York: Cambridge University Press, 1999, pp. 124–44.

Taylor, C., *Hegel*, Cambridge: Cambridge University Press, 1975.

Thomas, K., *Man and the Natural World*, London: Penguin, 1983.

Torrance, J., *Estrangement, Alienation and Exploitation*, London: Macmillan, 1977.

Tovey, H., *Environmentalism in Ireland: Movement and Activists*, Dublin: Institute of Public Administration, 2007.

Tovey, H., and P. Share, *A Sociology of Ireland*, Dublin: Gill and Macmillan, 2007.

Veblen, T., *A Theory of the Leisure Class*, London: George Allen & Unwin, 1970 [1899].

Walker, H., and I. Kavedžija (eds), *Values of Happiness: Toward an Anthropology of Purpose in Life*, Chicago: HAU Books, 2016.

Wallerstein, I., *World-Systems Analysis*, Durham, NC: Duke University Press, 2004.

Walzer, M., *Spheres of Justice*, Oxford: Blackwell, 1983.

Wang, X., *Social Media in Industrial China*, London: UCL Press, 2016.

Ward, M., and C. McGarrigle, 'The Contribution of Older Adults to Their Families and Communities', Dublin: TILDA, 2018 (https://

tilda.tcd.ie/publications/reports/pdf/w3-key-findings-report/Chapter%202.pdf).
Weiner, J., 'Anthropology Contra Heidegger Part 1: Anthropology's Nihilism', *Critique of Anthropology* 12(1) (1992): 75–90.
Wentzer, T., and C. Mattingly, 'Towards a New Humanism', *HAU: Journal of Ethnographic Theory* 8(1–2) (2018): 144–57.
White, M., 'The Virtues of a Kantian Economics', in J.A. Baker and M.D. White (eds), *Economics and the Virtues: Building a New Moral Foundation*, Oxford: Oxford University Press, 2016, pp. 94–115.
Whyte, D., 'Viral Intimacy and Catholic Nationalist Political Economy: COVID-19 and the Community Response in Rural Ireland', *Anthropology in Action* 27(3) (2021): 39–43.
Widlock, T., 'Virtue', in D. Fassin (ed.), *A Companion to Moral Anthropology*, Oxford: John Wiley and Sons, 2012, pp. 186–203.
Wiggershaus, R., *The Frankfurt School: Its History, Theories, and Political Significance*, Cambridge, MA: MIT Press, 1995.
Wilk, R., 'Taking Fun Seriously in Envisioning Sustainable Consumption', *Consumption and Society* 1(2) (2022): 255–72.
Wilkinson. R., and K. Pickett, *The Spirit Level*, London: Penguin, 2009.
Wills, C., 'Women, Domesticity and the Family: Recent Feminist Work in Irish Cultural Studies', *Cultural Studies* 15(1): 33–57.
Winnicott, D.W., *Babies and Their Mothers*, New York: Addison Wesley, 1987.
Wood, A.W., *Hegel's Ethical Thought*, Cambridge: Cambridge University Press, 1990.
Young, M., *The Rise of the Meritocracy*, London: Thames & Hudson, 1958.
Zigon, J., *Morality: An Anthropological Perspective*, Oxford: Berg, 2008.
Zuboff, S., *The Age of Surveillance Capitalism: The Fight for a Human Future at the New Frontier of Power*, London: Profile Books, 2019.

INDEX

a priori: Kant's appeal to, 26, 27–8, 234, 236; of sociality, 28, 30–1, 32
abortion rights, 15, 37, 45–6
Active Ageing Group, 130
Adorno, Theodor, 106, 111, 117, 272, 286, 287, 310n5; *Dialectic of Enlightenment*, 237, 287
aerobics, 189
After Virtue (MacIntyre), 297
ageing, 9, 44–5
agon: concept of, 202
Alcibiades, 201, 207
alcoholism, 137–8, 314n16
Alexander the Great, 265
alternative spirituality, 197
anomie, 72, 73, 76
anthropology: approaches to morality and freedom, 297–8; discipline of, 240–1; empathy and, 118; ethics and, 305n52; limitations of, 296; origins of, 31; philosophy and, 6, 24, 33, 76, 290, 295–7
anthropomorphism, 95, 96, 97–8
anti-consumption, 18, 78, 88, 91–3, 94, 103
Arensberg, Conrad, 160, 223
aretē (excellence/virtue), 1, 201, 204
aristocracies of culture, 109

Aristophanes, 199
Aristotle: on ethics, 305n52; on *eudaimonia*, 1; idea of habitus, 279; *kalokagathia* principle, 201; *Nicomachean Ethics*, 1, 69; philosophy of, 203, 210, 261; *Politics*, 69; *Rhetoric*, 201
asceticism, 105, 279–80
ASSA (Anthropology of Smartphones and Smart Ageing) project, 38, 255, 294, 321n5
Attenborough, David, 253
autism: attitude to people with, 163–4, 175; institutional response to, 164; sports and, 180–1

badminton, 178, 208, 255
Bakewell, Sarah, 65
Banshees of Inisherin, The (film), 213
Barry, Sebastian, 18; *The Secret Scripture*, 163
Baudrillard, Jean, 106; *A Critique of the Political Economy of the Sign*, 109–10
Beckett, Samuel, 72, 281.
Being (Dasein), 233, 234, 235, 236, 286
Being and Time (Heidegger), 231, 233, 234–6, 237, 241, 296

being human: definition of, 117
Benjamin, Walter, 106, 111–12, 114, 115
Bentham, Jeremy, 154
Berlin, Isaiah: study of freedom, 64, 66–9, 74, 76, 296; 'Two Concepts of Liberty', 66
beyond anthropomorphism: concept of, 101, 115
bingo, 130–3
Black migrants, 169
Bloody Sunday massacre, 182–3
blow-ins: arrival to Cuan, 215–17, 225, 229; background of, 88, 222, 229; citizenship status, 169; community activities, 21, 218–19, 221, 223, 224, 229–30, 238, 241, 288, 298; housing, 121; local attitude towards, 214–16, 219–20; population of, 10, 129, 179, 196; stories of, 222–4
blue jeans, 60, 80, 86
body: health and, 190; mind and, 193; sports and, 187, 196; sustainability of, 197
book reading group, 81, 82
Bourdieu, Pierre, 24, 79, 236, 277
bowling, 178, 179, 186
boxing, 178
brack (sweet fruit bread), 22
Brecht, Bertolt, 109
Brexit, 17, 46, 49–51
bridge (card game), 131–3, 134
Brittas Estate, 218–19, 221, 225
bucket lists, 244

Camino de Santiago pilgrimage trail, 188, 189, 198, 270, 273
Campbell, Colin, 79
Camus, Albert, 72
capabilities approach, 4, 64, 69, 70, 71, 75
capitalism, 6, 104, 106, 174, 311n34
Catholic Church: alternative spirituality and, 197; compassion of, 164; control of education, 14–15, 36–7; decline of authority of, 15, 36, 37, 204; emphasis on sin and guilt, 270; GAA and, 204–5; as heart of the community, 220; in Ireland, status of, 35–6, 38, 182, 304n35; local community and, 254, 255; portrayal in popular culture, 37; sexual scandals, 36, 37
'Celtic Tiger' period, 16
Chinese Traditional Medicine, 194
Christian Brothers, 14, 36–7
Christmas savings club, 127
Cicero, 265, 269, 279, 280
Citizens Advice Bureau, 220
citizenship, 168–72, 240
civil society, 283, 323n5
class (social), 134
clothing, 80–2, 180, 188
cocaine use, 139, 140, 141, 314n16
cognitive behavioural therapy (CBT), 146
Cohen, Leonard: songs of, 256, 257
comfortable middle class, 86, 129
commodity culture, 110
communitarianism, 289, 290
community gardens, 258
computer courses, 255
consciousness: Being in relation to, 234
conspicuous anti-consumption, 78, 88, 91–2, 119
conspicuous consumption, 78, 82, 83, 85, 86–7, 88, 96, 119
consumer society, 94, 105, 109, 278
consumption: academic characterizations of, 80; critique of, 94; emulation of, 88–9, 92–3; inequality and, 84; insatiable, 79–80, 110; mass, 18, 105, 278; satiable, 78, 82–9, 94; status marking and, 79, 85–6; vulgarity of, 83, 86

contracturalists: vs utilitarians, 165
cosmopolitanism, 271
Covid-19 pandemic, 30, 47, 74, 170
craic: ideal of good, 33, 83, 203, 214, 271, 278
creative writing groups, 257–8
cricket, 178, 184, 196
Critique of Practical Reason (Kant), 268
Critique of Pure Reason (Kant), 25–6
Croke Park, Dublin, 182–3
Cromwell, Oliver, 48
Cuan: attitudes to citizenship, 57, 168–72; Brexit referendum and, 46, 49–51; businesses, 88, 222, 225; caveats of, 292–3; children in, 86, 139, 216; civic responsibility, 75; class relations, 20, 128–30; in comparative perspective, 175; as contemporary *polis*, 76, 210, 240, 294, 299; contractual relationships, 162–3, 165–6, 168, 169; cosmology of, 254, 261, 268–9, 270, 274–9; cosmopolitanism of, 271–2; creation of community, 146, 217–20, 221–2, 223, 225–6, 228–30; digital divide, 125; drinking in, 278–9; entertainment, 36; ethnographic study of, 8, 12, 22–4, 55; family relations, 40–1; freedoms, 68, 73, 284; funerals, 30; gender differences, 58; geography of, 14, 30, 87–8, 224–5, 290; good enough life, 294, 300; health services, 191–2; history of, 211–12, 219; hobbies and interests, 29–30, 113–14; as holiday destination, 20, 216–17, 224, 246; housing, 20, 21, 212, 214, 217, 300; income level in, 49; inequalities, 3, 18–19, 120–1, 129, 147, 151–2, 299; infrastructure, 225; leisure activities, 11, 19, 30, 55, 114, 130–4, 254, 255, 258; liberalism, 36, 46, 166; lonely people in, 23; middle class, 129; modernization of, 216; neighbourly relations, 213–15; news media, 218, 220, 221; normative society of, 74–5; ownership of local retail outlet, 88; perception of retirement, 278; poetry festival, 114, 292; politics, attitude to, 21, 46–7, 48, 52–5, 56–7; population of, 3, 20–1, 57, 177, 211, 212, 215; property prices, 21, 124, 129, 134, 169; public safety, 11, 122; public transportation, 212; religious observance, 36, 37, 213; repair initiatives, 89, 90–1; reputation of, 10–11, 12, 228, 230; restaurants and pubs, 21; retirees, 72, 113; secondary schools, 211–12; secular organizations, 220; social services, 51–2; state's relationship to, 226–8; tourism, 211, 217; traditional culture, 212; transformation of, 218–20
'Cuan Against Coronavirus' Facebook group, 170, 221
Cuan Community Association (CCA): activities of, 53, 54, 225–6; disputes resolution in, 55–7; ethos and practice of, 55; Facebook group, 221; formation of, 218, 223; general meetings of, 53, 56, 57; leadership of, 148; mediation of local disputes, 55, 228–9, 291; members of, 55–6, 218–19; newsflash sponsored by, 220; politics and, 53, 54, 55–6
Cuan Historical Society, 218, 219–20
Cuan News, 95, 180, 218, 220, 221
cultural appropriation, 240

cultural pluralism, 76
cultural relativism, 306n69
culture industry, 107–8, 109
cycling, 178, 186–7, 188

dancing, 190, 195, 256
'Darkness Into Light' annual walk, 144
Das, Veena, 297
Dasein *see* Being (Dasein)
Davidson, James, 279; *Courtesans and Fishcakes*, 264
death: contemplation of, 265, 281; Stoics philosophy on, 264–5
de-commodification, 114
dementia, 41
depression, 142, 143–4, 151, 152, 166
Descartes, René, 234
dialectic, 310n5
Dialectic of Enlightenment (Adorno and Horkheimer), 106–9, 113, 117, 237, 287, 295
digital divide, 125
digital technologies, 94, 100, 241
disabled people, 167, 180–1
dogs, 95–6, 97, 98–9, 100, 116, 118
Douglas, Mary, 31, 79, 297
downsizing, 87
Dreyfus, Hubert, 234
drugs, 121, 139, 140
Dublin City: marathon, 187; population, 14, 172
Duque, Marília, 38
Durkheim, Émile, 31, 72, 294, 298, 324n33
dwelling, 231, 237, 238, 239, 241–2
dysfunctional households, 122

Easter Rising (1916 uprising), 20
Edict of Caracalla, 240
egalitarian practices, 147–8
Eighth Amendment of the Constitution Act, 37, 45–6

electronic goods, 84–5
emulation: anti-consumption, 78, 103; consumption, 79, 83, 88–9, 92–3; environmental, 89–94
Enlightenment, 106–7
entrepreneurs, 88
environmentalism: class differentiation and, 92; economic development and, 280; politics and, 89–90; private interests and, 91; rise of, 91, 118–19; status competition and, 92, 93; view of asceticism, 279–80
Epicurus: contemplations on life and death, 267, 281; on friendship, 267; hedonism of, 267, 268; Kant on, 268; moral philosophy of, 243, 261, 269; on pleasure, 266, 267, 268; school of, 265, 266–7, 268; vs Stoics 266, 267, 268, 295
ethnography: comparative, 29; examination of judgements, 31; limitations of, 294; methods, 9–10, 22, 24, 28, 29; philosophy and, 2, 24, 115, 117, 295; of retired population, 2; value of, 8
Etzioni, Amitai, 290
eudaimonia, 1, 6, 291, 293, 297, 298, 299
European identity, 18, 171–2, 239
existentialism, 64–5
expansion of culture, 288
expansionist cosmology, 271, 277

Facebook, 220–1
Fair Deal Scheme, 170, 171
fairness, 163, 167, 170–1
family, 159, 160, 161, 162, 166, 167
fascism, 271
Father Ted (TV series), 37
feminism, 59, 190, 275–6
Fianna Fáil (political party), 48
fictive kinship, 73–4

INDEX

Fine Gael (political party), 48
fishing, 179
football, 178
Foucault, Michel: *The History of Sexuality*, 142
Frankfurt School, 106, 111, 112, 113, 115
freedom: from age, 35, 44–5; as agency, 69–70; authority and, 67–8, 72; as collective endeavour, 62; colonial context, 35; from consumption, 78; cultural values and, 75, 76; definition of, 70, 284, 288; equality and, 70, 71; from family, 40–4; human rights and, 70–1; from identity, 35, 58–61; individual choice and, 284; justice and, 70; law as oppression of, 285–6; modern aspects of, 35, 45; negative and positive, 66–7, 68, 75, 76; philosophers of, 26–7, 64–72; from politics, 35, 45–53, 62, 75; as property of rational being, 305n50; radical, 66; from religion, 35–8; as responsibility, 65; of thought, 38; from work, 34–5, 38–40, 63
freedom *from* and freedom *to*, 40, 45, 52, 62
French Revolution, 68
friendship, 43, 74
fulfilling life, 325n35

Gaelic Athletics Association (GAA): club house of, 178; establishment of, 178; fundraising, 184; Irish nationalism and, 182–4, 204–5; sports centres, 183, 204–5, 206; teams of, 182, 183–4
Galbraith, J.K., 79, 107
gardening, 101
Garvey, Pauline, 3, 9, 23, 41, 87, 148, 255, 321n5; publications of, 34, 35, 37, 39, 44, 45, 191, 195, 197, 246, 247, 254

Gemeinschaft: concept of, 294
gender relations, 58–60, 275–6
Genet, Jean, 72
German *Völkisch* movement, 232
Gesellschaft: concept of, 294
Gilroy, Paul, 241
Glassie, Henry, 213, 256; *Passing the Time in Ballymenone*, 212
Global Irish Civic Forum, 303n23
Global Smartphone, The (Miller et al.), 294–5
Godbey, Geoffrey, 132
Goffman, Erving, 24, 297
Golden Generation, 63, 292
golf, 85, 178, 179, 181, 186, 208
good enough life: ethnographic study of, 1, 2, 299, 300; vs good life, 261; meaning of, 3, 4–5, 94; philosophical view of, 280–1; value of, 179
good life: philosophical writing about, 1, 2, 3–4, 7, 69, 261, 269, 282, 283, 293–5
Goodman, Benny, 108
Gramsci, Antonio, 106
grandparenting, 41–3, 59, 74, 275
Greenblatt, Stephen, 268; *The Swerve*, 266
Guys and Dolls (musical), 218, 223

habitus, 279
Hadot, Pierre, 203
happiness: definition of, 159, 270; of elderly and young people, 7; *eudaimonia* and, 6; fulfilment of, 291, 325n35; sources of, 2, 160
Haraway, Donna, 116
Harries, Karsten, 241
Harvey, David, 231, 233
Haug, Wolfgang Fritz, 109
Haughey, Charles, 170
Headspace app, 194
health services, 136, 175, 191, 192, 194–5, 197–8
Hegel, Georg Wilhelm Friedrich: on

civil society, 76, 323n5; concept of self-actualization, 282; concept of *Sittlichkeit*, 283; ethical philosophy of, 282–4, 290; idea of objectification, 238, 285–7, 288–9, 298; on institution of law, 285–6; *The Phenomenology of Spirit*, 283, 285; *Philosophy of Right*, 285

Heidegger, Martin: *Being and Time*, 231, 233, 234, 236, 237, 241, 296; Black Notebooks, 233; 'Building, Dwelling, Thinking', 237; concept of Dasein, 234–6, 286; on concept of *Heimat*, 232, 234, 237–8; concern with *a priori*, 235; critique of, 233, 236; on dwelling, 231, 237, 241–2; Nazi ideology and, 232–3; nostalgia of, 238; on objectification, 234; personal beliefs, 233; on sense-making, 234; on space, 233, 234, 235, 237; on state of being prior to consciousness, 234; on technology, 235, 237, 238

Heimat: ancient *polis* and, 240; concept of *Volk* and, 238–9; definition of, 232, 296; Heidegger and, 232, 234, 237–8; Irish state and, 239; Nazi ideology and, 232, 233; sense of place and, 234

Hesse, Herman, 109
Hippocrates, 208
hockey, 178
holidays, 84, 246, 269–70, 272–3, 291–2; *see also* travel
Homer: *Iliad*, 199–200
Horkheimer, Max, 106, 117, 272, 310n5; *Dialectic of Enlightenment*, 237
Horowitz, Daniel, 105
horse racing, 178, 180
housing, 212

identity, 38–9, 44–5, 58, 60–1
indigenous societies, 288
individualism, 29, 159
inequality, 120, 157
Inglis, Tom, 15, 239, 304n35
Ingold, Tim, 231, 241
Instagram influencers, 86–7, 143, 221
insult: as mechanism for social equality, 149–50
Internet, 271, 277
Ireland: anthropological studies of, 223; books about, 13–14, 18–19; Catholic Church in, 15, 304n35; civil war in, 35, 48; clerical scandals, 16; Constitution, 35, 303n24; divorce rates, 16; economic development, 14, 15–16; emigration from, 49; environmental policies, 89–90; EU membership, 14; family values, 160–1, 162, 212–13; freedoms in, 35; independence movement, 14, 35; inequality, 16, 17; IT corporations in, 174–5; liberal values, 37, 38; literacy rates, 257; music and literature, 18; national school exams, 143, 144; perception of Englishmen, 47–8, 49; political theocracy in, 35, 36; politics, 17, 46–8; population of, 14, 16–17; poverty, 16; property prices, 16, 17, 52; public housing, 175; repeal of ban on abortion, 15, 19; same-sex marriage, 15, 19; social development, 304n35; social services, 51–2; taxation policy, 175; unemployment benefits in, 303n29
Irish diaspora, 14, 17, 246
Irish egalitarianism, 172
Irish identity, 18, 60–1, 239
Irish language, 15, 182
Irish nationalism, 182–4, 196

INDEX

isolation, 29, 30
isonomia: principle of, 200

James, C.L.R., 178, 196
justice: as fairness, 153, 170; philosophical approach to, 172–3; theories of, 158–9, 163; utilitarian approach to, 154
Juvenal, 264

kalokagathia: concept of, 201
Kant, Immanuel: appeal to the *a priori*, 25, 26, 27–8, 233–4, 236, 284; categorical imperative of, 26; *Critique of Practical Reason*, 268; *Critique of Pure Reason*, 25–6; on Epicurus, 268; on freedom, 305n50; on individual autonomy, 31, 32; influence of, 25; on morality, 26, 27, 31, 72–3, 156; on pleasure, 269; on relationship between individuals and the universal, 296; view of space, 234
karate, 178
Kavedžija, Iza, 6
ketamine, 140
Keyes, Marian, 131; *Rachel's Holiday*, 140
Kimball, Solon, 160, 223
kinship: friendship and, 43, 73–4; grandparenting and, 41–3; social obligations of, 40, 41, 74
kitesurfing, 178
Klein, Melanie, 31

Laidlaw, James, 298
Lambek, Michael, 305n52, 325n35
Lang, Berel, 232
Lang, Fritz, 109
Late Late Show, The, 113
law: as oppression of freedom, 285–6
Lethe river, 12
Levmore, Saul, 273

Liberalism and the Limits of Justice (Sandel), 158
Lidl supermarket, 83
Line of Duty (TV serial), 49
loneliness, 29, 30, 146–7
Lucretius, 261, 266, 268; *The Nature of Things*, 266
Lukács, György, 106

Macfarlane, Alan, 29
Machiavelli, Niccoló, 206
MacIntyre, Alasdair, 7, 33, 298, 325n35; *After Virtue*, 4, 206, 297
Mackenzie, Catriona, 32
MacNamara, Brinsley: *The Valley of the Squinting Windows*, 213, 289
Malpas, Jeff, 233
Mann, Thomas, 109
Marcus Aurelius, 262–3, 264, 269; *Meditations*, 262, 263
marijuana, 140, 141
Marx, Karl, 68, 238, 285, 286–7
Marxism, 105, 106, 109, 295
masculine minimalism, 102
mass consumption, 18, 105, 278
mass culture, 112–15
Massey, Doreen, 233
Material Culture and Mass Consumption (Miller), 105, 285
Mattingly, Cheryl, 298
McCormack, Mike: *Solar Bones*, 257
McTell, Ralph, 256
MDMA (ecstasy), 140
Megasthenes, 265
Men's Shed community initiative: creation of, 146; leadership, 54; meetings, 250; social activities, 39–40, 59, 149, 256, 258, 291; success of, 276; voluntary work, 39
mental health, 163–4
meritocracy, 133, 173
Merleau-Ponty, Maurice, 296

INDEX

migrants: attitude towards, 169; contribution in local communities, 232, 239; dehumanizing of, 232; English-language classes for, 135; health services, 136; origin of, 4, 10, 120, 134–5, 136, 163; professions, 136–7; religion of, 136; search for good life, 4, 5; social networks, 135–6; use of social media, 136; *see also* blow-ins
Miller, Stephen, 200, 201
mindfulness, 193, 194, 195
morality, 26, 27, 239, 324n33
motorcycling, 178
Munoz-Dardé, Véronique, 160
music sessions, 256–7, 274

Nagle, Shane, 239
National Socialism, 232, 233
nativism, 232
neighbourly relations, 146–7, 213–15
Neiman, Susan, 297
Nietzsche, Friedrich Wilhelm, 297
Northern Irish border: debates about, 17
nouveaux riche: leisure activities of, 78–9
Nove, Alec, 155
Nussbaum, Martha: capabilities approach, 4, 64; *Frontiers of Justice*, 158, 172; on good life, 273, 290; philosophy of, 7, 33, 279, 296; study of freedom, 69–72, 74

objectification, 234, 235, 238, 285–9, 298
Olympic Games, 199, 200–1, 207
'the original position', 156, 157
O'Toole, Fintan, 113; *We Don't Know Ourselves*, 13, 14, 18–19, 36, 289

phenomenology, 64–5
Phenomenology of Spirit, The (Hegel), 283, 285
philosophy: in Ancient Greece, 1, 201, 204; anthropology and, 6, 24, 33, 76, 290, 295–7; as escape, 243, 262, 263; ethnography and, 2, 24, 115, 117; sport and, 200–3, 210; Western tradition of, 199, 210
Philosophy of Right (Hegel), 285
Pickett, Kate: *The Spirit Level*, 157
Piketty, Thomas, 157
Pilates, 192–3, 207
pilgrimage, 247
Plato, 203, 261; *Republic*, 201
pleasure, 264, 265–6, 267–8, 269, 270, 279–80
Plenty of Fish app, 44
pluralism, 70, 71, 289–90
polis, 2, 8, 240, 293
politics: as divisive force, 46–7; government and, 51–2; in international context, 48–51; in Irish context, 45–8; on local level, 52–7
post-humanism, 115–16, 118
poverty, 313n5; 'pockets of', 128, 140, 141, 165, 292
proletariat, 68
Protestant Church, 254
psychotherapy, 137, 144–5
pubs, 256, 257–8
Pullman, Philip: *His Dark Materials*, 101

racism, 169
Rawls, John: on capitalist system, 155; critique of, 153, 158, 173; on family, 159–62; on happiness, 159, 160; on justice and fairness, 3, 154–5, 156, 162–8, 170, 172–3; on least advantaged member of society, 157; on market system, 155; on relationship between

Rawls, John (*cont.*)
  individuals and the universal, 296;
  on right to egalitarian educational
  system, 156; on 'the original
  position', 156; *A Theory of
  Justice*, 153–4, 162
reasonable: conception of, 168, 291
regional councils, 226–7
Reid, Heather, 200, 201, 202, 203,
  267
religion: decline of, 73
retired people: access to public
  transport, 83–4; active agency of,
  167, 282; blue jeans population,
  86; consumption habits, 85,
  114–15, 278; decision to retire,
  250; desires and aspirations,
  114, 243–5, 273; emphasis
  upon the self and the body,
  198; former occupations of,
  88; freedoms of, 34, 40, 62–3,
  278; identity of, 38–9; life
  expectancy of, 40, 62; medical
  services for, 83; phobia around
  wasting time, 258; possession of
  property abroad, 248; pursuit
  of education, 251; quality of
  life, 258–60; realism of, 166–7,
  168; sense of the reasonable,
  168; sexual possibilities, 58–9;
  social and leisure activities, 39,
  254, 255–8, 274; social benefits,
  83–4; sociality of, 277; use of
  smartphones, 39–40, 288, 294
Robbins, Joel, 298, 324n33
Rooney, Sally, 18
Rousseau, Jean-Jacques, 67
rowing, 178, 179
rugby, 178, 181–2, 184
Ryan, Carrie, 131

Sahlins, Marshall, 79
sailing, 178, 179, 181, 208
'sampling' culture, 109
Samuel, Geoffrey, 209

Sandel, Michael, 173; *Liberalism
  and the Limits of Justice*, 158
Sartre, Jean-Paul, 64–6, 72, 296
satiable society, 78, 88, 249, 250,
  252–3, 281
Scheper-Hughes, Nancy,
  142; *Saints, Scholars and
  Schizophrenics*, 212
Schultz, Bruno, 109
Scott, David, 132
sea swimming, 178, 179, 187, 188,
  208
self-actualization, 282
self-alienation, 288
Sen, Amartya, 4, 7, 64, 69–72,
  74, 290, 296; *Development as
  Freedom*, 69; *The Idea of Justice*,
  158, 172
Seneca, 264, 265–7
Setiya, Kieran, 278
shopping, 110–11
Sidgwick, Henry: *The Methods of
  Ethics*, 154
Simmel, Georg, 94, 272, 288
Sinn Féin (political party), 47, 170
Sittlichkeit (ethical life), 283
small communities, 212–13
smartphones: as avatars, 101–2;
  as extension of cognition, 103;
  gender stereotypes and, 102;
  human relations to, 100–1, 103,
  116–17; as a loss of humanity,
  63; older people and, 9, 39–40,
  118, 276–7, 288, 294; studies of,
  101–2, 115
social contract, 155
social democratic capitalism, 174
social prescribing, 255–6, 321n5
social science, 32, 151
sociality, 30–1, 32, 274
Socrates, 3, 33, 201, 202–3, 207,
  210, 261, 264–5
solidarity, 294
Soper, Kate, 115
space, 234–6, 237

INDEX

Spirit Level, The (Wilkinson and Pickett), 51, 157
spiritual practices, 192–4, 197
sports: in Ancient Greece, 201–2; body image and, 187, 190–1, 196, 207–8; as character building, 205; children and, 84, 179–80, 185, 197, 205, 206, 208; in classical Greece, 199–201, 203–4; clubs, 178, 179; as communal activity, 195–6, 255; competitive nature of, 179–80, 181, 184, 192, 202–3, 206–7; cost of, 84; democracy and, 200, 201; disability and, 180–1; drinking and, 181–2, 185, 206–7; excellence and virtue in, 204; Gaelic, 18, 206; government initiatives, 191; health and, 188–90, 208–9; ideal icons in, 205–6; local teams, 181; morality and, 204; national identity and, 180–1, 182–4, 196; older people and, 185–7, 207–8; in philosophical discourse, 3, 200–3; philosophy and, 199, 200, 210; popularity of, 177–8, 198, 207, 208; press coverage, 209–10; social bonding and, 178, 206; social status and, 181, 184, 187; variety of, 178, 179, 180, 184; women and, 187
squash, 178
St Patrick's Day parade, 179, 225
state housing *see* Vartry Estate
step-counting apps, 186
stereotypes, 172
Stoics: vs Epicurus, 243, 266, 267, 268, 295; philosophy of, 261, 262, 269, 279, 280; view of death, 264–5, 270; view of pleasure, 279–80; on withdrawal from the world, 263–4
Strathern, Marilyn: *After Nature*, 29
streaming services, 254–5, 277

'Successful Ageing' movement, 191, 317n8
suicide, 145–6, 173
surveillance capitalism, 311n34
sustainability initiatives, 90, 91

Tai Chi, 192–3, 194
Tamagotchi, 101
targeted advertising, 311n34
Taylor, Charles, 283, 290, 297
television, 83, 113, 254–5, 271, 273, 277
tennis, 178, 208
theatrical group, 228
Theory of Justice, A (Rawls), 153–4, 162
things, people's relationship to, 94
Thomas, Keith, 99
Thucydides, 201
Thunberg, Greta, 91
Tidy Towns competition, 21, 52, 89, 90, 220, 221
Tönnies, Ferdinand, 294
'Transition Towns' movement, 90
travel: abroad, 244, 245–8, 250, 251, 272–3; charitable work during, 249; choice of destinations, 269–70, 272–3; competitive element of, 250–1; on cruise ships, 248–9; educational element of, 251; environmental cost of, 253; as escape, 246; to exotic places, 246, 247; frequency of, 250; hassle of, 252; idea of a bucket list and, 244; information exchange about, 259; local, 245, 273; pets and, 252; pilgrimage, 247; reasons for, 245, 246; refusal to, 252; as search for lost authenticity, 247–8, 249; sense of freedom, 248; social component of, 248–9; spending on, 249, 250, 251, 259, 270, 273; TV programmes about, 253; value of, 252–3; *see also* holidays
Trump, Donald, 46

353

'Unpacking my Library' (Benjamin), 111, 115
utilitarianism, 154

Valera, Éamon de, 14, 35, 61, 182, 239
Valley of the Squinting Windows, The (MacNamara), 147, 289
Varadkar, Leo, 51
Vartry Estate: alcohol problem, 127; community centre, 148, 166, 168–9; drug use, 140; feeling of community, 226; government initiatives, 123; health services, 195; houses, 121; integration of, 293; internal networks, 127–8; intruders, 126; living standards, 128; murder on, 123; neglect of, 147, 165; reputation of, 123–4, 128; residents, 121, 122–3, 125–8; single mothers at, 127; social support of, 166, 173; sports, 184
Veblen, Thorstein: *A Theory of the Leisure Class*, 78–9
virtue, 2, 7, 206, 280
visceral enlightenment, 38
Volk: concept of, 238–9, 271
volleyball, 178
volunteering, 99

Walker, Harry, 6
walking, 178, 186, 189, 195, 256
Wallerstein, Immanuel, 174
Wang, Xinyuan, 4
We Don't Know Ourselves (O'Toole), 36, 289
Weight Watchers, 192
Weimar Republic, 109
welfare states, 174
Welles, Orson, 108
wellness, 192–4, 195, 197, 198
WhatsApp, 101
Wilk, Richard, 280
Wilkinson, Richard: *The Spirit Level*, 157
Winnicott, Donald, 3
women: grandparenting, 275; meditation and relaxation activities, 193–4; social networks, 276; sports and, 187
Wood, Allen, 283, 285; *Hegel's Ethical Thought*, 282

yachting club, 181
Yoga, 192–3, 194, 195, 197, 208–9, 255
Young, Michael, 173
young people: activities, 143–4; consumer behaviour, 87; substance use, 314n16

Zorba the Greek (novel), 265
Zuboff, Shoshana, 311n34

Printed and bound by CPI Group (UK) Ltd, Croydon, CR0 4YY
04/12/2023
08200701-0001